Anfang
und
Fortschritt

An Introduction to German

Second Edition

Anfang und Fortschritt

An Introduction to German

Second Edition

ELLIN S. FELD
COLUMBIA UNIVERSITY

WILLY SCHUMANN
SMITH COLLEGE

ELLEN VON NARDROFF
UPSALA COLLEGE

THE MACMILLAN COMPANY
NEW YORK

COLLIER-MACMILLAN PUBLISHERS
LONDON

CREDITS

German Information Center for the posters on page 2, upper left and right and lower left, and on page 260.
Lufthansa German Airlines for the poster on page 2, lower right.
German Federal Railroad for the poster on page 246.
Constantin Film, Munich, for photos on page 332, lower left and right.
Heinz and Ursala Röhnert, Berlin, for the middle photo on page 332.

Cover design by Jacqueline Kahane

Copyright © 1968, 1973 The Macmillan Company

Library of Congress catalog card number: 72–94543

The Macmillan Company
Collier-Macmillan Canada, Ltd., Toronto, Ontario

Printed in the United States of America

Earlier edition copyright 1968 by The Macmillan Company

printing number
5   6   7   8   9   10

To
Professor Helen M. Mustard

Preface

Aims and Methods

Anfang und Fortschritt is designed to teach the four skills inherent in language learning: listening comprehension, speaking, reading, and writing, and, at the same time, to expose the students to many aspects of German life and culture. Although the emphasis in method is mainly audiolingual, some traditional techniques that we have found to be sound are also used. The lesson units lend themselves to adjustments in approach, so that those teachers who wish to stress any of the four skills over others will be able to do so.

There are twenty-five lessons, which can easily be covered in the normal college year. Four of these are strictly review lessons. Because they contain no new material, they can be omitted by teachers who wish to finish in less time.

The new features of this second edition of *Anfang und Fortschritt* include a grammar appendix and a numbering system in the end vocabulary to indicate the lesson in which active vocabulary words are introduced. The reading selections have been extensively revised to reduce the number of new lexical items included in each, to ease the level of difficulty in some, and to update the subject matter wherever necessary. Several exercises and drills have been rewritten, others have minor revisions.

The Lesson Unit

Following is a description of the format of each lesson with an indication of the purpose served by each section:

DIALOGUE: Each dialogue is short enough for students to memorize. It presents the characters in a natural situation revealing aspects of German life and culture. It also incorporates a unit of interrelated vocabulary and expressions. Illustrations of the grammatical constructions are given without sacrificing any of the naturalness of the dialogue. The language is normal, colloquial speech.

DIALOGUE TRANSLATION: Each dialogue is translated into colloquial, idiomatic English in order to convey the natural tone as well as the contextual meanings of the words and phrases. This translation is printed on the page backing the dialogue in order to make it easily accessible and yet prevent its use as a crutch.

READING TEXT: Because written German, and especially expository prose, is more complex than the colloquial spoken language, and because college students can and want to develop an ability to read mature material at an early stage, we introduce separate reading texts from the very beginning. These are provided with a visible vocabulary in which each new word is given. The texts gradually increase in difficulty (though at a faster rate than the dialogues) and length. They are, however, integrated with the dialogues to reinforce and further expand the vocabulary, to show additional examples of the constructions, and to provide continuity in the experiences of the characters. The cultural material was selected with the mature intellectual level and interests of college students in mind. There are selections that deal with events and figures of German history, literature, art, and music, as well as customs and traditions.

QUESTIONS AND ANSWERS: Following the dialogue and reading selection is a set of questions and answers that illustrate, in slightly varied form, the vocabulary, expressions, and constructions of the lesson. The questions concentrate primarily on the dialogue material, but useful material from the reading texts is brought into active use through them. The answers to the questions are always given because they too are formulated to provide further illustrations. It is expected that the students will learn this material by heart through repetition and drill.

EXPLANATION OF FORMS: The explanations of grammatical constructions are intended to be clear and full enough so that the teacher can assign this section for home study. In this way, class time can be spent practicing the constructions instead of discussing them. The approach in the explanations aims at satisfying the college students' desire for an organized analysis of grammar and, at the same time, at avoiding unnecessary detail. Contrasts with English are shown wherever they seem valuable. Each point is illustrated by examples from the dialogues and reading texts. The order of presentation of grammar points is based on their relative occurrence in the spoken language.

WORD STUDY AND USAGE:	This section is reserved primarily for explanations of special uses, word formation, certain idioms, vocabulary building, and so on. Here, too, the explanations use illustrations from the dialogues and reading texts.
CLASS DRILLS:	The class drills are easily cued pattern practices of the constructions explained in the lesson. Many varieties of substitution and transformation drills are used. Every construction that can be drilled through pattern practice is treated separately except in review lessons where drills are of the testing variety. Thus, the entire explanation section need not be covered before drill on individual grammar points can begin. In fact, it is possible to practice the drills before covering the explanation.
EXERCISES:	The exercises are meant to be used after the previous material of the lesson has been learned well. They use the vocabulary, idioms, and constructions of the current lesson and previous lessons in new variations, and the students should be able to do these exercises quite easily if they have learned the material. In each set there are several exercises that are specifically designed to give further practice in the constructions of the lesson, often tying them up with some learned earlier. Translation exercises appear regularly, because they are important devices for review. (In the early lessons, the student is asked, in connection with the German-English translation exercises, to translate the sentences first into English, then to reproduce the original sentence from his English translation. The rationale behind this technique is twofold: the material is reinforced by this double exercise, and the student has an immediate check on the accuracy of his translation. Naturally, it is understood that he will cover up the original German sentence while he is reproducing it, then compare his own German version with the one in the book in order to find any errors. In later lessons, where we wish to present more complex sentences, the student is asked to reproduce only some of the sentences, that is, the ones that are not too difficult.)

Beginning with the first lesson, each set of exercises contains a composition practice. In the first eight lessons this takes the form of questions, the answers to which, when written in a paragraph, present a simple composition. Beginning with Lesson 9, this exercise has a different, though still carefully controlled, form: key words are suggested for each of ten sentences, which, when written as a paragraph, produce a simple composition. Beginning with Lesson 19, an alternate form of composition exercise is offered for use if the teacher feels his class is ready for it: a topic is suggested, which is controlled only to the extent that it is based on the dialogue material.

ACTIVE VOCABULARY: The last section of each lesson consists of a list of all the new lexical items introduced in the lesson. Normally, new vocabulary is introduced only in the dialogues. This list does not include the passive vocabulary used only in the reading text.

Reviews

Lessons 6, 11, 16, and 22 are review lessons. Each of these contains a narrative summary of the previous dialogue material in the form of a letter. These summaries not only serve as additional reinforcement but provide good reading-practice passages. Because the students are familiar with the material in them, there is no comprehension problem, and they can concentrate on learning to read with proper intonation and sentence rhythm. The remainder of each review lesson is devoted to drills and exercises, which are labeled as to the constructions being reviewed. Those constructions that involve declensions and inflections are treated in progressive drills that can be assigned for self-study, because correct responses appear in each succeeding line. Constructions that do not lend themselves to this kind of drill are treated in other exercises.

Pronunciation

Pronunciation is a skill that is constantly practiced through imitation of the teacher in class and the native voices on the tapes. As an aid to teachers and students, we have provided a separate reference section in the appendix for pronunciation. *Those sounds which cause difficulties are practiced in special exercises on the tapes.*

Appendix

The appendix contains, in addition to a section on pronunciation, a summary of verb conjugation patterns, adjective, noun, and pronoun declensions, as well as lists of prepositions, conjunctions, and so forth, which the student may find helpful for reference.

Tapes and Workbook

The taped exercises for each lesson are four-phased: stimulus, pause for student response, confirmation, pause for student repetition. They are integrated with the textbook material. The dialogue and question-and-answer section of each lesson are included, but the remainder of the taped material consists of new drills (not the same ones appearing in the textbook) on constructions and pronunciation as well as dictations, reading practice, and aural comprehension exercises. The workbook, to be used with the tapes, provides the printed material needed for certain exercises, that is, reading passages, tests, discrimination exercises, and so on.

Acknowledgments

We wish to express our gratitude to our many colleagues who offered valuable suggestions and criticisms during the preparation of this book, and to our families and friends for their moral support.

E. S. F.
W. S.
E. V. N.

Contents

xiii

Anfang
und
Fortschritt

An Introduction to German

Second Edition

Glückliche
Ferientage in
Deutschland

Luftha

Erste Lektion

Im Flugzeug

[In einer Lufthansamaschine auf dem Wege nach Frankfurt. Ein Fluggast fragt die Stewardeß:]

EVANS — Verzeihung, haben Sie noch eine deutsche Zeitung?

STEWARDESS — Nein, leider nicht.

DER HERR NEBEN EVANS — Nehmen Sie meine Zeitschrift. Ich bin fertig damit.

EVANS — Vielen Dank. „Der Spiegel". Keine leichte Lektüre für mich.

DER HERR — Sind Sie kein Deutscher?

EVANS — Nein, Amerikaner. Ich komme aus Wisconsin. Ich heiße Tom Evans.

DER HERR — Mein Name ist Lorenz.

EVANS — Sind Sie in Frankfurt zu Hause?

LORENZ — Ja, ich arbeite bei der Firma Opel. Wollen Sie auch nach Frankfurt?

EVANS — Nein, ich fahre weiter nach Bonn.

LORENZ — Für die Politik sind Sie aber noch zu jung.

EVANS — Da haben Sie recht. Ich bin Student.

LORENZ — Was studieren Sie denn?

EVANS — Geschichte als Hauptfach. Deutsch ist mein Nebenfach.

LORENZ — Also darum sprechen Sie so gut deutsch.

In the Airplane

[In a Lufthansa plane on the way to Frankfurt. A passenger asks the stewardess:]

EVANS — Pardon me, do you have another German newspaper?

STEWARDESS — No, I'm sorry, I don't.

THE GENTLEMAN NEXT TO EVANS — Take my magazine. I'm through with it.

EVANS — Thank you very much. *Der Spiegel.* That's not easy reading for me.

THE GENTLEMAN — Aren't you German?

EVANS — No, American. I'm from Wisconsin. My name is Tom Evans.

THE GENTLEMAN — My name is Lorenz.

EVANS — Do you live in Frankfurt?

LORENZ — Yes, I work for the Opel Company. Are you going to Frankfurt, too?

EVANS — No, I'm going on to Bonn.

LORENZ — But you're too young for politics.

EVANS — You're right. I'm a student.

LORENZ — What are you studying?

EVANS — History as a major. German is my minor.

LORENZ — So that's why you speak such good German.

Note: The dialogues are rendered in colloquial, idiomatic English. Consult the vocabulary at the end of each lesson for the individual equivalents of German words, which have been translated here within the meaning of the context.

Tom Evans bleibt[1] ein Jahr[2] in Deutschland,[3] denn[4] er will[5] zwei[6] Semester an[7] der Universität Bonn studieren. Er möchte[8] privat wohnen,[9] nicht in einem Studentenheim.[10] Ein Zimmer[11] hat er schon[12] bei der Familie Thiele in Bonn. Gerd Thiele, der Sohn,[13] kennt[14] den Gast[15] aus Amerika schon aus Briefen.[16] Das Flugzeug fliegt[17] direkt nach Frankfurt. Um elf Uhr[18] landet es. Gerd 5 Thiele wartet[19] schon mit[20] dem Wagen[21] auf dem Flugplatz.[22]

[1] **bleiben** to remain, stay	[12] **schon** already
[2] **das Jahr** year	[13] **der Sohn** son
[3] **Deutschland** Germany	[14] **kennen** to know
[4] **denn** for, because	[15] **der Gast** guest
[5] **er will** he wants	[16] **aus Briefen** from letters
[6] **zwei** two	[17] **fliegen** to fly
[7] **an** at	[18] **um elf Uhr** at eleven o'clock
[8] **möchte** would like	[19] **warten** to wait
[9] **wohnen** to live, dwell	[20] **mit** with
[10] **das Studentenheim** dormitory	[21] **der Wagen** car
[11] **das Zimmer** room	[22] **der Flugplatz** airport

Fragen und Antworten

1. Wer (*who*) ist Tom Evans?
   Tom Evans ist der Student.

2. Wie (*how*) heißt der Herr neben Tom Evans?
   Der Herr heißt Lorenz.

3. Ist Herr Evans in Frankfurt zu Hause?
   Nein, er kommt aus Wisconsin.

4. Wie heißt die Zeitschrift?
   Sie heißt „Der Spiegel".

5. Wo (*where*) arbeitet Herr Lorenz?
   Er arbeitet bei der Firma Opel.

6. Was studiert Herr Evans?
   Er studiert Geschichte und Deutsch.

7. Ist Herr Lorenz Amerikaner?
   Nein, er ist Deutscher.

8. Wo ist Bonn?
   Bonn ist in Deutschland.

9. Fliegen Herr Lorenz und Herr Evans nach Bonn?
   Nein, sie fliegen direkt nach Frankfurt.
10. Wohnt Herr Evans in einem Studentenheim?
    Nein, er wohnt privat.

Structure and Practice

Explanation of Forms

I. CAPITALIZATION OF NOUNS

German nouns are always capitalized.

> Zum **Glück** hat er schon ein **Zimmer** bei der **Familie** Thiele.

II. DEFINITE ARTICLES (*the*) AND INDEFINITE ARTICLES (*a, an*)

The dialogue and reading text show that the definite and indefinite articles vary in form. These variations are determined by the gender and case (function) of the nouns they modify.

A. Gender

English generally distinguishes three natural genders for nouns: masculine (for male living beings), feminine (for female living beings), and neuter (for inanimate objects), but uses only one definite article (*the*) for all three.

German distinguishes three grammatical genders with the form of the definite article showing the distinction: **der** (masculine), **die** (feminine), **das** (neuter). The grammatical gender of living beings usually corresponds to the natural gender, but there are exceptions to this (**das Mädchen** — *girl*). Inanimate objects can be masculine, feminine, or neuter with no apparent logic. In view of these facts, it is imperative that you learn the gender of each new noun by memorizing the definite article given with it in the vocabulary.

EXAMPLES:

	LIVING BEINGS	INANIMATE OBJECTS
der (masculine)	**der Student** (student)	**der Brief** (letter)
die (feminine)	**die Stewardeß** (stewardess)	**die Zeitung** (newspaper)
das (neuter)	**das Kind** (child)	**das Flugzeug** (airplane)

B. *Case: Nominative*

The grammatical function (subject, object, etc.) of the noun in the sentence determines its case; and in German, unlike English, the form of the article frequently changes with the case. There are four cases in German, but for the present we will consider only one, the nominative.

1. FORMS OF THE NOMINATIVE: The nominative forms of the definite and indefinite articles are:

	MASCULINE	FEMININE	NEUTER
Definite Article (*the*)	**der** Name	**die** Zeitschrift	**das** Zimmer
Indefinite Article (*a, an*)	**ein** Name	**eine** Zeitschrift	**ein** Zimmer

The nominative form of the definite article is given with each noun in the vocabularies of this book.

2. USES OF THE NOMINATIVE: The uses of the nominative case are:

   a. Subject: The subject of the verb is in the nominative case.

   Der Student kommt nach Bonn.　*The student is coming to Bonn.*

   Ein Student kommt nach Bonn.　*A student is coming to Bonn.*

   Das Flugzeug landet.　*The airplane is landing.*

   Ein Flugzeug landet.　*An airplane is landing.*

   Die Stewardeß wartet auf mich.　*The stewardess is waiting for me.*

   Eine Stewardeß wartet auf mich.　*A stewardess is waiting for me.*

   b. Predicate Nominative: The predicate noun (or pronoun) after verbs such as **sein** (*to be*), **bleiben** (*to remain*), and **heißen** (*to be called*) is in the nominative case.

   Tom Evans ist **der Student.**　*Tom Evans is the student.*

3. OMISSION OF THE INDEFINITE ARTICLE: Generally German uses the indefinite article wherever English does. One exception, however, occurs when stating a person's nationality, profession, or religion. German then omits the indefinite article.

   Herr Evans ist **Amerikaner.**　*Mr. Evans is **an American.***

   Er ist **Student.**　*He is **a student.***

   Ich bin **Lutheraner.**　*I am **a Lutheran.***

III. VERBS: PRESENT TENSE

A. The Infinitive

Infinitives in German end in **-en** (occasionally in **-n**).

fragen (*to ask*)   tun (*to do*)

B. Present-Tense Conjugation

To conjugate a German verb in the present tense, personal endings (shown below in bold face) are added to the verb stem (the infinitive minus the **-en** or **-n** ending). Notice, in the example below, that German adds a personal ending for each person; English adds one only in the third person singular: *he comes.*

Most verbs follow this pattern in the present tense:

kommen	*to come*
ich komm**e**	*I come*
er, sie, es komm**t**	*he, she, it comes*
wir komm**en**	*we come*
sie komm**en**	*they come*
Sie komm**en**	*you come*

Verbs whose stems end in **-t, -d,** or a combination of consonants (**öffnen** — *to open*) add an additional **-e-** before the personal ending of the third person singular (**er, sie, es**) in order to facilitate pronunciation.

arbeiten (*to work*)

ich arbeite	wir arbeiten
er, sie, es arbeitet	sie arbeiten
	Sie arbeiten

A few verbs are irregular in the present tense. The most common of these are **haben** (*to have*) and **sein** (*to be*).

haben	**sein**
ich **habe**	ich **bin**
er, sie, es **hat**	er, sie, es **ist**
wir **haben**	wir **sind**
sie **haben**	sie **sind**
Sie **haben**	Sie **sind**

C. Meanings of the Present Tense

English has three ways of expressing present time, but German has only one.

He studies history.
  (simple present)
He is studying history.
  (progressive present)   } Er **studiert** Geschichte.
He does study history.
  (emphatic present)

Both English and German frequently use the present tense to express future time.

Tom Evans **bleibt** ein Jahr in Deutschland.
Tom Evans is staying (going to stay) in Germany for a year.

When rendering a German sentence into English, use the present-tense form which is most idiomatic in that particular context.

Ich arbeite bei der Firma Opel.
I work for the Opel Company.

Ich fahre weiter nach Bonn.
I am going on to Bonn.

Ja, **er wohnt** in einem Studentenheim.
Yes, he does live in a dormitory.

IV. PERSONAL PRONOUNS: NOMINATIVE CASE

The pronouns used in the sample conjugations above are the nominative case personal pronouns. Note the following:

ich (*I*) is not capitalized unless it begins a sentence;

sie (*she*) and **sie** (*they*) can be distinguished from each other by the personal ending of the verb:

Studiert sie Geschichte?   *Is she studying history?*
Studieren sie Geschichte?   *Are they studying history?*

Sie (*you*) is always capitalized and is used for both singular and plural:
Sind **Sie** in Frankfurt zu Hause?   *Do you live in Frankfurt?*

V. WORD ORDER

A. Statements

1. NORMAL WORD ORDER: In German, normal word order has the subject first and the verb second.

   Ich komme aus Wisconsin.
   Das Flugzeug fliegt direkt nach Frankfurt.

2. INVERTED WORD ORDER: When a German sentence does not begin
with the subject, the subject must then follow the verb. This is called
inverted word order. Notice the contrast with English in the following
example:

> Um elf Uhr **landet es** in Frankfurt.
> *At 11 o'clock **it lands** in Frankfurt.*

Thus in German, with either normal or inverted word order, the verb
will always be the second element. (The first element may consist of
several words, as in the example above.)

Words like **ja, nein,** and **Verzeihung** (set off by a comma), as well
as coordinating conjunctions like **und, aber,** and **denn** (not set off
by a comma) are not counted as elements and do not affect the
normal subject-verb word order.

> **Ja, ich arbeite** bei der Firma Opel.
> Um elf Uhr landet es, und **Gerd Thiele wartet** schon.

B. Questions

In both English and German questions, the verb precedes the subject.
(English present-tense questions usually use an auxiliary [*is, are; does,
do*], and it is this auxiliary which precedes the subject.)

Sind Sie kein Deutscher?	*Aren't you German?*
Haben Sie eine deutsche Zeitung?	*Do you have a German news-paper?*

This same word-order rule applies if the question begins with a question
word such as **wer** (*who*), **wie** (*how*), **wo** (*where*), **was** (*what*).

Was **studieren Sie?**	*What are you studying?*
Wo **arbeitet Herr Lorenz?**	*Where does Mr. Lorenz work?*

Word Study and Usage

I. FORMATION OF FEMININE NOUNS

German can often form a feminine from a masculine noun by simply adding
an **-in** suffix. However, this can only be done with nouns referring to living
beings.

der Student	the student (*m.*)
die Studentin	the student (*f.*)
der Amerikaner	the American (*m.*)
die Amerikanerin	the American (*f.*)

II. *COMMON ADVERBS WITH SPECIAL MEANINGS*

German has a number of adverbs that occur frequently and whose meanings are so subtle that they are often difficult and sometimes impossible to translate into English. Only through repeated contact with these words, the most common of which are **denn, doch, ja, schon,** and **wohl,** can the nuances they convey become clear enough for a non-native to learn to use them correctly. You have already seen **denn** used in the dialogue of this lesson:

Was studieren Sie **denn?**   *What are you studying?*

Here the **denn** gives to the question an emphasis that indicates a genuine interest on the part of the speaker.

No further attempt will be made to discuss the nuances of these words. Try to get a feeling for their use as you have more and more contact with them.

Class Drills

I. *Repeat the following sentences, substituting the nouns indicated:*

1. Wo ist der Wagen?
   Flugplatz
   „Spiegel"
   Amerikaner

2. Das ist das Zimmer.
   Studentenheim
   Flugzeug
   Haus

3. Wo ist die Zeitung?
   Firma
   Zeitschrift
   Universität

(*Watch the gender for each noun in the following group.*)
4. Wo ist der Wagen?
   die Zeitschrift
   das Flugzeug
   der Amerikaner
   die Universität
   das Studentenheim

5. Das ist ein Wagen.
   Flugplatz

Student
Name

6. Da ist noch ein Zimmer.
Studentenheim
Flugzeug
Haus

7. Das ist eine Zeitung.
Firma
Zeitschrift
Universität

(*Watch the gender of each noun in the following group.*)
8. Da ist noch ein Student.
eine Zeitschrift
ein Flugzeug
ein Wagen
ein Haus

II. Restate the following sentences, substituting the new pronoun or noun subject indicated:

1. Ich heiße Lorenz.
Er
Der Herr
Sie (*she*)
Die Stewardeß

Ich frage die Stewardeß.
Er
Herr Lorenz
Sie (*she*)
Die Amerikanerin

Ich bleibe in Deutschland.
Er
Der Fluggast
Sie (*she*)
Die Studentin

Ich komme aus Wisconsin.
Er
Tom Evans
Sie (*she*)
Die Stewardeß

Ich arbeite nicht.
Er
Der Herr
Sie (*she*)
Die Amerikanerin

Ich lande in Bonn.
Er
Das Flugzeug
Sie (*she*)
Die Studentin

Ich warte auf dem Flugplatz.
Er
Gerd Thiele
Sie (*she*)
Die Stewardeß

Ich habe recht.
Er
Der Fluggast
Herr Lorenz
Sie (*she*)
Die Stewardeß
Die Amerikanerin

Ich bin fertig damit.
Er
Herr Lorenz
Der Fluggast
Sie (*she*)
Die Studentin
Die Amerikanerin

2. Ich heiße Lorenz.
Wir
Er und ich heissen ←
Gerd und ich heissen

Ich frage die Stewardeß.
Wir
Herr Lorenz und ich
Er und ich

Ich bleibe in Deutschland.
Wir
Der Amerikaner und ich
Er und ich

Ich komme aus Wisconsin.
Wir
Die Studentin und ich
Tom Evans und ich

Ich arbeite nicht.
Wir
Tom und ich
Der Amerikaner und ich

Ich lande in Bonn.
Wir
Gerd und ich
Herr Evans und ich

Ich warte auf dem Flugplatz.
Wir
Gerd und ich
Herr Lorenz und ich

Ich habe recht.
Wir
Die Stewardeß und ich
Der Amerikaner und ich

Ich bin fertig damit.
Wir
Herr Lorenz und ich
Der Amerikaner und ich

3. Ich heiße Lorenz.
Sie (*you*)
Sie (*they*)
Der Herr und die Familie

Ich frage die Stewardeß.
Sie (*you*)
Sie (*they*)
Herr und Frau Lorenz
Gerd und Tom

Ich bleibe in Deutschland.
Sie (*they*)
Tom und die Stewardeß
Herr und Frau Lorenz

Ich komme aus Wisconsin.
Sie (*you*)

Der Amerikaner und die Amerikanerin
Tom und die Stewardeß

Ich arbeite nicht.
Sie (*you*)
Sie (*they*)
Der Student und die Studentin

Ich lande in Frankfurt.
Sie (*you*)
Sie (*they*)
Tom und Herr Lorenz

Ich warte auf dem Flugplatz.
Sie (*they*)
Gerd und Tom
Gerd und die Familie Lorenz

Ich habe recht.
Sie (*you*)
Herr und Frau Thiele
Herr Lorenz und die Stewardeß

Ich bin fertig damit.
Sie (*they*)
Gerd und Tom
Herr und Frau Lorenz

4. Sie heißen Lorenz.
Ich

Sie fragen die Stewardeß.
Ich

Sie bleiben in Deutschland.
Ich

Sie kommen aus Wisconsin.
Ich

Sie arbeiten nicht.
Ich

Sie landen in Bonn.
Ich

Sie warten auf dem Flugplatz.
Ich

Sie haben recht.
Ich

Sie sind fertig damit.
Ich

5. Ich komme aus Frankfurt.
Sie (*you*)
Sie (*she*)
Wir
Herr Lorenz

Herr und Frau Lorenz
Die Stewardeß
Ich
Sie (*they*)
Herr Lorenz und ich
Er

III. Restate the following sentences, beginning each sentence with the word or phrase in italics:

EXAMPLE: **Er ist *da*.**
          ***Da* ist er.**

1. Sie wollen auch *nach Frankfurt*.
2. Sie arbeitet *bei der Firma Opel*.
3. Ich bin *in Bonn* zu Hause.
4. Er ist *leider* noch zu jung.
5. Ich bin fertig *damit*.

IV. Change the following statements to questions:

EXAMPLE: **Sie ist jung.**
          Ist sie jung?

1. Er ist Student.
2. Sie kommt aus Wisconsin.
3. Ich habe recht.
4. Sie wohnen privat.
5. Der Herr heißt Evans.
6. Die Stewardeß kommt aus Bonn.
7. Das Flugzeug fliegt direkt nach Frankfurt.
8. Der Student ist noch zu jung.
9. Das ist eine deutsche Zeitschrift.
10. Er ist in Bonn zu Hause.

Exercises

I. Insert the appropriate form of the verb:

EXAMPLE: **Ich (nehmen) die Zeitschrift.**
Ich nehme die Zeitschrift.

1. Wo (landen) das Flugzeug? 2. Er (arbeiten) in Bonn. 3. Die Stewardeß (warten) noch. 4. Wir (sein) Amerikaner. 5. (Kennen) Sie die Familie Thiele? 6. Der Amerikaner (studieren) in Deutschland. 7. Wir (fliegen) direkt nach New York. 8. Wo (wohnen) sie (*she*)? 9. Ich (sprechen) gut deutsch. 10. Wo (studieren) Sie? 11. (Haben) er recht? 12. Sie (*they*) (nehmen) die Zeitschrift.

II. Translate into English. Then reproduce the German sentences from your English translations:

1. Wollen Sie auch eine Zeitschrift? 2. Sie hat recht, ich spreche nicht gut deutsch. 3. Er ist kein Deutscher, er ist Amerikaner. 4. Haben Sie noch eine deutsche Zeitung? 5. Eine deutsche Zeitschrift ist keine leichte Lektüre für mich. 6. Für die Politik bin ich noch zu jung. 7. Die Amerikanerin ist in Wisconsin zu Hause. 8. Sie studiert Deutsch als Hauptfach und Geschichte als Nebenfach. 9. Arbeitet der Herr auch bei der Firma Opel? 10. Verzeihung, fahren Sie nach Bonn?

III. Translate into German:

1. My name is Tom Evans. 2. We're from Germany. 3. The student is an American. 4. Does she live in a dormitory? 5. Is the plane going directly to Bonn? 6. Are you going to stay in Frankfurt? 7. Where does he work? 8. Excuse me, are you from Bonn? 9. You speak good German. — Thank you very much. 10. Unfortunately, they are right.

IV. Composition. Answer the following questions in complete German sentences. Write your answers in a paragraph, omitting ja and nein:

1. Wie heißen Sie?
2. Sind Sie Amerikaner(in)?
3. Kommen Sie aus Wisconsin?

4. Sind Sie in New York zu Hause?
5. Sind Sie Student(in)?
6. Sprechen Sie gut deutsch?
7. Ist Deutsch leicht?
8. Arbeiten Sie?
9. Wohnen Sie privat?

Active Vocabulary

aber	but, however	jung	young
als	as	kein	no, not a, not any
also	so, thus	kennen	to know
der Amerikaner	the American	kommen	to come
arbeiten	to work	landen	to land
auch	also, too	leicht	easy
auf	on	leider	unfortunately
aus	from	die Lektüre	reading material
bei	at	die Lufthansa-	airplane of the Luft-
da	there	maschine	hansa, the German
damit	with it		airline
der Dank	thanks	die Maschine	machine
vielen Dank	thank you very much	mein	my
darum	for that reason,	mich	me
	therefore	nach	to
das	that	der Name	name
deutsch	German	neben	next to
Deutscher	German (citizen)	das Nebenfach	minor subject
Deutschland	Germany	nehmen	to take
ein	a, an; one	nein	no
fahren	to drive, travel, go	nicht	not
	(by vehicle)	noch	still
die Familie	family	noch ein	another, one more
fertig	finished	der Platz	place, plaza
die Firma	firm, company	die Politik	politics
fliegen	to fly	privat	private
der Fluggast	airline passenger	recht	right
der Flugplatz	airport	recht haben	to be right
das Flugzeug	airplane	sein	to be
fragen	to ask	so	so, such
für	for	der Spiegel	mirror; name of
die Geschichte	history		German weekly
gut	good; well		magazine
haben	to have	sprechen	to speak
das Hauptfach	major subject	die Stewardeß	stewardess
das Haus	house	der Student	student
zu Hause	at home	das Studentenheim	dormitory
heißen	to be called, named	studieren	to study
der Herr	gentleman; Mr.	die Universität	university
im = in dem	in the	Verzeihung!	pardon me!
in	in	viel	much
ja	yes	der Wagen	car

warten	to wait		**wo**	where
was	what		**wohnen**	to live
der Weg	way		**wollen**	to want (to)
weiter	farther, further		**die Zeitschrift**	magazine
wer	who		**die Zeitung**	newspaper
wie	how		**das Zimmer**	room
			zu	at; too

Die Autobahn

Zweite Lektion

Nach Bonn

[*Gerd Thiele und Tom Evans fahren auf der Autobahn nach der Bundes-hauptstadt.*]

EVANS — Wie lange haben Sie den Wagen schon?

THIELE — Er ist noch so gut wie neu. Wir haben ihn seit Juni.

EVANS — Übrigens, gibt es hier keine Geschwindigkeitsbegrenzung?

THIELE — Doch, aber nicht auf der Autobahn. Fahre ich denn zu schnell?

EVANS — Nein, Sie nicht, aber die anderen.

THIELE — Ja, das ist eben die Autobahn. Mein Vater nennt sie eine Renn-bahn, und das ist sie auch.

EVANS — Aber eine gute Straße.

THIELE — Ja, für den Geschäftsmann ist sie ideal. Aber leider sieht man nichts vom Land.

EVANS — Das ist bei uns genauso. Man fährt den ganzen Tag und kennt nachher nichts von Amerika.

THIELE — Ja, aber wer will schon durch jedes kleine Dorf fahren?

EVANS — Wie weit ist es noch bis Bonn?

THIELE — Ungefähr siebzig Kilometer. Um zwei sind wir da.

On the Way to Bonn

[Gerd Thiele and Tom Evans are driving to the West German capital on the Autobahn.]

EVANS — How long have you had the car?

THIELE — It's still practically new. We've had it since June.

EVANS — By the way, isn't there a speed limit here?

THIELE — Of course there is. But not on the *Autobahn*. Am I driving too fast?

EVANS — No, you're not, but the others are.

THIELE — Yes, that's the *Autobahn* for you. My father calls it a racetrack and that's just what it is.

EVANS — But it's a good road.

THIELE — Yes. It's ideal for the businessman. But unfortunately you don't see anything of the country.

EVANS — It's just the same back home. You drive all day, and when you're through, you've seen nothing of America.

THIELE — Yes, but who wants to drive through every little village?

EVANS — How much farther is it to Bonn?

THIELE — About seventy kilometers. We'll be there at two.

Gerd und Tom fahren also noch ungefähr eine Stunde[1] mit dem Wagen nach Bonn. Die beiden[2] sprechen über[3] die deutsche Autobahn, die Universität in Deutschland und Amerika, das Studium[4] und die Bundeshauptstadt. Sie lachen[5] besonders[6] über das Wort[7] „Bundeshauptdorf". So nennt man die westdeutsche Hauptstadt manchmal.[8] Bonn, früher[9] eine kleine Stadt,[10] ideal 5 für Studenten und Pensionäre,[11] ist nun[12] ein Zentrum[13] der Weltpolitik.[14] Seit 1949 (neunzehnhundertneunundvierzig) wächst[15] sie von Jahr zu Jahr. Politiker,[16] Diplomaten und Journalisten kommen nach Bonn. Die große[17] Welt kommt in die kleine „provisorische"[18] Hauptstadt. Aber für Gerd Thiele und seine Generation ist dieser Zustand[19] nicht mehr[20] provisorisch. 10

Um zwei Uhr sind sie in Bonn, und Gerd fährt Tom einmal[21] durch die Stadt. Zu Hause[22] warten Gerds Eltern[23] schon auf den Gast aus Amerika, und nun begrüßen[24] sie ihn.

[1] **die Stunde** hour
[2] **beide** both
    die beiden the two
[3] **über** about
[4] **das Studium** study, studying
[5] **lachen** to laugh
[6] **besonders** especially
[7] **das Wort** word
[8] **manchmal** sometimes
[9] **früher** formerly
[10] **die Stadt** city, town
[11] **der Pensionär,** *pl.* **die Pensionäre** retired person
[12] **nun** now

[13] **das Zentrum** center
[14] **der Weltpolitik** of world politics
[15] **wachsen (ä)** to grow
[16] **der Politiker,** *pl.* **die Politiker** politician
[17] **groß** big, great
[18] **provisorisch** temporary
[19] **der Zustand** condition, state
[20] **nicht mehr** no longer
[21] **einmal** once
[22] **das Haus** house
    zu Hause at home
[23] **die Eltern** (*pl.*) parents
[24] **begrüßen** to greet, welcome

Fragen und Antworten

1. Hat Gerd Thiele den Wagen schon lange?
   Nein, er hat ihn seit Juni.
2. Ist Gerds Wagen schon alt (*old*)?
   Nein, er ist noch so gut wie neu.
3. Was ist Bonn?
   Bonn ist die deutsche Bundeshauptstadt.
4. Wie nennt man die Bundeshauptstadt manchmal?
   Man nennt sie manchmal das „Bundeshauptdorf".
5. Worüber (*about what*) sprechen Gerd und Tom?
   Die beiden sprechen über die Autobahn.

6. Was hat Gerd gegen (*against*) die Autobahn?
Man sieht nichts vom Land.
7. Für wen (*whom*) ist die Autobahn eine ideale Straße?
Für den Geschäftsmann; er will nicht durch jedes Dorf fahren.
8. Gibt es in Amerika keine Geschwindigkeitsbegrenzung?
Doch, bei uns gibt es auch eine Geschwindigkeitsbegrenzung.
9. Fahren Gerd und Tom direkt nach Hause (*home*)?
Nein, Gerd fährt den Amerikaner einmal durch die Stadt.
10. Wer begrüßt den Gast aus Amerika?
Die Familie Thiele begrüßt ihn.

Structure and Practice

Explanation of Forms

I. ACCUSATIVE CASE

A. *Forms of the Definite and Indefinite Article*

In the accusative case the definite and indefinite articles change only for masculine nouns.

	Nominative	
MASCULINE	FEMININE	NEUTER
der Wagen	**die** Stadt	**das** Zentrum
ein Wagen	**eine** Stadt	**ein** Zentrum
	Accusative	
den Wagen	**die** Stadt	**das** Zentrum
einen Wagen	**eine** Stadt	**ein** Zentrum

B. *Uses of the Accusative Case*

1. DIRECT OBJECT: The direct object of the verb is in the accusative case.

Wir haben **den Wagen** seit Juni.
We've had the car since June.
Wir haben **einen Wagen** seit Juni.
We've had a car since June.

Ich nehme **das Zimmer** bei Thieles.
I'm taking the room at the Thieles'.
Ich nehme **ein Zimmer** bei Thieles.
I'm taking a room at the Thieles'.
Er hat schon **die Zeitung.**
He already has the newspaper.
Er hat schon **eine Zeitung.**
He already has a newspaper.

2. OBJECT OF SOME PREPOSITIONS: The accusative case is always used after these prepositions: **durch** (*through*), **für** (*for*), **gegen** (*against*), **ohne** (*without*), **um** (*around*).

> **durch:** Gerd fährt **durch die Stadt.**
> *Gerd drives through the city.*
> **für:** **Für den Geschäftsmann** ist sie ideal.
> *For the businessman it's ideal.*
> **gegen:** Was hat Gerd **gegen die Autobahn?**
> *What does Gerd have against the* Autobahn?
> **ohne:** Er fährt **ohne den Amerikaner** nach Bonn.
> *He drives to Bonn without the American.*
> **um:** Sie fahren **um das Dorf.**
> *They drive around the village.*

Note: Other prepositions, such as **auf, über,** and **in,** sometimes take the accusative case. These will be explained in Lesson 7.

3. TIME EXPRESSIONS: For expressions denoting duration of time, German uses the accusative case.

> Man fährt **den** ganzen Tag.
> *You drive all day.*
> Tom Evans bleibt **ein** Jahr in Deutschland.
> *Tom Evans is staying in Germany for a year.*
> Gerd und Tom fahren also noch ungefähr **eine** Stunde.
> *So Gerd and Tom drive about one more hour.*

C. *Personal Pronouns: Accusative Case*

In both English and German the accusative case (English: *objective*) of the personal pronouns is often different from the nominative case.

	English		*German*	
NOMINATIVE	OBJECTIVE	NOMINATIVE	ACCUSATIVE
I	me	**ich**	**mich**
he	him	**er**	**ihn**
she	her	**sie**	**sie**
it	it	**es**	**es**
we	us	**wir**	**uns**
they	them	**sie**	**sie**
you	you	**Sie**	**Sie**

The accusative pronouns are used as:

Direct Object

Die Eltern begrüßen **ihn.**

Object of Prepositions

Keine leichte Lektüre **für mich.**

II. AGREEMENT OF PRONOUN WITH NOUN GENDER

In German a personal pronoun must agree in gender with the noun it replaces. Its case depends on its use in the sentence.

Er (der Student) ist in Wisconsin zu Hause.
He (the student) lives in Wisconsin.

Für ihn (den Amerikaner) ist „Der Spiegel" keine leichte Lektüre.
For him (the American) Der Spiegel is not easy reading.

Sie (die Stewardeß) hat keine deutsche Zeitung.
She (the stewardess) doesn't have a German newspaper.

This applies as well to inanimate objects.

Er (der Wagen) ist noch so gut wie neu.
It (the car) is still practically new.

Wir haben **ihn** (den Wagen) seit Juni.
We've had it (the car) since June.

Mein Vater nennt **sie** (die Autobahn) eine Rennbahn.
My father calls it (the Autobahn) *a racetrack.*

Um elf Uhr landet **es** (das Flugzeug).
At eleven o'clock it (the plane) lands.

III. INTERROGATIVE PRONOUNS

The nominative interrogative pronoun **wer** (*who*) changes to **wen** (*whom*) in the accusative case.

Wer begrüßt den Gast aus Amerika?
Who greets the guest from America?
Für wen ist die Autobahn eine ideale Straße?
For whom is the Autobahn *an ideal road?*

The nominative interrogative pronoun **was** (*what*) remains the same in the accusative case.

Was ist Bonn?
What is Bonn?
Was hat Gerd gegen die Autobahn?
What does Gerd have against the Autobahn?

IV. PRESENT TENSE WITH VOWEL CHANGE

In the dialogue and reading text of this lesson, you have noticed that some verbs show stem variations in the present tense.

geben: **Gibt** es hier keine Geschwindigkeitsbegrenzung?
sehen: Aber leider **sieht** man nichts vom Land.
fahren: Man **fährt** den ganzen Tag.

These verbs, among others, have a vowel change in the third person singular (**er, sie, es**) of the present tense. When such a vowel change occurs, it takes the following forms:

a to **ä** (fahren: ich fahre, er **fährt**)
au to **äu** (laufen: ich laufe, er **läuft**)
e to **i** or **ie** (geben: ich gebe, er **gibt**; sprechen: ich spreche, er **spricht**; sehen: ich sehe, er **sieht**)

Any verb that has this type of change in the present tense will follow this pattern:

fahren (*to drive, travel, go by vehicle*)

ich fahre	wir fahren
er, sie, es **fährt**	sie fahren
	Sie fahren

Occasionally there is a somewhat more radical change in the third-person singular stem:

nehmen (*to take*)

ich nehme	wir nehmen
er, sie, es **nimmt**	sie nehmen
	Sie nehmen

The vocabulary of each lesson will indicate the verbs that have a stem variation in the present tense.

Word Study and Usage

I. *ES GIBT*

Es gibt is an idiom meaning *there is* or *there are.* The object of **gibt** is in the accusative case.

> **Es gibt** hier eine Geschwindigkeitsbegrenzung.
> *There is a speed limit here.*
>
> **Gibt es** hier keine Geschwindigkeitsbegrenzung?
> *Isn't there a speed limit here?*
>
> **Es gibt** viele Diplomaten und Politiker in Bonn.
> *There are many diplomats and politicians in Bonn.*

II. *DOCH*

In replying affirmatively to a question, English generally uses *yes,* German uses **ja.**

> Sind Sie in Frankfurt zu Hause? — **Ja.**
> *Do you live in Frankfurt? — Yes.*

To answer a negative question affirmatively, English uses *yes,* but then must add something to clarify the *yes.*

> Isn't there a speed limit here? — **Yes, there is.**
> Don't you see the airport?— **Yes, I do.**

In German the affirmative reply to such a negative question is **doch,** which has the meaning of *yes, on the contrary; yes, there is; yes, I do;* etc.

> Gibt es hier keine Geschwindigkeitsbegrenzung? — **Doch.**
> Sehen Sie den Flugplatz nicht? — **Doch.**

negative question — doch

III. *SPECIAL USE OF THE PRESENT TENSE*

For an action begun in the past and still continuing in the present, German uses the present tense whereas English uses the present perfect. The word **schon** or **seit** frequently accompanies this idiomatic use of the present tense.

> Wie lange **haben Sie** den Wagen schon?
> *How long **have you had** the car?*
>
> **Wir haben** ihn seit Juni.
> *We've had it since June.*

Class Drills

I. *Repeat the following sentences, substituting the nouns indicated:*

a. 1. Er kennt den Amerikaner.
                Flugplatz
                „Spiegel"
                Gast
                Geschäftsmann

   2. Er kennt die Familie.
                Stadt
                Zeitschrift
                Stewardeß
                Firma

   3. Er kennt das Dorf.
                Studentenheim
                Land
                Haus

   (*Watch the gender for each noun in the following group.*)
   4. Er kennt den Flugplatz.
                Studentenheim
                Stadt
                Amerikaner
                Familie

b. 1. Sie fragt einen Amerikaner.
                Politiker
                Geschäftsmann
                Professor

   2. Hier gibt es eine Rennbahn.
                Universität
                Autobahn
                Geschwindigkeitsbegrenzung

   3. Hier sehen Sie noch ein Studentenheim.
                Flugzeug
                Dorf
                Zimmer

   (*Watch the gender for each noun in the following group.*)
   4. Gibt es hier eine Rennbahn?
                Professor

Studentenheim
Universität
Amerikaner

II. *Repeat the following sentences, substituting the new noun:*

1. Ich habe nichts gegen den Politiker.
   Geschäftsmann
   Amerikaner
   „Spiegel"

2. Ich habe nichts gegen die Firma.
   Stadt
   Familie
   Maschine

3. Ich habe nichts gegen das Haus.
   Dorf
   Flugzeug
   Studentenheim

4. Das ist ideal für den Politiker.
   Geschäftsmann
   Amerikaner
   Professor

5. Das ist ideal für die Firma.
   Familie
   Universität
   Stewardeß

6. Das ist ideal für das Studentenheim.
   Dorf
   Land
   Geschäft

III. *Repeat the following sentences, substituting the German for the pronouns indicated in parentheses:*

1. Gerd kennt mich nicht. (*him, her, us, them, me*)
2. Ist das für mich? (*him, her, us, them, you, me*)
3. Was hat Gerd gegen sie? (*me, them, him, you, us, her*)

IV. *Repeat the following sentences, substituting the appropriate pronouns for the noun subjects:*

EXAMPLE: **Hier ist *der Spiegel*.** *masculine noun*
Hier ist *er*. *masculine pronoun*

1. Der Student wohnt privat.
   Der Flugplatz ist in Frankfurt.
   Wo ist der „Spiegel"?
   Der Wagen ist so gut wie neu.
   Der Amerikaner spricht zu schnell.

2. Ist die Firma in Frankfurt?
   Die Stewardeß spricht deutsch.
   Die Zeitschrift heißt „Der Spiegel".
   Die Lufthansamaschine fliegt nach Frankfurt.
   Da ist die Universität.

3. Wo ist das Haus?
   Das Zimmer ist zu klein.
   Wo ist das Studentenheim?
   Das Flugzeug fliegt nach Frankfurt.
   Das Dorf ist klein.

4. Der Wagen ist so gut wie neu.
   Das Flugzeug ist so gut wie neu.
   Da ist die Zeitschrift.
   Wo ist die Autobahn?
   Da ist das Studentenheim.

V. *Answer affirmatively, substituting the appropriate pronoun for each noun:*

EXAMPLE: **Kennt er *den Geschäftsmann* nicht?**
Doch, er kennt *ihn.*

1. Sieht sie den Flugplatz nicht?
   Sieht sie den Wagen nicht?
   Sieht sie den Professor nicht?

2. Kennt er die Autobahn nicht?
   Kennt er die Stewardeß nicht?
   Kennt er die Zeitschrift nicht?

3. Kennt sie das Studentenheim nicht?
   Kennt sie das Land nicht?
   Kennt sie das Dorf nicht?

VI. *Repeat the following sentences, substituting the pronouns indicated:*

1. Ich sehe das Dorf. (**er**)
   Ich sehe die Universität. (**er**)

Ich sehe nichts. (**sie** — *she*)
Ich sehe nicht gut. (**sie** — *she*)

2. Ich nehme das Zimmer. (**er**)
Ich nehme den Wagen. (**er**)
Ich nehme die Zeitschrift. (**sie** — *she*)
Ich nehme den „Spiegel". (**sie** — *she*)

3. Ich fahre nach Frankfurt. (**er**)
Ich fahre zu schnell. (**er**)
Ich fahre weiter nach Bonn. (**sie** — *she*)
Ich fahre auf der Autobahn. (**sie** — *she*)

4. Ich laufe schnell. (**er**)
Ich laufe durch die Stadt. (**er**)
Ich laufe durch das Dorf. (**sie** — *she*)
Ich laufe zu schnell. (**sie** — *she*)

läuft is pronounced "loift"

5. Ich sehe das Dorf. (**wir**)
Ich fahre nach Frankfurt. (**wir**)
Ich nehme das Zimmer. (**sie** — *they*)
Ich laufe schnell. (**sie** — *they*)

Exercises

I. *Rewrite the following sentences, substituting the German for the new subject pronouns given in English:*

1. Sie fahren den ganzen Tag und sehen nichts. (*he, I*)   2. Wir arbeiten bei der Firma Opel. (*she, they*)   3. Sie läuft zu schnell. (*they, we*)
4. Sie wohnen bei Thieles. (*he, I*)   5. Fliegen Sie auch nach Frankfurt? (*he, she*)   6. Sie nehmen die Zeitschrift. (*she, he*)   7. Ich studiere in Berlin. (*we, she*)   8. Wo ist er? (*they, she*)   9. Sie sprechen über die Autobahn. (*we, he*)   10. Wo studiert sie? (*they, you*)

II. *Translate into English. Then reproduce the German sentences from your English translations:*

1. Übrigens, gibt es hier ein Studentenheim?   2. Wie lange kennt sie den Amerikaner schon?   3. Wer will schon den ganzen Tag arbeiten?
4. Die Geschwindigkeitsbegrenzung haben sie seit Juni.   5. Ist es noch weit bis Frankfurt?   6. Wen fährt Gerd durch Bonn?   7. Er hat recht, es ist ungefähr siebzig Kilometer bis Bonn.   8. Ist er nicht in Bonn zu Hause? — Doch.   9. Die beiden fahren einmal um die Stadt.   10. Sie arbeiten den ganzen Tag.

den – accusative

III. *Translate into German:*

1. He has had the car since June. 2. Does she work all day? 3. Unfortunately he drives too fast. 4. She is going without him. 5. What does he have against her? 6. We are driving through the capital. 7. He is a businessman; do you know him? 8. How far is it to Frankfurt? 9. By the way, whom do you know in Bonn? 10. There is a speed limit.

IV. *Composition. Answer the following questions in complete German sentences, using as much of the question in your answer as possible. Write your answers in a paragraph, omitting* ja *and* nein:

1. Wer begrüßt in Frankfurt den Gast aus Amerika?
2. Wohin (*where to*) fahren Gerd und Tom?
3. Wie heißt die Straße?
4. Wie nennt Gerds Vater die Straße?
5. Hat Gerds Vater recht?
6. Fährt Gerd zu schnell?
7. Wie weit ist es bis Bonn?
8. Wann (*when*) sind Gerd und Tom in Bonn?
9. Fährt Gerd den Amerikaner direkt nach Hause?
10. Wer begrüßt Tom in Bonn?

Active Vocabulary

alt	old	genau	exact
die anderen	the others	genauso	just the same
das Auto	automobile	das Geschäft	business, store
die Autobahn	superhighway	der Geschäftsmann	businessman
die Bahn	lane, track, way	die Geschwindig-	speed
die Begrenzung	limitation, limit	keit	
begrüßen	to greet, welcome	die Geschwindig-	speed limit
beide	both	keitsbegren-	
die beiden	the two	zung	
bis	to, until	die Hauptstadt	capital
die Bundeshaupt-	capital of the Federal	das Haus	house
stadt	Republic	nach Hause	home
das Dorf	village	hier	here
durch	through	ihn	him; it
einmal	once	jeder	every, each
ganz	whole, entire	der Juni	June
der Gast	guest	der Kilometer	kilometer
geben (i)	to give	klein	small
es gibt	there is	das Land	country
gegen	against	lang(e)	long

laufen (äu)	to run	der Tag	day
man	one	über	about
manchmal	sometimes	übrigens	by the way
der Mann	man	um	around; at
nachher	afterward	und	and
nennen	to call, name	ungefähr	approximately
neu	new	uns	us
nichts	nothing	der Vater	father
ohne	without	vom = von dem	of the
der Politiker	politician, statesman	von	of, from
der Professor	professor	wann	when
die Rennbahn	racetrack	weit	far
schnell	fast	wen	whom
sehen (ie)	to see	wie	as
seit	since	will	wants
siebzig	seventy	*from* wollen	to want (to)
so . . . wie	as . . . as	wohin	where (to)
die Stadt	city	worüber	about what
die Straße	road, street	zwei	two

German Information Center

In Bonn

Lyonel Feininger: Am Strand

Dritte Lektion

Bei Thieles

[*Gerd und seine Schwester Sabine helfen Frau Thiele in der Küche. Tom Evans und Herr Thiele sitzen auf der Terrasse vor dem Wohnzimmer.*]

EVANS — Ihr Haus ist wirklich sehr modern. Bei uns glauben viele, hier gibt es nur altmodische Wohnungen.

THIELE — Das stimmt aber nicht! Ich prahle nicht gern, aber die moderne Architektur verdankt uns sehr viel. Das darf man nicht vergessen.

EVANS — Wieso?

THIELE — Sie kennen doch sicher den Namen „Bauhaus"?

EVANS — Den Namen schon. Aber ich weiß nicht viel darüber. Können Sie mir mehr davon erzählen?

THIELE — Selbstverständlich. Aber Sie möchten doch sicher zuerst einen Rundgang machen.

EVANS — Sehr gerne.

THIELE — Hier ist das Arbeitszimmer. Antike Möbel. Sie sollen als Kontrast wirken.

EVANS — Bei uns sieht man das auch oft.

THIELE — Dort neben der Küche ist die Tür zum Bad. Kommen Sie, gehen wir jetzt nach oben in die Schlafzimmer.

FRAU THIELE — [*aus der Küche*] Und dann ins Eßzimmer bitte!

At the Thieles

[*Gerd and his sister Sabine are helping Mrs. Thiele in the kitchen. Tom Evans and Mr. Thiele are sitting on the terrace outside the living room.*]

EVANS — Your house is really very modern. At home a lot of people think there are only old-fashioned houses here.

THIELE — But that's not so. I don't like to boast, but modern architecture owes us a lot. One mustn't forget that.

EVANS — In what way?

THIELE — I'm sure you know the name *Bauhaus*.

EVANS — I do know the name. But I don't know much about it. Can you tell me more about it?

THIELE — Certainly. But I'm sure you'd like to take a tour around first.

EVANS — I'd like to very much.

THIELE — Here's the study. Antique furniture. It's supposed to serve as a contrast.

EVANS — We see that a lot at home, too.

THIELE — Over there next to the kitchen is the door to the bathroom. Come, let's go upstairs to the bedrooms now.

MRS. THIELE — [*from the kitchen*] And then to the dining room please.

Lesestück III

Nach dem Essen[1] spricht Herr Thiele über ein interessantes[2] Kapitel[3] aus der Geschichte der modernen deutschen Architektur.

Im Jahre 1919 (neunzehnhundertneunzehn) gründet[4] Walter Gropius eine Hochschule[5] für Architektur, das „Bauhaus“. Er will die Architektur modernisieren, denn sie soll in das Maschinenzeitalter[6] passen.[7] Gropius will die Verbindung[8] von Industrie und Kunst:[9] der Architekt, der Ingenieur,[10] und der Künstler[11] sollen zusammen[12] arbeiten und konstruieren[13] — praktisch, harmonisch und schön[14] — das „Einheitskunstwerk“.[15] Man lehrt[16] Architektur, Stadtplanung[17] und Innendekoration:[18] man konstruiert Möbel und Lampen, experimentiert mit Farben[19] und Formen. Das Material für den Hausbau[20] ist Stahl,[21] Glas und Beton,[22] für die Möbel Stahl, Holz,[23] Glas und Textilien.

Große Künstler wie Klee, Kandinsky und Feininger lehren an der Bauhaus–Schule.[24] In der ganzen Welt hat der neue Stil[25] großen Einfluß.[26] Aber 1934 (neunzehnhundertvierunddreißig) muß[27] die Hochschule schließen.[28] Die Nationalsozialisten nennen den Stil „dekadent“. Gropius und andere emigrieren nach Amerika, wo sie weiterarbeiten. Im Jahre 1937 (neunzehnhundertsiebenunddreißig) gründen sie dann ein „New Bauhaus“ in Chicago.

[1] **das Essen** meal
[2] **interessant** interesting
[3] **das Kapitel** chapter
[4] **gründen** to found
[5] **die Hochschule** academy
[6] **das Maschinenzeitalter** machine age, era of technology
[7] **passen** to fit
[8] **die Verbindung** union
[9] **die Kunst** art
[10] **der Ingenieur** engineer
[11] **der Künstler,** *pl.* **die Künstler** artist
[12] **zusammen** together
[13] **konstruieren** to construct
[14] **schön** beautifully

[15] **das Einheitskunstwerk** (not translatable) work of art combining the skills of all the participants
[16] **lehren** to teach
[17] **die Stadtplanung** city planning
[18] **die Innendekoration** interior decorating
[19] **die Farbe,** *pl.* **die Farben** color
[20] **der Hausbau** construction of a house
[21] **der Stahl** steel
[22] **der Beton** concrete
[23] **das Holz** wood
[24] **die Schule** school
[25] **der Stil** style
[26] **der Einfluß** influence
[27] **müssen** must, to have to
[28] **schließen** to close, shut

Innendekoration, 1930

Stuhl, 1925 **Vier Tische, 1926**

Fragen und Antworten

1. Sitzt Gerd auf der Terrasse?
   Nein, er ist in der Küche und hilft Frau Thiele.
2. Ist Gerds Schwester nicht in der Küche?
   Doch, sie ist auch dort.
3. Was weiß Tom Evans über das „Bauhaus"?
   Er kennt den Namen, aber er weiß nicht viel darüber.
4. Möchte Tom Evans mehr über das „Bauhaus" wissen?
   Ja, Herr Thiele soll Tom Evans mehr davon erzählen.
5. Kennt Tom Evans die Wohnung schon?
   Nein, er muß zuerst einen Rundgang machen.
6. Was für (*what kind of*) Möbel hat das Arbeitszimmer?
   Antike Möbel. Sie wirken als Kontrast.
7. Warum (*why*) gehen die beiden nach oben?
   Sie wollen die Schlafzimmer sehen.
8. Dürfen sie lange oben bleiben (*stay*)?
   Nein, sie sollen bald (*soon*) ins Eßzimmer kommen.
9. Gibt es in Amerika nur altmodische Wohnungen?
   Nein, hier gibt es auch moderne Wohnungen.
10. Worüber spricht Herr Thiele nach dem Essen?
    Er spricht über Walter Gropius und die moderne Architektur.

Structure and Practice

Explanation of Forms

I. MODAL AUXILIARIES

German has a group of six modal auxiliary verbs. They express the manner (mode) in which an action is performed. For example, in the sentence "You can explain it to me," ability is indicated; in the sentence "I have to fly to Berlin," necessity is indicated.

A. Basic Meanings of the Modals

dürfen expresses *permission:* to be permitted to, be allowed to, may
können expresses *ability:* to be able to, can

mögen expresses *liking:* to like (to)
müssen expresses *necessity:* to have to, must
sollen expresses *obligation:* to be supposed to
wollen expresses *wish, desire, intention:* to want (to), intend to

Some of the modals have additional idiomatic meanings, which will be dealt with as they occur in each lesson.

B. *Forms of the Modals*

The present-tense conjugation of modals is different from that of regular verbs. In the singular each modal except **sollen** has a vowel change, and there is no personal ending in the first and third person; in the plural the modals follow the pattern of regular verbs.

dürfen		**können**	
ich er sie es	**darf**	ich er sie es	**kann**
wir sie Sie	**dürfen**	wir sie Sie	**können**

mögen		**müssen**	
ich er sie es	**mag**	ich er sie es	**muß**
wir sie Sie	**mögen**	wir sie Sie	**müssen**

sollen		**wollen**	
ich er sie es	**soll**	ich er sie es	**will**
wir sie Sie	**sollen**	wir sie Sie	**wollen**

C. Use of the Modals

1. WITH A DEPENDENT INFINITIVE: The modals are usually used as auxiliary verbs with a dependent infinitive, which in German is placed at
the end of the clause.

> **dürfen** (*permission*)
>
> **Darf** ich das Arbeitszimmer **sehen?**
> *May I see the study?*

Note: The negative of **dürfen** may mean *not allowed to:*

> Ich darf nicht in Gerds Zimmer gehen.
> *I am not allowed to go into Gerd's room.*

Often, however, it means *must not:*

> Das darf man nicht vergessen.
> *One must not forget that.*

> **können** (*ability*)
>
> **Können** Sie mir mehr davon **erzählen?**
> *Can you tell me more about it?*

> **mögen** (*liking*)
>
> Ich **mag** das nicht **sehen.**
> *I don't like to see that.*

Note: **Mögen** is less frequently used than the other modals. It has been replaced
in its meaning of *to like* by other constructions. (See **gern** in the section "Word Study
and Usage" of this lesson.) When it is used, it is generally in the negative, as in the
above example.

The only frequent use of **mögen** occurs in the subjunctive **möchte.** It means *would like*
and has the following forms:

$$\left.\begin{array}{l} \text{ich} \\ \text{er} \\ \text{sie} \\ \text{es} \end{array}\right\} \textbf{möchte} \qquad \left.\begin{array}{l} \text{wir} \\ \text{sie} \\ \text{Sie} \end{array}\right\} \textbf{möchten}$$

Aber Sie **möchten** doch sicher zuerst einen Rundgang **machen.**
But I'm sure you'd like to take a tour around first.

> **müssen** (*necessity*)
>
> Im Jahre 1934 **muß** die Hochschule **schließen.**
> *In 1934 the school has to close.*

> **sollen** (*obligation*)
>
> Sie **sollen** als Kontrast **wirken.**
> *They are supposed to serve as a contrast.*

> **wollen** (*wish, desire, intention*)
>
> Er **will** die Architektur **modernisieren.**
> *He wants to modernize architecture.*

Er **will** an der Universität Bonn **studieren.**
He intends to study at the University of Bonn.

2. WITHOUT A DEPENDENT INFINITIVE: The dependent infinitive may be omitted with a modal when its meaning is clear from the context.

Wollen Sie auch nach Frankfurt?
Do you intend to go to Frankfurt, too?

Wer will schon durch jedes kleine Dorf?
Who wants to go through every little village?

II. WISSEN (TO KNOW A FACT)

The verb **wissen** has a present-tense conjugation similar to that of the modals:

$$
\left.\begin{array}{l} \text{ich} \\ \text{er} \\ \text{sie} \\ \text{es} \end{array}\right\} \textbf{weiß} \qquad \left.\begin{array}{l} \text{wir} \\ \text{sie} \\ \text{Sie} \end{array}\right\} \textbf{wissen}
$$

III. IMPERATIVE

The command or request is expressed in German by inverting the order of the subject and verb.

Nehmen Sie meine Zeitschrift!   *Take my magazine.*
Kommen Sie!   *Come.*

The first person plural imperative, the English *let us* form, also uses this inverted word order:

Gehen wir jetzt nach oben!   *Let's go upstairs now.*

Note: The punctuation for a command or request in German is either a period or an exclamation mark.

Since German questions (except those beginning with a question word) use the same word order as commands, in written German it is important to note the punctuation and in spoken German to note the intonation. (The voice goes up at the end of a question and down at the end of a command.) Compare the following questions with the commands given above.

Nehmen Sie meine Zeitschrift?   *Are you taking my magazine?*
Gehen wir jetzt nach oben?   *Shall we go (are we going) upstairs now?*

Word Study and Usage

I. GERN(E)

Gern(e) literally means *gladly*. When used in combination with a verb, however, it means *to like to* (do whatever the verb specifies).

Ich prahle nicht gern.   *I don't like to boast.*

In this use, **gern** occurs more frequently than **mögen.**

Ich **mag** das nicht **sehen.** }
Ich **sehe** das nicht **gern.** } *I don't like to see that.*

Gern is not restricted to use in the negative, as **mögen** has come to be.

Ich sehe das gern.   *I like to see that.*

II. KENNEN AND WISSEN

The two verbs **kennen** and **wissen,** meaning *to know,* have different uses: **kennen** means *to know by acquaintance, be acquainted with.*

Sie kennen doch sicher den Namen „Bauhaus".
I'm sure you know (are acquainted with) the name Bauhaus.
Gerd Thiele kennt den Gast schon.
Gerd Thiele already knows the guest.

wissen means *to know a fact* (or *facts*).

Ich weiß nicht viel darüber.   *I don't know much about it.*

III. OBEN AND UNTEN

Oben means *upstairs;* **unten** means *downstairs.* When motion toward those places is indicated, then **nach** must be used before those words.

Welche Zimmer sind **oben?**   *Which rooms are upstairs?*
Gehen wir jetzt **nach oben!**   *Let's go upstairs now.*
Welche Zimmer sind **unten?**   *Which rooms are downstairs?*
Gehen wir jetzt **nach unten!**   *Let's go downstairs now.*

Class Drills

I. a. Restate the following sentences, substituting <u>wir</u> as the subject:

Ich soll Gerd helfen.
Ich kann hier sitzen.

Ich darf das nicht erzählen.
Ich will nach oben gehen.
Ich muß deutsch sprechen.
Ich mag das nicht.
Ich weiß nicht viel.

b. Restate the following sentences, substituting <u>er</u> *as the subject:*

Sie sollen hier bleiben.
Sie können mehr davon erzählen.
Sie dürfen hier sitzen.
Sie wollen nach Frankfurt kommen.
Sie müssen in Bonn bleiben.
Sie mögen das nicht.
Sie wissen mehr.

II. Restate the following sentences, using each of the following modals — müssen, dürfen, wollen, können, sollen:

EXAMPLE: **Ich frage sie.**
Ich muß sie fragen; ich darf sie fragen; etc.

1. Er hilft Sabine.
2. Ich fahre nach Bonn.
3. Sie erzählen Gerd davon.
4. Wir gehen ins Eßzimmer.
5. Sie fragt den Professor.
6. Gehen Sie jetzt nach oben?

III. Restate the following sentences, substituting the German for the modals given in English:

1. Er will über Architektur sprechen.
      (*must*)
      (*would like to*)
      (*is supposed to*)

2. Sie können das nicht machen.
      (*must not*)
      (*do not want to*)
      (*are not supposed to*)

3. Ich möchte ihn fragen.
      (*can*)
      (*am allowed to*)
      (*want to*)

4. Wir müssen es erzählen.
   (*would like to*)
   (*are supposed to*)
   (*want to*)

IV. *Change the following to the <u>Sie</u> and <u>wir</u> imperatives:*

EXAMPLE: **Sie fahren nach Bonn.**
   Fahren Sie **nach Bonn!**
   Fahren wir **nach Bonn!**

1. Sie gehen direkt nach Hause.
2. Sie vergessen das nicht.
3. Sie nehmen eine deutsche Zeitung.
4. Sie nehmen meinen Wagen.
5. Sie gehen nach oben.
6. Sie fahren auf der Autobahn.
7. Sie machen einen Rundgang.
8. Sie gehen ins Eßzimmer.
9. Sie fahren durch die Stadt.
10. Sie sprechen nicht darüber.

V. *Change the following sentences, adding <u>gern</u>:*

EXAMPLE: **Gerd fährt auf der Autobahn.**
   Gerd fährt *gern* **auf der Autobahn.**

1. Ich fahre durch jedes Dorf.
2. Er sitzt auf der Terrasse.
3. Sie hilft in der Küche.
4. Sie fahren durch die Stadt.
5. Wir arbeiten bei der Firma Opel.
6. Er wohnt in Bonn.
7. Sie sprechen über Amerika.
8. Sie studiert Geschichte.

Exercises

I. *Rewrite the following sentences, substituting the pronouns given in English:*

1. Ich will in Berlin studieren. (*they, she*)   2. Wir müssen die Stewardeß fragen. (*he, you*)   3. Wann sollen sie kommen? (*I, we*)   4. Sie kann den Wagen nicht fahren. (*he, we*)   5. Ich mag das nicht sehen.

(*they, she*)   6. Dürfen Sie das machen? (*I, they*)   7. Wir möchten hier arbeiten. (*he, I*)   8. Wir wissen nicht viel. (*she, they*)

II. *a. Translate the following sentences:*   ~~Sie hilft Gerd.~~

1. Er muß darüber sprechen.   2. Sie soll Gerd helfen.   3. Er darf nicht so schnell fahren.   4. Er kann nichts darüber erzählen. 5. Tom möchte das wissen.   6. Sie will einen Rundgang machen. 7. Das darf man nicht vergessen.   8. Sie möchte bei der Lufthansa arbeiten.   9. Es soll als Kontrast wirken.   10. Sie dürfen nicht so schnell laufen.

b. Rewrite the sentences in exercise a. *without modals.*

EXAMPLE: **Er soll nach Bonn fahren.**
            Er *fährt* nach Bonn.

III. *Translate into English. Then reproduce the German sentences from your English translations:*

1. Darf ich jetzt nach unten gehen?   2. Ich weiß, er ist Professor, aber ich kenne ihn nicht.   3. Das muß der Gast aus Amerika sein. Er ist seit Juni hier.   4. Wohnt sie gern im Studentenheim?   5. Will er auch durch das Dorf? — Nein, er kann nicht, er muß um zwei in Frankfurt sein. 6. Kommen Sie, fahren wir jetzt durch die Stadt.   7. Das kann nicht stimmen.   8. Sie vergißt oft die Zeitung.   9. Ich glaube, nicht viele kennen ihn hier.   10. Antike Möbel mag er nicht.

IV. *Translate:*

1. He likes to brag, but he doesn't know the name *Bauhaus*.   2. Do you want to help Mrs. Thiele? — Certainly.   3. Let's drive to Berlin. 4. Doesn't she want to see the living room?   5. You mustn't forget that. 6. Please don't drive too fast. 7. Let's go downstairs.   8. That's right, the bedroom is upstairs.   9. At two o'clock he is supposed to be here.   10. Whom would you like to see?

V. *Composition. Answer the following questions in German, using as much of the question in your answer as possible. Write your answers in a paragraph, omitting* ja *and* nein:

1. Wo sitzen Tom Evans und Herr Thiele vor dem Essen?
2. Wo ist Frau Thiele?
3. Wer hilft Frau Thiele?

4. Wie ist Thieles Haus?
5. Welche (*which*) Zimmer sind unten?
6. Was ist vor dem Wohnzimmer?
7. Welche Zimmer sind oben?
8. Welches Zimmer hat antike Möbel?
9. Sieht man antike Möbel als Kontrast nur in Deutschland?
10. In welches Zimmer gehen Tom und Herr Thiele nach dem Rundgang?

Active Vocabulary

altmodisch	old-fashioned	**oben**	above; upstairs
antik	antique	**oft**	often
das Arbeitszimmer	study	**prahlen**	to boast
die Architektur	architecture	**der Rundgang**	tour
das Bad	bathroom, bath	**das Schlafzimmer,**	bedroom
bald	soon	*pl.* **die Schlaf-**	
bitte	please	**zimmer**	
bleiben	to stay	**schon**	already
dann	then	**die Schwester**	sister
darüber	about it	**sehr**	very
davon	about it, of it	**sein**	his
dort	there	**selbstverständ-**	of course, certainly
dürfen	to be allowed to	**lich**	
erzählen	to tell, narrate	**sicher**	sure, certain
das Essen	meal	**sitzen**	to sit
das Eßzimmer	dining room	**sollen**	to be supposed to
die Frau	woman; Mrs.	**stimmen**	to be correct
gehen	to go	**die Terrasse**	terrace
gern(e)	gladly	**die Tür**	door
glauben	to believe	**unten**	below; downstairs
helfen (i)	to help	**verdanken**	to owe
Ihr	your	**vergessen (i)**	to forget
ins = in das	into the	**viele**	many
jetzt	now	**vor**	in front of, before
können	can, to be able to	**warum**	why
der Kontrast	contrast	**was für**	what kind of
die Küche	kitchen	**welch-**	which
machen	to make, do	**wieso**	in what way
mehr	more	**wirken**	to have an effect
mir	me, to me	**wirklich**	real
die Möbel (*pl.*)	furniture	**wissen**	to know
möchte	would like (to)	**die Wohnung**	apartment; dwelling; house
from **mögen**	to like (to)		
modern	modern	**das Wohnzimmer**	living room
mögen	to like (to)	**wollen**	to want (to)
müssen	to have to	**zuerst**	first, at first
nach	after	**zum = zu dem**	to the
nur	only		

Die Burgruine Drachenfels

Vierte Lektion

Auf dem Drachenfels

[*Gerd und Tom machen einen Ausflug. Sie folgen einem Fußweg. Er führt zu der Ruine Drachenfels. Sie sind kurz vor der Höhe.*]

TOM — So eine Fußtour macht mir Spaß.

GERD — Ja, bei dem vielen Autofahren ist das gerade das Richtige.

TOM — Woher hat der Berg eigentlich den Namen?

GERD — Von einem Drachen im Mittelalter. So heißt es wenigstens in einer Legende.

TOM — Hat jede Burg eine Legende oder Sage?

GERD — Fast alle. Sehen Sie den Mauerrest dort drüben auf der anderen Seite? Das ist der „Rolandsbogen". Er hat mit dem Drachenfels eine Sage gemeinsam. Ich erzähle sie Ihnen später.

TOM — Da sind wir ja schon. Was für eine Aussicht!

GERD — Gefällt Ihnen der romantische Rhein?

TOM — Und ob! Wie aus einem Film!

GERD — Der Turm dort im Wald neben dem Weinberg, das ist eine Schloß-ruine. Warten Sie, ich gebe Ihnen das Fernglas.

TOM — Jetzt sehe ich sie.

GERD — Hier ist übrigens eine Bank. Sie sind sicher auch müde.

At the *Drachenfels*

[*Gerd and Tom are on an outing. They are following a footpath. It leads to the* Drachenfels *castle ruin. They are almost at the top.*]

TOM — I enjoy a hike like this.

GERD — Yes, with all the driving we do, this is just the right thing.

TOM — By the way, where did the mountain get its name?

GERD — From a dragon in the Middle Ages. Or at least that's what the legend says.

TOM — Does every castle have a legend?

GERD — Almost all of them. Do you see the remains of a wall over there on the other side? That's the *Rolandsbogen*.[1] There is one legend about it and the *Drachenfels*. I'll tell it to you later.

TOM — Well, here we are. What a view!

GERD — Do you like the romantic Rhine?

TOM — And how! It's like a movie.

GERD — The tower over there in the woods next to the vineyard is a castle ruin. Wait, I'll give you the binoculars.

TOM — Now I see it.

GERD — By the way, here's a bench. I'm sure you're tired, too.

[1] **der Bogen** — *arch.* All that remains of the former castle is a window arch.

Lesestück IV

Gerd erzählt seinem Gast die Sage:

Zur Zeit[1] Karls des Großen lebt[2] in der Burg auf dem Drachenfels ein Ritter[3] mit seiner Tochter[4] Hildegund. Auf der anderen Rheinseite, auf der Burg Rolandseck, wohnt ein junger Ritter. Roland — so heißt er — ist jeden Tag mit Hildegund zusammen. Nach einigen[5] Jahren muß Roland zum Heer[6] Karls des Großen. Er bleibt manchmal lange Zeit weg,[7] aber wenn[8] er heimkommt,[9] geht er zuerst zum Drachenfels, zu Hildegund. Sie lieben sich,[10] und bald wollen sie heiraten.[11] Die Hochzeit[12] soll nach Rolands nächster[13] Heimkehr[14] sein.

Das Mädchen[15] ist glücklich,[16] aber sie hat auch Angst.[17] Roland kämpft[18] weit von Deutschland für seinen Kaiser.[19] Nach langer Wartezeit kommt Nachricht:[20] der Ritter ist in Spanien[21] gefallen.[22] Das ist für Hildegund das Ende ihres Glückes.[23]

Es ist ein Jahr später. Hildegund lebt jetzt als Nonne[24] im Kloster.[25] So will sie ihrem Geliebten[26] treu[27] bleiben. Aber ihr Leid[28] ist noch nicht zu Ende. Eines Tages ist Roland am Kloster. Die Nachricht aus Spanien war falsch.[29] Aber Hildegund muß im Kloster bleiben, denn sie darf ihr Gelübde[30] nicht brechen.[31] Roland geht zum Kaiser und zum Papst[32] in Rom. Es ist umsonst.[33] Auch sie können ihm und Hildegund nicht helfen, und so kehrt[34] er auf seine Burg zurück.[34] Dort sitzt er am Fenster[35] und sieht auf das Kloster, von wo manchmal eine junge Nonne ihm zuwinkt.[36] Eines Abends[37] hört[38] Roland die Sterbeglocke[39] im Kloster. Er weiß, Hildegund ist tot,[40] und da bricht auch ihm das Herz.[41]

---

[1] **die Zeit** time
  zur Zeit at the time of
[2] **leben** to live
[3] **der Ritter** knight
[4] **die Tochter** daughter
[5] **einige** some, a few
[6] **das Heer** army
[7] **weg** away
[8] **wenn** when
[9] **heimkommen** to come home
[10] **sich lieben** to love each other
[11] **heiraten** to marry
[12] **die Hochzeit** wedding
[13] **nächst-** next
[14] **die Heimkehr** return home
[15] **das Mädchen** girl
[16] **glücklich** happy
[17] **die Angst** fear
[18] **kämpfen** to fight
[19] **der Kaiser** emperor
[20] **die Nachricht** news
[21] **Spanien** Spain

[22] **fallen (ä)** to fall, die in battle
  ist . . . gefallen has died in battle
[23] **das Glück** happiness
[24] **die Nonne** nun
[25] **das Kloster** cloister
[26] **der Geliebte** lover, beloved
[27] **treu** true, faithful
[28] **das Leid** suffering, sorrow
[29] **falsch** false, wrong
[30] **das Gelübde** vow
[31] **brechen (i)** to break
[32] **der Papst** pope
[33] **umsonst** in vain
[34] **kehrt . . . zurück** returns
[35] **das Fenster** window
[36] **zuwinken** to wave at
[37] **der Abend** the evening
  eines Abends one evening
[38] **hören** to hear
[39] **die Sterbeglocke** funeral bell
[40] **tot** dead
[41] **das Herz** heart

Fragen und Antworten

1. Mit wem macht Gerd einen Ausflug?
   Er macht einen Ausflug mit dem Amerikaner.
2. Was macht Tom Spaß?
   Ihm macht die Fußtour Spaß.
3. Gefällt der romantische Rhein dem Amerikaner?
   Ja, er gefällt ihm.
4. Wo ist die Bank?
   Auf der Höhe, bei der Ruine.
5. Was sagt (*says*) Tom über den Rhein?
   Er sagt, er ist wie aus dem Film.
6. Was will Gerd dem Amerikaner erzählen?
   Er will dem Amerikaner eine Sage erzählen.
7. Wann will er ihm die Sage erzählen?
   Er will sie ihm später erzählen.
8. Was für eine Sage ist das?
   Es ist die Sage von einem Ritter und einer Nonne.
9. Wo lebt der Vater mit seiner Tochter?
   Er lebt mit ihr auf dem Drachenfels.
10. Wer besucht (*visits*) Hildegund oft?
    Roland kommt oft zu ihr.

Structure and Practice

Explanation of Forms

I. DATIVE CASE

A. *Forms of the Definite and Indefinite Articles*

In the dative case the definite and indefinite articles show a change in form for each gender.

	MASCULINE	FEMININE	NEUTER
Definite Article	**dem** Weg(e)	**der** Stadt	**dem** Dorf(e)
Indefinite Article	**einem** Weg(e)	**einer** Stadt	**einem** Dorf(e)

An optional **-e** is added to monosyllabic masculine and neuter nouns in the dative case. It is consistently used in such idioms as **nach Hause,** except in colloquial speech where there is a tendency to drop such endings.

B. Uses of the Dative Case

1. THE INDIRECT OBJECT: The indirect object of the verb is in the dative case.

> Er erzählt **dem Amerikaner (der Frau, dem Kind)** die Sage.
> *He tells the American (the woman, the child) the legend.*
> *He tells the legend to the American (to the woman, to the child).*
>
> Er erzählt **einem Amerikaner (einer Frau, einem Kind)** die Sage.
> *He tells an American (a woman, a child) the legend.*
> *He tells the legend to an American (to a woman, to a child).*

Note that English has no distinct dative form, in contrast to German, but has two ways of expressing the indirect object: (1) by placing it before the direct object and (2) by placing it after the direct object with the preposition *to.* German has only one way of expressing the indirect object — through the use of the dative case.

2. OBJECT OF SOME PREPOSITIONS: The dative case is always used after the following prepositions: **aus** (*out of, from*); **bei** (*at, with, near*); **mit** (*with*); **nach** (*after, to*); **seit** (*since, for*); **von** (*from, of*); **zu** (*to*).

Note: Many prepositions, including some of the above, have special idiomatic meanings in addition to the basic ones given. You will note these as they occur in the dialogues and reading selections.

> **aus:** Frau Thiele kommt **aus der Küche.**
> *Mrs. Thiele comes out of the kitchen.*
>
> **bei:** Die Bank ist auf der Höhe **bei der Ruine.**
> *The bench is at the top near the ruin.*
>
> **mit:** Er wartet schon **mit dem Wagen.**
> *He is already waiting with the car.*
>
> **nach:** **Nach dem Essen** spricht Herr Thiele von Walter Gropius.
> *After dinner Mr. Thiele talks about Walter Gropius.*
>
> **seit:** Er hat den Wagen **seit einem Jahr.**
> *He's had the car for a year.*

von: Man sieht nichts **vom (von dem) Land.**
           One sees nothing of the country.

zu: Hier ist die Tür **zum (zu dem) Bad.**
           Here is the door to the bathroom.

Note: Other prepositions, such as **auf, über, in, vor,** sometimes take the dative case. These will be explained in Lesson 7.

Contractions: Some combinations of prepositions and definite articles are usually contracted in German.

Man sieht nichts **vom (von dem)** Land.
Hier ist die Tür **zum (zu dem)** Bad.

3. OBJECT OF SOME VERBS: Although most verbs require an accusative case object, a few verbs can take only a dative object. Of these you have encountered the following in the text:

folgen: Sie **folgen einem Fußweg** zu der Ruine.
helfen: Sie **helfen der Mutter** in der Küche.
gefallen: Der romantische Rhein **gefällt dem Amerikaner.**
glauben (dative only with persons): Er **glaubt dem Amerikaner** nicht.
           but: Er glaubt **es.** (*acc.*)

C. Personal Pronouns: Dative Case

Whereas English uses the same forms of the personal pronouns for all objects — direct, indirect, and prepositional — German distinguishes between accusative and dative pronouns in most persons.

English	*German*	
OBJECTIVE CASE (for all objects)	ACCUSATIVE CASE	DATIVE CASE
me	**mich**	**mir**
him	**ihn**	**ihm**
her	**sie**	**ihr**
it	**es**	**ihm**
us	**uns**	**uns**
them	**sie**	**ihnen**
you	**Sie**	**Ihnen**

Dative personal pronouns have the same uses as dative nouns:

Indirect Object
Ich gebe **Ihnen** das Fernglas.

Object of Some Prepositions
> Roland kommt oft **zu ihr.**

Object of Some Verbs
> Der Rhein gefällt **ihm.**

D. Interrogative Pronouns: Dative Case

The dative form of the nominative interrogative pronoun **wer** (accusative: **wen**) is **wem.**

> Mit **wem** macht Gerd einen Ausflug?
> *With whom does Gerd go on an outing?*

The dative form of the interrogative pronoun **was** does not exist. Substitutes for it will be explained in a later lesson.

II. WORD ORDER OF DIRECT AND INDIRECT OBJECTS

There is a rule governing the position of direct and indirect objects in German when both occur in a sentence: the indirect object (dative) precedes the direct object (accusative), unless the direct object is a pronoun.

> Er will **dem Amerikaner eine Sage** erzählen.
> Ich gebe **Ihnen das Fernglas.**
> Ich erzähle **sie Ihnen** später.
> Ich verdanke **es dem Amerikaner.**

III. WEAK NOUNS

Usually, when a German noun is used in the accusative or dative case, it retains the same form as the nominative (**der Berg, den Berg, dem Berg**); there are a few masculine nouns, however, which add an **-n** or **-en** when they are used in any case other than the nominative. Of these so-called weak nouns you have had the following in the dialogues:

> **der Name, den Namen, dem Namen**
> **der Student, den Studenten, dem Studenten**
> **der Herr, den Herrn, dem Herrn**
> **der Drache, den Drachen, dem Drachen**

Woher hat der Berg **den Namen?** *Where did the mountain get its name?*

Additional weak nouns will be indicated in the vocabulary of the lessons in which they occur.

Word Study and Usage

I. GERUNDS (VERBAL NOUNS)

The gerund (-*ing* noun formed from a verb: *The driving* was difficult) is formed in German by making a neuter noun of the infinitive.

> **das Arbeiten,** *the working:*
>> Manchmal ist **das Arbeiten** nicht leicht.
>> *Sometimes working is not easy.*

> **das Autofahren,** *the* (*car*) *driving:*
>> Bei **dem vielen Autofahren** ist das gerade das Richtige.
>> *With all the driving* (*we do*), *this is just the right thing.*

II. WAS FÜR EIN

In a question, the expression **was für ein** means *what kind of a:*
> **Was für eine Sage** ist das?   *What kind of a legend is that?*

In an exclamation the same phrase means *what a:*
> **Was für eine Aussicht!**   *What a view!*

The case of the noun after **für** is not governed by the preposition **für** but by the function of the entire phrase in the sentence:

> Was für **ein Wagen** (*nom.*) ist das?
> *What kind of a car is that?*
> Was für **einen Wagen** (*acc.*) haben Sie?
> *What kind of a car do you have?*
> Von was für **einer Zeitung** (*dat.*) spricht er?
> *What kind of a newspaper is he talking about?*

III. GEFALLEN

The verb **gefallen** literally means *to please, be pleasing to.* It is frequently translated most idiomatically as *to like.* The object of the verb (the person who is pleased) is in the dative case.

> Es gefällt mir.
> *It pleases me.* (or) *I like it.*
> Der romantische Rhein gefällt ihm.
> *He likes the romantic Rhine.*
> Gefällt Ihnen der romantische Rhein?
> *Do you like the romantic Rhine?*

Class Drills

I. Repeat the following sentences, substituting the nouns indicated:

1. Er erzählt dem Amerikaner die Sage.
> Gast
> Vater
> Geschäftsmann
> Herrn
> Kind
> Mädchen

2. Er erzählt der Familie die Sage.
> Frau
> Tochter
> Studentin
> Schwester

(Watch the gender for each noun in the following group.)

3. Er erzählt dem Vater die Sage.
> Frau
> Kind
> Geschäftsmann
> Tochter
> Herrn

4. Sie gibt einem Fluggast die Zeitschrift.
> Amerikaner
> Studenten
> Herrn
> Geschäftsmann
> Kind
> Mädchen

5. Sie gibt einer Studentin die Zeitschrift.
> Frau
> Amerikanerin
> Stewardeß

(Watch the gender for each noun in the following group.)

6. Sie gibt einem Amerikaner die Zeitschrift.
> Frau
> Kind
> Studentin
> Studenten
> Mädchen

II. Repeat the following sentences, substituting the nouns indicated:

1. Das ist der Weg zum Drachenfels.
   >Flugplatz
   >Weinberg
   >Wald
   >Turm

2. Das ist der Weg zum Dorf.
   >Studentenheim
   >Schloß
   >Haus

3. Das ist der Weg zur Rennbahn.
   >Stadt
   >Autobahn
   >Schloßruine
   >Höhe

(Watch the gender for each noun in the following group.)

4. Das ist der Weg zum Schloß.
   >Schloßruine
   >Dorf
   >Turm
   >Stadt
   >Wald

5. Der Weg führt zu einem Wald.
   >Flugplatz
   >Weinberg
   >Turm

6. Der Weg führt zu einem Haus.
   >Schloß
   >Dorf
   >Studentenheim

7. Der Weg führt zu einer Schloßruine.
   >Bank
   >Stadt
   >Rennbahn

(Watch the gender for each noun in the following group.)

8. Der Weg führt zu einem Turm.
   >Schloßruine
   >Haus
   >Bank

              Wald
              Dorf

9. Er spricht von dem Film.
              Ausflug
              Rundgang
              Drachenfels
              Berg

10. Er spricht von dem Mädchen.
              Schloß
              Essen
              Land
              Zimmer

11. Er spricht von der Universität.
              Fußtour
              Wohnung
              Burg
              Hauptstadt

III. Answer each question affirmatively, substituting a pronoun for each dative noun:

EXAMPLE: **Erzählt sie *dem Amerikaner* die Sage?**
              Ja, sie erzählt *ihm* die Sage.

1. Erzählt sie dem Studenten die Sage?
   Gibt sie dem Fluggast die Zeitung?
   Verdankt sie dem Amerikaner so viel?
   Erzählt sie dem Kind die Legende?

2. Erzählt sie der Tochter die Sage?
   Gibt sie der Frau die Zeitung?
   Verdankt sie der Amerikanerin so viel?
   Erzählt sie der Studentin die Legende?

3. Gibt er dem Herrn die Zeitung?
   Gibt sie der Studentin die Zeitschrift?
   Erzählt sie dem Kind die Legende?
   Gibt sie dem Studenten die Zeitschrift?

IV. Repeat the following sentences, substituting the nouns indicated:

1. Er hilft dem Amerikaner.
              Studenten
              Herrn

> Kind
> Mädchen

2. Er hilft der Studentin.
> Amerikanerin
> Tochter
> Frau
> Schwester

(*Watch the gender for each noun in the following group.*)

3. Er hilft dem Amerikaner.
> Kind
> Frau
> Studenten
> Studentin

4. Der romantische Rhein gefällt dem Amerikaner.
> Studenten
> Herrn
> Geschäftsmann
> Mädchen

5. Der romantische Rhein gefällt der Amerikanerin.
> Studentin
> Tochter
> Frau
> Schwester

(*Watch the gender for each noun in the following group.*)

6. Der romantische Rhein gefällt dem Amerikaner.
> Studentin
> Frau
> Studenten
> Mädchen

V. Repeat the following sentences, substituting the German for the object pronouns given in English:

1. Er erzählt mir die Legende. (*him, her, us, them, you, me*)
2. Er fährt mit mir nach Frankfurt. (*him, her, us, them, you, me*)
3. Er folgt mir zu der Ruine. (*him, her, us, them, you, me*)
4. Die Stadt gefällt mir. (*I like the city.*)
> (*He*)
> (*She*)
> (*We*)
> (*They*)

(You)
(I)

5. So eine Fußtour macht mir Spaß. (*I enjoy a hike like this.*)
        (He)
        (She)
        (We)
        (They)
        (You)
        (I)

VI. Form questions from the following statements according to the example:

EXAMPLE: **Das ist ein Wagen.**
          Was für ein Wagen ist das?

1. Das ist ein Name.
  Das ist ein Flugplatz.
  Das ist ein Weinberg.
  Das ist ein Studentenheim.
  Das ist ein Dorf.
  Das ist eine Schloßruine.
  Das ist eine Firma.
  Das ist eine Rennbahn.

2. Er hat einen Wagen.
  Er hat einen Weinberg.
  Er hat einen Professor.
  Er hat ein Haus.
  Er hat ein Zimmer.
  Er hat ein Fernglas.
  Er hat eine Wohnung.
  Er hat eine Zeitung.
  Er hat eine Zeitschrift.

Exercises

I. Answer affirmatively, substituting a pronoun for the object in each sentence:

1. Erzählt sie die Sage oft?   2. Helfen Sie dem Professor oft?   3. Sehen Sie die Ruine?   4. Sehen Sie den Berg?   5. Hilft er dem Amerikaner?   6. Glaubt er der Studentin?   7. Gefällt es dem Gast?   8. Be-

sucht er Gerd und Sabine oft? 9. Macht es Gerd und Tom Spaß?
10. Ist das für Gerd und Sabine?

II. Rewrite the following sentences according to the example:

EXAMPLE: **Sie gibt *dem Gast die Zeitung.***
Sie gibt *ihm die Zeitung.*
Sie gibt *sie dem Gast.*
Sie gibt *sie ihm.*

1. Gerd gibt dem Herrn den „Spiegel".
2. Sie erzählen der Amerikanerin die Sage.
3. Geben Sie dem Professor die Zeitschrift!
4. Kann er der Studentin den Wagen geben?
5. Ich soll dem Studenten das Fernglas geben.

III. Translate into English. Then reproduce the German sentences from your English translations.

1. Mit dem Fernglas können Sie das Schloß dort im Wald sehen.
2. Kurz vor zwei kommt der Politiker nach Bonn; so heißt es wenigstens
in der Zeitung. 3. Folgen Sie der Straße durch den Wald, dann sind Sie
um zwei da. 4. Der Fußweg führt direkt zum Rhein. 5. Bei dem
vielen Studieren ist so ein Ausflug gerade das Richtige. 6. Wem gefällt
so eine Aussicht nicht! 7. Mir macht es Spaß. Ihnen auch? 8. Sehen
Sie das Haus dort drüben? Tom hat dort ein Zimmer bei einer deutschen
Familie. 9. Woher kommt er eigentlich? — Aus einer Stadt in Kali-
fornien. 10. Was für einen Wagen möchten Sie? — Einen Volkswagen
oder einen Opel.

IV. Translate:

1. Wait, he'll give you the newspaper. 2. He knows me and he can
help me. 3. He is enjoying the hike, but he is tired and wants to go
home. 4. She has to follow them. 5. By the way, the dormitory is
not far from (*von*) the university. 6. What kind of a newspaper does
she have? 7. After the outing I must tell you a legend. 8. Let's drive
through the forest; later we can visit the castle on the other side.
9. With whom would you like to go? 10. That's for you. Do you like it?

V. Composition. Answer the following questions in German, using as much of the question in your answer as possible. Write your answer in a paragraph, omitting ja and nein:

1. Wo sind Gerd und Tom?
2. Sind sie schon auf der Höhe?
3. Wie findet (*finds*) Tom die Fußtour?
4. Woher hat der Drachenfels den Namen?
5. Was kann man auf der anderen Rheinseite sehen?
6. Wie heißt die Ruine auf der anderen Rheinseite?
7. Was gefällt Tom?
8. Was sieht man von der Höhe?
9. Was gibt Gerd seinem Gast?
10. Was erzählt er ihm später?

Active Vocabulary

alle	all	**die Mauer**	wall
ander-	other	**der Mauerrest**	remains of a wall
der Ausflug	outing, excursion	**mit**	with
die Aussicht	view	**das Mittelalter**	Middle Ages
das Autofahren	driving	**müde**	tired
die Bank	bench	**nach**	after, to
bei	at, with, near	**die Nonne**	nun
der Berg	mountain	**ob**	whether
besuchen	to visit	**und ob!**	and how!
die Burg	castle	**richtig**	right, correct
der Drache, den	dragon	**das Richtige**	the right thing
Drachen, dem		**der Ritter**	knight
Drachen		**romantisch**	romantic
der Drachenfels	*lit.*, dragon's cliff	**die Ruine**	ruin
	(*name of mountain*	**die Sage**	legend
	on the Rhine)	**sagen**	to say
drüben	over there	**das Schloß**	castle
eigentlich	actual	**die Schloßruine**	castle ruin
es heißt	it says	**seit**	since, for
fast	almost	**die Seite**	side
das Fernglas	binoculars	**so ein**	such a
der Film	film, movie(s)	**der Spaß**	fun
finden	to find	**es macht mir**	I enjoy it
folgen	to follow	**Spaß**	
führen	to lead	**spät**	late
die Fußtour	hike	**später**	later
der Fußweg	footpath	**die Tochter**	daughter
gefallen (ä)	to be pleasing to, like	**die Tour**	tour
gemeinsam	in common	**der Turm**	tower
gerade	just	**von**	from, of
die Höhe	peak, top	**der Wald**	forest
das Kind	child	**der Wein**	wine
kurz	short	**der Weinberg**	vineyard
leben	to live	**wenigstens**	at least
die Legende	legend	**woher**	from where
das Mädchen	girl		

In einer Weinstube

Fünfte Lektion

In der Weinstube

[*Nach ihrem Ausflug sitzen Gerd und Tom in einer alten Weinstube und bestellen ein Glas Wein.*]

GERD — Wir kennen uns schon ziemlich gut, Herr Evans, und wir sind ja auch Kommilitonen. Sagen wir doch „du" zueinander.

TOM — Gern. Gibt es nicht bei euch eine richtige Zeremonie? Wie nennt ihr das?

GERD — Brüderschafttrinken. Da kommt unser Wein. Ich zeige dir, wie man das macht. Hier, nimm dein Glas in die Hand, häng deinen Arm in meinen Arm, Prost! Siehst du, jetzt bist du mein „Bruder" und darfst mich beim Vornamen nennen.

TOM — Seid ihr immer so umständlich?

GERD — Das tut man nur zum Spaß.

TOM — [*zeigt auf die Fotografie einer Kirche an der Wand*] Dieses Bild, das ist euer berühmter Kölner Dom, nicht wahr?

GERD — Stimmt, ich will dich ja noch nach Köln fahren! Da müssen wir noch vor Semesterbeginn hin.

TOM — Die Stadt Köln möchte ich unbedingt sehen, besonders ihr weltbekanntes Wahrzeichen.

GERD — [*sieht auf seine Uhr*] Schon fünf! Jetzt wird's aber Zeit, sonst gibt's kein Abendessen.

In the *Weinstube*[1]

[*After their outing, Gerd and Tom are sitting in an old* Weinstube, *and they order a glass of wine.*]

GERD — We know each other pretty well by now, Mr. Evans, and we're fellow students besides. Let's say *du*[2] to each other.

TOM — I'd like to very much. Isn't there an actual ceremony here? What do you call it?

GERD — *Brüderschafttrinken.*[3] Here comes our wine. I'll show you how it's done. Here, take your glass in your hand, link your arm in mine. Cheers! You see, now you're my "brother" and are allowed to call me by my first name.

TOM — Are you Germans always so formal?

GERD — That's only done for fun.

TOM — [*points to a photograph of a church on the wall*] This picture here — that's your famous Cologne Cathedral, isn't it?

GERD — That's right, I still want to drive you to Cologne. We'll have to go there before the beginning of the semester.

TOM — I'd certainly like to see Cologne, especially its famous landmark.

GERD — [*looks at his watch*] Five o'clock already. It's time to go now, or else we won't get any dinner.

---

[1] **die Weinstube:** (*lit.* "wine room"). There is no English equivalent for this word. Although there are new, modern ones, most are old, atmospheric places full of historic mementos, pictures, etc. Wines are the specialty.   [2] **du:** familiar form of address used between close friends. (See "Explanation of Forms" in this lesson.)   [3] **das Brüderschafttrinken:** (*lit.* "drink to brotherhood") a pledge of close friendship made over a glass of wine.

Lesestück V

Der Kölner Dom hat eine interessante Geschichte. Man beginnt den Bau in der Zeit der Frühgotik[1] im 13. (dreizehnten) Jahrhundert.[2] Im Jahre 1248 (zwölfhundertachtundvierzig) legt man den Grundstein[3] zu dieser großen Kathedrale. Sie soll den Dreikönigsschrein[4] aufnehmen,[5] eine der heiligsten[6] Reliquien[7] der ganzen Christenheit.[8] Kaiser Barbarossa hatte[9] diesen Schrein im 12. (zwölften) Jahrhundert von Italien nach Köln gebracht.[9] Der Chor des Doms[10] ist 1322 (dreizehnhundertzweiundzwanzig) fertig, und aus der ganzen Welt kommen die Pilger[11] in die Stadt. Hoch[12] wächst der Torso in den Himmel.[13] Die Stadt Köln möchte einen Dom haben, so groß und schön wie die Notre–Dame–Kathedrale in Paris. Aber dann wird die Stadt arm,[14] und Köln verliert[15] das Interesse am Dom. Seit dem Jahre 1511 (fünfzehnhundertelf) arbeitet man nicht mehr an dem Bau.

Über[16] 300 (dreihundert) Jahre lang[16] steht[17] der halbfertige[18] Dom im Zentrum von Köln. Man macht manchen[19] schwachen[20] Versuch,[21] ihn zu erhalten,[22] aber solche[23] Versuche sind umsonst. Jetzt ist der Dom fast eine Ruine, und die Ratten[24] laufen durch den Bau. Man vergißt die großen Pläne,[25] denn gotische Architektur ist jetzt unmodern.

Aber dann kommt die romantische Epoche, und sie hat wieder[26] Interesse an der Gotik. Man findet die alten Pläne wieder und will jetzt die Vollendung[27] des Doms. Im Jahre 1842 (achtzehnhundertzweiundvierzig) legt man zum zweiten[28] Mal[28] den Grundstein. Vierzig (40) Jahre später ist das große Werk fertig. Im Jahre 1888 (achtzehnhundertachtundachtzig), über 600 (sechshundert) Jahre nach dem Baubeginn, steht der Kölner Dom in seiner heutigen[29] Gestalt[30] da.

---

[1] **die Frühgotik** early Gothic period (in art and architecture)
[2] **das Jahrhundert** century
[3] **den Grundstein legen** to lay the cornerstone
[4] **der Dreikönigsschrein** shrine of the Three Wise Men
[5] **aufnehmen (i)** to receive, house
[6] **heilig** holy
   heiligst- most sacred
[7] **die Reliquie,** *pl.* **die Reliquien** relic
[8] **der Christenheit** of Christianity
[9] **hatte . . . gebracht** had brought
[10] **der Chor des Doms** choir of the cathedral (*arch.*)
[11] **der Pilger,** *pl.* **die Pilger** pilgrim
[12] **hoch** high
[13] **der Himmel** sky, heaven
[14] **arm** poor
[15] **verlieren** to lose

[16] **über** over
   über 300 Jahre lang for more than 300 years
[17] **stehen** to stand
[18] **halbfertig** half-finished
[19] **manch-** many a
[20] **schwach** weak, feeble
[21] **der Versuch** attempt
[22] **erhalten (ä)** to preserve, maintain
[23] **solch-** such
[24] **die Ratte,** *pl.* **die Ratten** rat
[25] **der Plan,** *pl.* **die Pläne** plan
[26] **wieder** again
[27] **die Vollendung** completion
[28] **zweit-** second
   zum zweiten Mal for the second time
[29] **heutig** present
[30] **die Gestalt** shape

69

Der Kölner Dom

Lufthansa Archiv

Fragen und Antworten

1. Wo ist Gerd nach dem Ausflug?
   Er sitzt mit seinem Freund (*friend*) in der Weinstube.
2. Trinken Tom und Gerd keinen Wein?
   Doch, die beiden trinken ein Glas Rheinwein.
3. Was zeigt Gerd seinem Gast?
   Er zeigt ihm, wie man Brüderschaft trinkt.
4. Bei welchem Namen nennt Gerd seinen Gast jetzt?
   Er nennt ihn jetzt beim Vornamen.
5. Was sieht man auf dem Bild?
   Köln mit seiner berühmten Kirche.
6. Ist jede Weinstube im Rheinland alt?
   Nein, manche Weinstube ist neu und modern.
7. Wann wollen Gerd und Tom nach Köln?
   Sie wollen vor ihrem Semesterbeginn hin.
8. Hat nur Köln ein Wahrzeichen?
   Nein, fast jede Stadt hat ihr Wahrzeichen.
9. Warum müssen Gerd und Tom schon gehen?
   Sie haben keine Zeit, sie müssen nach Hause.
10. Welchen Dom möchte Tom unbedingt sehen?
    Den Kölner Dom, denn diese Kirche hat eine interessante Geschichte.

Structure and Practice

Explanation of Forms

I. DER-WORDS

There is a group of six adjectives that are used before a noun in place of the article to limit or specify the noun more closely.

dieser	this	*plural:* these
jeder	each, every	*no plural*
jener	that	*plural:* those (*jener* rarely used in modern German)
mancher	many a	*plural:* some
solcher	such a	*plural:* such (German singular is rarely used)
welcher	which	*plural:* which

The endings of these adjectives change to agree in case and gender with the nouns they modify. Since these inflected forms resemble those of the definite article, they are called **der**-words.

EXAMPLE: **dieser**

	MASCULINE	FEMININE	NEUTER
	(der)	**(die)**	**(das)**
Nom.	dies**er** Wagen	dies**e** Studentin	dies**es** Kind
	(den)	**(die)**	**(das)**
Acc.	dies**en** Wagen	dies**e** Studentin	dies**es** Kind
	(dem)	**(der)**	**(dem)**
Dat.	dies**em** Wagen	dies**er** Studentin	dies**em** Kind

dieser: **Diese Kirche** hat eine interessante Geschichte.
This church has an interesting history.

jeder: Wer will durch **jedes Dorf** fahren?
Who wants to drive through every village?

mancher: **Manche Weinstube** ist neu und modern.
Many a Weinstube *is new and modern.*

solcher: **Solche Versuche** sind umsonst.
Such attempts are in vain.

welcher: **Welchen Dom** möchte Tom sehen?
Which cathedral would Tom like to see?

II. FAMILIAR FORMS OF ADDRESS

The pronoun **Sie** (*you*), which has been used in the previous dialogues, is the normal polite form of address in German.

Haben Sie eine deutsche Zeitung?   *Do you have a German newspaper?*

Among members of a family, close friends, for children, animals and the Deity a familiar form of address is used: **du** (singular), **ihr** (plural).

A. Present-Tense Verb Forms: Familiar

1. REGULAR PRESENT TENSE: In the present tense the characteristic personal verb ending for the **du** form is **-(e)st,** for the **ihr** form it is **-(e)t.** The **(e)** is used when the stem ends in **-t, -d,** or a difficult consonant combination.

kommen (*to come*)		**arbeiten** (*to work*)	
ich komme	wir kommen	ich arbeite	wir arbeiten
du kommst	**ihr kommt**	**du arbeitest**	**ihr arbeitet**
er, sie, es kommt	sie kommen	er, sie, es arbeitet	sie arbeiten
	Sie kommen		Sie arbeiten

Verbs whose stem ends in any s-sound (**-s, -ß, -z, -tz**) add only **-t** instead of **-st** in the **du** form.

heißen: du heißt   **sitzen:** du sitzt

2. VERBS WITH VOWEL CHANGE: Verbs that have a vowel change in the present tense (e.g., **geben, sehen, fahren**) show the vowel change with **du** but not with **ihr.**

sehen: du siehst, ihr seht   **fahren:** du fährst, ihr fahrt

3. MODALS: With modals the **du** forms have the same vowels as the other singular forms; the **ihr** forms follow the plural pattern.

dürfen: du darfst, ihr dürft   **können:** du kannst, ihr könnt

4. IRREGULAR VERBS **haben** (TO HAVE) AND **sein** (TO BE): The verbs **haben** and **sein** show some irregularities in the familiar forms.

haben: du hast, ihr habt   **sein: du bist, ihr seid**

B. Familiar Personal Pronouns: Case Forms

Du and **ihr** are the nominative forms of the familiar pronouns. Like other personal pronouns, they change in the accusative and dative.

NOMINATIVE	ACCUSATIVE	DATIVE
du	**dich**	**dir**
ihr	**euch**	**euch**

Ich will **dich** nach Köln fahren.
I want to drive you to Cologne.
Ich will **dir** zeigen, wie man das macht.
I want to show you how it's done.
Gibt es nicht bei **euch** eine richtige Zeremonie?
Isn't there an actual ceremony here (in your country)?

C. Imperative: Familiar

1. SINGULAR FAMILIAR (**du** FORM): The singular familiar imperative for most verbs is formed by adding **-e** to the verb stem. This **-e** is usually dropped in normal conversation. As in English, the pronoun is not expressed.

> **Häng(e)** deinen Arm in meinen Arm.   *Link your arm in mine.*

Exceptions: Verbs that have a present-tense vowel change from **e** to **i** or **ie** (e.g., **geben, sprechen, nehmen, sehen**) show this vowel change in the singular familiar imperative. They have no ending.

> **Nimm** dein Glas in die Hand.   *Take your glass in your hand.*
> **Gib** mir das Fernglas.   *Give me the binoculars.*

The verb **sein** simply uses the infinitive stem and adds no ending.

> **Sei** nicht so umständlich.   *Don't be so formal.*

2. PLURAL FAMILIAR (**ihr** FORM): All verbs form their plural familiar imperative by using the regular present-tense **-(e)t** ending on the stem, except **sein** whose **ihr** form is **seid**.

> **Kommt** ins Eßzimmer!   *Come into the dining room.*
> **Helft** mir in der Küche, Kinder!   *Help me in the kitchen, children.*
> **Seid** nicht so umständlich!   *Don't be so formal.*

III. THE VERB *WERDEN* (*TO BECOME, GET*)

The verb **werden** is the third of the three irregular German verbs. (The others are **haben** and **sein.**)

ich **werde**	wir **werden**
du **wirst**	ihr **werdet**
er, sie, es **wird**	sie **werden**
	Sie **werden**

IV. *EIN-WORDS* (*POSSESSIVE ADJECTIVES AND KEIN*)

To denote relationship, a possessive adjective is used before a noun in place of an article: *my mother, his sister,* and so on.

The negative form of the indefinite article **ein** is **kein.**

A. Meanings and Forms of the <u>ein</u>-Words

mein	*my*	**unser**	*our*
dein	*your (sing. fam.)*	**euer**	*your (pl. fam.)*
sein	*his, its*	**ihr**	*their*
ihr	*her, its*	**Ihr**	*your (polite)*

kein *no, not a, not any* (used when negating a noun that has an indefinite article or no article):

Haben Sie einen Wagen? — Nein, ich habe **keinen** Wagen.
Do you have a car? — No, I have no car. (I don't have a car.)

Haben Sie Zeit? — Nein, ich habe **keine** Zeit.
Do you have time? — No, I have no time. (I haven't any time.)

The endings added to possessive adjectives and **kein** change to agree in case and gender with the nouns they modify. Since these endings are the same as those of the indefinite article, they are called **ein**-words.

EXAMPLE: **mein**

	MASCULINE	FEMININE	NEUTER
	(ein)	**(eine)**	**(ein)**
Nom.	mein Wagen	meine Schwester	mein Kind
	(einen)	**(eine)**	**(ein)**
Acc.	meinen Wagen	meine Schwester	mein Kind
	(einem)	**(einer)**	**(einem)**
Dat.	meinem Wagen	meiner Schwester	meinem Kind

Jetzt bist du **mein „Bruder"**.
Now you're my "brother."
Häng **deinen Arm** in **meinen Arm**.
Link your arm in mine.
Gerd und **seine Schwester** helfen Frau Thiele in der Küche.
Gerd and his sister are helping Mrs. Thiele in the kitchen.
Sonst gibt's **kein Abendessen**.
Otherwise there won't be any dinner.

B. Agreement of Possessive with Antecedent

The third person singular possessives **sein** (*his*) and **ihr** (*her*) both also mean *its*. **Sein** means *its* when the antecedent is a masculine or neuter inanimate object; **ihr** means *its* when the antecedent is a feminine inanimate object.

Die Stadt (*f.*) Köln möchte ich sehen, besonders **ihr Wahrzeichen.**
*I'd like to see the city of Cologne, especially **its** landmark.*

Woher hat **der Berg** (*m.*) **seinen Namen?**
*Where did the mountain get **its** name?*

Man sieht **Köln** (*n.*) mit **seiner Kirche.**
*You see Cologne with **its** church.*

The endings added to these possessives agree, as always, with the noun being modified.

Word Study and Usage

I. NICHT WAHR

The expression **nicht wahr** is frequently used in German when the speaker wants confirmation of a statement he has just made. Its English equivalent will depend on the context.

Das ist euer berühmter Kölner Dom, **nicht wahr?**
*That's your famous Cologne Cathedral, **isn't it?***

Wir kennen uns schon ziemlich gut, **nicht wahr?**
*We know each other pretty well, **don't we?***

II. CONTRACTION OF ES

In conversation, when the pronoun **es** follows a verb, the combination is often contracted. The **e** is omitted and an apostrophe is used in its place.

Jetzt **wird's** aber Zeit, sonst **gibt's** kein Abendessen.

III. THE PRONOUN MAN

The pronoun **man** (equivalent to the English indefinite pronoun *one*) takes a third-person singular verb form. Since in English *one* is usually felt to be somewhat stiff, **man** is rendered into English in various ways, depending on the context.

Man fährt den ganzen Tag und kennt nachher nichts von Amerika.
***You** drive all day, and when you're through, you've seen nothing of America.*

Man macht manchen schwachen Versuch, ihn zu erhalten.
***They** make many a weak attempt to preserve it.*

Ich zeige dir, **wie man das macht.**
*I'll show you **how it's done.*** (English: *passive*)

Die moderne Architektur verdankt uns sehr viel. Das darf **man** nicht
vergessen.
*Modern architecture owes us a lot. **One** mustn't forget that.*

Class Drills

*I. a. Restate each of the following sentences, substituting alter-
nately the appropriate form of* dieser, jeder *and* mancher *for
the definite article:*

EXAMPLE: *Der Amerikaner* möchte ein Schloß sehen.
Dieser Amerikaner möchte ein Schloß sehen.
Jeder Amerikaner möchte ein Schloß sehen.
Mancher Amerikaner möchte ein Schloß sehen.

1. Der Student möchte Köln sehen.
   Das Schloß hat eine Sage.
   Die Stadt hat ein Wahrzeichen.
2. Für den Geschäftsmann ist das ideal.
   Durch das Dorf will er nicht fahren.
   Die Stadt möchte er sehen.
3. Von dem Professor spricht er gern.
   Zu dem Mädchen darf man „du" sagen.
   Bei der Familie kann man das sehen.
4. Für den Politiker ist Bonn interessant.
   Die Kirche hat eine interessante Geschichte.
   Dem Mädchen hilft er gern.

b. Formulate questions from the statements in exercise a. *by
using the appropriate form of* welcher *in place of the definite
article:*

EXAMPLE: *Der Amerikaner* möchte ein Schloß sehen.
Welcher Amerikaner möchte ein Schloß sehen?

*II. a. Formulate questions from the following statements, using
the* du *form:*

EXAMPLE: *Ich gehe nach Hause.*
Gehst du nach Hause?

Ich wohne privat.
Ich kenne ihn schon lange.

Ich bestelle ein Glas Wein.
Ich trinke gern Rheinwein.
Ich warte schon lange.
Ich arbeite den ganzen Tag.
Ich finde es leicht.
Ich lande in Frankfurt.
Ich sitze gern auf der Terrasse.
Ich vergesse das immer.
Ich esse gern Sauerkraut.
Ich begrüße den Gast.
Ich fahre gern schnell.
Ich spreche von diesem Studenten.
Ich sehe das oft.
Ich nehme eine deutsche Zeitung.
Ich habe eine deutsche Zeitung.
Ich bin müde.
Ich will nach Köln fahren.
Ich kann das machen.
Ich muß immer arbeiten.
Ich darf ihn beim Vornamen nennen.
Ich werde müde.

b. Formulate questions from the sentences in exercise a., this time using the ihr form:

EXAMPLE: *Ich gehe* nach Hause.
         Geht ihr nach Hause?

c. Follow the same procedure, using the Sie form:

EXAMPLE: *Ich gehe* nach Hause.
         Gehen Sie nach Hause?

III. a. Answer the following questions affirmatively, using the form of the object pronoun called for by the context:

EXAMPLE: **Willst du mich sehen?**
         Ja, ich will dich sehen.

1. Willst du mich nach Köln fahren?
   Kannst du mich besuchen?
   Gehst du ohne mich?
   Tust du das für mich?

EXAMPLE: **Willst du uns sehen?**
Ja, ich will euch sehen.

2. Willst du uns nach Köln fahren?
Kannst du uns besuchen?
Gehst du ohne uns?
Tust du das für uns?

EXAMPLE: **Wollen Sie mich sehen?**
Ja, ich will Sie sehen.

3. Wollen Sie mich nach Köln fahren?
Können Sie mich besuchen?
Gehen Sie ohne uns?
Tun Sie das für uns?

b. *Do the same with the following questions, this time using the appropriate dative pronouns:*

1. Kannst du mir die Stadt zeigen?
Willst du mir helfen?
Sprichst du von mir?
Kommst du jetzt zu mir?

2. Kannst du uns die Stadt zeigen?
Willst du uns helfen?
Sprichst du von uns?
Kommst du jetzt zu uns?

3. Können Sie mir die Stadt zeigen?
Wollen Sie mir helfen?
Sprechen Sie von uns?
Kommen Sie jetzt zu uns?

IV. *Form commands from the following statements. Use the appropriate form of the command called for by the statement:*

EXAMPLE: *Du gehst nach oben.*
Geh(e) nach oben.

1. Du erzählst die alte Legende.
Du kommst jetzt nach Hause.
Du fährst mit uns.
Du vergißt das.
Du nimmst das Glas in die Hand.

EXAMPLE: *Ihr geht* nach oben.
Geht nach oben.

2. Ihr erzählt die alte Legende.
   Ihr kommt jetzt nach Hause.
   Ihr fahrt mit uns.
   Ihr vergeßt das.
   Ihr nehmt das Glas in die Hand.

EXAMPLE: *Sie gehen* nach oben.
Gehen Sie nach oben.

3. Sie erzählen die alte Legende.
   Sie kommen jetzt nach Hause.
   Sie fahren mit uns.
   Sie vergessen das.
   Sie nehmen das Glas in die Hand.

EXAMPLE: *Wir gehen* nach oben.
Gehen wir nach oben.

4. Wir sagen „du" zueinander.
   Wir fahren nach Bonn.
   Wir trinken ein Glas Wein.
   Wir helfen dem Kind.

V. *Restate each of the following sentences, substituting alternately the appropriate form of* mein, Ihr, unser, *and* kein *for the indefinite article:*

1. Ein Professor hat immer recht.
   Ein Schlafzimmer ist oben.
   Das ist eine Zeitschrift.

2. Für einen Studenten ist das leicht.
   Ich sehe ein Flugzeug.
   Ich habe eine Zeitung.

3. Ich erzähle einem Professor die Geschichte.
   Ich gebe es einem Kind.
   Ich wohne bei einer Familie.

4. Ein Kind läuft schnell.
   Er wohnt bei einer Familie.
   Für einen Professor ist das leicht.

VI. Answer affirmatively, replacing the indefinite article with the proper third-person singular possessive:

EXAMPLE: **Jede Kirche hat *eine Geschichte,* nicht wahr?**
Ja, jede Kirche hat *ihre Geschichte.*

1. Jeder Geschäftsmann hat einen Wagen, nicht wahr?
Jeder Wald hat einen Fußweg, nicht wahr?
Jeder Dom hat eine Geschichte, nicht wahr?
Jeder Berg hat einen Wald, nicht wahr?

2. Jedes Kind muß eine Familie haben, nicht wahr?
Jedes Schloß hat eine Sage, nicht wahr?
Jedes Haus hat eine Terrasse, nicht wahr?
Jedes Flugzeug hat eine Stewardeß, nicht wahr?

3. Jede Studentin hat ein Hauptfach, nicht wahr?
Jede Stadt hat ein Wahrzeichen, nicht wahr?
Jede Burg hat eine Sage, nicht wahr?
Jede Familie hat eine Wohnung, nicht wahr?

4. Jedes Wahrzeichen hat eine Geschichte, nicht wahr?
Jede Stadt hat eine Kirche, nicht wahr?
Jeder Dom hat einen Turm, nicht wahr?

Exercises

I. Rewrite the following sentences, substituting the <u>der-</u> and <u>ein-</u> words given in English:

1. Dieses Haus ist alt. (*our, many a*)   2. Unser Wagen ist nicht neu. (*this, which . . . ?*)   3. Kennen Sie jeden Professor? (*this, his*) 4. Glauben Sie dem Professor? (*your, no*)   5. Gefällt Ihnen dieser Wagen? (*my, her*)   6. Sie fahren durch manches Dorf. (*a, every*) 7. Ich habe den Wagen. (*no, their*)   8. Das ist ideal für diesen Studenten. (*every, a*)

II. Translate into English. Then reproduce the German sentences from your English translations:

1. Deutsch ist ihr Hauptfach, und darum will sie dieses Jahr in München studieren.   2. Haben Sie kein Arbeitszimmer? — Doch, es ist oben. 3. Diese Zeitschrift macht ihr Spaß, aber sie findet sie nicht leicht.   4. Er kann Ihnen zeigen, wie man nach Köln kommt.   5. Die Burg verdankt einem Drachen ihren Namen.   6. Ich habe keine Uhr, ich ver-

gesse sie immer.   7. Kennen Sie diesen Studenten gut? — Nein, aber ich weiß ziemlich viel über ihn.   8. Glaub ihm nicht, er sagt das nur zum Spaß.   9. Stimmt, Sie müssen ungefähr um zwei zu Hause sein und Ihren Gast begrüßen.   10. Warum will er ihr die Fotografie nicht zeigen?

III. *Translate:*

1. Gerd, may I visit you (*fam.*) after your outing?   2. I know her pretty well, and I call her by her first name.   3. Is that only done for fun?   4. That's right, he has no car.   5. Does she want a room in Bonn?   6. Many a student lives with (*bei*) his family.   7. Which picture do you like?   8. Can you show them how it's done?   9. Excuse me, Mr. Thiele, is that your newspaper? — Please take it.   10. She is right, isn't she?

IV. *Composition. Answer the following questions in German, using as much of the question in your answer as possible. Write your answers in a paragraph, omitting* ja *and* nein:

1. Was tun Gerd und Tom in der Weinstube?
2. Was ist Tom nach dem Brüderschafttrinken?
3. Sagen sie noch „Sie" zueinander?
4. Bei welchem Namen nennt Tom jetzt seinen Freund?
5. Was hängt an der Wand?
6. Was ist auf diesem Bild?
7. Was ist der Kölner Dom?
8. Wann will Gerd seinen Freund nach Köln fahren?
9. Was will Tom in dieser Stadt unbedingt sehen?
10. Können die beiden lange in der Weinstube bleiben?

Active Vocabulary

der Abend	evening	die Fotografie	photograph
das Abendessen	dinner, evening meal	der Freund	friend
der Arm	arm	fünf	five
der Beginn	beginning	das Glas	glass
berühmt	famous	hängen	to hang, link
besonders	especially	die Hand	hand
bestellen	to order	hin	there
das Bild	picture	immer	always
der Bruder	brother	interessant	interesting
die Brüderschaft	brotherhood	jeder	every, each
denn	for, because	jener	that
dieser	this	die Kirche	church
der Dom	cathedral	der Kommilitone	fellow student

mancher	many a	**wahr**	true
Prost!	cheers! your health! (informal toast)	**nicht wahr?**	isn't it so?
das Semester	semester	**das Wahrzeichen**	landmark
der Semesterbeginn	beginning of the semester	**die Wand**	wall
		die Weinstube	(*lit.* "wine room")
solcher	such a	**welcher**	which
sonst	otherwise, or else	**weltbekannt**	world-renowned, famous
zum Spaß	for fun	**werden (i)**	to become, get
trinken	to drink	**zeigen**	to show
tun	to do	**die Zeit**	time
die Uhr	clock; watch; o'clock	**die Zeremonie**	ceremony
umständlich	formal, fussy	**ziemlich**	rather, quite
unbedingt	absolutely, by all means	**zueinander**	to each other
der Vorname, den Vornamen, dem Vornamen	first name		

Review

Reading Practice

Tom schreibt (*writes*) an einen deutschen Freund in Amerika.

Lieber (*dear*) Peter,

jetzt bin ich schon seit einem Monat (*month*) in der Bundeshauptstadt! (Übrigens, hier nennt man Bonn oft zum Spaß „Bundeshauptdorf", aber das weißt Du[1] sicher schon aus dem „Spiegel".) Ich wohne bei Thieles — eine nette (*nice*) Familie, und gar nicht umständlich. Der Sohn Gerd und ich nennen uns schon beim Vornamen, und wir sagen „du" zueinander. Seine Schwester Sabine nenne ich auch beim Vornamen, aber ich sage noch „Sie" zu ihr. Thieles Haus gefällt mir, eine sehr moderne Wohnung; oben sind die Schlafzimmer und ein Bad, unten Wohn-, Eß- und Arbeitszimmer, Küche und Bad. Herr Thiele weiß viel über Architektur und erzählt mir oft davon. Manchmal mache ich mit Gerd einen Ausflug, z. B. (zum Beispiel — *e.g.*) auf den „Drachenfels"; den Namen hat dieser Berg aus einer Legende. Von der Höhe hat man eine Aussicht wie im Film. Von dort oben kann man auch den „Rolandsbogen" sehen. Das ist eine berühmte Ruine; sie hat mit dem Drachenfels eine Sage gemeinsam. Nach einem Ausflug geht man hier gern in eine Weinstube, denn so eine Fußtour macht müde. Jetzt weiß ich auch, wie man Brüderschaft trinkt. Die Autobahn kenne ich auch schon — eine richtige Rennbahn. Du weißt, hier gibt es keine Geschwindigkeitsbegrenzung auf der Autobahn, und alle fahren zu schnell. Vom Land sieht man dann nicht viel, genau wie in Amerika. Vor Semesterbeginn will Gerd mich noch nach Köln fahren, denn ich möchte unbedingt den Kölner Dom sehen.

Hast Du viel Zeit zum Autofahren? Arbeite nicht so viel, sonst kommst Du nach Deutschland zurück und kennst nichts von Amerika. Schreib mir bald!

Herzliche Grüße, (*best regards*)
Dein Freund
Tom

[1] In letters, pronouns and possessives referring to the person addressed are capitalized.

Drills

The following drills are intended to help you review and tie together the main constructions you have learned in the previous lessons. In each set of drills, you will be asked to make various substitutions. In doing these at home, cover the lines following the one you are working on, since the correct new form is given in the succeeding line. By this method you can check your own work immediately. If you find that you have made an error, be sure you understand the correct form before going on. If you discover that you have not mastered a particular construction, go back to the lesson that deals with it. Each individual set of drills indicates the grammatical constructions being reviewed.

I. NOMINATIVE CASE AND PRESENT-TENSE VERB FORMS

Substitute the element indicated. At times, the element is cued in English:

EXAMPLE: **Der Student kommt auch. (*dieser*)**
Dieser Student kommt auch. (*nach Hause*)
Dieser Student kommt nach Hause. (*wollen*)
Dieser Student will nach Hause.

A. Der Politiker kommt auch. (**ein**)
Ein Politiker kommt auch. (**dieser**)
Dieser Politiker kommt auch. (**nach Bonn**)
Dieser Politiker kommt nach Bonn. (**jeder**)
Jeder Politiker kommt nach Bonn. (**wollen**)
Jeder Politiker will nach Bonn. (**Herr und Frau Thiele**)
Herr und Frau Thiele wollen nach Bonn. (**fahren**)
Herr und Frau Thiele fahren nach Bonn. (**nach Hause**)
Herr und Frau Thiele fahren nach Hause. (**ich**)
Ich fahre nach Hause. (**er**)
Er fährt nach Hause. (**müssen**)
Er muß nach Hause. (**du**)
Du mußt nach Hause. (**der Professor**)
Der Professor muß nach Hause. (**unser**)
Unser Professor muß nach Hause. (**Tochter**)
Unsere Tochter muß nach Hause.

B. Ich spreche zu schnell. (**der Professor**)
Der Professor spricht zu schnell. (**Amerikanerin**)
Die Amerikanerin spricht zu schnell. (**dieser**)
Diese Amerikanerin spricht zu schnell. (**deutsch**)
Diese Amerikanerin spricht deutsch. (**Kind**)
Dieses Kind spricht deutsch. (**wer**)

Wer spricht deutsch? (**hier**)
Wer spricht hier? (**arbeiten**)
Wer arbeitet hier? (**der Student**)
Der Student arbeitet hier. (**welcher**)
Welcher Student arbeitet hier?

C. Ein Amerikaner wohnt hier. (**Familie**)
Eine Familie wohnt hier. (**Geschäftsmann**)
Ein Geschäftsmann wohnt hier. (**dieser**)
Dieser Geschäftsmann wohnt hier. (**in Frankfurt**)
Dieser Geschäftsmann wohnt in Frankfurt. (**sie** — *they*)
Sie wohnen in Frankfurt. (**landen**)
Sie landen in Frankfurt. (**du**)
Du landest in Frankfurt. (**er**)
Er landet in Frankfurt. (**sein** — *to be*)
Er ist in Frankfurt. (**alt**)
Er ist alt. (**die Kirche**)
Die Kirche ist alt. (*it*)
Sie ist alt. (**der Turm**)
Der Turm ist alt. (*it*)
Er ist alt. (**berühmt**)
Er ist berühmt. (**du**)
Du bist berühmt. (**werden**)
Du wirst berühmt. (**er**)
Er wird berühmt. (**die beiden**)
Die beiden werden berühmt.

D. Ich kann das nicht. (**sie** — *they*)
Sie können das nicht. (**man**)
Man kann das nicht. (**ihr**)
Ihr könnt das nicht. (**wer**)
Wer kann das nicht? (**haben**)
Wer hat das nicht? (**du**)
Du hast das nicht. (**wissen**)
Du weißt das nicht. (**der Vater**)
Der Vater weiß das nicht. (**mein**)
Mein Vater weiß das nicht. (**man**)
Man weiß das nicht. (**ihr** — *you*)
Ihr wißt das nicht.

II. *VERB OBJECTS: ACCUSATIVE AND DATIVE CASE*

Substitute the new object or verb indicated. The cue for nouns and pronouns is given in the nominative case or in English:

Er kennt den Herrn. (**Student**)
Er kennt den Studenten. (**dieser**)
Er kennt diesen Studenten. (**er**)
Er kennt ihn. (**glauben**)
Er glaubt ihm. (**sie** — *she*)
Er glaubt ihr. (**der Professor**)
Er glaubt dem Professor. (**dieser**)
Er glaubt diesem Professor. (**sein** — *his*)
Er glaubt seinem Professor. (**Freundin**)
Er glaubt seiner Freundin. (**besuchen**)
Er besucht seine Freundin. (**das Dorf**)
Er besucht das Dorf. (**jeder**)
Er besucht jedes Dorf. (**Dom**)
Er besucht jeden Dom. (**kein**)
Er besucht keinen Dom. (**mancher**)
Er besucht manchen Dom. (**Universität**)
Er besucht manche Universität. (**kennen**)
Er kennt manche Universität. (**ich**)
Er kennt mich. (**helfen**)
Er hilft mir. (**das Kind**)
Er hilft dem Kind. (**jeder**)
Er hilft jedem Kind. (**wir**)
Er hilft uns. (**vergessen**)
Er vergißt uns. (**ich**)
Er vergißt mich. (**der Name**)
Er vergißt den Namen. (**jeder**)
Er vergißt jeden Namen. (**kein**)
Er vergißt keinen Namen. (**ihr** — *you*)
Er vergißt euch. (**folgen**)
Er folgt euch. (**der Fußweg**)
Er folgt dem Fußweg. (*it*)
Er folgt ihm. (**sehen**)
Er sieht ihn. (**die Ruine**)
Er sieht die Ruine. (*it*)
Er sieht sie.

III. INDIRECT OBJECT: DATIVE CASE

Substitute the new verb or indirect object element, which is cued in the nominative case:

Er gibt der Stewardeß die Zeitung. (**dieser**)
Er gibt dieser Stewardeß die Zeitung. (**ein**)
Er gibt einer Stewardeß die Zeitung. (**sie** — *she*)

Er gibt ihr die Zeitung. (**er**)
Er gibt ihm die Zeitung. (**der Herr**)
Er gibt dem Herrn die Zeitung. (**dieser**)
Er gibt diesem Herrn die Zeitung. (**wir**)
Er gibt uns die Zeitung. (**sie** — *they*)
Er gibt ihnen die Zeitung. (**zeigen**)
Er zeigt ihnen die Zeitung. (**die Familie**)
Er zeigt der Familie die Zeitung. (**unser**)
Er zeigt unserer Familie die Zeitung. (**sein** — *his*)
Er zeigt seiner Familie die Zeitung.

IV. PREPOSITIONS: DATIVE AND ACCUSATIVE

*Substitute the new verb or prepositional phrase element, which is
cued in the nominative case:*

A. Sie kommt aus der Weinstube. (**dieser**)
   Sie kommt aus dieser Weinstube. (**ein**)
   Sie kommt aus einer Weinstube. (**Dorf**)
   Sie kommt aus einem Dorf. (**dieser**)
   Sie kommt aus diesem Dorf. (**müssen**)
   Sie muß aus diesem Dorf. (**durch**)
   Sie muß durch dieses Dorf. (**ein**)
   Sie muß durch ein Dorf. (**unser**)
   Sie muß durch unser Dorf. (**Stadt**)
   Sie muß durch unsere Stadt. (**mancher**)
   Sie muß durch manche Stadt. (**jeder**)
   Sie muß durch jede Stadt.

B. Wir fahren um das Dorf. (**Stadt**)
   Wir fahren um die Stadt. (**Dom**)
   Wir fahren um den Dom. (**dieser**)
   Wir fahren um diesen Dom. (**ein**)
   Wir fahren um einen Dom. (**Berg**)
   Wir fahren um einen Berg. (**der**)
   Wir fahren um den Berg. (**Universität**)
   Wir fahren um die Universität. (**zu**)
   Wir fahren zu der Universität. (**unser**)
   Wir fahren zu unserer Universität. (**Freund**)
   Wir fahren zu unserem Freund. (**dein**)
   Wir fahren zu deinem Freund. (**Wohnung**)
   Wir fahren zu deiner Wohnung. (**er**)

Wir fahren zu ihm. (**das Schloß**)
Wir fahren zu dem Schloß. (**sie** — *they*)
Wir fahren zu ihnen.

C. Er wohnt bei einer Familie. (**dieser**)
Er wohnt bei dieser Familie. (**sein**)
Er wohnt bei seiner Familie. (**Freund**)
Er wohnt bei seinem Freund. (**sie** — *they*)
Er wohnt bei ihnen. (**wir**)
Er wohnt bei uns. (**er**)
Er wohnt bei ihm. (**warten**)
Er wartet bei ihm. (**ohne**)
Er wartet ohne ihn. (**der Freund**)
Er wartet ohne den Freund. (**ich**)
Er wartet ohne mich. (**die Freundin**)
Er wartet ohne die Freundin. (**sie** — *they*)
Er wartet ohne sie.

D. Ist das für mich? (**er**)
Ist das für ihn? (**der Vater**)
Ist das für den Vater? (**unser**)
Ist das für unseren Vater? (**Freund**)
Ist das für unseren Freund? (**Freundin**)
Ist das für unsere Freundin? (**ihr** — *her*)
Ist das für ihre Freundin? (**von**)
Ist das von ihrer Freundin? (**Professor**)
Ist das von ihrem Professor? (**er**)
Ist das von ihm? (**sie** — *they*)
Ist das von ihnen? (**Sie**)
Ist das von Ihnen?

E. Sie fährt gegen die Mauer. (**ein**)
Sie fährt gegen eine Mauer. (**Turm**)
Sie fährt gegen einen Turm. (**Haus**)
Sie fährt gegen ein Haus. (**sein** — *his*)
Sie fährt gegen sein Haus. (**Wagen**)
Sie fährt gegen seinen Wagen. (**mit**)
Sie fährt mit seinem Wagen. (**er**)
Sie fährt mit ihm. (**wir**)
Sie fährt mit uns. (**der Professor**)
Sie fährt mit dem Professor. (**ihr** — *her*)
Sie fährt mit ihrem Professor. (**Freund**)
Sie fährt mit ihrem Freund.

Exercises

I. *DER- AND EIN-WORDS*

Substitute the new der- and ein-words indicated:

1. Sie fährt durch dieses Dorf. (**unser, jeder, kein**) 2. Er kennt eine Weinstube. (**euer, mancher, unser**) 3. Wollen Sie einen Film sehen? (**kein, dieser, jeder, sein**) 4. Möchten Sie das Fernglas? (**mein, dieser, Ihr, unser**) 5. Sie wohnt bei einer Familie. (**dieser, mein, ihr, unser**) 6. Was sagen Sie zu diesem Wagen? (**mein, ihr, sein, der**)

II. *VERBS; WORD ORDER IN QUESTIONS*

Change each sentence according to the example:

EXAMPLE: **Sie landen in Bonn.**
Landet er in Bonn?
Landest du in Bonn?
Landet ihr in Bonn?

1. Sie arbeiten in Frankfurt. 2. Sie helfen ihm gern. 3. Sie fahren oft nach Bonn. 4. Sie geben ihm die Zeitschrift. 5. Sie sprechen gut deutsch. 6. Sie vergessen das oft. 7. Sie sehen die Ruine. 8. Sie zeigen es dem Professor. 9. Sie kennen sie. 10. Sie wissen das nicht.

III. *MODALS*

Add the modals indicated:

1. Sehen Sie es? (**können**) 2. Er tut es wirklich nicht. (**dürfen**) 3. Sie studiert Geschichte. (**sollen**) 4. Ich sehe den Dom. (**wollen**) 5. Findet sie die Zeitschrift nicht? (**können**) 6. Wir gehen nach Hause. (**müssen**) 7. Sie gehen nach oben. (**sollen**) 8. Ich bin um fünf zu Hause. (**müssen**)

IV. *DATIVE AND ACCUSATIVE PREPOSITIONS*

Substitute the new prepositional objects:

1. Das ist für das Kind. (*her professor, him, us, the stewardess, them*)
2. Er spricht oft von der Stewardeß. (*me, his family, you [polite and fam.] their house, him, her*)
3. Wir fahren mit diesem Autobus. (*her car, them, him, our car*)

V. INVERTED WORD ORDER

a. Begin each sentence with the italicized expression:

1. Er will unbedingt *vor dem Semesterbeginn* nach Köln.   2. Sie sind sicher auch *müde*.   3. Es gibt hier auch *moderne Wohnungen*.   4. Er kann Ihnen sicher *den Dom* zeigen.   5. Sie hilft *ihrem Freund* gern. 6. Sie studieren *den ganzen Tag*.   7. Wir machen *manchmal* einen Ausflug.   8. Sie fahren nicht *zu schnell*.

b. Change the following sentences according to the example:

EXAMPLE: **Sie besuchen ihn *bald*.**
          Bald besuchen Sie ihn.
          Besuchen Sie ihn bald!
          Besuchen Sie ihn bald?

1. Du sprichst nicht *darüber*.
2. Ihr erzählt ihm das *zuerst*.
3. Wir gehen auch *nach Köln*.

VI. TRANSLATION

Translate the following sentences:

1. Do you like the capital?   2. Let's help this student.   3. She is getting old.   4. Don't you know him?   5. Here is my newspaper. Give it to him. 6. She likes to work all day.   7. What kind of a room do you have? 8. You can ride with them.   9. Show me my room, please.   10. Her room is upstairs, isn't it?   11. Whom would you like to see?   12. To whom does he owe that?

Ludwig van Beethoven

Beethoven-Haus

Die Beethovenhalle

Siebte Lektion

In der Beethovenhalle

[*Konzertpause. Sabine und Tom gehen in die Vorhalle.*]

SABINE — Dieses Orchester spielt heute zum erstenmal hier. Gut, nicht wahr?

TOM — Ausgezeichnet, vor allem die Streicher. Der Dirigent erinnert mich
an einen bekannten New Yorker Dirigenten.

SABINE — Er ist noch sehr jung, aber begabt. Seine Konzerte sind alle ausverkauft. Man liest schon in jeder Zeitung über ihn. — Sind Sie
musikalisch, Tom? Ich meine, spielen Sie Klavier oder sonst ein
Instrument?

TOM — Ein wenig Geige. Ich *höre* lieber Musik, besonders Jazz.

SABINE — Darüber muß ich Sie gelegentlich allerlei fragen.

TOM — Worüber, über Jazz? Ich denke, Ihr Gebiet ist klassische Musik?

SABINE — Ich will aufs Konservatorium, und eine Musikerin muß auch in
der modernen Musik Bescheid wissen.

TOM — Ich muß mal im Programm nachsehen. Vielleicht steht für Sonntag eine Jazz-Sinfonie drauf. Darf ich Sie dazu einladen, Sabine?

SABINE — Danke, gern, Tom. Hoffentlich bekommen wir noch Karten dafür.

In Beethoven Hall

[*Concert intermission. Sabine and Tom go into the lobby.*]

SABINE — Today this orchestra is playing here for the first time. Good, isn't it?

TOM — Excellent, especially the strings. The conductor reminds me of a well-known New York conductor.

SABINE — He's still very young, but talented. His concerts are all sold out. You already read about him in every newspaper. — Are you musical, Tom? I mean, do you play the piano or some other instrument?

TOM — I play the violin a little. I prefer to *listen* to music, especially jazz.

SABINE — I have to ask you all sorts of questions about that when we have a chance.

TOM — About what? Jazz? I thought your field was classical music.

SABINE — I want to go to the conservatory, and a musician must know something about modern music, too.

TOM — I'll have to take a look at the program. Maybe there's a jazz symphony scheduled for Sunday. Would you like to go with me?

SABINE — Thank you, Tom, I would. I hope we can still get tickets for it.

Lesestück VII

Die Bonner Bürger[1] nennen ihre Stadt gern „Beethovenstadt" nach ihrem größten[2] Sohn. Auf diesen Namen sind sie genauso stolz wie[3] auf den neuen Titel „Bundeshauptstadt".

Im Jahre 1770 (siebzehnhundertsiebzig) kommt Ludwig van Beethoven in der Bonngasse zur Welt. Wie[4] sein Vater and Großvater[5] soll auch der kleine 5 Ludwig Musiker werden. Seine Instrumente sind vor allem das Klavier und die Orgel,[6] aber er lernt[7] auch Geige und Viola. Wir wissen nicht sehr viel über seine Jugend,[8] und es gibt auch fast keine Anekdoten darüber. Der Vater will aus Ludwig ein Wunderkind[9] wie Mozart machen. Schon als kleines Kind muß Ludwig viele Stunden auf einer Bank vor dem Klavier stehen und 10 üben.[10] Mit acht (8) Jahren gibt er schon ein Konzert. Auf dem Programm steht aber, daß er sechs (6) Jahre alt ist. Er komponiert[11] auch schon, und manchmal sind es schwere[12] Stücke;[13] seine kleine Hand kann die Akkorde[14] noch nicht greifen.[15] „Das kannst du doch nicht spielen, Ludwig", sagt sein Lehrer.[16] Der junge Künstler antwortet:[17] „Aber wenn ich größer[18] bin." 15 Mit dreizehn (13) Jahren wird er zweiter Hoforganist.[19] Zuerst bekommt er noch kein Geld[20] dafür. Er hat diese Stelle[21] neun Jahre lang.[22]

In den alten Biographien liest man über den strengen[23] Vater Beethovens: er tyrannisiert das junge Genie[24] und hat kein Mitleid[25] mit ihm. Heute aber sehen wir den Vater nicht mehr als bösen[26] Haustyrannen, sondern[27] nur als 20 schwachen, egoistischen Mann.

Mit 22 (zweiundzwanzig) Jahren verläßt[28] Beethoven seine Heimat[29] am Rhein. Sein Ziel[30] ist Wien, die Musikhauptstadt Europas.

---

[1] **der Bürger,** *pl.* **die Bürger** citizen
[2] **größt-** greatest
[3] **genauso stolz wie** just as proud as
[4] **wie** like
[5] **der Großvater** grandfather
[6] **die Orgel** organ
[7] **lernen** to learn
[8] **die Jugend** youth
[9] **das Wunderkind** child prodigy
[10] **üben** to practice
[11] **komponieren** to compose
[12] **schwer** difficult
[13] **das Stück,** *pl.* **die Stücke** piece
[14] **der Akkord,** *pl.* **die Akkorde** chord
[15] **greifen** to span (a chord)

[16] **der Lehrer** teacher
[17] **antworten** to answer
[18] **größer** bigger
[19] **der Hoforganist** court organist
[20] **das Geld** money
[21] **die Stelle** position
[22] **neun Jahre lang** for nine years
[23] **streng** strict
[24] **das Genie** genius
[25] **das Mitleid** sympathy, pity
[26] **böse** bad, wicked
[27] **sondern** but
[28] **verlassen (ä)** to leave
[29] **die Heimat** home town, homeland
[30] **das Ziel** destination

Fragen und Antworten

1. Wohin gehen Tom und Sabine?
   Sie gehen heute in die Beethovenhalle.
2. Worüber sprechen sie in der Halle?
   Sie sprechen über das Orchester und Musik.
3. An wen erinnert der Dirigent den Amerikaner?
   Er erinnert ihn an einen berühmten Dirigenten.
4. Wo liest man etwas (*something*) über die Konzerte?
   In der Zeitung liest man etwas darüber.
5. Wo möchte Sabine studieren?
   Sie möchte auf einem Konservatorium studieren.
6. Wofür will Tom Karten kaufen (*buy*)?
   Er möchte Karten für das Jazzkonzert kaufen.
7. Worin weiß Sabine Bescheid?
   Sie weiß in der klassischen Musik Bescheid.
8. Kommt dieses Orchester oft nach Bonn?
   Nein, es spielt nur heute und am Sonntag dort.
9. Auf wen ist Bonn stolz?
   Bonn ist stolz auf seinen größten Sohn, Beethoven.
10. Worauf ist Bonn stolz?
    Bonn ist stolz auf den Namen „Beethovenstadt".

Structure and Practice

Explanation of Forms

I. PREPOSITIONS WITH DATIVE AND ACCUSATIVE

You have previously learned two groups of prepositions: those that are always followed by the accusative case (see Lesson 2) and those that are always followed by the dative case (see Lesson 4). You now will be introduced to a third group of prepositions that sometimes take the dative, sometimes the accusative case. We will refer to these as dative/accusative prepositions.

A. Meanings of Dative/Accusative Prepositions

The dative/accusative prepositions with their basic meanings are:

> **an** (*at, to, on*)   **über** (*over, above, across*)
> **auf** (*on, to, at*)   **unter** (*under, among*)
> **hinter** (*behind*)   **vor** (*in front of, before*)
> **in** (*in, into, to*)   **zwischen** (*between*)
> **neben** (*next to*)

In German, as in other languages, the choice of prepositions for particular situations is highly idiomatic. Note the use of the prepositions as they occur in the dialogues and reading selections.

B. Use of Dative/Accusative Prepositions

1. WITH LOCATION: The case after dative/accusative prepositions depends on whether there is a change of location.

   a. Accusative: The accusative case is used after these prepositions when motion toward a new location is indicated.

      Sabine und Tom gehen **in die Vorhalle.**
      Sabine and Tom walk into the lobby.

      Er geht **an die Tür.**
      He walks to the door.

      Sie will **aufs (auf das) Konservatorium.**
      She wants to go to the conservatory.

   b. Dative: The dative case is used after these prepositions when stationary position or motion with no change to a new location is indicated.

      Er will **an der Universität** Bonn studieren.
      He wants to study at the University of Bonn.

      Sie sitzen **auf der Terrasse vor dem Wohnzimmer.**
      They are sitting on the terrace in front of the living room.

      Gerd und Sabine helfen Frau Thiele **in der Küche.**
      Gerd and Sabine are helping Mrs. Thiele in the kitchen.

      Gerd und Tom fahren **auf der Autobahn.**
      Gerd and Tom are driving on the Autobahn.

      Neben der Küche ist die Tür zum Bad.
      Next to the kitchen is the door to the bath.

2. TIME: When the dative/accusative prepositions are used in answer to the question *when?*, they are followed by the dative case.

Das Orchester spielt **am (an dem) Sonntag** dort.
The orchestra is playing there on Sunday.

In einer Stunde sind sie in Bonn.
In an hour they'll be in Bonn.

3. FIGURATIVE: In many idiomatic expressions, the dative/accusative prepositions have figurative, rather than literal, meanings. In such cases the above rules do not apply, and it is best to learn the case for each expression individually.

It will be helpful to note that **auf** and **über,** when they are used figuratively, usually take the accusative case.

Man liest schon in jeder Zeitung **über ihn.**
You already read about him in every newspaper.

Sie sprechen **über das Orchester.**
They talk about the orchestra.

Sie warten **auf den Gast.**
They are waiting for the guest.

Sie sind stolz **auf den Titel.**
They are proud of the title.

The other prepositions in the group vary the case with the expression.

Der Dirigent erinnert mich **an einen New Yorker Dirigenten.**
(*acc.*)
The conductor reminds me of a New York conductor.

Sie verlieren das Interesse **am (an dem) Dom.** (*dat.*)
They lose interest in the cathedral.

II. DA- AND WO- COMPOUNDS

A. The Pronoun Substitute da-

When the pronoun object of a preposition refers to a living being (or beings), the regular personal pronoun is used in the appropriate case.

„Der Spiegel" ist keine leichte Lektüre **für mich.**
Der Spiegel isn't easy reading for me.

Man liest in jeder Zeitung **über ihn.**
You read about him in every newspaper.

When the pronoun object of a preposition refers to an inanimate object (or objects), the personal pronoun is replaced by **da-** (**dar-** when the preposition begins with a vowel), which is prefixed to the preposition.

This **da-** remains the same for any case, number, or gender, and it means *it, that,* or *them,* depending on the context.

> Er kennt den Namen „Bauhaus", aber er weiß nicht viel **darüber.**
> *He knows the name* Bauhaus, *but he doesn't know much about it.*

> Für Sonntag steht eine Jazz-Sinfonie auf dem Programm. Hoffentlich bekommen wir noch Karten **dafür.**
> *There's a jazz symphony scheduled for Sunday. I hope we can still get tickets for it.*

> Wo liest man über die Konzerte? In der Zeitung liest man **darüber.**
> *Where do you read about the concerts? You read about them in the newspaper.*

Note: In colloquial conversation, the **-a-** in **dar-** is often slurred, and this form, when written, omits the **-a-.**

> Vielleicht steht für Sonntag eine Jazz-Sinfonie **drauf.**

B. The Interrogative Substitute <u>wo</u>-

When the interrogative **was** is the object of a preposition, it is replaced by **wo- (wor-),** which is prefixed to the preposition. Like **da-,** it does not change its form, no matter what case the preposition takes.

> **Worüber** sprechen sie in der Pause?
> *What do they talk about during the intermission?*

> **Wofür** will Tom Karten kaufen?
> *For what does Tom want to buy tickets?*

> **Worin** weiß Sabine Bescheid?
> *What does Sabine know something about?*

III. WORD ORDER OF ADVERBS

Like many other elements, an adverb or adverbial phrase can begin a German sentence for emphasis or other stylistic reasons.

> **Kurz nach zwei Uhr** sind sie in Bonn.
> *Shortly after two o'clock they are in Bonn.*

When several adverbs or adverbial phrases are used together, time comes before place.

> Sie gehen **heute in die Beethovenhalle.**
> *They are going to Beethoven Hall today.*

> Er will **zwei Semester an der Universität Bonn** studieren.
> *He wants to study at the University of Bonn for two semesters.*

When there are two time elements, the more general one comes first.

> Das Orchester spielt **heute um zwei Uhr** in der Beethovenhalle.
> *The orchestra is playing in Beethoven Hall today at two o'clock.*

Other adverbial elements, such as manner, generally come after time and before place.

> Gerd Thiele wartet **jetzt mit dem Wagen auf dem Flugplatz.**
> *Now Gerd Thiele is waiting at the airport with the car.*

Word Study and Usage

I. WO, WOHIN AND WOHER

German has two interrogatives meaning *where:* **wo** indicates stationary position or motion with no change to a new location; **wohin** indicates direction or motion toward a new location (as in older English *whither*). A **wo** question will always elicit the dative case after a dative/accusative preposition in the answer; a **wohin** question will elicit an accusative.

> Wo liest man über die Konzerte? **In der Zeitung** liest man darüber.
> Wo möchte Sabine studieren? Sie möchte **auf einem Konservatorium** studieren.
> Wohin gehen Tom und Sabine? Sie gehen heute **in die Beethovenhalle.**

Woher means *from where.*

> **Woher** hat der Berg eigentlich den Namen?

II. CARDINAL NUMBERS: 1 TO 20

The cardinal numbers from 1 to 20 are:

eins	(1)	**sechs**	(6)	**elf**	(11)	**sechzehn**	(16)
zwei	(2)	**sieben**	(7)	**zwölf**	(12)	**siebzehn**	(17)
drei	(3)	**acht**	(8)	**dreizehn**	(13)	**achtzehn**	(18)
vier	(4)	**neun**	(9)	**vierzehn**	(14)	**neunzehn**	(19)
fünf	(5)	**zehn**	(10)	**fünfzehn**	(15)	**zwanzig**	(20)

Notice that the "teens" are formed by adding **-zehn** to the unit number, except for slight changes in **sechzehn** and **siebzehn.**

III. DAYS OF THE WEEK

The days of the week are all masculine and are almost always used with the definite article:

der Sonntag	Sunday
der Montag	Monday
der Dienstag	Tuesday
der Mittwoch	Wednesday
der Donnerstag	Thursday
der Freitag	Friday
der Samstag, der Sonnabend	Saturday

The preposition **an** is used to mean *on* with the days of the week. It is always contracted with the definite article and takes the dative case.

Es spielt **am Sonntag** zum erstenmal dort.
It's playing there for the first time on Sunday.

Class Drills

I. Repeat the following sentences, substituting the nouns indicated:

1. Er ist auf dem Berg.
   Turm
   Flugplatz
   Fußweg
   Konservatorium
   Schloß
   Zimmer

2. Er ist auf der Terrasse.
   Autobahn
   Burg
   Ruine

(*Watch the gender for each noun in the following group.*)

3. Er ist auf dem Flugplatz.
   Terrasse
   Burg
   Schloß
   Turm
   Konservatorium

4. Er geht auf den Berg.
   Turm
   Flugplatz
   Fußweg

5. Er geht auf das (aufs) Konservatorium.
                    Schloß
                    Zimmer

6. Er geht auf die Terrasse.
                    Autobahn
                    Burg
                    Ruine

(Watch the gender for each noun in the following group.)

7. Er geht auf den Turm.
                    Schloß
                    Burg
                    Autobahn
                    Konservatorium
                    Berg

8. Sie ist in dem (im) Wagen.
                    Dom
                    Wald
                    Haus
                    Wohnzimmer
                    Konzert
                    Studentenheim

9. Er ist in der Kirche.
                    Wohnung
                    Küche
                    Vorhalle

(Watch the gender for each noun in the following group.)

10. Sie ist in dem Dom.
                    Konzert
                    Wohnung
                    Vorhalle
                    Wald
                    Haus
                    Wohnzimmer

11. Sie will in den Wagen.
                    Dom
                    Wald

12. Sie will in das (ins) Haus.
                    Wohnzimmer
                    Konzert
                    Studentenheim

13. Sie will in die Kirche.
        Wohnung
        Küche
        Vorhalle

(*Watch the gender for each noun in the following group.*)
14. Sie will in den Wald.
        Kirche
        Dom
        Wohnzimmer
        Wagen
        Küche

II. Repeat the following sentences, substituting the German equivalent for the English words:

Am Sonntag kommt das Orchester.
        (*Tuesday*)
        (*Friday*)
        (*Wednesday*)
        (*Monday*)
        (*Thursday*)
        (*Saturday*)

III. Repeat the following sentences, substituting the nouns indicated. Notice that the prepositions are being used here in a figurative meaning:

1. Ich warte auf den Amerikaner.
        Musiker
        Dirigenten
        Herrn

2. Ich warte auf das (aufs) Abendessen.
        Mädchen
        Flugzeug

3. Ich warte auf die Stewardeß.
        Musikerin
        Studentin
        Zeitung

(*Watch the gender for each noun in the following group.*)
4. Ich warte auf den Dirigenten.
        Abendessen

Zeitung
Musikerin
Musiker
Mädchen

5. Er spricht über den Ausflug.
Film
Rundgang
Dom

6. Er spricht über das Autofahren.
Orchester
Konservatorium
Konzert

7. Er spricht über die Architektur.
Geschichte
Legende
Sinfonie

(*Watch the gender for each noun in the following group.*)
8. Er spricht über den Film.
Orchester
Konservatorium
Architektur
Ausflug
Legende

IV. *Restate the following sentences, replacing the noun in the prepositional phrase with a <u>da-</u> pronoun substitute:*

EXAMPLE: **Er kommt *mit dem Wagen* nach Bonn.**
Er kommt *damit* nach Bonn.

Sie weiß in der Musik Bescheid.
Er fragt sie allerlei über Jazz.
Ich kaufe Karten fürs Konzert.
Das erinnert ihn an den Ausflug.
Sie spricht oft vom „Bauhaus".
Sie kommt nach dem Konzert zu mir.

V. *Form questions from the following sentences, using the <u>wo-</u> substitute:*

EXAMPLE: **Ich fahre *mit dem Wagen.***
Womit fahren Sie?

Ich spreche über Musik.
Ich warte auf die Zeitung.
Ich spreche von dem Ausflug.
Ich fahre mit dem Wagen.
Ich kaufe Karten fürs Konzert.
Ich weiß in der Architektur Bescheid.

VI. Restate the following sentences, inserting in its proper place each of the words or phrases in parentheses:

EXAMPLE: **Sie wollen nach Köln fahren. (*jetzt*)**
Sie wollen *jetzt* nach Köln fahren.

Sie wollen nach Köln fahren. (**am Sonntag, vor Semesterbeginn, heute, bald**)
Dieses Orchester spielt am Sonntag. (**in Bonn, hier, in der Stadt, in der Konzerthalle**)
Wir gehen um zwei Uhr hin. (**am Sonntag, am Freitag, am Mittwoch, am Montag**)

VII. Form questions from the following statements, using <u>wo</u>, <u>wohin</u>, *or* <u>woher</u> *appropriately:*

EXAMPLE: **Sie ist *im Schloß. Wo* ist sie?**
Sie geht *in die Stadt. Wohin* geht sie?
Sie kommt *aus der Stadt. Woher* kommt sie?

1. Sie sitzt am Klavier.
   Sie steht an der Tür.
   Er liest im Arbeitszimmer.
   Sie arbeitet in der Küche.

2. Sie fährt in die Stadt.
   Er geht in die Kirche.
   Sie möchte aufs Konservatorium.
   Wir gehen ins Konzert.

3. Er kommt aus dem Studentenheim.
   Sie kommt aus Wisconsin.
   Sie kommen von der Beethovenhalle.
   Er kommt vom Flugplatz.

Exercises

I. a. Substitute the pronouns in parentheses for the one in the original sentence:

1. Gerd kommt oft zu mir. (*her, us, them, you* [*fam.* and *polite*], *him*)
2. Das ist keine leichte Lektüre für mich. (*her, us, them, you* [*fam.* and *polite*], *him*)
3. Sabine sitzt zwischen mir und ihm. (*you and me, her and them, you* [*fam.*] *and us*)

b. Substitute the <u>der</u>- and <u>ein</u>-words in parentheses for the definite article:

1. Ihr Bild hängt an der Wand. **(mancher, unser, dieser, ihr)**
2. Er erinnert mich an den Professor. **(ein, Ihr, dieser, euer)**
3. Neben dem Schloß finden Sie einen Wald. **(dieser, sein, jeder, unser)**
4. Er spricht über die Firma. **(ein, jeder, sein, dieser)**

II. Rewrite the following sentences, starting with the subject:

1. Heute geht Sabine in die Beethovenhalle. 2. Jetzt will sie nach Bonn. 3. Um elf Uhr müssen wir nach Hause. 4. Ins Konzert gehen sie oft. 5. Auf der Terrasse sitzen wir manchmal. 6. Nur am Sonntag essen wir im Eßzimmer. 7. Mit dem Wagen will sie dann nach Bonn. 8. Ohne mich geht er nicht oft ins Konzert.

III. Translate into English. Then reproduce the German sentences from your English translations:

1. Hoffentlich bekomme ich noch eine Karte für sie. 2. Er möchte sie ins Konzert einladen. 3. Auf der Autobahn fährt man oft zu schnell. 4. Dort sehen Sie einen Turm; daneben steht eine Schloßruine. 5. Gehen wir auf die Terrasse. Oder sitzen Sie nicht gern auf der Terrasse? 6. Wissen Sie etwas über diesen Berg? Leider weiß ich nicht viel darüber. 7. Gerd studiert an der Universität Bonn. Später möchte er an eine andere Universität gehen. 8. Politik macht ihm Spaß, aber er ist noch zu jung dafür. 9. Er sitzt am Klavier und spielt etwas darauf. 10. Für einen Studenten ist das gerade das Richtige.

IV. Translate:

1. Today he is visiting her for the first time. 2. Where are they going? They are going to (*auf*) the *Drachenfels*. 3. Where is she? She is

helping Mrs. Thiele in the kitchen. 4. Gerd and Tom go to (*in*) a *Weinstube* after their outing. 5. Let's go to (*in*) a concert on Monday. 6. She is waiting at (*auf*) the airport. 7. Take the binoculars.—Are you through with them? 8. Do you want to take a look at the program? 9. This orchestra is excellent. You read about it in every newspaper. 10. He reminds her of a professor.

V. Composition. *Answer the following questions in complete German sentences, using as much of the question in your answer as possible. Write your answers in a paragraph, omitting* <u>ja</u> *and* <u>nein</u>:

- 1. Was tun Tom und Sabine in der Konzertpause?
  2. Wie finden sie das Konzert?
  3. Wer gefällt Tom besonders?
  4. An wen muß Tom denken?
  5. Ist der Dirigent schon berühmt?
  6. Ist Tom musikalisch?
  7. Ist Sabine musikalisch?
  8. Worin möchte Sabine Bescheid wissen?
  9. Wen muß sie darüber fragen?
  10. Was möchte Tom am Sonntag hören?
  11. Wen will er dazu einladen?

Active Vocabulary

allerlei	all kinds of (things)	der Donnerstag	Thursday
an	at, to, on	einladen (ä)	to invite
auf	on, to, at	erinnern (an +	to remind (of)
ausgezeichnet	excellent	acc.)	
ausverkauft	sold out	etwas	something
begabt	talented	der Freitag	Friday
bekannt	well-known	das Gebiet	field, subject
bekommen	to get, obtain	die Geige	violin
Bescheid	to be informed (in a	gelegentlich	occasionally, at the
wissen (in +	field)		first opportunity
dat.)		größt-	greatest
danke!	thank you!	die Halle	hall, auditorium
denken (an +	to think (of)	heute	today
acc.)		hinter	behind
der Dienstag	Tuesday	hoffentlich	I hope; it is to be
der Dirigent, den	conductor		hoped
Dirigenten,		hören	to hear
dem Dirigenten		das Instrument	instrument

der Jazz	jazz	**der Samstag, Sonn-**	Saturday
die Karte	ticket; card	**abend**	
kaufen	to buy	**die Sinfonie**	symphony
klassisch	classical	**der Sohn**	son
das Klavier	piano	**der Sonntag**	Sunday
das Konserva-	conservatory	**sonst ein**	some other
torium		**spielen**	to play
das Konzert	concert	**stehen**	to stand
die Konzertpause	concert intermission	**stolz auf**	proud of
lesen (ie)	to read	**der Streicher**	player of a stringed
lieber	rather		instrument
meinen	to mean	**über**	over, above, about
der Mittwoch	Wednesday	**unter**	under, among
der Montag	Monday	**vielleicht**	perhaps
die Musik	music	**vor allem**	especially, above all
musikalisch	musical	**die Vorhalle**	lobby
der Musiker	musician	**warten (auf +**	to wait (for)
nachsehen (ie)	to look up, check	**acc.)**	
oder	or	**wenig**	little
das Orchester	orchestra	**zum erstenmal**	for the first time
die Pause	pause, intermission	**zwischen**	between
das Programm	program		

Achte Lektion

Vor der ersten Vorlesung

[*Tom steht am Eingang zum Hörsaal. Er bittet einen Studenten um Auskunft.*]

TOM — Entschuldigen Sie, liest hier der englische Gastprofessor?

STUDENT — Ja, über die wirtschaftliche Lage Europas vor dem zweiten Weltkrieg.

TOM — Erst zehn vor neun, ich komme immer zu früh.

STUDENT — Bestimmt nicht, eher zu spät, wenn Sie einen guten Platz wollen. Das ist kein großer Saal.

TOM — Hält er die Vorlesung auf englisch?

STUDENT — Ja. Ich belege sie nur als Gasthörer, weil Englisch mich interessiert. Ich bin Jurist. Und Sie?

TOM — Mein Fach ist Geschichte. Ich bin ein amerikanischer Austauschstudent.

STUDENT — Kaum zu glauben! Sie sprechen ein fehlerloses Deutsch.—Vielleicht kann ich Sie nach meiner letzten Vorlesung treffen? Um Viertel nach fünf in der Mensa? — Übrigens, mein Name ist Hans Krüger.

TOM — Tom Evans. Also schön, bis dann. — Einen Augenblick bitte, wo ist eigentlich die Mensa?

STUDENT — Wissen Sie was? Warten Sie vor dem Audimax. Dann gehen wir zusammen hin.

TOM — Abgemacht. Auf Wiedersehen bis heute nachmittag.

Before the First Lecture

[*Tom is standing at the entrance to the lecture hall. He asks a student for information.*]

TOM — Excuse me, is this where the English visiting professor is lecturing?

STUDENT — Yes, on the economic conditions in Europe before World War II.

TOM — It's only ten to nine. I'm always too early.

STUDENT — Not at all. In fact, you're late if you want to get a good seat. This is not a big room.

TOM — Is he lecturing in English?

STUDENT — Yes. I'm just taking it as an auditor because I'm interested in English. I'm a law student. And you?

TOM — My field is history. I'm an American exchange student.

STUDENT — Amazing! Your German is perfect. Maybe I can meet you after my last lecture? At 5:15 in the *Mensa*?[1] By the way, my name is Hans Krüger.

TOM — I'm Tom Evans. Fine, see you then. — Just a second, please, where exactly is the *Mensa*?

STUDENT — I'll tell you what. Wait in front of the *Audimax*.[2] Then we'll go over together.

TOM — Good. See you this afternoon.

[1] **die Mensa:** The students' dining hall at German universities.   [2] **das Audimax:** Abbreviated form of the Latin *auditorium maximum,* the main auditorium at German universities.

Lesestück VIII

Tom Evans weiß, daß die deutsche Universität anders als[1] die amerikanische ist, aber vieles überrascht[2] ihn an diesem ersten Tag. Am Nachmittag trifft er Hans Krüger vor dem Auditorium Maximum. Sein neuer Freund erklärt[3] ihm, was er nicht versteht.[4] Sie gehen nicht in die Mensa, weil[5] sie immer so voll[6] ist, sondern in ein kleines Lokal[7] in der Nähe.[8]

Hans Krüger zeigt Tom Evans seine Visitenkarte.[9] Darauf steht hinter seinem Namen „stud. jur.". Das ist der lateinische[10] Ausdruck[11] für „Student der Rechte".[12] Wenn Tom Evans will, darf er hinter seinen Namen „stud. phil." setzen,[13] d.h.[14] (das heißt) „Student der Philosophie". Er lernt noch einen lateinischen Ausdruck: „c.t.". Das ist das berühmte „akademische Viertel" und bedeutet,[15] daß der Professor eine Viertelstunde nach der vollen Stunde zu lesen beginnt.

Hans Krüger erzählt dem neuen Kommilitonen von anderen akademischen Sitten.[16] Zum Beispiel[17] klopfen[18] die Studenten, wenn der Professor in den Hörsaal kommt und auch, wenn seine Vorlesung zu Ende ist. Das ist die akademische Art[19] zu applaudieren. Wenn den Studenten etwas nicht gefällt, scharren[20] sie mit den Füßen. Ein neuer Ausdruck für Tom Evans ist auch das „schwarze Brett".[21] Es ist für die Studenten sehr wichtig,[22] denn sie können nur dort erfahren,[23] wo und wann der Professor liest. Im Vorlesungsverzeichnis[24] stehen nur der Titel der Vorlesung und der Name des Dozenten.[25] Da[26] Hans Krügers Eltern nicht in Bonn wohnen, hat er eine „Bude", d.h. ein möbliertes[27] Zimmer. Es gibt hier einige Studentenheime, aber keinen wirklichen Campus wie in Amerika.

---

[1] **anders als** different from
[2] **überraschen** to surprise
[3] **erklären** to explain
[4] **verstehen** to understand
[5] **weil** because, since
[6] **voll** full, crowded
[7] **das Lokal** restaurant, inn
[8] **die Nähe** vicinity
[9] **die Visitenkarte** calling card
[10] **lateinisch** Latin
[11] **der Ausdruck** expression
[12] **das Recht,** *pl.* **die Rechte** law, jurisprudence
[13] **setzen** to put, place
[14] **d.h.** i.e. (that is)
[15] **bedeuten** to mean, signify
[16] **die Sitte** custom, habit

[17] **das Beispiel** example
　　zum Beispiel for example
[18] **klopfen** to knock, rap
[19] **die Art** manner, way(s)
[20] **scharren** to scrape
　　mit den Füßen scharren to scrape one's feet
[21] **das „schwarze Brett"** bulletin board
[22] **wichtig** important
[23] **erfahren (ä)** to learn, find out
[24] **das Vorlesungsverzeichnis** university catalogue
[25] **des Dozenten** of the university lecturer or instructor
[26] **da** since, because
[27] **möbliert** furnished

BITTE

In der Mensa

Fragen und Antworten

1. Kann der Student dem Amerikaner sagen, wer hier liest?
   Ja, das kann er ihm sagen; hier liest ein englischer Gastprofessor.
2. Worüber spricht der Professor?
   Er spricht über die wirtschaftliche Lage Europas.
3. Warum kommt der deutsche Student so früh?
   Weil er einen guten Platz möchte.
4. Was kann Hans Krüger kaum glauben?
   Er kann kaum glauben, daß Tom Amerikaner ist.
5. Warum will Tom diese Vorlesung belegen?
   Er möchte sie belegen, weil Geschichte sein Hauptfach ist.
6. Was studiert der deutsche Student?
   Er ist Jurist, aber Englisch interessiert ihn.
7. Was fragt Tom den deutschen Studenten?
   Er fragt ihn, ob er ihm sagen kann, wo die Mensa ist.
8. Wann gehen die beiden in die Mensa?
   Wenn die letzte Vorlesung vorbei (*over*) ist, gehen sie hin.
9. Gehen sie wirklich in die Mensa?
   Nein, sie gehen in das kleine Lokal in der Nähe.
10. Wie lange dauert (**dauern** — *to last*) eine deutsche Vorlesung?
    Sie dauert fünfundvierzig Minuten (*minutes*) (dreiviertel Stunde).

Structure and Practice

Explanation of Forms

I. DECLENSION OF ADJECTIVES

A. Predicate Adjectives

In German, predicate adjectives (those which refer back to the subject) add no endings.

Ihr Haus ist sehr **modern.** *Your house is very modern.*
Der Wagen ist so gut wie **neu.** *The car is practically new.*

B. *Attributive Adjectives (I)*

In German, unlike English, attributive adjectives (those which precede the nouns they modify) always add endings.

Memorize the following six adjective phrases:

MASCULINE	FEMININE	NEUTER
der neue Wagen	die alte Firma	das moderne Haus
ein neuer Wagen	eine alte Firma	ein modernes Haus

Whenever the form of the article changes from what it is in the pattern above, the adjective ending changes to **-en.** Notice how this works out in the following sentences:

> **Der neue Wagen** ist schön.
> Sie haben **den neuen Wagen** seit Juni.
> Sie fahren mit **dem neuen Wagen** nach Bonn.
>
> Das ist **eine alte Firma.**
> Er arbeitet bei **einer alten Firma.**
>
> Sie haben **ein modernes Haus.**
> Sie wohnen in **einem modernen Haus.**

The system as just described is seen in the following paradigm of adjective phrases showing all the cases you have learned. In the boldfaced phrases the adjective ending is **-en.** These are the cases in which the articles are different from the forms that you were asked to memorize.

	MASCULINE	FEMININE	NEUTER
Nom.	der neue Wagen	die alte Firma	das moderne Haus
	ein neuer Wagen	eine alte Firma	ein modernes Haus
Acc.	**den neuen Wagen**	die alte Firma	das moderne Haus
	einen neuen Wagen	eine alte Firma	ein modernes Haus
Dat.	**dem neuen Wagen**	**der alten Firma**	**dem modernen Haus**
	einem neuen Wagen	**einer alten Firma**	**einem modernen Haus**

Any **der**-word can be substituted for the definite article in the paradigm above, and the adjective-ending pattern will remain the same; any **ein-**word can be substituted for the indefinite article in the paradigm, and the adjective-ending pattern will likewise remain the same. In the original six adjective phrases to be memorized, a substitution of a new **der**-word and **ein**-word would work out as follows:

dieser neue Wagen	diese alte Firma	dieses moderne Haus
ihr neuer Wagen	ihre alte Firma	ihr modernes Haus

II. WORD ORDER: CONJUNCTIONS

A. Coordinating Conjunctions

The most common coordinating conjunctions are:

> **und** (*and*)   **oder** (*or*)
> **aber** (*but*)   **denn** (*because, for*)

Note: Other coordinating conjunctions will be listed in the vocabulary as they occur.

Coordinating conjunctions used to connect independent clauses are not counted as elements and have no effect on the word order of either clause.

> Ich prahle nicht gern, aber **die moderne Architektur verdankt** uns sehr viel.
> Ich will aufs Konservatorium, und **eine Musikerin muß** auch in der modernen Musik Bescheid wissen.
> Er kommt früh, denn **er will** einen guten Platz.

B. Subordinating Conjunctions

The most common subordinating conjunctions are:

> **daß** (*that*)   **da** (*since*)
> **wenn** (*if, whenever*)   **ob** (*whether, if*)
> **weil** (*because, since*)

Note: Other subordinating conjunctions will be listed in the vocabulary as they occur.

Subordinating conjunctions introduce dependent clauses and do have an effect on the word order: every dependent clause in German has the inflected verb (the one which is normally in second position) in final position.

> Ich belege sie nur als Gasthörer, weil Englisch mich **interessiert.**
> Sie kommen zu spät, wenn Sie einen guten Platz **wollen.**

The subordinating conjunction **daß,** like its English equivalent *that,* may be omitted. In such a case the verb in that clause will be in second position. Notice the word-order contrast in the following sentences:

> Ich glaube, daß **ihr Gebiet** klassische Musik **ist.**
> *I think that her field is classical music.*
> Ich glaube, **ihr Gebiet ist** klassische Musik.
> *I think her field is classical music.*

When the dependent clause precedes the independent clause, it is considered to be the first element, and the independent clause has inverted word order (verb before the subject).

Wenn die letzte Vorlesung vorbei ist, **gehen sie** in die Mensa.

C. Indirect Questions

In indirect questions the interrogative word functions as a subordinating conjunction, and the verb, therefore, will be placed at the end of the clause. In the following examples, notice the different word order in direct and indirect questions.

DIRECT QUESTION	INDIRECT QUESTION
Wo ist die Mensa?	Er fragt ihn, **wo** die Mensa **ist.**
Wann gehen sie in die Mensa?	Ich weiß nicht, **wann** sie in die Mensa **gehen.**

When there is no interrogative word in the direct question, the conjunction **ob** (*whether, if*) is used to introduce the indirect question.

Können Sie es mir erzählen?   Ich frage ihn, **ob** er es mir erzählen **kann.**

III. PUNCTUATION: CLAUSES

All complete clauses in German are set off by commas. A comma is not used between two independent clauses joined by a coordinating conjunction if the subject in the second clause is not expressed.

Mein Freund kommt nach Deutschland und bleibt bis Juni.
Mein Freund kommt nach Deutschland, und er bleibt bis Juni.

Word Study and Usage

I. CARDINAL NUMBERS (II)

The remaining cardinal numbers are formed according to the following pattern:

zwanzig (20)   fünfundzwanzig (25)
einundzwanzig (21)   sechsundzwanzig (26)
zweiundzwanzig (22)   siebenundzwanzig (27)
dreiundzwanzig (23)   achtundzwanzig (28)
vierundzwanzig (24)   neunundzwanzig (29)

dreißig (30)
vierzig (40)
fünfzig (50)
sechzig (60)
siebzig (70)
achtzig (80)
neunzig (90)
hundert (100)
hunderteins (101)
hundertzwei (102)
hundertzehn (110)
hundertzweiundachtzig (182)

zweihundert (200)
zweihunderteins (201)
dreihundert (300)
sechshundert (600)
siebenhundert (700)
tausend (1000)
(ein) tausendachthundert or achtzehn-
hundert (1800)
zweitausend (2000)
eine Million (*one million*)
eine Milliarde (*one billion*)

II. EXPRESSIONS OF TIME (I)

Some expressions of time are:

Wieviel Uhr ist es? or **Wie spät ist es?**   What time is it?
Um wieviel Uhr?   At what time?
Um vier Uhr.   At 4:00.
Um Viertel nach vier.   At 4:15.
Um halb fünf.   At 4:30.
Um Viertel vor fünf.   At 4:45.
Um fünf Uhr.   At 5:00.

III. USE OF ALS

The German word **als** has several uses, one of which has the meaning *as a*
or *as an.* ("They looked upon him as a stranger.") German does not use
the indefinite article after **als** in this meaning, unless the noun is modified
by an adjective, in which case the article is optional.

Ich belege sie nur **als Gasthörer.**
Sie sehen den Vater **als bösen Haustyrannen.** (or: Sie sehen den
Vater **als einen bösen Haustyrannen.**)

Class Drills

*I. Restate the following sentences, substituting, in turn, each of
the given adjectives for the one in the original sentence:*

1. Der englische Gastprofessor liest hier. ⎱ **deutsch, neu, jung,**
   Ein englischer Gastprofessor liest hier. ⎰ **bekannt**

2. Das alte Lokal ist nicht weit von hier. ⎫ **groß, bekannt,**
Ein altes Lokal ist nicht weit von hier. ⎬ **modern, klein**

3. Er spricht über die alte Legende. ⎫ **bekannt, berühmt, deutsch,**
Er spricht über eine alte Legende. ⎬ **englisch**

4. Er wartet vor dem neuen Lokal. ⎫ **alt, bekannt, klein, groß**
Er wartet vor einem neuen Lokal. ⎬

5. Er fragt den deutschen Studenten. ⎫ **amerikanisch, englisch,**
Er fragt einen deutschen Studenten. ⎬ **neu, deutsch**

6. Er arbeitet bei der großen Firma. ⎫ **klein, neu, alt, bekannt**
Er arbeitet bei einer großen Firma. ⎬

II. *Restate the following sentences, substituting, in turn,* <u>dieser</u>, <u>jeder</u>, *and* <u>mancher</u> *for the definite article in the original sentence:*

Der bekannte Dirigent ist sehr begabt.
Das junge Mädchen spielt gern.
Die alte Legende ist sehr bekannt.
Er erzählt uns von dem neuen Politiker.
So heißt es in der deutschen Zeitung.

III. *Restate the following sentences, substituting, in turn,* <u>kein</u>, <u>unser</u>, *and* <u>Ihr</u> *for the indefinite article in the original sentence:*

Ist das ein neuer Wagen?
Er möchte ein altes Klavier kaufen.
Eine moderne Küche gefällt ihr.
Er spielt auf einem neuen Klavier.
Er will bei einer neuen Firma arbeiten.

IV. *Connect each of the following sets of sentences, first with* **und,** *then with* <u>aber</u>:

Sie wartet vor dem Lokal. Er kommt nicht.
Er kommt zu spät. Er will einen guten Platz.
Ich bin Jurist. Englisch interessiert mich auch.
Er will mich um fünf Uhr treffen. Dann ist es zu spät.

V. *Connect each of the following sets of sentences, first with* <u>wenn</u>, *then with* <u>da</u>. *Make the appropriate word order change each time:*

Ich fahre mit ihm. Er will nach Frankfurt.
Ich möchte ihn hören. Er liest auf englisch.
Wir müssen nach oben. Er will die Schlafzimmer sehen.
Er kommt um vier Uhr. Er will einen guten Platz.

VI. **Connect each of the following sets of sentences, first with the coordinating conjunction** <u>denn</u> **(because), then with the subordinating conjunction** <u>weil</u> **(because). Make word order changes when necessary:**

Ich kann ihn nicht besuchen. Ich fahre nach Berlin.
Ich will nach Amerika. Dieses Land interessiert mich.
Er bekommt keinen guten Platz. Er kommt zu spät.
Er wartet vor dem Audimax. Er weiß nicht, wo die Mensa ist.

VII. **Restate each of the following sentences by introducing it with — (1)** **Er weiß, daß** *. . .* **(2)** **Er weiß,** *. . . Make word order changes when necessary:*

Ihr Hauptfach ist Geschichte.
Hier gibt es moderne Wohnungen.
Sie kann nicht kommen.
Sie möchten die Vorlesung belegen. *Er weiss, dass Sie die Vorlesung belegen möchten.*
Er weiss, Sie möchten die Vorlesung belegen.

VIII. **Restate each of the following sentences, reversing the order of the clauses by placing the dependent clause first. Make the appropriate word order change each time:**

Ich gehe mit ihm, wenn er will.
Er kommt so früh, weil er einen guten Platz will. *Weil er einen guten Platz will, kommt er so früh.*
Sie gehen schon nach Hause, da es sonst kein Essen gibt. *Da es sonst kein Essen gibt, gehen sie schon nach Hause.*
Er weiß schon, daß es zu spät ist. *Dass es zu spät ist, weiss er schon.*

IX. **Form indirect questions by introducing each of the following direct questions with —** **Er fragt mich,** *. . . :*

Wann beginnt die Vorlesung?
Wo ist die Mensa?
Wer ist der Student? *Er fragt mich, wer der Student ist.*
Wie spät ist es?
Was möchte sie hören? *Er fragt mich, was sie hören möchte.*
Warum kommt sie so früh?
Hält er die Vorlesung auf englisch? *Er fragt mich, ob er die Vorlesung auf englisch hält.*
Wohnt die Familie in Bonn? *Er fragt mich, ob die Familie in Bonn wohnt.*
Weiß sie, wo die Mensa ist? *Er fragt mich, ob sie weiss wo die Mensa ist.*

X. *Restate the following sentences, substituting the new times for the one in the original sentence:*

Es ist vier Uhr. (5:00; 8:00; 11:00; 2:00)
Er kommt um Viertel nach vier. (2:15; 6:15; 9:15; 12:15)
Er beginnt um halb fünf. (3:30; 7:30; 9:30; 10:30)
Es ist Viertel vor fünf. (6:45; 8:45; 11:45; 1:45)

Es ist 10 minuten nach —

Exercises

I. Translate the following prepositional phrases:

1. **für**

   for our German student
      every
   for this little child
      her
   for their new car
      which
   for his old firm
      this

2. **von**

   about your old house
      the
   about a famous conductor
      each
   about which famous legend
      its (**sein**)
   about her German professor
      this

3. **in**

   into this famous cathedral
      our
   into my new kitchen
      each
   into which old-fashioned house
      our

II. Rewrite the following sentences, substituting each of the new conjunctions for the one in the original sentence:

1. Er belegt die Vorlesung, weil Englisch ihn interessiert. (**denn, da**)
2. Sie können es mir erzählen, denn sie wissen viel darüber. (**weil, da**)
3. Wir kommen früh, da wir einen guten Platz wollen. (**wenn, denn, weil, und**)

III. *Translate into English. Then reproduce the German sentences 1–7 from your English translations.*

1. Können Sie uns sagen, wie weit es noch bis Bonn ist? 2. Vielleicht treffe ich sie nach dem Konzert. 3. Wie lange hat er den alten Wagen schon? 4. Darf ich Sie um Auskunft bitten? Ich möchte wissen, wie alt dieses Haus ist. 5. Sie weiß nicht, ob sie die Vorlesung als Gasthörerin belegen kann. 6. Ich muß ihn fragen, warum er antike Möbel nicht mag. 7. Bei uns glauben viele, daß es hier keine altmodischen Wohnungen gibt. 8. Daß er schon ein berühmter Dirigent ist, wissen wir aus der Zeitung. 9. Jetzt wird's aber Zeit, weil es sonst kein Abendessen gibt. 10. Auf der Autobahn sieht man nichts vom Land, weil man zu schnell fährt. Ist das bei Ihnen auch so?

IV. *Translate:*

1. Please tell me what he wants to know. 2. That is the big lecture hall, isn't it? 3. Since he is late, he can't get a good seat. 4. Do you know where the *Audimax* is? 5. Just a second please, are you the American exchange student? 6. He asks the German professor for information. 7. They are standing at the entrance to the big lecture hall. 8. Perhaps they can meet you after your lecture? 9. A classical symphony is on the program. Let's buy tickets for it. 10. See you this afternoon in the *Mensa*.

V. *Composition. Answer the following questions in complete German sentences, using as much of the question in your answer as possible. Write your answers in a paragraph, omitting* ja *and* nein:

1. Wann beginnt Toms erste Vorlesung?
2. Wann kommt Tom zum Hörsaal?
3. Kommt er zu früh?
4. Ist es eine Vorlesung über Literatur?
5. Warum hält der Professor die Vorlesung auf englisch?
6. Wen trifft Tom am Eingang?
7. Warum belegt Hans Krüger diese Vorlesung?
8. Was sagt Hans über Toms Deutsch?
9. Wann und wo will Hans den Amerikaner treffen?
10. Warum soll Tom vor dem Audimax warten?

Active Vocabulary

abgemacht!	agreed! all right! settled!
das Audimax = **Auditorium** **Maximum**	main lecture hall
der Augenblick	moment
die Auskunft	information
der Austausch- **student**	exchange student
beginnen	to begin
belegen	to register for, take (a course)
bestimmt	certain, definite
bitten (um)	to ask (for)
da (*subord. conj.*)	since
daß (*subord. conj.*)	that
dauern	to last
eher	rather
der Eingang	entrance
englisch	English
auf englisch	in English
entschuldigen	to excuse
erst-	first
erst (*adv.*)	only, not until
das Fach	field, specialty
fehlerlos	flawless, perfect
früh	early
der Gasthörer	auditor
der Gastprofessor	visiting professor
groß	big; great
halb	half
halten (ä)	to hold; give (a lecture)
der Hörsaal	lecture hall
interessieren	to interest
der Jurist, den **Juristen, dem** **Juristen**	law student, jurist, one versed in the law

kaum	scarcely, hardly
der Krieg	war
die Lage	situation
lesen (ie)	to read; lecture
letzt-	last
das Lokal	restaurant, inn
die Mensa	students' dining hall
die Minute	minute
der Mittag	noon
der Nachmittag	afternoon
heute nach- **mittag**	this afternoon
die Nähe	vicinity
der Platz	seat
der Saal	room, hall
schön	beautiful; fine, nice
die Stunde	hour
treffen (i)	to meet
das Viertel	quarter, section
vorbei	over, finished
die Vorlesung	lecture
weil (*subord. conj.*)	because, since
die Welt	world
der Weltkrieg	world war
wenn (*subord. conj.*)	if, whenever
das Wiedersehen	meeting again, reunion
auf Wieder- **sehen**	good-by
wieviel Uhr	what time
um wieviel **Uhr**	at what time
wirtschaftlich	economic
zusammen	together

German Information Center

Die Universität Bonn

Thomas Mann

Neunte Lektion

Auf dem Alten Zoll

[*Auf einem Spaziergang kommen Hans und Tom an die Mauer der alten Festung.*]

TOM — Endlich mal keine Menschen und keine Autos, nur das Rauschen des Wassers . . .

HANS — Der Alte Zoll gehört zu den historischen Stätten. Leider verschwinden sie allmählich. Bonn braucht jetzt mehr Wohnungen, Straßen und Hotels.

TOM — Aber hier muß man an die alten Zeiten denken. Bonn war sicher idyllisch, als es noch ziemlich unbekannt war.

HANS — Gewiß, aber interessante Studenten waren damals auch hier. Karl Marx zum Beispiel.

TOM — Karl Marx??

HANS — [*ironisch*] Ja, darüber schweigen manche Leute gern. Sie betrachten das als einen dunklen Punkt in der Chronik unserer Stadt. Aber dafür können wir ja nichts.

TOM — Bestimmt nicht!

HANS — Aber die andere Geschichte ist schlimmer: die Sache mit Thomas Mann.

TOM — Sie meinen während der Nazizeit. Ja, das war unglaublich. Aber es gibt fast keine alten Universitäten ohne ihre Skandalgeschichten.

HANS — Schon, aber das war mehr als ein Skandal. — Zum Glück kann man auch solche Namen wie Beethoven und Heine erwähnen. Sie waren ja auch Studenten in Bonn.

At the *Alte Zoll*[1]

[*On a stroll, Hans and Tom come to the wall of the old fortification.*]

TOM — At last — no people and no cars. Just the sound of the water . . .

HANS — The *Alte Zoll* is one of the historic spots. Unfortunately, they're gradually disappearing. Now Bonn needs more houses, streets, and hotels.

TOM — But here you're still reminded of the old days. Bonn must have been idyllic when it was still fairly unknown.

HANS — That's true, but there were interesting students here then, too. Karl Marx, for example.

TOM — Karl Marx??

HANS — [*ironically*] Yes, some people don't like to talk about it. They consider it a black spot in the history of our city. But there's nothing we can do about that.

TOM — Of course not.

HANS — But the other story is worse: the incident with Thomas Mann.

TOM — You mean during the Nazi period. Yes, that was unbelievable. But there are hardly any old universities without their scandals.

HANS — That's true. But that was more than a scandal. Fortunately, we can also mention names like Beethoven[2] and Heine. They were also students in Bonn.

---

[1] **der Zoll** — *customs.* The *Alte Zoll* is a former customs station used to collect duties from ships on the Rhine.   [2] Beethoven was enrolled at the *Kurfürstliche Universität* in Bonn from 1788 to 1791. This was actually the parent institution of the *Rheinische Friedrich-Wilhelms-Universität Bonn*, which was not founded in its present form until 1818.

Lesestück IX

Bonn gehört nicht zu den alten deutschen Universitäten wie Heidelberg oder Leipzig. Aber seit der Gründung[1] im Jahre 1818 findet man berühmte Namen unter den Professoren und Studenten aller Fakultäten.[2] Auch unter den Ehrendoktoren[3] gibt es manche bekannten Leute, unter ihnen den großen Schriftsteller[4] Thomas Mann. Die Universität ist besonders stolz auf ihn. 5
Aber 1933 kommen die Nationalsozialisten in Deutschland an die Regierung,[5] und Thomas Mann, ein bitterer Feind[6] dieser Partei,[7] muß das Land verlassen. Drei Jahre später erklärt[8] die Universität Bonn, daß er nicht mehr zu ihren Ehrendoktoren gehört. Damit zeigen die Nazis, daß die Interessen der Partei und ihrer Ideologie wichtiger sind als[9] Kunst und Kultur. 10

Die Antwort Manns ist ein interessantes Dokument aus dieser schlimmen Zeit. Das Datum[10] des Briefes ist „Neujahr 1937". Darin klagt[11] Thomas Mann die Universitäten an,[11] daß sie schweigen, während[12] die Nazis „Deutschland moralisch, kulturell und wirtschaftlich verwüsten".[13] Wie viele andere Dichter[14] und Schriftsteller weiß auch Thomas Mann, daß die Politik 15 der Nazis Krieg bedeutet, und er warnt: „Dieser Krieg ist unmöglich.[15] Deutschland kann ihn nicht führen."[16] Am Ende seines Briefes heißt es: „Gott helfe unserem Lande und lehre[17] es, seinen Frieden[18] zu machen mit der Welt und mit sich selbst."[19] Heute wissen wir, wie prophetisch Thomas Manns Brief war: der zweite Weltkrieg verwüstet die halbe Welt und kommt 20 erst nach großem Leid zu einem Ende.

Zehn Jahre nach dem ersten Brief schreibt Thomas Mann wieder an die Universität Bonn, denn er ist jetzt wieder ihr Ehrendoktor. Er dankt der Universität höflich[20] aber sehr formell dafür. Trotz[21] des höflichen Tons[22] aber hören wir die Ironie und Resignation zwischen den Zeilen[23] dieses 25 Briefes.

---

[1] **die Gründung, –, –en** founding
[2] **die Fakultät, –, –en** branch of university learning and teaching
[3] **der Ehrendoktor, –s, –en** honorary doctor
[4] **der Schriftsteller, –s, –** writer
[5] **die Regierung, –, –en** government
[6] **der Feind, –(e)s, –e** enemy
[7] **die Partei, –, –en** (political) party
[8] **erklären** to declare
[9] **wichtiger . . . als** more important than
[10] **das Datum, –s, Daten** date
[11] **klagt . . . an** accuses
[12] **während** while

[13] **verwüsten** to devastate, wreck
[14] **der Dichter, –s, –** poet, fiction writer
[15] **unmöglich** impossible
[16] **(einen Krieg) führen** to fight (a war)
[17] **lehren** to teach
[18] **der Friede(n), –ns** peace
[19] **selbst** self
　　mit sich selbst with itself
[20] **höflich** politely
[21] **trotz** in spite of
[22] **der Ton, –(e)s, ⸚e** tone
[23] **die Zeile, –, –n** line

Fragen und Antworten

1. Wohin kommen Hans und Tom?
   Sie kommen an die Mauer einer alten Festung.
2. Warum ist es auf dem Alten Zoll so still (*quiet*)?
   Man sieht keinen Menschen und kein Auto.
3. Was verschwindet allmählich?
   Die historischen Stätten Bonns verschwinden allmählich.
4. Was braucht Bonn heute?
   Anstatt (*instead of*) der historischen Stätten braucht Bonn mehr Wohnungen.
5. An welche Zeiten muß man denken?
   An die alten Zeiten, als Bonn noch unbekannt war.
6. Wann war Bonn sicher sehr idyllisch?
   Während der alten Zeiten war es sicher idyllisch.
7. Worüber schweigen manche Leute gern?
   Sie erwähnen nicht gern, daß Karl Marx Student in Bonn war.
8. Hat Bonn keine berühmten Studenten?
   Doch, man kann die Namen mancher bekannten Leute nennen.
9. Wessen Name gehört auch zu den berühmten Namen?
   Beethovens Name gehört auch dazu.
10. Warum ist die Bonner Universität auch in der Politik unseres Jahrhunderts (*century*) bekannt?
    Wegen (*because of*) der Sache mit Thomas Mann.

Structure and Practice

Explanation of Forms

I. GENITIVE CASE

A. Forms

1. NOUNS AND THEIR MODIFIERS (**der-** AND **ein**-WORDS): Unlike the other cases, the genitive case shows distinctions not only in the forms of the **der-** and **ein**-words but in the nouns as well.

MASCULINE	FEMININE	NEUTER
des (dieses) Wagens	**der (dieser)** Wohnung	**des (dieses)** Kindes
eines (ihres) Wagens	**einer (ihrer)** Wohnung	**eines (ihres)** Kindes

Masculine and neuter nouns add **-s** (usually on nouns of more than one syllable) or **-es** (usually on monosyllabic nouns or nouns ending in one of the following: **s, ß, z, tz, st, zt, sch**) in the genitive case. Modern colloquial German tends to use **-s** rather than **-es** even on monosyllabic nouns except for those that end in one of the sibilants mentioned above.

A most important exception to this rule occurs in the group of weak masculine nouns, which add **-n** or **-en** in the genitive: **des Studenten, des Herrn.**

Feminine nouns add no ending in the genitive case.

2. PROPER NAMES: Proper names, which are normally used without an article, simply add **-s** (with no apostrophe) in the genitive: **Beethovens Name.**

3. ATTRIBUTIVE ADJECTIVES: In the genitive case, adjective endings after **der-** and **ein**-words will always be **-en** in accordance with the formula given in the last lesson: **der alten Festung, einer alten Festung.**

4. INTERROGATIVE PRONOUN: The genitive form of the interrogative pronoun is **wessen** (*whose*): **Wessen Name ist das?**

B. Uses

1. RELATIONSHIP BETWEEN PERSONS OR THINGS: The relationship between persons and/or things, expressed in English by an *of* or *'s* construction, in German is in the genitive case. The *of* is not expressed but is implied in the genitive form.

> Sie hören das Rauschen **des Wassers.**
> *They hear the murmur **of the water.***

> Der Name **des Studenten** ist Krüger.
> *The name **of the student** (**the student's** name) is Krüger.*

> Sie kommen an die Mauer **einer alten Festung.**
> *They come to the wall **of an old fortification.***

Beethovens Name gehört auch dazu.
Beethoven's name is also among them.

Note: The conventional genitive word order may also be used with proper names:
Der Name Beethovens gehört auch dazu.

2. WITH CERTAIN PREPOSITIONS: There are some prepositions that are followed by the genitive case. Of these you have met:

anstatt (*instead of*)
trotz (*in spite of*)
während (*during*)
wegen (*because of*)

Sie meinen **während der Nazizeit.**
You mean during the Nazi period.

Trotz des höflichen Tons hören wir die Ironie zwischen den Zeilen.
In spite of the polite tone, we hear the irony between the lines.

Anstatt der historischen Stätten braucht Bonn mehr Wohnungen.
Instead of historical spots, Bonn needs more houses.

Note: Other prepositions in this group will be listed in the vocabulary as they occur.

II. PLURALS

In English, plurals are indicated by a change in the noun (usually an **-s** or **-es** ending; occasionally a vowel change: *foot, feet; man, men;* sometimes no plural indication: *sheep, sheep; fish, fish*). Articles and other adjectives remain the same as they are in the singular.

In German, plurals are indicated by the form of the article, **der**-words, **ein**-words, and other adjectives as well as in the form of the noun.

A. Articles, <u>der</u>- and <u>ein</u>- Words

German has no distinction in gender in the plural. The forms of the definite article (there is no indefinite article in the plural) as well as **der**- and **ein**-words are the same for masculine, neuter, and feminine nouns. These forms are shown in the following paradigm. We have used **Straßen** as the example of a plural noun with which these modifiers can be used. Any plural noun can be substituted.

	DEFINITE ARTICLE	**der**-WORDS	**ein**-WORDS
Nom.	**die**	**diese**	**keine, ihre** Straßen

Acc.	**die**	**diese**	**keine, ihre** Straßen
Dat.	**den**	**diesen**	**keinen, ihren** Straßen
Gen.	**der**	**dieser**	**keiner, ihrer** Straßen

B. Nouns (I)

In German there are five ways in which the plural of nouns is formed. The rules and their exceptions are numerous. Therefore, it is best to learn the plural of each noun as you learn the singular. The following systematized presentation of the plural formation of nouns, however, will help you to learn them.

Nouns are traditionally divided into five different groups, or classes, according to the way they form their plurals:

Class I nouns adding no plural ending, some adding umlaut: **der Amerikaner, die Amerikaner; der Bruder, die Brüder.**

Class II nouns adding plural ending **-e,** some also adding umlaut: **der Freund, die Freunde; der Sohn, die Söhne.**

Class III nouns adding plural ending **-er** and umlaut whenever possible: **das Bild, die Bilder; das Glas, die Gläser.**

Class IV nouns adding plural ending **-n** or **-en,** never adding umlaut: **die Schwester, die Schwestern; die Universität, die Universitäten.**

Class V nouns adding plural ending **-s,** never adding umlaut: **das Auto, die Autos; das Hotel, die Hotels.**

If you are in doubt about the plural of a noun, you can check it in the end vocabulary, which lists most nouns with two endings, for example: **der Freund, -es, -e.** The first of these is the genitive singular ending; the second is the plural ending. Beginning with this lesson, both the genitive and plural of new nouns are also given in the reading and active vocabularies.

In this lesson we will describe classes IV and V since they are the simplest to learn. The remaining groups will be described in the next lesson. There will be no attempt at completeness in the description of each group. Only the most helpful rules will be given, and you should keep in mind that there are usually exceptions to these, too.

Class IV:

Plural formed by adding **-n** or **-en.** In this group you will find:

(1) most feminine nouns: **die Schwester, die Schwestern; die**

Frau, die Frauen; die Tür, die Türen; die Universität, die Universitäten. (Feminine nouns with **-in** suffixes add **-nen** in the plural: **die Studentin, die Studentinnen**)

(2)   all weak masculine nouns (those that add **-en** or **-n** in all cases of the singular except the nominative): **der Herr, die Herren; der Student, die Studenten; der Name, die Namen**

(3)   nouns ending in **-or: der Professor, die Professoren** (the accent in these nouns shifts in the plural to the **-or** syllable)

Class V:

Plural formed by adding **-s**. In this group, which is a very small one, you will find some nouns of foreign origin: **das Auto, die Autos; das Hotel, die Hotels**

C. Attributive Adjectives

After **der-** and **ein-**words in all cases of the plural, attributive adjectives add **-en.**

Die historischen Stätten Bonns verschwinden allmählich.
Es gibt fast **keine alten Universitäten** ohne ihre Skandalgeschichten.
Der Alte Zoll gehört zu **den historischen** Stätten.
Man kann die Namen **mancher bekannten Leute** nennen.

Word Study and Usage

I. ALS, WENN AND WANN

There are three German words meaning *when:* **als, wenn** and **wann.** They are not interchangeable; each one has a specific use.

Als is used to refer to one time in the past.

Bonn war sicher idyllisch, **als** es noch ziemlich unbekannt war.
Bonn must have been idyllic when it was still fairly unknown.

Wenn is used with the present or future tense or for repeated times in the past (as in English: *whenever*). It also has the meaning *if.*

Wenn die letzte Vorlesung vorbei ist, gehen sie in ein Lokal.
***When** the last lecture is finished, they go to a restaurant.*
Die Studenten klopfen, **wenn** der Professor in den Hörsaal kommt.

The students rap (with their knuckles on the desks) **whenever** *the professor comes into the lecture hall.*

Wenn ich ihn sehe, erzähle ich ihm davon.
If (when) I see him, I'll tell him about it.

Wann is used only in questions, direct or indirect.

Wann war Bonn sicher idyllisch?
When must Bonn have been idyllic?

Er fragt ihn, **wann** die Vorlesung beginnt.
He asks him **when** *the lecture begins.*

II. THE PREFIX UN- WITH ADJECTIVES

Like English, German often uses an **un**-prefix with adjectives to indicate the negative form.

bekannt (well-known)	*un*bekannt (unknown)
glaublich (believable, credible)	*un*glaublich (unbelievable, incredible)
bestimmt (certain, definite)	*un*bestimmt (uncertain, indefinite)
interessant (interesting)	*un*interessant (uninteresting)

III. COMPOUND NOUNS

A characteristic feature of German is the compound noun. A number of them have already appeared in the dialogues and reading texts. These compounds usually consist of two or more nouns, but can also include verb stems, prepositions, adjectives, and adverbs. The last component determines the gender of the compound.

> **das Auto** (car), **die Bahn** (road) = **die Autobahn**
> **vor** (before), **der Name** (name) = **der Vorname**
> **rennen** (to run), **die Bahn** (road) = **die Rennbahn**

Sometimes an **-s-** or **-es-** connects the components.

> **der Bund** (confederation), **das Haupt** (head), **die Stadt** (city) = **die Bund*es*hauptstadt**
> **die Geschwindigkeit** (speed), **die Begrenzung** (limit) = **die Geschwindigkeitsbegrenzung**

The plural of a compound noun is formed by pluralizing the last component.

> **die Skandalgeschichte, die Skandalgeschichte*n***

Class Drills

I. a. Restate the following sentence, substituting each new noun, given in the nominative case. Make any necessary changes in the article and the noun:

Das ist der Name des Flugplatzes.
>(der Wein)
>(der Turm)
>(der Professor)
>(der Dirigent)
>(der Student)
>(das Kind)
>(das Orchester)
>(das Land)
>(das Studentenheim)
>(die Universität)
>(die Firma)
>(die Zeitung)
>(die Straße)

b. Using the sentence in exercise a., substitute for each definite article the correct form of <u>dieser</u>, <u>ein</u>, and <u>unser</u>:

II. Restate the following sentence, substituting each new noun, given in the nominative case. Make any necessary changes in the article and the noun:

Während des Ausflugs wird er müde.
>(der Spaziergang)
>(der Film)
>(der Nachmittag)
>(das Konzert)
>(das Abendessen)
>(das Programm)
>(die Vorlesung)
>(die Fußtour)
>(die Zeremonie)

III. Restate the following sentence, substituting the correct form of the names shown:

Er weiß nichts über die Geschichte Bonns.
>(Frankfurt)
>(Berlin)

(Europa)
(Amerika)

IV. a. Restate the following sentences, changing the noun in each to the plural. Make the necessary changes in the definite article. In the case of noun subjects, you will also have to change the verb to a plural form:

1. Der Professor hat immer recht.
   Der Student kennt das nicht.
   Der Jurist schweigt darüber.
   Die Zeitung kommt am Montag.
   Die Universität ist schon alt.
   Die Straße ist nicht so gut.
   Die Stewardeß spricht gut deutsch.

2. Kennen Sie den Professor?
   Das ist nicht so leicht für den Studenten.
   Das ist etwas für den Juristen.
   Kommen Sie auch in die Vorlesung?
   Besuchen Sie die Burg!
   Möchten Sie die Zeitschrift haben?
   Kennen Sie die Kirche?

3. Wir gehen mit dem Professor hin.
   Das verdanken wir dem Studenten.
   Was sagen Sie zu der Geschichte?
   Wir sprechen von der Studentin.
   So heißt es in der Zeitung.
   Waren Sie nicht in der Vorlesung?

(*In the following group, change only the genitive nouns to the plural.*)
4. Wer kommt anstatt des Professors?
   Das war die Auskunft des Juristen.
   Das ist die Lektüre des Studenten.
   Kennen Sie die Skandalgeschichten der Universität?
   Wir kommen wegen der Karte.
   Das war der Beginn der Skandalgeschichte.

b. Restate the sentences in exercise a. in the plural, using first <u>dieser</u>, *then* <u>unser</u> *in place of the definite article:*

V. Restate the following sentences, inserting before each plural noun the correct form of the adjective:

Manche Skandalgeschichten sind unglaublich. (**alt**)
Die Hotels sind zu klein. (**alt**)
Wir denken an unsere Gastprofessoren. (**neu**)
Er kennt manche Universitäten. (**berühmt**)
Er erzählt uns von seinen Professoren. (**bekannt**)
Er geht mit den Studenten hin. (**deutsch**)
Das ist der Skandal dieser Universitäten. (**alt**)
Köln ist bekannt wegen seiner Kirchen. (**viel**)

Exercises

I. Rewrite the following sentences, changing all nouns to the plural. Make any other changes necessary to agree with the plural nouns:

1. Sein Kommilitone erzählt ihm die Skandalgeschichte der Universität.
2. Sie hört gern diese alte Legende von dem großen Drachen.   3. Diese Fußtour machen wir oft; wir besuchen gern die alte Ruine auf der Höhe.   4. Manche englische Familie wohnt jetzt in Bonn.   5. Welche alte Universität ist sehr berühmt?   6. Von diesem bekannten Dirigenten liest man oft in der Berliner Zeitung.   7. Auf dieser Seite ist keine Tür.
8. Diese Stewardeß ist seine Freundin.

II. Rewrite the following pairs of sentences, connecting the two clauses with <u>als</u> or <u>wenn</u>, as called for by the sentence:

1. Bonn war eine kleine Stadt. Beethoven war hier Student.
2. Man hört das Rauschen des Wassers. Man sitzt hier.
3. Die Universität war ziemlich unbekannt. Marx war Student in Bonn.
4. Ich war in Frankfurt. Er war Gastprofessor an der Universität.
5. Eine Stadt braucht mehr Wohnungen. Sie wird die Hauptstadt.

III. Translate into English. In sentences 1–5, reproduce the German sentences from your English translations:

1. Es ist unglaublich, daß Mathematik sie nicht interessiert.   2. Er vergißt es immer, aber er kann ja nichts dafür.   3. Leider hat er noch keinen Wagen.   4. Fotografien von den alten Kirchen können Sie hier kaufen.   5. Wegen des Berges dort kann man die Ruinen nicht sehen.
6. Während der Konzertpausen geht man oft in die Vorhalle und spricht über das Orchester.   7. Hier ist es so still, weil diese historische Stätte so weit von der Stadt ist.   8. Weil Sabines Gebiet klassische Musik ist,

weiß sie nicht sehr viel über Jazz-Sinfonien, aber sie hört sie gelegentlich gern. 9. Sie können in dieser Chronik nachsehen; darin finden Sie sicher etwas über die Geschichte dieser alten Festungen. 10. Beim Autofahren darf man nicht vergessen, daß es auch Geschwindigkeitsbegrenzungen gibt.

IV. *Translate:*

1. Please mention that he wants to visit us. 2. We consider that a scandal; it is unbelievable. 3. Let's go to (*in*) the cathedral when we are in Cologne. 4. By the way, what's her name? 5. Do you know anything about (*über*) this student? 6. No, I know nothing about him. 7. Where was he when she was in Bonn? 8. I have to say "good-by"; my friend is waiting for me. 9. You are right. I am late, but I can't help it. 10. That was the scandal of this century.

V. *Composition. Write ten sentences in the form of a composition about what Hans and Tom do and discuss after their last lecture. For each sentence use the words given below:*

1. Hans und Tom   Lokal   Nähe   Universität
2. dann   der Alte Zoll
3. Festung   historisch   Stätte
4. leider   verschwinden
5. Bundeshauptstadt   Wohnung
6. Hans   dunkler Punkt
7. Karl Marx   Student
8. Thomas Mann   schlimmer
9. alt   Universität   Skandal
10. berühmt   Student

Active Vocabulary

allmählich	gradual	**die Chronik, –, –en**	chronicle
als (*subord. conj.*)	when	**damals**	then, at that time, in those days
als (*after comparative*)	than	**dunkel**	dark
anstatt	instead of	**endlich**	at last, finally
das Beispiel, –s, –e	example	**erwähnen**	to mention
zum Beispiel	for example	**die Festung, –, –en**	fortress
betrachten als	to consider	**gehören (zu)**	to belong to
brauchen	to need	**die Geschichte, –, –n**	story

gewiß	certain	schon!	that's true!
das Glück, –(e)s	luck, fortune	schweigen	to be silent
zum Glück	fortunately	der Skandal, –s, –e	scandal
historisch	historic	die Skandalge-	scandal
das Hotel, –s, –s	hotel	schichte, –,	
idyllisch	idyllic	–n	
ironisch	ironic	der Spaziergang,	stroll, walk
das Jahr, –(e)s, –e	year	–s, ⸚e	
das Jahrhundert,	century	die Stätte, –, –n	spot, place
–s, –e		still	quiet
können für et-	can help it	trotz	in spite of
was		unglaublich	unbelievable
ich kann	I can't help it	verschwinden	to disappear
nichts dafür		während	during
die Leute	people	war, waren	was, were
der Mensch, –en,	man, human being	das Wasser, –s, –	water
–en		wegen	because of
die Nazizeit, –	Nazi period	wessen	whose
der Punkt, –(e)s, –e	point, spot	der Zoll, –(e)s, ⸚e	customs
das Rauschen, –s	rushing, rustle, mur-mur		
die Sache, –, –n	thing, matter, incident		
schlimm	bad, evil		
schlimmer	worse		

Zehnte Lektion

Am Kamin

[*Herr Thiele und Tom im Wohnzimmer. Sie sitzen gemütlich in Klubsesseln und trinken Tee.*]

HERR THIELE — Heißer Tee mit Rum ist einfach das beste Getränk. Bei kühlem Wetter ist es besser als kaltes Bier. Oder möchten Sie eisgekühlte Limonade?

TOM — Nein danke, der Tee schmeckt gut. Ich trinke nicht gern süße kalte Getränke.

HERR THIELE — Na, und wie war der erste Tag?

TOM — Etwas anstrengend. In den Vorlesungen verstehe ich fast alles. Aber die Seminare machen mir Schwierigkeiten. Wenn ich Fachausdrücke gebrauche, mache ich Fehler.

HERR THIELE — So schlimm ist es sicher nicht. Haben Sie auch schon Bekannte?

TOM — Einen Juristen. Er hat mir von berühmten Bonner Studenten erzählt.

HERR THIELE — Man kann auch bekannte Lehrer erwähnen, Männer wie August Wilhelm Schlegel. Heinrich Heine war damals Student bei ihm.

TOM — Heine ist auch in Amerika beliebt. Ich kenne einige Gedichte und Lieder von ihm.

HERR THIELE — Dann wissen Sie auch, wie ironisch er sein kann. Sie müssen unbedingt mal lesen, was er über Schlegel schreibt.

In Front of the Fireplace

[*Mr. Thiele and Tom in the living room. They are sitting comfortably in arm-chairs, drinking tea.*]

MR. THIELE — Hot tea with rum is certainly the best drink. In cool weather it's better than cold beer. Or would you like some cold soda?

TOM — No, thank you. The tea is good. I don't like sweet cold drinks.

MR. THIELE — Well, how was the first day?

TOM — A little strenous. I understand almost everything in the lectures. But the seminars are giving me trouble. When I use technical terms, I make mistakes.

MR. THIELE — I'm sure it's not that bad. Have you made any friends yet?

TOM — A law student. He told me about some famous Bonn students.

MR. THIELE — You can also mention famous teachers — men like August Wilhelm Schlegel. Heinrich Heine was one of his students at the time.

TOM — Heine is popular in America, too. I know a few of his poems and songs.

MR. THIELE — Then you know how ironic he can be. When you get a chance, you really must read what he writes about Schlegel.

Lesestück X

Wie die Universitäten in anderen Ländern sind auch die deutschen in einer Phase des Übergangs.[1] Die Studenten rebellieren gegen die Professoren, die junge Generation rebelliert gegen die alte. Man kann nicht mehr wie früher[2] sagen, daß der deutsche Professor der letzte Feudalherr[3] unserer Zeit ist. Er ist immer noch[4] eine Autorität auf seinem Gebiet, und in der deutschen Gesellschaft[5] ist er hoch angesehen.[6] Aber die Studenten nennen ihn manchmal ohne Respekt den „Fachidioten".[7] Er liest oft vor tausend und mehr Studenten, aber seine Hörer[8] schreiben nicht mehr jedes Wort[9] mit.[10] Sie sind kritisch und skeptisch. Theoretisch lernen und forschen[11] Professoren und Studenten zusammen. Das ist die Idee und das Ideal, doch[12] die Wirklichkeit ist oft anders. Die Professoren sind nicht mehr die „kleinen Könige"[13] wie früher. Die jungen Leute protestieren gegen die absolute Autorität der Universitätslehrer, denn sie wollen „mitbestimmen"[14] über ihre Lehrpläne,[15] über die Themen[16] der Vorlesungen usw. (und so weiter), und sie tun es auch.

Früher war das anders. In seinem Essay „Die Romantische Schule" (1833) erzählt der Dichter Heinrich Heine von seiner Studentenzeit in Bonn. Wie die meisten Studenten damals war auch er sehr beeindruckt[17] von den Professoren, zum Beispiel dem berühmten Romantiker August Wilhelm Schlegel. Er nennt ihn einen ausgezeichneten Übersetzer,[18] besonders der Werke Shakespeares. Allerdings[19] sieht Heine ihn auch in einem ironischen Licht.[20] Wir lesen in seinem Essay, daß Schlegels Verse manchmal „wie geschlagene Sahne"[21] sind, und daß man nicht weiß, „ob man sie essen oder trinken soll". Schlegel trägt[22] elegante Kleider,[23] und er ist „ganz parfümiert von guter Gesellschaft".[24] Im Hörsaal steht sein Diener[25] in Schlegelscher Hausuniform[26] hinter ihm, und auf dem Katheder[27] vor ihm stehen goldene

[1] **der Übergang, –s, ⁓e** transition
[2] **wie früher** as in the past
[3] **der Feudalherr, –n, –en** feudal lord
[4] **immer noch** still
[5] **die Gesellschaft, –, –en** society
[6] **angesehen** respected, esteemed
[7] **der „Fachidiot"** narrow specialist
[8] **der Hörer, –s, –** listener; student
[9] **das Wort, –es, –e** word
[10] **schreiben . . . mit** write down, take down
[11] **forschen** to do research
[12] **doch** but, yet, nevertheless
[13] **der König, –s ⁓e** king
[14] **mitbestimmen** to share in decisions
[15] **der Lehrplan, –s, ⁓e** curriculum
[16] **das Thema, –s, Themen** subject, topic
[17] **beeindruckt** impressed
[18] **der Übersetzer, –s, –** translator
[19] **allerdings** to be sure, it is true
[20] **das Licht, –(e)s, –er** light
[21] **die geschlagene Sahne, –** whipped cream
[22] **tragen, (ä)** to wear
[23] **das Kleid, –(e)s, –er** garment, dress
   pl. clothing
[24] **er ist „ganz parfümiert von guter Gesellschaft"** he "reeks of good society"
[25] **der Diener, –s, –** servant, footman
[26] **die Hausuniform, –, –en** livery
[27] **das Katheder, –s, –** lectern

Heinrich Heine

German Information Center

Armleuchter[28] und ein Glas Zuckerwasser.[29] Es ist also nicht nur eine Vorlesung, sondern auch eine Schau.[30]

So weit[31] der Ironiker Heine. Heute ist das alles anders. „Kleine Könige" gibt es nicht mehr. Die Universität wie die ganze Gesellschaft ist jetzt demokratischer.

[28] **der Armleuchter, –s, –** candelabrum
[29] **das Zuckerwasser, –s, –** sugar water

[30] **die Schau, –, –en** show, spectacle
[31] **so weit** so much for

Fragen und Antworten

1. Wo sitzt Tom?
   Er sitzt in einem Klubsessel.
2. In welchem Zimmer stehen die Sessel?
   Sie stehen im Wohnzimmer.
3. Was trinken Herr Thiele und Tom?
   Sie trinken heißen Tee.
4. Wann trinkt Herr Thiele gern Tee?
   An kühlen Tagen trinkt er gern Tee.
5. Was macht Tom Schwierigkeiten?
   Deutsche Seminare machen ihm Schwierigkeiten.
6. Wann macht Tom manchmal noch einen Fehler?
   Wenn er einen Fachausdruck gebrauchen muß.

7. Wann war Heinrich Heine in Bonn?
   Er war dort Student, als Schlegel ein bekannter Lehrer war.
8. Kennt Tom ein Gedicht oder ein Lied von Heine?
   Ja, denn Heine ist auch in Amerika beliebt.
9. Was soll Tom unbedingt lesen?
   Heines ironische Worte (**das Wort**—*word*) über den berühmten Schlegel.
10. Sind die deutschen Professoren wirklich „kleine Könige"?
    Nein, aber sie sind absolute Autoritäten auf ihren Gebieten.

Structure and Practice

Explanation of Forms

I. ATTRIBUTIVE ADJECTIVES (II)

A. Unpreceded Adjectives

The adjective endings you learned earlier were dependent on the **der**- or **ein**-words which preceded them. There are times, although not frequent, when the adjective will have no **der**- or **ein**-word before it (as in English: "I like hot coffee"). In such cases the adjective itself takes on the **der**-word ending, thereby showing the case and gender of the noun.

The masculine and neuter genitive adjective endings (see underlined forms in the paradigm below) are the only exceptions to this adjective declensional pattern. According to the **der**-word declension, one would expect **-es** in both places.

	MASCULINE	FEMININE	NEUTER	PLURAL
Nom.	heiß**er** Tee	eisgekühlt**e** Limonade	kalt**es** Bier	bekannt**e** Lehrer
Acc.	heiß**en** Tee	eisgekühlt**e** Limonade	kalt**es** Bier	bekannt**e** Lehrer
Dat.	heiß**em** Tee	eisgekühlt**er** Limonade	kalt**em** Bier	bekannt**en** Lehrern
Gen.	<u>heiß**en** Tees</u>	eisgekühlt**er** Limonade	<u>kalt**en** Biers</u>	bekannt**er** Lehrer

Notice the contrast in the following pairs of sentences. Those in Group I have adjectives preceded by **der**-words; those in Group II have unpreceded adjectives and take the **der**-word ending on the adjective.

<table>
<tr><td align="center">GROUP I</td><td align="center">GROUP II</td></tr>
</table>

GROUP I	GROUP II
Dieser heiße Tee schmeckt gut.	Heißer Tee schmeckt gut.
Dieses kalte Bier schmeckt gut.	Kaltes Bier schmeckt gut.
Diese moderne Musik gefällt ihm.	Moderne Musik gefällt ihm.
Diese süßen Getränke schmecken nicht gut.	Süße Getränke schmecken nicht gut.

B. Series of Adjectives

Several descriptive adjectives preceding the same noun have the same adjective ending. This applies to unpreceded adjectives as well as to those following a **der-** or **ein-**word.

> Ich trinke nicht gern süße kalte Getränke.
> Schlegel war ein bekannter und beliebter Lehrer.

II. NOUN PLURALS (II)

In the following explanation you will find some helpful details about the classification of nouns in the remaining three groups (Class I, II and III) mentioned in the previous lesson. You should keep in mind that not every noun can be dealt with here, for there are many minor rules and exceptions.

Class I:

Nouns in this group add no ending to form the plural. Some, however, umlaut the stem vowel. In this group you will find:

(1) masculines and neuters ending in **-el, -er,** or **-en: der Wagen, die Wagen; der Vater, die Väter; der Sessel, die Sessel**

(2) all nouns ending in **-chen** and **-lein: das Mädchen, die Mädchen**

(3) only two feminines: **die Mutter** (*mother*), **die Mütter; die Tochter, die Töchter**

Class II:

Plural formed by adding **-e.** Some nouns also umlaut the stem vowel. In this group you will find:

(1) most monosyllabic masculines: **der Krieg, die Kriege; der Gast, die Gäste**

(2) a small group of monosyllabic feminines: **die Stadt, die Städte; die Wand, die Wände; die Hand, die Hände**

Note: In this group there are also a number of neuters and polysyllabic masculines which are difficult to classify and must be learned individually: **das Konzert, die Konzerte; das Programm, die Programme; der Ausdruck, die Ausdrücke.**

Class III:

Plural formed by adding **-er.** Nouns umlaut the stem vowel whenever possible (i.e., when the stem vowel is **a, o, u,** or **au**). In this group you will find:

(1) most monosyllabic neuters: **das Haus, die Häuser; das Kind, die Kinder**

(2) a few common monosyllabic masculines: **der Mann, die Männer; der Wald, die Wälder**

There are no feminine nouns in this group.

III. DATIVE PLURAL

In the dative plural all nouns except those in Class V (which add **-s** to form the plural) must end in **-n.** If their plural form already ends in **-n,** they add nothing in the dative plural.

> Man kann **bekannte Lehrer** erwähnen.
> Er erzählt ihm **von bekannten Lehrern.**
>
> Ich kenne **seine Gedichte und Lieder.**
> Er spricht **von seinen Gedichten und Liedern.**

Word Study and Usage

I. ADJECTIVES FROM NAMES OF CITIES

Adjectives are formed from names of cities by adding **-er** to the name. No adjective endings are used.

> Er ist Jurist an der **Bonner** Universität.
> *He's a law student at the University of Bonn.*
>
> Das ist der berühmte **Hamburger** Professor.
> *That's the famous Hamburg professor.*
>
> Er erzählt ihm von berühmten **Frankfurter** Studenten.
> *He tells him about famous Frankfurt students.*

II. ORDINAL NUMBERS

Except for three irregularities, the ordinal numbers are formed by adding
-t (the numbers 1–19) and **-st** (the numbers from 20 on) to the cardinal
number.

zweit-	**zwanzigst-**
fünft-	**hundertst-** etc.
neunzehnt-	

The three irregulars are:

erst- (*first*) **dritt-** (*third*) **acht-** (*eighth*)
but: **sieb(en)t-** (*seventh*) has alternate forms

In addition to the **-t** or **-st,** ordinal numbers, unlike cardinals, add adjective
endings in accordance with the rules for attributive adjectives.

Wie war **der erste Tag?**
Er spricht über die wirtschaftliche Lage **vor dem zweiten Weltkrieg.**

Class Drills

I. Restate the following sentences, substituting the correct form of the given adjectives:

1. Als spanischer Gastprofessor ist er bei uns bekannt.
   (deutsch)
   (amerikanisch)
   (englisch)

2. Als kaltes Getränk ist das sehr gut.
   (warm)
   (heiß)
   (eisgekühlt)

3. Als deutsche Austauschstudentin hat sie Schwierigkeiten.
   (amerikanisch)
   (englisch)
   (neu)

4. Möchten Sie heißen Tee?
   (kalt)
   (eisgekühlt)
   (englisch)

5. Trinken Sie gern kaltes Bier?
   (englisch)

(deutsch)
(warm)

6. Er studiert moderne Politik.
   (englisch)
   (deutsch)
   (amerikanisch)

7. Mit heißem Tee trinkt man oft Rum.
   (warm)
   (englisch)
   (chinesisch)

8. Bei schönem Wetter sitzen wir auf der Terrasse.
   (warm)
   (heiß)
   (gut)

9. Er spricht von alter Musik.
   (modern)
   (amerikanisch)
   (klassisch)

10. Deutsche Seminare machen ihm Schwierigkeiten.
    (englisch)
    (viel)
    (bestimmt)

11. Ich mache viele Fehler.
    (unglaublich)
    (klein)
    (schlimm)

12. Er erzählt ihm von berühmten Lehrern.
    (bekannt)
    (deutsch)
    (amerikanisch)

13. Davon liest man in der Chronik berühmter Städte.
    (bekannt)
    (groß)
    (klein)

II. ***Restate the following sentences, adding the correct form of the given adjective between the adjective and the noun in the original sentence:***

Sie trinkt heißen Tee mit Rum. (**englisch**)

Kaltes Bier schmeckt gut. (**deutsch**)
Ich trinke gern süße Getränke. (**kalt**)
Das ist ein guter Fachausdruck. (**neu**)
Ihr erstes Seminar macht ihr Schwierigkeiten. (**deutsch**)
Er wohnt in einem idyllischen Dorf. (**alt**)

III. a. Restate the following sentences, changing the noun in each to the plural. Make the necessary changes in the definite article. In the case of noun subjects, you will also have to change the verb to the plural form:

   1. Das Bild ist mir zu modern.
       Das Lied gefällt ihm.
       Das Kind ist noch zu klein.
       Gefällt Ihnen das Dorf?

   2. Kennen Sie den Lehrer?
       Verstehen Sie den Politiker?
       Wir können nichts für den Fehler.
       Ich zeige Ihnen das Zimmer.

   3. In der Stadt gibt es das nicht.
       Er spricht mit dem Gast.
       Wir verdanken es dem Freund.
       Wer sitzt auf dem Platz?

(In the following group, change only the genitive nouns to the plural.)
   4. Das ist die Geschichte des Krieges.
       Er spricht über die Architektur der Stadt.
       Das sind die Skandalgeschichten des Politikers.
       So ist die Lage des Landes.

    b. Restate the sentences in exercise a. in the plural, substituting the correct form of <u>dieser</u>, *then* <u>unser</u> *for the definite article:*

IV. Restate the following sentence, substituting the adjectival form of the cities:

Das ist eine Bonner Zeitung.
         (Frankfurt)
         (Berlin)
         (New York)
         (London)

V. Restate the following sentence, substituting the correct form of the new ordinal number given in English:

sechsten ← dative case

Am ersten Tag schreibt sie nach Hause.

   (*6th*)
   (*8th*)
   (*14th*)
   (*22nd*)
   (*30th*) dreissigsten

erste
zweite
dritte
vierte
fünfte
sechste

Exercises

I. Rewrite the following sentences, changing all nouns to the plural. Make whatever changes are necessary to agree with the plural nouns:

1. Zeigen Sie dem amerikanischen Gast das Zimmer! 2. Das Orchester spielt immer in dieser Stadt, wenn es ein europäisches Land besucht. 3. Er fährt nicht gern durch diesen Wald. 4. Er möchte seinen alten Freund und seinen Bruder in Berlin besuchen. 5. Mancher Amerikaner möchte ein deutsches Auto haben. 6. Über welches modernen Haus sprechen Sie? 7. Hoffentlich bekommen Sie einen guten Platz. 8. Es gibt fast kein Schloß ohne Turm. 9. Dieses Mädchen ist seine Tochter. 10. Jeder Weg führt nach Rom.

II. Rewrite the following sentences, using, in turn, the correct form of each of the given <u>der</u>- and <u>ein</u>-words. Make any necessary changes in the adjective endings:

1. Wir bestellen deutschen Wein. (**kein, der, dieser**)
   Ist das alter Wein? (**kein, der, ein**)
   Wir sprechen von deutschem Wein. (**der, Ihr, ein**)

2. Ich bestelle warmes Essen. (**kein, dieser, ein**)
   Sie sprechen von gutem Essen. (**das, Ihr, unser**)
   Deutsches Essen ist fast wie das Essen bei uns. (**das, Ihr, dieser**)

3. Moderne Musik gefällt mir. (**die, sein, dieser**)
   Sie sprechen über moderne Musik. (**sein, dieser, ihr**)
   In moderner Musik findet man das oft. (**die, ihr, unser**)

4. Antike Möbel gefallen mir. (**dieser, Ihr, mancher**)
   Das wirkt als Kontrast zu modernen Möbeln. (**sein, dieser, unser**)
   Mögen Sie antike Möbel nicht? (**mein, dieser, unser**)

III. Translate into English. In sentences 1–5, reproduce the German sentences from your English translations:

1. Diesen Studenten können Sie fragen. 2. Möchten Sie etwas über unsere berühmten Lehrer hören? 3. Sie sitzt gemütlich im Klubsessel und spricht über Heines Gedicht. 4. Wenn man will, kann man hier auch heiße Getränke bestellen. 5. Wir haben oft kühle Tage hier in Bonn. 6. Den guten Lehrern verdankt die Universität sehr viel. 7. Daß er in der Vorlesung alles versteht, glaubt sie nicht. 8. Wissen Sie, ob er diesen Herrn kennt? — Nein, er kennt keinen Menschen hier in Bonn. 9. Während dieser Zeit sollen sie die Hauptstädte Europas besuchen. 10. Wenn du willst, kannst du ihn nach dem Konzert fragen.

IV. Translate:

1. The seminars are still giving them trouble. 2. You know how ironic they can be. 3. Unfortunately, the economic conditions (*sing.*) are getting worse. 4. He believes he knows everything, but he always makes mistakes. 5. My second day in Bonn was especially strenuous. 6. This is a beautiful room, and I like the modern furniture. 7. How many cars does he have? — Two, and he wants a third, small car. 8. Can you tell me whether he is still living with his brothers? 9. I cannot understand him because he uses so many technical terms. 10. I owe a lot to my old friends. I mustn't forget that.

V. Composition. Write ten sentences in the form of a composition about Tom's first day as a student in Germany. For each sentence, use the words given below:

1. Tom   erst-   Vorlesung   neun Uhr
2. Gastprofessor   lesen über
3. Tom   verstehen   weil   englisch
4. auch   Seminar   europäisch   Geschichte
5. deutsch   Fachausdruck   Schwierigkeiten
6. Fehler
7. nicht   schlimm
8. Viertel nach fünf   deutscher Student   Audimax
9. Lokal   dann   nach Hause
10. Tom   Herr Thiele   anstrengend   Tag

Active Vocabulary

absolut	absolute	**heiß**	hot
acht-	eighth	**kalt**	cold
alles	everything	**der Kamin, –s, –e**	fireplace
anstrengend	strenuous	**der Klubsessel, –s,**	armchair
der Ausdruck,	expression	**–**	
–s, ⸚e		**der König, –s, –e**	king
die Autorität, –,	authority	**kühl**	cool
–en		**der Lehrer, –s, –**	teacher
der Bekannte, –n,	acquaintance, friend	**das Lied, –(e)s, –er**	song
–n		**die Limonade, –,**	lemonade, soda, soft
beliebt	popular	**–n**	drink
besser	better	**na!**	well! now then!
best-	best	**der Rum, –s, –s**	rum
das Bier, –(e)s, –e	beer	**schmecken**	to taste
chinesisch	Chinese	**schreiben**	to write
dritt–	third	**die Schwierigkeit,**	difficulty
einfach	simple	**–, –en**	
einige	some, a few	**das Seminar, –s, –e**	seminar
eisgekühlt	cold, iced	**der Sessel, –s, –**	easy chair
etwas	somewhat, a little	**siebt–, siebent–**	seventh
europäisch	European	**spanisch**	Spanish
der Fachausdruck,	technical term	**süß**	sweet
–s, ⸚e		**der Tee, –s, –s**	tea
der Fehler, –s, –	mistake	**verstehen**	to understand
gebrauchen	to use	**warm**	warm
das Gedicht, –s, –e	poem	**das Wetter, –s, –**	weather
gemütlich	comfortable	**das Wort, –(e)s, –e**	word
das Getränk, –s, –e	drink, beverage		

Review

Reading Practice

Tom schreibt an Fred Johnson, einen Bekannten aus Wisconsin. Fred studiert in München.

Lieber Fred,

nun habe ich den ersten Vorlesungstag hinter mir und schreibe Dir wieder einen Brief (*letter*). Vielleicht ist es komisch, aber meine erste Vorlesung in Deutschland war über *The Economic Conditions in Europe Before the Second World War*. Warum gebe ich den Titel auf englisch? Weil Professor Thompson Engländer ist und auf englisch liest. Ich bin also in Deutschland und höre Englisch. Ich tue das aber nur zum Spaß. Meine anderen Vorlesungen und Seminare sind alle auf deutsch. Das ist natürlich anstrengend für mich. Im Seminar sage ich nicht viel, denn die Fachausdrücke machen mir noch Schwierigkeiten.

Das Musikleben hier in Bonn ist besonders aktiv. Das ist kein Wunder. Ich wohne ja in der „Beethovenstadt". Die großen Konzerte sind in der Beethovenhalle. Das ist eine neue Konzerthalle direkt am Rhein. Dort spielen oft ausgezeichnete Orchester mit berühmten Dirigenten. Übrigens, die Geschichte der Universität ist nicht uninteressant. Weißt Du zum Beispiel, wer hier einmal Student war? Karl Marx. Marx und ich haben also etwas gemeinsam: wir haben die gleiche Alma Mater. Ein anderer berühmter Bonner Student ist Heine. Erinnert Dich der Name an unsere Deutschklasse bei Professor Schulz? Wie oft hat er „Du bist wie eine Blume (*flower*)" zitiert (*recited*)! Der dritte „alte Herr" (*alumnus*) der Universität ist Ludwig van Beethoven. Viele wissen es nicht, aber wir finden seinen Namen auf der Studentenliste der alten Kurfürstlichen (*electoral*) Universität.

Ich fahre bald auch nach Frankfurt. Dann schreibe ich Dir wieder und erzähle davon.

Sehr herzlich
Dein
Tom

Drills

I. PREPOSITIONS: ALL CASES

Substitute the new verb and/or prepositional phrase element. Prepositional objects are cued in the nominative case. Use contractions wherever possible:

A. Sie geht in die Vorhalle. (**sitzen**)
Sie sitzt in der Vorhalle. (**Hörsaal**)
Sie sitzt im Hörsaal. (**dieser**)
Sie sitzt in diesem Hörsaal. (**gehen in**)
Sie geht in diesen Hörsaal. (**die Mensa**)
Sie geht in die Mensa. (**zu**)
Sie geht zur Mensa. (**Professor**)
Sie geht zum Professor. (**er**)
Sie geht zu ihm. (**sprechen über**)
Sie spricht über ihn. (**die Vorlesung**)
Sie spricht über die Vorlesung. (**Vorlesungen**)
Sie spricht über die Vorlesungen. (**sein** — *his*)
Sie spricht über seine Vorlesungen. (**von**)
Sie spricht von seinen Vorlesungen. (**Konzert**)
Sie spricht von seinem Konzert. (**Konzerte**)
Sie spricht von seinen Konzerten. (**der Drachenfels**)
Sie spricht vom Drachenfels. (**gehen auf**)
Sie geht auf den Drachenfels. (**Konservatorium**)
Sie geht aufs Konservatorium. (**Terrasse**)
Sie geht auf die Terrasse. (**sitzen**)
Sie sitzt auf der Terrasse. (**unser**)
Sie sitzt auf unserer Terrasse.

B. Warten Sie am Eingang! (**dieser**)
Warten Sie an diesem Eingang! (**Hotel**)
Warten Sie an diesem Hotel! (**unser**)
Warten Sie an unserem Hotel! (**kommen**)
Kommen Sie an unser Hotel! (**der Flugplatz**)
Kommen Sie an den Flugplatz! (**Wagen**)
Kommen Sie an den Wagen! (**mit**)
Kommen Sie mit dem Wagen! (**Ihr**)
Kommen Sie mit Ihrem Wagen! (**Freund**)
Kommen Sie mit Ihrem Freund! (**Freunde**)
Kommen Sie mit Ihren Freunden! (**ohne**)
Kommen Sie ohne Ihre Freunde! (**Freundin**)
Kommen Sie ohne Ihre Freundin! (**sie**)

Kommen Sie ohne sie! (**er**)
Kommen Sie ohne ihn!

C. Er wartet vor der Konzerthalle. (**Hotel**)
Er wartet vor dem Hotel. (**sein** — *his*)
Er wartet vor seinem Hotel. (**kommen**)
Er kommt vor sein Hotel. (**aus**)
Er kommt aus seinem Hotel. (**der Wald**)
Er kommt aus dem Wald. (**fahren durch**)
Er fährt durch den Wald. (**Stadt**)
Er fährt durch die Stadt. (**vor**)
Er fährt vor die Stadt. (**in**)
Er fährt in die Stadt. (**um**)
Er fährt um die Stadt. (**dieser**)
Er fährt um diese Stadt. (**der Berg**)
Er fährt um den Berg. (**dieser**)
Er fährt um diesen Berg. (**Dorf**)
Er fährt um dieses Dorf. (**jeder**)
Er fährt um jedes Dorf. (**die Dörfer**)
Er fährt um die Dörfer.

D. Er iiest es während der Pause. (**Abend**)
Er liest es während des Abends. (**Vorlesung**)
Er liest es während der Vorlesung. (**sein** — *his*)
Er liest es während seiner Vorlesung. (**vor**)
Er liest es vor seiner Vorlesung. (**Seminar**)
Er liest es vor seinem Seminar. (**das**)
Er liest es vor dem Seminar. (**in**)
Er liest es im Seminar. (**erwähnen**)
Er erwähnt es im Seminar. (**Seminare**)
Er erwähnt es in den Seminaren. (**während**)
Er erwähnt es während der Seminare. (**Seminar**)
Er erwähnt es während des Seminars. (**schreiben**)
Er schreibt es während des Seminars. (**Krieg**)
Er schreibt es während des Krieges. (**Abend**)
Er schreibt es während des Abends. (**an**)
Er schreibt es am Abend. (**dieser**)
Er schreibt es an diesem Abend. (**Dienstag**)
Er schreibt es an diesem Dienstag.

II. DECLENSION OF ADJECTIVES

Substitute the new element:

A. Eine moderne Sinfonie gefällt mir. (**kein**)
Keine moderne Sinfonie gefällt mir. (**dieser**)

Diese moderne Sinfonie gefällt mir. (**Lied**)
Dieses moderne Lied gefällt mir. (**mancher**)
Manches moderne Lied gefällt mir. (**Lieder**)
Manche modernen Lieder gefallen mir. (**kein**)
Keine modernen Lieder gefallen mir. (**solcher**)
Solche modernen Lieder gefallen mir. (**alt**)
Solche alten Lieder gefallen mir. (**der Film**)
Der alte Film gefällt mir. (**kein**)
Kein alter Film gefällt mir. (**jeder**)
Jeder alte Film gefällt mir.

B. Ich möchte ein altes Haus kaufen. (**dieser**)
Ich möchte dieses alte Haus kaufen. (**Fotografie**)
Ich möchte diese alte Fotografie kaufen. (**Fotografien**)
Ich möchte diese alten Fotografien kaufen. (**sein** — *his*)
Ich möchte seine alten Fotografien kaufen. (**der Wagen**)
Ich möchte den alten Wagen kaufen. (**kein**)
Ich möchte keinen alten Wagen kaufen. (**Auto**)
Ich möchte kein altes Auto kaufen. (**das Lokal**)
Ich möchte das alte Lokal kaufen. (**deutsch**)
Ich möchte das deutsche Lokal kaufen.

C. Er erzählt uns von seinem neuen Haus. (**Professor**)
Er erzählt uns von seinem neuen Professor. (**die Sinfonie**)
Er erzählt uns von der neuen Sinfonie. (**Lokal**)
Er erzählt uns von dem neuen Lokal. (**schön**)
Er erzählt uns von dem schönen Lokal. (**Wohnung**)
Er erzählt uns von der schönen Wohnung. (**ihr**)
Er erzählt uns von ihrer schönen Wohnung. (**dieser**)
Er erzählt uns von dieser schönen Wohnung. (**Wohnungen**)
Er erzählt uns von diesen schönen Wohnungen. (**Schlösser**)
Er erzählt uns von diesen schönen Schlössern.

D. So heißt es in der Geschichte der alten Burg. (**dieser**)
So heißt es in der Geschichte dieser alten Burg. (**Schloß**)
So heißt es in der Geschichte dieses alten Schlosses. (**ein**)
So heißt es in der Geschichte eines alten Schlosses. (**Kirche**)
So heißt es in der Geschichte einer alten Kirche. (**berühmt**)
So heißt es in der Geschichte einer berühmten Kirche. (**ihr**)
So heißt es in der Geschichte ihrer berühmten Kirche. (**König**)
So heißt es in der Geschichte ihres berühmten Königs. (**Könige**)
So heißt es in der Geschichte ihrer berühmten Könige.

E. Heißer Tee schmeckt gut. (**englisch**)
Englischer Tee schmeckt gut. (**Bier**)
Englisches Bier schmeckt gut. (**kalt**)

Kaltes Bier schmeckt gut. (**Limonade**)
Kalte Limonade schmeckt gut. (**eisgekühlt**)
Eisgekühlte Limonade schmeckt gut. (**Getränke**)
Eisgekühlte Getränke schmecken gut.

F. Ich trinke gern heißen Tee. (**englisch**)
Ich trinke gern englischen Tee. (**Bier**)
Ich trinke gern englisches Bier. (**kalt**)
Ich trinke gern kaltes Bier. (**Limonade**)
Ich trinke gern kalte Limonade. (**eisgekühlt**)
Ich trinke gern eisgekühlte Limonade. (**Getränke**)
Ich trinke gern eisgekühlte Getränke.

G. Er spricht von deutscher Architektur. (**Politik**)
Er spricht von deutscher Politik. (**Wein**)
Er spricht von deutschem Wein. (**alt**)
Er spricht von altem Wein. (**Möbel,** *pl.*)
Er spricht von alten Möbeln.

Exercises

I. DA- AND WO-COMPOUNDS AND PREPOSITIONS

a. Substitute the prepositional objects in place of the <u>da</u>-compound:

1. Denken Sie bitte daran! (**die Karte, das Programm, der „Spiegel"**)
2. Bitten Sie ihn darum! (**die Fotografie, das Fernglas, der Wagen**)
3. Kommen Sie bitte danach zu uns! (**das Konzert, der Ausflug, die Vorlesung**)
4. Sprechen Sie bitte nicht darüber! (**der Skandal, die Sache, das Autofahren**)
5. Was soll ich damit tun? (*sing.* and *pl.:* **die Zeitschrift, der Sessel, das Programm**)

b. Answer the following questions, using the given nouns:

1. Worauf sitzen die Kinder? (*sing.* and *pl.:* **die Bank, der Sessel**)
2. Worauf warten sie? (**die Zeitung, das Flugzeug, der „Spiegel"**)
3. Woran erinnert ihn das? (**ein Film, ein Bild, eine Sinfonie**)

II. DECLENSION OF ADJECTIVES

Add the adjective indicated:

1. Er trinkt gern Wasser. (**kalt**)   2. Ich kenne einen Gastprofessor.

(**beliebt**) 3. Gefällt Ihnen dieses Gedicht? (**alt**) 4. Sie wohnt in einem Haus. (**modern**) 5. Das ist ein Hotel. (**berühmt**) 6. Fahren wir mit unserem Wagen! (**neu**) 7. Ist das Ihr Fernglas? (**neu**) 8. Ist das der Platz? (**richtig**) 9. Er geht in keinen Film. (**englisch**) 10. Ich sitze gern in einer Weinstube. (**idyllisch**) 11. Das sind Hotels. (**modern**) 12. Sie besucht gern Schlösser. (**alt**) 13. Er erzählt uns manche Geschichte. (**unglaublich**) 14. Sessel sind nicht immer schön. (**modern**) 15. Er hat keine Schwierigkeiten. (**groß**)

III. DIRECT AND INDIRECT QUESTIONS

Change the following statements to direct questions and indirect questions, according to the example:

EXAMPLE: **Er besucht seine Freundin oft. (wen)**
Wen besucht er oft?
Ich weiß nicht, wen er oft besucht.

1. Er kommt vor Semesterbeginn nach Hause. (**wann**) 2. Sie war heute auf dem Drachenfels. (**wo**) 3. Sie lesen diese Zeitung gern. (**was**) 4. Der Gastprofessor hält die Vorlesung. (**wer**) 5. Er tut das wegen seiner Eltern. (**warum**) 6. Er verdankt es seinem Professor. (**wem**)

IV. GENITIVE CASE

Rewrite the following sentences, substituting the <u>der</u>- or <u>ein</u>-words in parentheses:

Er tut es wegen seines alten Professors. (*her, our, their, this*)
seiner neuen Freundin. (*her, your* [polite], *our*)
des jungen Mädchens. (*this, their, a*)

V. TRANSLATION

Translate the following sentences:

1. Where is she sitting? 2. Where are you going after your lecture? 3. I don't know whether the lecture begins at eight. 4. Is that the famous Frankfurt newspaper? 5. Can you tell me what time it is? 6. At what time do you have to go home? 7. She is meeting him at a quarter of eight. 8. Wait in front of the *Mensa* at a quarter past six or six-thirty. 9. Is he sitting next to your friend? 10. Can you visit us on Tuesday or Wednesday? 11. This (*das*) is their third concert. 12. He makes mistakes when he speaks German.

Dezemberabend

Zwölfte Lektion

Am Neujahrsmorgen

[*Tom kommt ins Eßzimmer, wo Frau Thiele den Frühstückstisch schon gedeckt hat.*]

TOM — Prost Neujahr, Frau Thiele!

FRAU THIELE — Prost Neujahr, Tom! Schon munter?

TOM — Wo sind denn die anderen?

FRAU THIELE — Sie schlafen noch alle. Sie sind der erste. War der Sylvesterabend bei Mayers schön?

TOM — Ja, bei einer Sylvesterparty am Rhein geht's lustig zu. Ich habe viel Interessantes gelernt, auch Lieder . . . „Einmal am Rhein . . .“ — Haben wir Sie beim Heimkommen geweckt?

FRAU THIELE — Nein, ich habe gar nichts gehört.

TOM — Gerd wollte Ihnen ein Ständchen bringen, aber Sabine war dagegen. Sie war müde; sie hatte zuviel getanzt.

FRAU THIELE — Und dann der weite Heimweg zu Fuß.

TOM — Wir sind auch noch am Rhein entlang spaziert. Dort haben wir die Schiffe beobachtet.

FRAU THIELE — Warum sind Sie eigentlich schon so früh auf?

TOM — Ich habe riesigen Hunger, Frau Thiele.

FRAU THIELE — Gut! Ich habe schon Kaffee gekocht. Bitte warten Sie nicht auf die Langschläfer. Nach einer Feier braucht man etwas Kräftiges im Magen.

On New Year's Morning

[*Tom comes into the dining room, where Mrs. Thiele has already set the breakfast table.*]

TOM — Happy New Year, Mrs. Thiele.

MRS. THIELE — Happy New Year, Tom. Up already?

TOM — Where are the others?

MRS. THIELE — They're all still asleep. You're the first. Was New Year's Eve at the Mayers' nice?

TOM — Yes. A New Year's Eve party in the Rhine country is a lot of fun. I learned a number of interesting things, including songs — „*Einmal am Rhein* . . ." Did we wake you when we got home?

MRS. THIELE — No, I didn't hear a thing.

TOM — Gerd wanted to serenade you, but Sabine was against it. She was tired — she had danced too much.

MRS. THIELE — And then the long walk home.

TOM — We even strolled along the Rhine. We watched the ships there.

MRS. THIELE — Tell me, why are you up so early?

TOM — I'm famished, Mrs. Thiele.

MRS. THIELE — Good. I've already made some coffee. Please don't wait for the sleepyheads. After a party you need some nourishing food.

Lesestück XII

Tom schreibt an einen Kommilitonen in Amerika. Sie haben zusammen Deutsch in Wisconsin gelernt.

Lieber[1] Bob,

hier ist mein erster Brief auf deutsch. Hoffentlich kannst Du alles verstehen.

Ich muß Dir vor allem vom Jahresende hier in Deutschland erzählen. [5] Weihnachten[2] habe ich bei der Familie Thiele gefeiert.[3] Besonders hat mich der Tannenbaum[4] beeindruckt. Herr Thiele hat mir erklärt, daß die Deutschen trotz der Feuersgefahr[5] einen Baum mit wirklichen Kerzen[6] vorziehen.[7]

Die Sylvesterfeier war das zweite große Fest[8] in einer Woche.[9] Eine Freundin hatte Gerd, Sabine und mich eingeladen. In Deutschland feiert man [10] das Ende des alten Jahres gründlich[10] und lange. Wir sind erst am nächsten Morgen um halb sechs Uhr nach Hause gekommen, und das ist in dieser Nacht[11] nichts Ungewöhnliches.[12] Zuerst hat es bei Mayers ein gutes Sylvesteressen gegeben. Danach haben wir getanzt und Gesellschaftsspiele[13] gespielt. Das traditionelle „Bleigießen"[14] hat mich besonders fasziniert. Man [15] macht etwas Blei flüssig,[15] dann gießt jeder etwas von diesem flüssigen Blei in kaltes Wasser. Natürlich wird das Metall schnell hart, und man sieht oft sehr komische Figuren und Formen. Dann deutet[16] man diese Figuren. Sabine hat man eine Hochzeit prophezeit, weil ihre Bleifigur ein Ring war, und mir eine Reise,[17] weil man in meiner Bleifigur mit etwas Phantasie[18] ein [20] Flugzeug sehen konnte.

Um 12 Uhr haben wir das neue Jahr begrüßt und haben einander[19] „Prost Neujahr" gewünscht.[20] Mayers servierten eine Pfirsichbowle.[21] Das ist ein kaltes Getränk aus Pfirsichen, Wein und Sekt.[22] Die Kirchenglocken haben geläutet[23] und die Schiffssirenen geheult.[24] Herr Mayer hat mir erzählt, daß [25] dieser Lärm[25] eine Sitte aus primitiven Zeiten ist. Man wollte die bösen Geister[26] damit vertreiben.[27]

---

[1] **lieb** dear
[2] **die Weihnacht(en), –** Christmas
[3] **feiern** to celebrate
[4] **der Tannenbaum, –s, ⸚e** Christmas tree
[5] **die Feuersgefahr, –, –en** fire hazard
[6] **die Kerze, –, –n** candle
[7] **vorziehen** to prefer
[8] **das Fest, –es, –e** celebration, festival
[9] **die Woche, –, –n** week
[10] **gründlich** thorough
[11] **die Nacht, –, ⸚e** night
[12] **ungewöhnlich** unusual
[13] **das Gesellschaftsspiel, –s, –e** party game
[14] **das „Bleigießen", –s** pouring of molten lead into water

[15] **flüssig** liquid
[16] **deuten** to interpret, read
[17] **die Reise, –, –n** trip, journey
[18] **die Phantasie, –, –n** imagination
[19] **einander** each other
[20] **wünschen** to wish
[21] **die Pfirsichbowle, –, –n** punch made with peaches
[22] **der Sekt, –(e)s, –e** champagne
[23] **läuten** to ring, toll
[24] **heulen** to hoot, scream
[25] **der Lärm, –(e)s** noise
[26] **der Geist, –es, –er** spirit, ghost
[27] **vertreiben** to drive out, expel

Eine deutsche Weihnachtskarte

Bei dem Feuerwerk über dem Rhein — auch eine alte Sylvestersitte — mußte ich an die Feier in Amerika am 4. Juli denken, und ich hatte ein wenig Heimweh.[28] Aber ich hatte keine Zeit, melancholisch zu werden, denn 30
die Party ging weiter[29] — fast bis zum Sonnenaufgang.[30]

Soviel für heute. Schreib bald mal wieder.

> Herzlichen[31] Gruß[32]
> Dein
> Tom   35

---

[28] **das Heimweh, –s** homesickness, nostalgia
[29] **ging weiter** continued
[30] **der Sonnenaufgang, –s, ¨e** sunrise

[31] **herzlich** cordial
[32] **der Gruß, –es, ¨e** greeting, regards

Fragen und Antworten

1. Wer ist schon im Eßzimmer?
   Frau Thiele, sie deckt den Frühstückstisch.
2. Wie hat Tom Gerds Mutter (*mother*) begrüßt?
   Er hat sie mit „Prost Neujahr" begrüßt.
3. Was hat er Frau Thiele erzählt?
   Er hat ihr über die Sylvesterfeier erzählt; sie hat ihm Spaß gemacht.
4. Was hat Tom auch erwähnt?
   Er hat erwähnt, daß sie am Rhein entlang spaziert sind.

5. Was hatte Sabine zu Gerd gesagt?
   Sie hatte gesagt: „Ich bin müde, weil ich so viel getanzt habe."
6. Warum war Tom schon auf?
   Er hat riesigen Hunger gehabt.
7. Auf wen hat er nicht gewartet?
   Er hat nicht auf die anderen gewartet.
8. Was hat Tom nach der Feier gebraucht?
   Er hat ein kräftiges Frühstück gebraucht.
9. Was ist am Sylvesterabend nicht ungewöhnlich?
   Es ist nichts Ungewöhnliches, wenn man spät nach Hause kommt.
10. Bei wem hat Tom Weihnachten gefeiert?
    Dieses Fest hat er bei Thieles gefeiert.

Structure and Practice

Explanation of Forms

THE PERFECT TENSES (I)

In English, the present perfect tense is formed with the present tense of the auxiliary *to have* and the past participle of the main verb: *I have seen, I have gone, I have read.* The past perfect uses the past tense of the auxiliary *to have* and the past participle of the main verb: *I had seen, I had gone, I had read.* German follows the same pattern in the formation of these tenses, except that there are two possible auxiliaries: **haben** and **sein.** Most verbs use the auxiliary **haben**; intransitive verbs (those which cannot take an accusative object) that show motion (**spazieren** — *to walk, stroll;* **kommen** — *to come*), change of location (**landen** — *to land*), or change of condition (**wachsen** — *to grow,* **sterben** — *to die*) use **sein** as their auxiliary in the perfect tenses.

Note: There are a few exceptions to this rule for the choice of auxiliary as well as occasional differences between English and German usage with regard to transitive and intransitive verbs. You should, therefore, make note of the comparatively few verbs that use **sein**. The ones you have already had will be listed in this lesson and the next.

Weak Verbs: Perfect Tenses

Weak (regular) verbs are those that have no stem changes and form their various tenses by simply adding to the stem (as in English: *love, loved, loved,* in contrast to *go, went, gone*).

A. Forms

Most weak verbs in German form their past participle by adding a **ge-** prefix and **-(e)t** suffix to the stem: **kochen, gekocht; landen, gelandet; wecken, geweckt.** There are two exceptions to this: verbs whose stem ends in **-ier** do not add the **ge-** prefix (**spazieren, spaziert; studieren, studiert**), and verbs that have unaccented prefixes on their infinitives (**emp-, ent-, er-, ge-, be-, ver-**) also add no **ge-** prefix to form the past participle (**beobachten, beobachtet; gehören, gehört; erzählen, erzählt**).

The irregular verb **haben** forms its past participle as weak verbs do: **gehabt.**

1. PRESENT PERFECT: Weak verbs follow one of the following patterns in forming the present perfect tense, depending on whether they take **haben** or **sein** as their auxiliary. (Of the weak verbs you have had in your active vocabularies thus far, only the following use the auxiliary **sein: landen, spazieren, folgen.**)

kochen	landen
ich **habe gekocht**	ich **bin gelandet**
du **hast gekocht**	du **bist gelandet**
er, sie, es **hat gekocht**	er, sie, es **ist gelandet**
wir **haben gekocht**	wir **sind gelandet**
ihr **habt gekocht**	ihr **seid gelandet**
sie **haben gekocht**	sie **sind gelandet**
Sie **haben gekocht**	Sie **sind gelandet**

2. PAST PERFECT: By simply changing the auxiliary to the past tense, we have the past perfect tense of the same verbs. (Note the past tense forms of **haben** and **sein.**)

ich **hatte gekocht**	ich **war gelandet**
du **hattest gekocht**	du **warst gelandet**
er, sie, es **hatte gekocht**	er, sie, es **war gelandet**
wir **hatten gekocht**	wir **waren gelandet**
ihr **hattet gekocht**	ihr **wart gelandet**
sie **hatten gekocht**	sie **waren gelandet**
Sie **hatten gekocht**	Sie **waren gelandet**

B. Word Order

1. INDEPENDENT CLAUSES: In independent clauses the auxiliary is in the normal verb (second) position, and the past participle is last.

Ich **habe** schon Kaffee **gekocht.**
Wir **sind** am Rhein entlang **spaziert.**
Dort **haben** wir die Schiffe **beobachtet.**

2. DEPENDENT CLAUSES: In dependent clauses the auxiliary, as the inflected form of the verb, is last and the past participle just before it.

> Ich bin müde, weil ich so viel **getanzt habe.**
> Er hat erwähnt, daß sie am Rhein entlang **spaziert sind.**
> Er hat ihn gefragt, ob sie ihn **geweckt haben.**

3. QUESTIONS: In questions the auxiliary takes the normal position of the inflected verb; the past participle is last.

> **Haben** wir Sie beim Heimkommen **geweckt?**
> Wie **hat** Tom Frau Thiele **begrüßt?**
> Was **hatte** Sabine zu Gerd **gesagt?**

C. Uses

1. PRESENT PERFECT: Although the formation of the present perfect in German and English is similar, this tense has broader usage in German. It is the normal past tense used in conversation when speaking of single past events where English would use the simple past. (The German simple past tense is mostly restricted to continuous narrative, as in stories and novels.) The following sentences, in the context of the dialogue of this lesson, require the past tense in English, whereas German uses the present perfect.

> **Ich habe** viel Interessantes **gelernt.**
> *I learned a lot of interesting things.*
> **Wir sind** auch noch am Rhein entlang **spaziert.**
> *We even strolled along the Rhine.*

In another context these same sentences might also be translated into present perfect in English.

The exceptions to this use of the present perfect for conversation occur with the verb **sein** and the modals. They are usually used in the simple past tense, as you can see from the following sentences taken from the dialogue.

> **War** der Sylvesterabend bei Mayers schön?
> Gerd **wollte** Ihnen ein Ständchen bringen, aber Sabine **war** dagegen.

In addition, the present perfect in German is used in most places where English uses it (except for actions begun in the past and continuing in the present: see Lesson 2, "Word Study and Usage").

> **Ich habe** schon Kaffee **gekocht.**
> *I've already **made** some coffee.*

2. PAST PERFECT: German uses the past perfect tense as English does, that is, for past actions completed before other past actions.

> Sie war müde, sie **hatte** zuviel **getanzt.**
> *She was tired — she **had danced** too much.*

Word Study and Usage

I. ADJECTIVAL NOUNS (I)

Adjectives after **etwas** (*something*), **nichts** (*nothing*), **viel** (*much*) and **wenig** (*little*) are capitalized since they function as nouns, but they take the endings of neuter unpreceded adjectives.

> Nach einer Feier braucht man **etwas Kräftiges** im Magen.
> *After a party you need some good food.*
> Das ist **nichts Ungewöhnliches.**
> *That's nothing unusual.*
> Ich habe **viel Interessantes** gelernt.
> *I learned a lot of interesting things.*
> Er hat **wenig Neues** gehört.
> *He's heard little news (little that is new).*

II. THE VERBS GEHEN, FAHREN AND FLIEGEN

Although English uses the verb *to go* no matter what means of travel is used, German requires a specific verb for each type.

> **gehen:** only for travel on foot
> **fahren:** for land vehicles, boats, and ships
> **fliegen:** for planes

When the means of travel is stated, **mit** is the preposition used for all vehicles, and in contrast to English, the definite article must be used after it.

Er fliegt **mit der Lufthansamaschine.**
*He's going **by Lufthansa plane.***
Er fährt **mit dem Wagen.**
*He's going **by car.***
Er fährt **mit dem Schiff.**
*He's going **by ship.***

But: Wir gehen **zu Fuß.** *We're walking (going **on foot**).*

III. MONTHS OF THE YEAR

The months of the year are all masculine and are almost always used with the definite article:

der Januar	January
der Februar	February
der März	March
der April	April
der Mai	May
der Juni	June
der Juli	July
der August	August
der September	September
der Oktober	October
der November	November
der Dezember	December

The preposition **in** must be contracted with the definite article (dative case) in the expression *in January, in February, etc.*

im Januar, im Februar

IV. DATES IN LETTERS

The date in the heading of a letter is always in the accusative case.

den 4. Januar (den vierten Januar) 1973

Notice that the day is given before the month. This applies also if a numeral is used in place of the name of the month. The above date would then read:

den 4. 1. 1973

The periods used after the numerals indicate that these are ordinal numbers.

Class Drills

I. ***Restate the following sentence, substituting the past participle
of each new infinitive given:***

Er hat das letztes Jahr gemacht.
>   (sagen)
>   (hören)
>   (kaufen)
>   (brauchen)
>   (gebrauchen)
>   (erwähnen)
>   (bestellen)
>   (studieren)

II. ***Restate the following sentences, substituting, in turn, <u>er</u>, <u>wir</u>,
<u>sie</u> (they) for the subject. Make the necessary changes in the
verb form:***

Ich habe gar nichts gehört.
Ich habe schon Kaffee gekocht.
Ich habe viel Interessantes gelernt.
Ich habe die Schiffe beobachtet.
Ich habe ihm die Legende erzählt.
Ich habe lange in Bonn studiert.

III. ***Change the following statements to questions addressed first to
<u>Sie</u> (you), then <u>du</u>:***

EXAMPLE: **Ich habe etwas gehört.**
          Haben Sie etwas gehört?
          Hast du etwas gehört?

Ich habe den Tisch schon gedeckt.
Ich habe ihn begrüßt.
Ich habe zuviel getanzt.
Ich bin in Bonn gelandet.
Ich bin am Rhein entlang spaziert.
Ich bin ihm nach Frankfurt gefolgt.

IV. ***Change the following sentences to the past perfect tense:***

Ich habe das nicht gesagt.
Ich habe den Vater geweckt.

Ich bin in Hamburg gelandet.
Ich bin ihm gefolgt.
Sie hat das nicht gesagt.
Sie hat den Vater geweckt.
Sie ist in Hamburg gelandet.
Sie ist ihm gefolgt.
Wir haben das nicht gesagt.
Wir haben den Vater geweckt.
Wir sind in Hamburg gelandet.
Wir sind ihm gefolgt.
Sie haben das nicht gesagt.
Sie haben den Vater geweckt.
Sie sind in Hamburg gelandet.
Sie sind ihm gefolgt.

V. Change the following sentences, using first the present perfect, then the past perfect in the dependent clause:

Ich weiß, daß sie es kauft.
Ich weiß, daß sie es braucht.
Ich weiß, daß sie es spielt.
Ich weiß, daß sie es kocht.
Ich weiß, daß sie es bestellt.

Er fragt, wo ich wohne.
Er fragt, wo ich studiere.
Er fragt, wo ich arbeite.
Er fragt, wo ich warte.
Er fragt, wo ich spiele.

VI. Restate the following sentences, substituting the adjectival noun form of the given adjectives:

Er spielt etwas Klassisches.
       (modern)
       (schön)
       (lustig)
       (bekannt)

Er hat mir nichts Gutes erzählt.
       (neu)
       (interessant)
       (bestimmt)
       (schlimm)

Exercises

I. *Rewrite the following sentences in the present perfect tense:*

1. Er studiert Literatur an der Bonner Universität.   2. Sie arbeitet in Hamburg.   3. Ich mache Fehler, wenn ich Fachausdrücke gebrauche. 4. Er gehört zu den Bonner Studenten.   5. Klassische Musik interessiert ihn.   6. Sie erinnert mich an eine Stewardeß.   7. Dieses Orchester spielt oft dort.   8. Schmeckt der Wein gut?   9. Wo kaufen Sie Ihre Zeitung?   10. Sie folgt uns.   11. Die Lufthansamaschine landet um acht Uhr.   12. Ich besuche ihn oft.   13. Wir bestellen ein Glas Bier. 14. Wir machen einen Rundgang, und dann zeige ich ihm sein Zimmer. 15. Es wirkt als Kontrast.

II. *Rewrite the following sentences, using the adjectives in parentheses as adjectival nouns:*

EXAMPLE: **Ich lese etwas.** (*interessant*)
Ich lese etwas *Interessantes.*

1. Er erzählt viel. (**neu**)
2. Er spielt nichts. (**modern**)
3. Ich möchte etwas essen. (**kräftig**)
4. Bestellen wir etwas. (**warm**)
5. Er will etwas sehen. (**lustig**)
6. Möchten Sie etwas lesen? (**romantisch**)
7. Er hat viel gelernt. (**neu**)
8. Wir haben viel über ihn gehört. (**unglaublich**)
9. Das war wirklich nichts. (**schlimm**)
10. Er soll nichts trinken. (**kalt**)
11. Das ist nichts. (**ungewöhnlich**)
12. Haben Sie nichts? (**antik**)

III. *Translate into English. In sentences 1–5, reproduce the German sentences from your English translations:*

1. Woran hat dich das erinnert? — An amerikanischen Jazz.   2. Sein Deutsch war fehlerlos; er hat alles richtig gesagt.   3. Bei heißem Wetter machen sie nicht gern eine Fußtour.   4. Was für ein romantisches kleines Lokal! Selbstverständlich gefällt es mir!   5. Möchten Sie den „Spiegel" oder sonst eine Zeitschrift lesen?   6. Hoffentlich kommt er nicht zu spät, sonst bekommt er keinen guten Platz.   7. Spiel etwas Modernes, denn in der klassischen Musik weiß ich nicht Bescheid. 8. Nach dem Ausflug auf den Drachenfels waren sie durch den dunklen

Wald nach Hause spaziert.   9. Nach einer Feier ist ein kräftiges Frühstück gerade das Richtige.   10. Am Sylvesterabend geht's lustig zu,
besonders wenn man dieses Fest bei guten Freunden feiert.

IV. *Translate:*

1. Would you like to serenade her?   2. I like to watch the ships when
I walk along the Rhine.   3. Did you hear something? — No, nothing
unusual.   4. What woke you? — My friends, they were celebrating upstairs.   5. We mentioned that we had been waiting at (*an*) the airport.
6. Did he use technical terms in his lecture?   7. He reminded me of a
popular New York conductor.   8. Can you tell me why he said that?
9. What did he have against his professor?   10. Please set the breakfast table in the kitchen. (*sing. fam.* and *polite*)

V. *Composition. Write ten sentences in the form of a composition about Tom's New Year's Eve. For each sentence, use the words given below:*

1. Gerd, Sabine und Tom   Sylvester   Mayers
2. am Rhein   Sylvesterparty   lustig
3. tanzen
4. nach   Party   müde
5. aber   Rhein   spazieren   Schiff
6. Gerd   Mutter   Ständchen
7. Sabine   Mutter   nicht   wecken
8. Frau Thiele   nichts
9. Neujahrsmorgen   Tom   früh
10. nach   Feier   Hunger

Active Vocabulary

der **April**	April	das **Frühstück, –s,**	breakfast
aufsein	to be up, be out of bed	**–e**	
der **August**	August	der **Frühstücks-**	breakfast table
beobachten	to watch, observe	**tisch, –es, ⁀e**	
bringen	to bring	der **Fuß, –es, ⁀e**	foot
decken	to set (the table)	**zu Fuß**	on foot
der **Dezember**	December	**gar nichts**	nothing at all
entlang	along	**heimkommen**	to come home
der **Februar**	February	der **Heimweg, –s,**	way home
die **Feier, –, –n**	celebration, party	**–e**	
feiern	to celebrate	der **Hunger, –s**	hunger
das **Fest, –es, –e**	celebration, festival	**Hunger**	to be hungry
		haben	

der Januar	January
der Juli	July
der Kaffee, –s	coffee
kochen	to cook, boil
kräftig	strong; substantial; nourishing
der Langschläfer, –s, –	sleepyhead
lernen	to learn
lustig	merry, gay, funny
der Magen, –s, – *or* ⁔	stomach
der Mai	May
der März	March
der Morgen, –s, –	morning
munter	awake; lively
die Mutter, –, ⁔	mother
das Neujahr, –s	New Year
der Neujahrsmorgen, –s, –	New Year's morning
der November	November
der Oktober	October

riesig	gigantic, immense, enormous
das Schiff, –(e)s, –e	ship
schlafen (ä)	to sleep
der September	September
spazieren	to walk (leisurely), stroll
das Ständchen, –s, –	serenade
der Sylvesterabend, –s, –e	New Year's Eve
die Sylvesterfeier, –, –n	New Year's Eve celebration
die Sylvesterparty, –, –s	New Year's Eve party
tanzen	to dance
der Tisch, –es, –e	table
ungewöhnlich	unusual
wecken	to wake
die Weihnachten	Christmas
zugehen	to go on, happen
es geht lustig zu	there is a lot of fun

German Information Center

Goethes Schreibtisch

Dreizehnte Lektion

Frankfurt am Main

[*Tom mit einer Studentin in einem Bonner Café. Sie haben Torte gegessen und Kaffee getrunken und sprechen nun über Toms Besuch in Frankfurt.*]

BRIGITTE — Hat Ihnen die „Kaiserstadt" gefallen?

TOM — Sehr! Vor allen Dingen, wie man die historischen Gebäude wieder aufgebaut hat.

BRIGITTE — Waren Sie auch im Goethehaus?

TOM — Natürlich! Ich habe sogar an Goethes Schreibtisch gesessen. Gerd hat mich so fotografiert.

BRIGITTE — Haben Sie auch das berühmte Rathaus gesehen?

TOM — Ja, dort haben wir an einer Besichtigungstour teilgenommen. Das ganze Viertel um das Rathaus war wirklich sehenswert. — Sie haben doch meine Ansichtskarte bekommen?

BRIGITTE — Noch nicht, aber besten Dank im voraus.

TOM — Bitte sehr. — Danach haben wir von Mainz aus die Rheinfahrt gemacht. Um fünf vor halb fünf sind wir abgefahren. Die Rheindampfer sind pünktlich wie die Züge!

BRIGITTE — Ich wette, Sie sind auch fahrplanmäßig angekommen.

TOM — Jawohl! Zweiundzwanzig Uhr fünfundzwanzig!

BRIGITTE — Apropos Pünktlichkeit, Tom, ich muß zum Zahnarzt.

TOM — Ich komme ein Stück mit. Ich muß die Bilder abholen, ehe das Geschäft zumacht.

BRIGITTE — Hoffentlich sind die Aufnahmen aus dem Goethehaus etwas geworden.

Frankfurt am Main

[*Tom with a student in a Bonn café. They have had cake and coffee and are now talking about Tom's visit to Frankfurt.*]

BRIGITTE — Did you like the "City of Emperors"?

TOM — Very much — especially the way they've reconstructed the historical buildings.

BRIGITTE — Were you in the Goethe house?

TOM — Certainly. I even sat at Goethe's desk. Gerd took a picture of me there.

BRIGITTE — Did you see the famous city hall, too?

TOM — Yes, we took a sightseeing tour there. The whole section around the city hall was really worth seeing. You did get my picture postcard, didn't you?

BRIGITTE — Not yet, but thanks for sending it.

TOM — You're welcome. After that we took the Rhine trip, starting from Mainz. We left at 4:25. The Rhine boats are as punctual as the trains.

BRIGITTE — I'll bet you arrived on schedule, too.

TOM — We certainly did. 10:25.

BRIGITTE — Speaking of punctuality, Tom, I have to go to the dentist.

TOM — I'll walk part of the way with you. I have to pick up the pictures before the shop closes.

BRIGITTE — I hope the Goethe house snapshots turned out.

Lesestück XIII

Lieber Bob,

vielen Dank für Deinen Brief. Du hast wirklich schnell geantwortet.
Natürlich bin ich sehr froh,[1] daß Dir die „Graduate School" so gut gefällt.
Ich habe in der letzten Woche eine kleine Reise nach Frankfurt gemacht.
Du weißt, ich bin vor vier Monaten[2] dort angekommen, aber damals sind wir 5
gleich[3] nach Bonn weitergefahren. Ich hatte schon viel über Frankfurt gehört.
Zum Beispiel hat man es nach 1945 die „amerikanischste[4] Stadt" Deutsch-
lands genannt.[5] Frankfurt und Heidelberg waren Hauptquartier[6] der ameri-
kanischen Armee in Deutschland. Viele unserer Soldaten[7] haben in und um
Frankfurt ihre Dienstzeit[8] verbracht[9] und sind auch vom „Rhein—Main— 10
Flughafen" wieder nach Hause geflogen.[10] Auch ist Frankfurt heute eine
Handels- und Industriestadt,[11] und für viele Deutsche ist „kommerziell"
identisch mit „amerikanisch". Das Wirtschaftszentrum Frankfurt ist beinahe[12]
auch einmal politisches Zentrum geworden. Das war 1948 bei der Gründung
der westdeutschen Bundesrepublik, als Frankfurt oder Bonn die neue Haupt- 15
stadt werden sollte. Viele Parlamentarier waren für Frankfurt, aber man hat
dann doch Bonn gewählt,[13] weil es nur eine provisorische Hauptstadt sein
sollte, und Frankfurt hatte zu viel politisch—historische Tradition.
Davon habe ich auf einer Besichtigungstour fast zu viel gehört. Unser
Fremdenführer[14] war sehr gründlich und sehr genau. Immer wieder[15] hat er 20
stolz von der „Kaiserstadt" gesprochen.[16] Hier hat man im Mittelalter den
deutschen König gewählt. Seit 1562 fand in dem Rathaus, dem „Römer",
auch die Krönungszeremonie[17] für den deutschen Kaiser statt.[18] Eine dieser
Feiern hat der junge Johann Wolfgang Goethe gesehen, und er hat später
davon in seiner Autobiographie „Dichtung[19] und Wahrheit" erzählt. Goethe 25
wurde 1749 in Frankfurt geboren,[20] und wir haben natürlich sein Geburts-
haus besichtigt.[21] Goethe hat zwar den größeren Teil[22] seines 82–jährigen

---

[1] **froh** happy, glad
[2] **der Monat, –s, –e** month
[3] **gleich** directly, at once
[4] **amerikanischst–** most American
[5] **nennen, hat genannt** to call
[6] **das Hauptquartier, –s, –e** headquarters
[7] **der Soldat, –en, –en** soldier
[8] **die Dienstzeit, –, –en** tour of duty
[9] **verbringen, hat verbracht** to spend
[10] **fliegen, ist geflogen** to fly
[11] **die Handels- und Industriestadt, –, ⁼e**
commercial and industrial city
[12] **beinahe** almost
[13] **wählen** to choose
[14] **der Fremdenführer, –s, –** guide
[15] **immer wieder** again and again
[16] **sprechen (i), hat gesprochen** to speak
[17] **die Krönungszeremonie, –, –n** coronation
[18] **fand . . . statt** took place
[19] **„Dichtung und Wahrheit"** *Poetry and Truth*
[20] **wurde . . . geboren** was born
[21] **besichtigen** to visit
[22] **der Teil, –(e)s, –e** part

Lebens in Weimar verbracht, aber viele seiner Ideen und Pläne gehen auf
seine Frankfurter Zeit zurück. Zum Beispiel hat er sein großes Drama
„Faust" dort begonnen.   30

Das ist nun wieder ein langer Brief geworden. Hoffentlich ist er nicht so
trocken[23] wie unser Fremdenführer.

Grüße[24] alle Bekannten.
Sehr herzlich
Dein   35
Tom

P.S. Weimar möchte ich unbedingt noch besuchen, bevor ich nach Amerika
zurückkomme.

---

[23] **trocken** dry   [24] **grüßen** to give regards, send greetings

Fragen und Antworten

1. Wo waren Tom und Brigitte?
   Sie haben im Café gesessen und über Frankfurt gesprochen.
2. Was hat Tom erzählt?
   Er hat erzählt, daß er Frankfurt besucht und eine Rheinfahrt gemacht
   hatte.
3. Was hat Brigitte ihn gefragt?
   Sie hat ihn gefragt, ob er im Goethehaus gewesen ist und das Rathaus
   gesehen hat.
4. Hat Brigitte die Ansichtskarte schon bekommen?
   Nein, aber sie bekommt sie sicher später.
5. Warum sind Tom und Gerd nach Mainz gefahren?
   Der Rheindampfer fährt in Mainz ab.
6. Ist der Dampfer pünktlich angekommen?
   Ja, denn er war pünktlich abgefahren.
7. Kommt der Dampfer um fünf vor halb elf an?
   Ja, wenn er fahrplanmäßig abfährt.
8. Was hat Tom nach dem Besuch im Café getan?
   Er hat die Bilder abgeholt.
9. Wem hat Tom einen Brief geschrieben?
   Er hat seinem amerikanischen Freund einen Brief geschrieben.
10. Hat Tom vor vier Monaten Frankfurt besucht?
    Nein, er ist damals gleich nach Bonn weitergefahren.

Structure and Practice

Explanation of Forms

I. PERFECT TENSES (II)

Strong Verbs

There is a large group of German verbs that have stem changes in one or more tenses and whose formation of the simple past, as well as the past participle, is different from weak verbs. These are called strong verbs, and they are roughly equivalent to English irregular verbs (e.g. *sing, sang, sung*). As in English, there is no way of telling from the infinitive which verbs are weak and which are strong. Therefore, the strong verbs and their forms must be learned. In word order and use, strong verbs follow the same rules as weak verbs in all tenses.

A. The Auxiliary

The rule for the use of **haben** or **sein** as the auxiliary for weak verbs in the perfect tenses applies also to strong verbs. Because of the exceptions to this rule, we repeat the recommendation that you learn which verbs use **sein.** In the following list of strong verbs, each past participle is shown with its proper auxiliary. As is traditional, the third-person singular of the auxiliary is given.

B. The Past Participle

Past participles of strong verbs in German have a **ge-** prefix (except for those verbs with **ent-, emp-, er-, ge-, be-, ver-** prefixes mentioned in the previous lesson) and an **-en** suffix. Like English irregular verbs, some strong verbs in German have the same stem in their past participle as they have in their infinitive: **kommen, gekommen; laufen, gelaufen.** Others have a different stem in the past participle: **trinken, getrunken; gehen, gegangen.**

The following is a list of the infinitives and past participles of all strong verbs you have had through this lesson (except for verbs with separable prefixes, which will be explained later in this lesson). Beginning with this lesson, the past participle of each new strong verb is indicated in the reading and active vocabularies.

181

INFINITIVE	PAST PARTICIPLE
beginnen (to begin)	hat begonnen
bekommen (to receive)	hat bekommen
bitten (to ask, request)	hat gebeten
bleiben (to remain)	*ist* geblieben
essen (to eat)	hat gegessen
fahren (to go, drive)	**ist* (hat) gefahren
finden (to find)	hat gefunden
fliegen (to fly)	**ist* (hat) geflogen
geben (to give)	hat gegeben
gefallen (to be pleasing to, like)	hat gefallen
gehen (to go)	*ist* gegangen
halten (to hold, stop)	hat gehalten
heißen (to be called)	hat geheißen
helfen (to help)	hat geholfen
kommen (to come)	*ist* gekommen
laufen (to run)	*ist* gelaufen
lesen (to read)	hat gelesen
nehmen (to take)	hat genommen
schlafen (to sleep)	hat geschlafen
schreiben (to write)	hat geschrieben
schweigen (to be silent)	hat geschwiegen
sehen (to see)	hat gesehen
sein (to be)	*ist* gewesen
sitzen (to sit)	hat gesessen
sprechen (to speak)	hat gesprochen
stehen (to stand)	hat gestanden
treffen (to meet)	hat getroffen
trinken (to drink)	hat getrunken
tun (to do)	hat getan
vergessen (to forget)	hat vergessen
verschwinden (to disappear)	*ist* verschwunden
verstehen (to understand)	hat verstanden
werden (to become)	*ist* geworden

* These verbs, among others, are sometimes used transitively and take the auxiliary **haben,** sometimes intransitively and take the auxiliary **sein.**

Er **ist** mit dem Wagen nach Bonn **gefahren.**
He went to Bonn by car.
Er **hat** meinen Wagen nach Bonn **gefahren.**
He drove my car to Bonn.
Er **ist** von New York nach Frankfurt **geflogen.**
He flew from New York to Frankfurt.
Der Pilot **hat** das Flugzeug nach Frankfurt **geflogen.**
The pilot flew the plane to Frankfurt.

C. Omission of Auxiliary

If one subject is used with several verbs in a perfect tense, the auxiliary, if it is the same for all verbs, need be stated only once.

1. IN INDEPENDENT CLAUSES: In independent clauses the auxiliary is used with the first verb and omitted for the others.

> Sie **haben** Torte **gegessen** und Kaffee **getrunken.**

2. IN DEPENDENT CLAUSES: In dependent clauses the auxiliary is used only after the last past participle.

> Er hat erzählt, daß er Frankfurt **besucht** und eine Rheinfahrt **gemacht hatte.**

If the verbs take different auxiliaries, however, each one must be stated.

> Sie hat ihn gefragt, ob er im Goethehaus **gewesen ist** und das Rathaus **gesehen hat.**

II. SEPARABLE PREFIXES

English often uses an adverb or preposition in such close connection with a verb that it is felt to be an integral part of the verb: *to stand up, to sit down, to look at.* In German, such elements connected with verbs are actually attached to the infinitives as prefixes: **aufbauen** (*to build up, construct*), **mitkommen** (*to come along*). It is sometimes possible to figure out the meanings of these verbs from the separate meanings of the prefixes, which are words in themselves, and the verbs, as in the examples just given. In other cases it is not quite so simple: **zumachen** (*to close*), **abmachen** (*to settle*).

These prefixes are accented and are called separable (in contrast to the unaccented prefixes **ent-, emp-, er-, ge-, be-, ver-** mentioned earlier, which are called inseparable) because under certain conditions they are completely separated from the verb.

A. When the Prefix Is Separated

When the verb to which the prefix belongs is in first or second position in the clause (direct questions in simple tenses, commands, present and simple past tense in independent clauses), the prefix is detached from the verb and placed at the end of the clause.

Question: **Kommt** der Dampfer um fünf Uhr **an?** (**ankommen** — *to arrive*)

Command: **Kommen** Sie jetzt **mit!** (**mitkommen** — *to come along*)

Present tense in independent clause: Der Dampfer **fährt** in Mainz **ab.** (**abfahren** — *to leave*)

B. When the Prefix Is Not Separated

When the verb to which the prefix belongs comes at or near the end of the clause (past participle, infinitive, inflected verb in dependent clauses), the prefix is attached to the verb.

Past Participle: Um fünf Uhr sind wir **abgefahren.**

Infinitive: Ich muß die Bilder **abholen.**

Inflected verb in dependent clause: Er kommt pünktlich an, wenn er fahrplanmäßig **abfährt.**

C. List of Verbs with Separable Prefixes

The following is a list of verbs with separable prefixes you have had through this lesson. They are given with their past participles. Notice that some are strong verbs, others weak. In all cases the **ge-** prefix on the past participle is placed between the separable prefix and the stem of the verb. Beginning with this lesson, all new verbs with separable prefixes are indicated in the reading and active vocabularies by a hyphen between prefix and verb. The end vocabulary will make the same indication for all such verbs.

INFINITIVE	PAST PARTICIPLE
ab-fahren (to leave)	*ist* **abgefahren**
ab-holen (to fetch, pick up)	**hat abgeholt**
ab-machen (to settle)	**hat abgemacht**
an-kommen (to arrive)	*ist* **angekommen**
auf-bauen (to build up, construct)	**hat aufgebaut**
auf-sein (to be up)	*ist* **aufgewesen**
ein-laden (to invite)	**hat eingeladen**
heim-kommen (to come home)	*ist* **heimgekommen**
hin-gehen (to go over)	*ist* **hingegangen**
mit-kommen (to come along)	*ist* **mitgekommen**
nach-sehen (to look, look up, check)	**hat nachgesehen**
teil-nehmen (to take part, participate)	**hat teilgenommen**
weiter-fahren (to drive on)	*ist* **weitergefahren**
zu-gehen (to take place, happen)	*ist* **zugegangen**
zu-machen (to close)	**hat zugemacht**

*III. Restate the following sentence, substit**ss** en verbs:*

Er kommt heute an.
(abfahren)
(zumachen)
(hingehen)
(mitfahren)
(mitkommen)

*IV. Answer the following questions in the present tense, om
the modal:*

EXAMPLE: **Wollen Sie das Geschäft zumachen?**
Ja, ich mache das Geschäft zu.

Wollen Sie ihn einladen?
Können Sie ihn mitnehmen?
Müssen Sie wirklich abfahren?
Dürfen Sie auch mitgehen?
Wollen Sie die Bilder abholen?

V. Form polite commands in answer to the following questions:

EXAMPLE: **Soll ich die Bilder abholen?**
Ja, holen Sie die Bilder ab.

Soll ich ihn einladen?
Soll ich auch hingehen?
Soll ich jetzt mitkommen?
Soll ich an der Tour teilnehmen?
Soll ich das Geschäft zumachen?

*VI. Form questions addressed to <u>Sie</u> (you) from the following
statements:*

EXAMPLE: **Ich fahre heute ab.**
Fahren Sie heute ab?

Ich komme heute mit.
Ich lade ihn ein.
Ich nehme an der Tour teil.
Ich gehe nach der Vorlesung hin.
Ich hole die Kinder jetzt ab.

..he following sentences in the present perfect tense:

VII. ..den es wieder auf.

..olen es heute ab.

..machen das Geschäft zu.

..e laden ihn sicher ein.

Sie nehmen das Kind mit.

Sie kommen heute an.

Sie fahren um fünf Uhr ab.

Sie gehen heute hin.

b. Restate the sentences in exercise a. in the past perfect tense.

VIII. *Restate the following sentences, inserting* <u>daß</u> *before the second clause in each. Make the appropriate word order changes:*

Er weiß, ich nehme daran teil.

Er weiß, sie macht das Geschäft zu.

Er weiß, sie bauen es wieder auf.

Er weiß, sie fahren früh ab.

Er weiß, wir kommen spät an.

Er weiß, ich habe daran teilgenommen.

Er weiß, sie hat das Geschäft zugemacht.

Er weiß, sie haben es wieder aufgebaut.

Er weiß, wir sind früh abgefahren.

Er weiß, wir sind spät angekommen.

IX. *Add* <u>doch</u> *to the following questions, and change them accordingly:*

EXAMPLE: **Haben Sie meine Karte bekommen?**
Sie haben doch meine Karte bekommen?

Haben Sie meine Ansichtskarte bekommen?

Hat man die historischen Gebäude wieder aufgebaut?

Waren Sie auch im Goethehaus?

Haben Sie das berühmte Rathaus gesehen?

War das Viertel um das Rathaus sehenswert?

Haben Sie die Bilder abgeholt?

Exercises

I. Rewrite the following sentences in the present perfect tense:

1. Wann kommen Sie in New York an?   2. Der Spaziergang macht uns Spaß.   3. Der Zug fährt immer pünktlich ab.   4. Ich sehe in der Zeitung nach.   5. Ich komme gleich mit.   6. Ich spaziere gern durch die Stadt.   7. Ich bekomme manchmal eine Ansichtskarte von ihm.   8. Wir folgen Ihnen mit dem Auto.   9. Er läuft in die Mensa.   10. Sie wartet am Flugplatz auf mich.   11. Bleibt sie lange in Frankfurt?   12. Die alten Gebäude verschwinden allmählich.   13. Jazz interessiert ihn sehr.   14. Hält er die Vorlesung auf englisch?   15. Hoffentlich wird alles besser.

II. Rewrite the following sentences, omitting daß:

1. Ich weiß, daß er im Programm nachgesehen hat.   2. Ich weiß, daß es ihm nicht gefällt.   3. Ich weiß, daß er an der Besichtigungstour teilgenommen hat.   4. Ich weiß, daß sie spät heimgekommen ist.   5. Ich weiß, daß das Geschäft um sieben Uhr zumacht.   6. Ich weiß, daß man das Gebäude bald wieder aufbaut.   7. Ich weiß, daß er sie nicht eingeladen hat.   8. Ich weiß, daß der Zug pünktlich abfährt.   9. Ich weiß, daß sie fahrplanmäßig angekommen sind.   10. Ich weiß, daß er gern mitkommt.

III. Translate into English. In sentences 1–5, reproduce the German sentences from your English translations:

1. Hoffentlich nimmt er auch daran teil.   2. Jetzt wird's aber Zeit, sonst machen die Geschäfte zu.   3. Als sie mit dem Abendessen fertig war, hat sie ihrer Mutter geholfen.   4. Kommt das Flugzeug pünktlich an?   5. Sie hat sie nicht um Auskunft gebeten.   6. Bist du nicht mit ihm ins Goethehaus gegangen? — Doch, aber ich bin nicht lange dort geblieben.   7. Wißt ihr was? Laden wir auch den Professor ein! Oder seid ihr dagegen?   8. Möchten Sie nicht zuerst Frankfurt besuchen, ehe Sie die Rheinfahrt machen?   9. Wer hat die Vorlesung gehalten? — Ein englischer Professor; leider habe ich vergessen, wie er heißt.   10. Sie haben ihn doch getroffen? — Nein, er war schon nach Hause gegangen.

IV. Translate:

1. Would you like to take a Rhine trip?   2. We'll pick you up at 9:30. (*present tense*)   3. Did he like Bonn?   4. We met him in a café at 4:20.   5. Why didn't he speak German?   6. I don't know whether

he gave this lecture in German.   7. I did not understand him because he spoke too fast.   8. She got your letter today; it arrived too late.   9. You did give her the binoculars, didn't you?   10. We don't know whether they drove or flew to Bonn.   11. He would like to take part in a German seminar.

V. *Composition. Write ten sentences in the form of a composition about Tom's visit to Frankfurt. In each sentence, use the words given below:*

1. Tom und Gerd   Sonntag   Frankfurt
2. Tom   gefallen
3. Goethehaus   Schreibtisch
4. Rathaus   Besichtigungstour
5. Ansichtskarte   Brigitte   schreiben
6. Rheindampfer   Rheinfahrt
7. abfahren   ankommen
8. Montag   Tom und Brigitte
9. Tom   erzählen
10. Tom und Brigitte   hoffen (*to hope*)   Bilder   etwas werden

Active Vocabulary

apropos	speaking of	ehe (*subord. conj.*)	before
der Arzt, –es, ⸚e	physician	essen (i), hat gegessen	to eat
ab-fahren (ä), ist abgefahren	to leave, depart	fahrplanmäßig	as scheduled, on schedule
ab-holen	to pick up	die Fahrt, –, –en	trip
an-kommen, ist angekommen	to arrive	fotografieren	to take a photograph
		das Gebäude, –s, –	building
die Ansichtskarte, –, –n	picture postcard	gleich	directly, at once
auf-bauen	to build up, construct	hoffen	to hope
		jawohl	yes (indeed)
die Aufnahme, –, –n	photograph, snapshot	mit-kommen, ist mitgekommen	to come along
die Besichtigungstour, –, –en	sightseeing tour	der Monat, –s, –e	month
der Besuch, –s, –e	visit	vor vier Monaten	four months ago
bitte	you are welcome	natürlich	natural
der Brief, –(e)s, –e	letter	noch nicht	not yet
das Café, –s, –s	café	pünktlich	punctual
der Dampfer, –s, –	steamer, ship	die Pünktlichkeit, –	punctuality
das Ding, –(e)s, –e	thing		
vor allen Dingen	above all, especially		

das Rathaus, –es, ⸚er	city hall	die Torte, –, –n	cake, pastry, pie
		von . . . aus	from
der Rheindampfer, –s, –	Rhine boat	voraus	beforehand
		im voraus	in advance
die Rheinfahrt, –, –en	Rhine trip	weiter-fahren (ä), ist weitergefahren	to drive on, continue
der Schreibtisch, –es, –e	desk		
		werden (i), ist geworden	to become
sehenswert	worth seeing, remarkable	etwas werden	to turn out (well)
		wetten	to bet
sogar	even	der Zahnarzt, –es, ⸚e	dentist
das Stück, –(e)s, –e	piece, part, bit		
teil-nehmen (an + *dat.*) (i), hat teilgenommen	to take part (in), participate (in)	der Zug, –(e)s, ⸚e	train
		zu-machen	to close

Karneval in KÖLN

Vierzehnte Lektion

Der Kölner Karneval

[*Im Hörsaal. Ricardo Tudisco, ein spanischer Austauschstudent, setzt sich neben Tom. Tom sieht schlecht aus. Ricardo erkundigt sich teilnahmsvoll.*]

RICARDO — Waren Sie krank, Tom?

TOM — Nein, ich war in Köln auf dem Karneval. Ich sollte eigentlich gestern wieder hier sein. Aber ich wollte mir den Rosenmontagszug ansehen.

RICARDO — Ist das tatsächlich ein so tolles Fest?

TOM — Das können Sie sich gar nicht vorstellen. Alles tanzte auf den Straßen und brüllte im Chor: „Kölle — Alaaf!" Man mußte sich die Ohren zuhalten.

RICARDO — Stimmt es, daß manche Leute von Fastnachtsonntag bis Aschermittwoch nicht schlafen?

TOM — Das glaube ich schon. Kein Wunder, es gibt tagsüber Umzüge, abends Maskenball und morgens Katerfrühstück. Und dann fängt es wieder von vorne an.

RICARDO — Haben Sie das alles mitgemacht?

TOM — Na klar, so etwas habe ich ja noch nie erlebt. Ich bin aber auch vollkommen erschöpft und habe Kopfschmerzen. Nach der Vorlesung kaufe ich mir Aspirin.

RICARDO — Na, Sie sind eben noch kein echter Rheinländer!

The Cologne Carnival

[*In the lecture hall. Ricardo Tudisco, a Spanish exchange student, sits down next to Tom. Tom looks bad. Ricardo inquires sympathetically:*]

RICARDO — Have you been sick, Tom?

TOM — No, I was in Cologne at the carnival. Actually, I was supposed to be back here yesterday. But I wanted to see the *Rosenmontag*[1] parade.

RICARDO — Is it really such a wild festival?

TOM — You just can't imagine. Everyone was dancing in the streets and shouting in chorus: "Kölle — Alaaf!"[2] You had to hold your ears closed.

RICARDO — Is it true that some people don't sleep from the Sunday before Lent until Ash Wednesday?

TOM — I think so. And no wonder. During the day there are parades, in the evening fancy-dress balls, in the morning breakfast for hang-over victims. And then it begins all over again.

RICARDO — Did you join in everything?

TOM — Of course. I've never experienced anything like it before. I'm completely exhausted though, and I have a headache. After class I'm going to buy some aspirin.

RICARDO — Well, you're just not a real Rhinelander yet.

[1] **Rosenmontag:** The name for the Monday before Ash Wednesday, explained in the reading text of this lesson. [2] „**Kölle — Alaaf!**": Cologne dialect for a cheer meaning "Hooray for Cologne!"

194

Lesestück XIV

Vor langer Zeit durfte die Stadt Köln sich mit Erlaubnis[1] des Papstes „das heilige Köln" nennen. Es gibt aber eine Zeit im Jahr, wo es dort gar nicht heilig zugeht — beim Karneval. Er beginnt am 11.11. um 11 Uhr, d. h., am elften November vormittags[2] um elf Uhr, und dauert bis zum Aschermittwoch, vierzig Tage vor Ostern.[3] Höhepunkt[4] ist der Rosenmontag mit den 5 Umzügen, Maskenbällen, „Büttenreden"[5] usw. Es ist der Montag vor Aschermittwoch. Der Name „Rosenmontag" hat nichts mit Rosen zu tun. Früher hieß[6] der Tag „rasender[7] Montag", und allmählich machte das Volk daraus „Rosenmontag".

Tom Evans hatte schon manches über den Karneval und den Fasching[8] 10 gehört. Fasching ist ein anderes Wort für Karneval, und als Tom seinen Freund nach dem Unterschied[9] fragte, erklärte ihm dieser, daß die Rheinländer den Münchner Fasching langweilig[10] nennen, während die Münchner den Kölner Karneval vulgär finden. Tom suchte im Wörterbuch[11] nach[12] der Erklärung des Wortes Karneval. Da er etwas Latein konnte, glaubte er, 15 daß es von *carne valis* kommt, also „dem Fleisch[13] Lebewohl sagen".[14] Aber im Wörterbuch hieß es, daß das Wort vielleicht von dem italienischen *carrus navalis* („Schiffswagen"[15]) kommt. In alten Zeiten führten[16] die Menschen in den Umzügen Schiffe auf Wagen mit.[16] Das bedeutete, daß man bald wieder auf den eisfreien[17] Wasserwegen fahren konnte. 20

In Köln ist der Karneval ein richtiges Volksfest. Tom freute sich besonders über[18] die vielen Karnevalsschlager.[19] Gerd wunderte sich,[20] wie schnell sein amerikanischer Freund die Stimmung[21] dieses Festes erfaßte.[22] Bald tanzten und sangen die beiden wie geborene Kölner und machten viele Bekanntschaften.[23] Ganz Köln war in großartiger[24] Stimmung, und Gerd und Tom 25

---

[1] **die Erlaubnis, –** permission
[2] **vormittags** in the morning, before noon
[3] **das Ostern** Easter
[4] **der Höhepunkt, –s, –e** high point, climax
[5] **die Büttenrede, –, –n** funny speech, mostly improvised, delivered during carnival. The speaker stands in a "Bütt," i.e., a vat
[6] **hieß** was called
  from **heißen** to be called
[7] **rasen** to rage; rave
[8] **der Fasching, –s** carnival, Shrovetide
[9] **der Unterschied, –s, –e** difference
[10] **langweilig** boring, dull
[11] **das Wörterbuch, –s, ⁀er** dictionary

[12] **suchen nach** to look for
[13] **das Fleisch, –es** flesh; meat
[14] **Lebewohl sagen** to bid farewell
[15] **der Wagen, –s, –** *here* wagon
[16] **mit-führen** to carry along
[17] **eisfrei** icefree
[18] **sich freuen über** to enjoy
[19] **der Karnevalsschlager, –s, –** hit tune at carnival time
[20] **sich wundern** to be surprised
[21] **die Stimmung, –, –en** mood
[22] **erfassen** to catch, grasp
[23] **die Bekanntschaft, –, –en** acquaintance
[24] **großartig** splendid, great

195

hatten das Gefühl,[25] daß sie richtig dazu gehörten. Zuerst ärgerte[26] Tom sich,[26] daß er von den „Büttenreden" vieles nicht verstehen konnte, denn der Kölner Dialekt machte ihm Schwierigkeiten. Aber bald lachte und klatschte[27] er wie die anderen über die Witze[28] und Schlager. Es war wirklich die „großartigste Party in ganz Europa", wie es vor einigen Jahren im „Life Magazine" hieß. [30]

[25] **das Gefühl, –s, –e** feeling
[26] **sich ärgern** to be annoyed

[27] **klatschen** to applaud
[28] **der Witz, –es, –e** joke

German Information Center

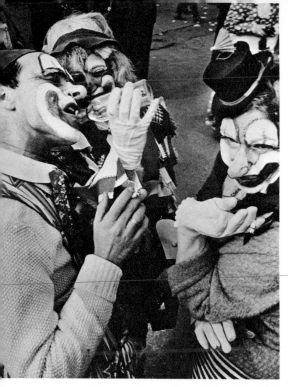

German Information Center

German Tourist Information Office

Karneval am Rhein

German Tourist Information Office

German Tourist Information Office

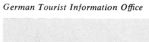

Fragen und Antworten

1. Wer erkundigte sich, ob Tom krank war?
   Ricardo Tudisco, der spanische Austauschstudent.
2. Warum konnte Tom am Montag nicht in die Vorlesung?
   Er war in Köln, weil er sich den Rosenmontagszug ansehen wollte.
3. Warum kaufte Tom sich Aspirin?
   Er hatte Kopfschmerzen.
4. Warum hat Tom sich die Ohren zugehalten?
   Die Leute brüllten so laut (*loud*).
5. Warum wollte Tom alles mitmachen?
   Weil er so ein Fest noch nie erlebt hatte.
6. Was war das tolle Fest in Köln?
   Man feierte den Karneval.
7. Warum hat Ricardo sich so teilnahmsvoll erkundigt?
   Tom hat schlecht ausgesehen.
8. Können wir Amerikaner uns das Karnevalsfest vorstellen?
   Nein, das können wir uns nicht vorstellen.
9. Wann fängt der Karneval an?
   Er beginnt am elften November, vormittags um elf Uhr.
10. Warum ärgerte Tom sich zuerst auf dem Karneval?
    Er konnte vieles nicht verstehen.

Structure and Practice

Explanation of Forms

I. SIMPLE PAST TENSE (I)

A. Forms

The simple past tense is so called because it has only one verb component in contrast to the compound past tenses (present perfect and past perfect), which have two. In this lesson the formation of the simple past tense of weak verbs and modals will be explained. Strong verbs will be treated in the next lesson.

1. WEAK VERBS: The simple past tense of weak verbs is formed by adding to the stem the endings shown in the examples below. The sign of the past tense of weak verbs in German is the **-t-** before each personal ending, just as the *-ed* is the sign of the past tense of regular verbs in English (e.g., *to live, lived; to follow, followed*).

folgen (*to follow*)	**kaufen** (*to buy*)
ich folg**te**	ich kauf**te**
du folg**test**	du kauf**test**
er, sie, es folg**te**	er, sie, es kauf**te**
wir folg**ten**	wir kauf**ten**
ihr folg**tet**	ihr kauf**tet**
sie folg**ten**	sie kauf**ten**
Sie folg**ten**	Sie kauf**ten**

Exception: Verbs whose stems end in **-t, -d,** or a combination of consonants (**atmen** — *to breathe*) add an extra **-e-** between the stem and the endings, shown above, in order to facilitate pronunciation, as in the example of **warten:**

warten (*to wait*)	
ich wart**ete**	wir wart**eten**
du wart**etest**	ihr wart**etet**
er, sie, es wart**ete**	sie wart**eten**
	Sie wart**eten**

2. MODALS: Modals in the simple past tense use the same endings as weak verbs, but some have stem changes: those modals that have umlauts in the infinitive drop this umlaut in the past tense; the only additional stem change occurs in the verb **mögen** (see below). In the following list (the present tense is given as a review) the third-person singular forms are shown:

INFINITIVE	SIMPLE PAST	PRESENT
dürfen	er **durfte**	er darf
können	er **konnte**	er kann
mögen	er **mochte**	er mag
müssen	er **mußte**	er muß
sollen	er **sollte**	er soll
wollen	er **wollte**	er will

The complete past-tense conjugation of modals will follow the pattern of **können:**

ich **konn*te***	wir **konn*ten***
du **konn*test***	ihr **konn*tet***
er, sie, es **konn*te***	sie **konn*ten***
	Sie **konn*ten***

3. HABEN: The simple past tense of **haben,** although irregular in its stem, has the same personal endings as weak verbs.

ich **hat*te***   wir **hat*ten***
du **hat*test***   ihr **hat*tet***
er, sie, es **hat*te***   sie **hat*ten***
         Sie **hat*ten***

B. Uses

The simple past is the narrative tense in German. As such, it can be the equivalent of any of the four English past tense forms, depending on the context.

Ich **wohnte** da.
{
*I **lived** there.*
*I **was living** there.*
*I **did live** there.*
*I **used to live** there.*

As the narrative past it is used, orally or written, for an entire or partial story or description, but it can also be used for single statements that are part of a narrative or description. Within a conversation, therefore, where most of the exchange is in the present or present perfect, there may be occasion to employ the simple past for one of these uses. In the dialogue of this lesson, for example, Tom describes a few of the things he saw at the Cologne carnival:

Alles **tanzte** auf den Straßen und **brüllte** im Chor.
Everyone was dancing in the streets and shouting in chorus.

II. REFLEXIVE VERBS

A reflexive verb is one for which the subject and pronoun object (direct or indirect) are the same person or thing: "He washed himself (*direct object*); he bought himself (*indirect object*) a new car."

A. Forms

In English the reflexive pronouns are: *myself, yourself, himself, herself,* etc. In German the reflexive pronouns are identical with the personal pronouns (accusative for direct object; dative for indirect object), except for the third-person singular and plural, where the form in both cases is **sich.** Note that the polite form (**Sie**) does not capitalize its reflexive pronoun. Following are examples of verbs used reflexively.

1. REFLEXIVE PRONOUN USED AS DIRECT OBJECT:

> **Ich** betrachte **mich** im Spiegel. *I look at myself in the mirror.*
> **Du** betrachtest **dich** im Spiegel. *You look at yourself in the mirror.*
> **Er, sie, es** betrachtet **sich** im Spiegel. *He . . . etc.*
> **Wir** betrachten **uns** im Spiegel.
> **Ihr** betrachtet **euch** im Spiegel.
> **Sie** betrachten **sich** im Spiegel.
> **Sie** (*you*) betrachten **sich** im Spiegel.

2. REFLEXIVE PRONOUN USED AS INDIRECT OBJECT:

> **Ich** kaufe **mir** Aspirin. *I am buying myself some aspirin.*
> **Du** kaufst **dir** Aspirin. *You are buying yourself some aspirin.*
> **Er, sie, es** kauft **sich** Aspirin. *He . . . etc.*
> **Wir** kaufen **uns** Aspirin.
> **Ihr** kauft **euch** Aspirin.
> **Sie** kaufen **sich** Aspirin.
> **Sie** (*you*) kaufen **sich** Aspirin.

B. Uses

In German, as in English, there are verbs that can be used reflexively or not: "I bought myself a present"; "I bought her a present." German, however, also has a number of verbs that are always used reflexively to convey a particular meaning (e.g., **setzen** [non-reflexive], *to put, place;* **sich setzen** [reflexive], *to sit down*). In such cases the reflexive pronoun is a grammatical necessity and is not translated into English. Some of these are dative reflexives, others are accusative. Following is a list of reflexives of this type that you have had thus far. (NOTE: A verb that is reflexive is identified by **sich** before the infinitive.)

> **sich** (*dat.*) **ansehen** (to look at, take a look at)
> **sich** (*acc.*) **ärgern** (to get annoyed)
> **sich** (*acc.*) **erkundigen** (to inquire)
> **sich** (*acc.*) **setzen** (to sit down)
> **sich** (*dat.*) **vorstellen** (to imagine)

EXAMPLES:

Das kann ich mir nicht vorstellen. *I can't imagine that.*
Ich erkundige mich nach ihm. *I'm inquiring about him.*

C. Word Order

In independent clauses (statements and questions), the reflexive pronoun has the same position as a personal pronoun (i.e., after the subject-verb or verb-subject unit).

REFLEXIVE PRONOUN	PERSONAL PRONOUN
Ich kaufe **mir** Aspirin.	Ich kaufe **ihm** Aspirin.
Kaufen Sie **sich** Aspirin?	Kaufen Sie **ihm** Aspirin?

This applies even when the reflexive verb is an infinitive.

Ich wollte **mir** den Rosenmontagszug **ansehen.**

In polite commands the reflexive pronoun is placed after the subject.

Kaufen Sie **sich** Aspirin!

In familiar commands the reflexive pronoun follows the verb.

Kauf **dir** Aspirin!   Kauft **euch** Aspirin!

In dependent clauses the reflexive pronoun follows a pronoun subject but may precede or follow a noun subject.

Ich weiß, daß er **sich** Aspirin kauft.
Ich weiß, daß Herr Schmidt **sich** Aspirin kauft. (*or:* Ich weiß, daß **sich** Herr Schmidt Aspirin kauft.)

Word Study and Usage

I. PARTS OF THE DAY

The German words for the various parts of the day are:

der Morgen (morning)
der Vormittag (forenoon, morning)
der Mittag (noon)
der Nachmittag (afternoon)
der Abend (evening)
die Nacht (night)

II. TIME EXPRESSIONS FOR REPEATED OCCURRENCES

To indicate that something occurs repeatedly or regularly at the same time of day, German uses an adverbial form constructed from the above nouns by adding **-s** to the noun. (The adverbial form is, of course, not capitalized.)

> **morgens** (in the morning[s])
> **vormittags** (in the morning[s])
> **mittags** (at noon)
> **nachmittags** (in the afternoon[s])
> **abends** (in the evening[s])
> **nachts** (at night)
> but: **tagsüber** (during the day)

The same construction can be used for days of the week.

> **sonntags** (on Sunday[s])
> **montags** (on Monday[s])
> **dienstags** (on Tuesday[s])
> **mittwochs** (on Wednesday[s])
> **donnerstags** (on Thursday[s])
> **freitags** (on Friday[s])
> **samstags, sonnabends** (on Saturday[s])

Class Drills

I. Restate the following sentences in the simple past tense:

1. Ich zeige ihm den Kölner Dom.
   Ich erzähle ihm die Legende.
   Ich mache um acht Uhr zu.
   Ich warte lange auf ihn.

2. Du glaubst das doch nicht.
   Du verdankst ihm viel.
   Du machst sehr früh zu.
   Du arbeitest zu schwer.

3. Er studiert Geschichte.
   Er bestellt eine Torte.
   Er macht alles mit.
   Er arbeitet bei der Firma Opel.

4. Wir tanzen den ganzen Abend.
   Wir belegen diese Vorlesung.
   Wir bauen die Stadt wieder auf.
   Wir landen in Bonn.

5. Sie wecken mich um acht.
   Sie erwähnen das oft.
   Sie holen es am Mittag ab.
   Sie betrachten das als Skandal.

6. Ich sage ihr das.
   Er kauft die Zeitung.
   Du meinst das nicht.
   Sie lernen Deutsch.
   Wir wohnen lange dort.

II. Restate the following sentences in the simple past tense:

1. Ich will den Kölner Dom sehen.
   Ich soll um fünf da sein.
   Ich darf nicht hingehen.
   Ich kann mir das vorstellen.
   Ich muß zum Zahnarzt.

2. Er muß die Bilder abholen.
   Er kann ihn nicht verstehen.
   Er darf am Karneval teilnehmen.
   Er soll ihn in der Mensa treffen.
   Er will mich fotografieren.

3. Wir wollen nicht mitmachen.
   Wir müssen die Bilder abholen.
   Wir dürfen ihn sehen.
   Wir können mit dem Rheindampfer hin.
   Wir sollen um fünf hier sein.

4. Sie können das verstehen.
   Sie wollen uns besuchen.
   Sie müssen zum Zahnarzt.
   Sie sollen ihn wecken.
   Sie dürfen lange schlafen.

5. Ich kann das nicht glauben.
   Wir wollen nach Köln.
   Er muß sich die Ohren zuhalten.
   Sie sollen die Zeitungen abholen.
   Sie darf mich um acht Uhr wecken.

III. ***Restate the following sentences, substituting the German for the modals given in English:***

1. Er durfte die Bilder abholen.
   (*had to*)
   (*wanted to*)
   (*was supposed to*)
   (*could*)

2. Ich sollte am Karneval teilnehmen.
   (*was allowed to*)
   (*wanted to*)
   (*was able to*)
   (*had to*)

3. Wir mußten nach Bonn.
   (*wanted to*)
   (*were supposed to*)
   (*were allowed to*)
   (*were able to*)

4. Sie wollten früh zumachen.
   (*had to*)
   (*were supposed to*)
   (*were allowed to*)
   (*were able to*)

IV. a. ***Restate the following sentences, substituting, in turn,*** <u>er</u>, <u>wir</u>, <u>sie</u> ***(they) in place of the subject:***

Ich frage mich das oft.
Ich erkundige mich nach ihm.
Ich betrachte mich im Spiegel.
Ich setze mich neben ihn.
Ich kaufe mir Aspirin.
Ich sehe mir das Goethehaus an.
Ich stelle mir das vor.
Ich halte mir die Ohren zu.

b. ***Restate the sentences in exercise a. first in the present perfect, then past perfect.***

V. a. Answer the following questions by using, in turn, the singular familiar imperative, then polite imperative:

EXAMPLE: **Soll ich mich neben ihn setzen?**
Ja, *setz dich* **neben ihn!**
Ja, *setzen Sie sich* **neben ihn!**

Soll ich mich im Spiegel betrachten?
Soll ich mich danach erkundigen?
Soll ich mich neben ihn setzen?
Soll ich mir das Gebäude ansehen?
Soll ich mir so etwas kaufen?
Soll ich mir die Ohren zuhalten?

b. Answer the following questions as in exercise a., but with a familiar plural imperative:

Sollen wir uns im Spiegel betrachten?
Sollen wir uns danach erkundigen?
Sollen wir uns neben sie setzen?
Sollen wir uns das Gebäude ansehen?
Sollen wir uns so etwas kaufen?
Sollen wir uns die Ohren zuhalten?

VI. Restate the following sentences, adding the given modals:

EXAMPLE: **Ich halte mir die Ohren zu.** (*müssen*)
Ich *muß* **mir die Ohren** *zuhalten.*

Ich erkundige mich danach. (**wollen**)
Ich kaufe mir Aspirin. (**sollen**)
Ich setze mich neben ihn. (**dürfen**)
Ich stelle mir das vor. (**können**)
Ich sehe mir das Goethehaus an. (**wollen**)
Ich halte mir die Ohren zu. (**müssen**)

VII. Restate the following sentence, substituting the new adverbial element given in English:

Vormittags kann ich nie arbeiten.
(*in the morning*)
(*in the afternoon*)
(*in the evening*)
(*on Saturday*)
(*on Sunday*)

Exercises

I. Rewrite the following sentences, using <u>ich</u> as the subject:

1. Er fragt sich, ob er das tun kann.   2. Er stellt sich das leicht vor.
3. Er kauft sich bald einen neuen Wagen.   4. Er betrachtet sich oft
im Spiegel.   5. Er hält sich die Ohren zu.   6. Er ärgert sich über den
Professor.   7. Er setzt sich auf einen Sessel.   8. Er möchte sich erkundigen, wie es war.   9. Er soll sich die Zeitschrift ansehen.

II. Rewrite the following sentences in the singular familiar im-perative and polite imperative:

1. Fragt euch zuerst, wie ihr das tun wollt!   2. Stellt euch das nicht so
leicht vor!   3. Kauft euch Aspirin!   4. Betrachtet euch mal im Spiegel!
5. Setzt euch in dieses Zimmer!   6. Erkundigt euch, wie man das
macht!   7. Haltet euch die Ohren zu!   8. Seht euch das neue Programm an!   9. Ärgert euch nicht darüber!

III. Rewrite the following sentences in the same tense without modals:

1. Ich wollte abends auf dem Maskenball tanzen.   2. Die Leute mußten auf den Umzug warten.   3. Er sollte die Tür zumachen.   4. Tom
durfte die Vorlesung nicht belegen.   5. Sie wollten ihm das alte Rathaus
zeigen.   6. Ich konnte ihm nicht glauben.   7. Sie mußte sich in
Köln erkundigen.   8. Ich konnte mir das nicht so vorstellen.   9. Wir
sollten uns neben sie setzen.   10. Er durfte alles mitmachen.

IV. Translate into English. In sentences 1–5, reproduce the German sentences from your English translations:

1. Es stimmt, daß er schlecht aussieht; vielleicht hat er Kopfschmerzen.
2. Auf dem Karneval geht's wirklich lustig zu; wir haben alles mitgemacht.   3. Sie können sich gar nicht vorstellen, was für ein tolles
Fest das ist.   4. Ich mußte ins Geschäft, ehe es zumachte.   5. Sie
haben sich doch neben ihn gesetzt?   6. Die antiken Möbel in seinem
Arbeitszimmer sollten als Kontrast wirken.   7. Sehen wir uns zuerst
den Film an; ins Café können wir später gehen.   8. Sie wollten ihm
eine Ansichtskarte schreiben, aber sie hatten vergessen, wo er wohnt.
9. Während des Umzugs in Köln mußte er sich die Ohren zuhalten.
10. Hoffentlich machen ihm die Seminare keine großen Schwierigkeiten.

V. Translate:

1. You don't look well. 2. Buy yourself (*some*) aspirin. 3. I could not imagine what he wanted. 4. Did he pick up the newspaper? (*present perfect*) 5. I want to tell you something interesting. 6. In the afternoons he always walked through the village. (*simple past*) 7. I'd like to take a look at a program. 8. We were allowed to start again from the beginning. 9. He mentioned the name of a student. (*simple past*) 10. They were completely exhausted because they had not slept.

VI. Composition. Write ten sentences in the form of a composition on this topic — „Tom auf dem Karneval". For each sentence, use the words given below:

1. Tom   Köln   Karneval
2. Rosenmontag
3. tolles Fest
4. nicht schlafen   Fastnachtsonntag   Aschermittwoch
5. tagsüber   abends
6. morgens   anfangen   von vorne
7. Tom   mitmachen   Spaß machen
8. Dienstag   Vorlesung
9. erschöpft   Kopfschmerzen
10. Tom   erzählen   Ricardo   Karneval

Active Vocabulary

abends	in the evening	**eben**	just
alles	everyone (*coll.*)	**echt**	real, genuine
an-fangen (ä), hat ange-fangen	to begin	**sich** (*acc.*) **erkundi-gen**	to inquire
sich (*dat.*) **an-sehen (ie), hat ange-sehen**	to (have a) look at	**erleben**	to experience
		erschöpft	exhausted
		so etwas	such a thing
sich (*acc.*) **ärgern**	to be annoyed	**der Fastnacht-sonntag, –s, –e**	Sunday before Lent
der Aschermitt-woch, –s, –e	Ash Wednesday	**gar nicht**	not at all
		gestern	yesterday
das Aspirin, –s	aspirin	**der Karneval, –s, –e**	carnival
aus-sehen (ie), hat aus-gesehen	to look, appear	**das Katerfrüh-stück, –s, –e**	breakfast for hang-over victims
brüllen	to roar, shout	**klar**	clear, plain
der Chor, –(e)s, ⁼e	chorus, choir	**na klar!**	of course, certainly

die Kopfschmer-	headache	tagsüber	during the day
zen (*pl.*)		tatsächlich	real, actual
krank	sick	teilnahmsvoll	concerned, sympa-
laut	loud		thetic
der Maskenball,	fancy-dress	toll	mad, wild
–s, –̈e	ball	der Umzug,	parade
mit-machen	to join in	–s, –̈e	
mittags	at noon	vieles	many things
der Morgen, –s, –	morning	vollkommen	complete
morgens	in the morning	der Vormittag, –s,	forenoon, morning
die Nacht, –, –̈e	night	–e	
nie	never	vormittags	in the morning
noch nie	never (before)	vorn(e)	in front
das Ohr, –(e)s, –en	ear	von vorn(e)	over again
der Rheinländer,	Rhinelander	sich (*dat.*) vor-	to imagine
–s, –		stellen	
der Rosenmon-	parade on the Mon-	das Wunder, –s, –	wonder, miracle
tagszug, –s, –̈e	day before Lent	zu-halten (ä),	to hold closed, keep
schlecht	bad	hat zugehalten	closed
sich (*acc.*) setzen	to sit down		

Im Kom(m)ödchen

Fünfzehnte Lektion

Das Kabarett

[*Nach einer Kabarettvorstellung in Düsseldorf. Gerd und Tom fahren zurück nach Bonn. Sie haben sich gut amüsiert und unterhalten sich über das Programm.*]

TOM — Mir kamen die Tränen vor Lachen!

GERD — Mir ging's genauso. Heute war es wirklich einmalig.

TOM — Waren das nicht sehr gewagte politische Witze?

GERD — Schon, aber das gehört zur Kabarett-Tradition.

TOM — Gab es das auch während der Nazizeit?

GERD — Anfangs ja. Später wurde die Zensur zu streng. Da verloren viele Darsteller den Mut. Nach und nach schlossen die meisten Kabaretts. — Hast du alles verstanden?

TOM — Manchmal war es schwer, mitzukommen.

GERD — Das ist verständlich. Selbst mir fällt es oft schwer, alles zu verstehen. Was hat dir am besten gefallen?

TOM — Der Sketch über die Amerikanisierung der deutschen Sprache. Und dir?

GERD — Die Parodie über ein literarisches Cocktailgespräch. „Dem Dichter ist es gelungen, die Realität der Dinge ins Metaphysische zu transponieren." Großartig!

TOM — Den blasierten Ton kannst du ja gut nachahmen.

GERD — Das habe ich gerade selbst bemerkt! Vielleicht sollte ich Kabarettist werden.

The Cabaret[1]

[*After a cabaret performance in Düsseldorf. Gerd and Tom are driving back to Bonn. They've had a good time and are talking about the program.*]

TOM — I laughed until the tears ran down my face.

GERD — The same with me. It really was exceptional today.

TOM — Weren't those rather daring political jokes?

GERD — They were, but that's part of cabaret tradition.

TOM — Did that go on during the Nazi period too?

GERD — At the beginning it did. Later the censorship got too strict. Then a lot of performers lost their courage. Gradually most of the cabarets closed. — Did you understand it all?

TOM — At times it was hard to follow.

GERD — That's understandable. Even I often find it hard to understand everything. What did you like best?

TOM — The sketch about the Americanization of the German language. How about you?

GERD — The parody on a literary conversation at a cocktail party. "The poet succeeded in transporting the reality of things into the realm of the metaphysical." Great!

TOM — You really imitate the blasé tone very well.

GERD — I was just noticing that myself. Maybe I should become a cabaret performer.

[1] A very popular form of entertainment in Germany. Usually in a theater-like setting, the performers satirize political, social, and literary figures, trends and situations.

Lesestück XV

In Amerika hatte Tom oft gehört: „Die Deutschen haben keinen Humor."
Schon damals hatte er sich über diese Behauptung[1] gewundert, und jetzt, da
er Deutschland und die Deutschen besser kannte,[2] ärgerte er sich manchmal
darüber. Die Familie Thiele und auch seine anderen Freunde waren nicht
humorlos. Er sprach[3] dann mit Gerd darüber, und dieser lud ihn ein,[4] sich 5
eine besonders populäre Form der humoristischen Kunst anzusehen, das
Kabarett. In Düsseldorf, nicht weit von Bonn, gibt es ein gutes Kabarett, das
„Kom(m)ödchen",[5] und so fuhren die beiden Freunde mit dem Wagen hin.
Auf der Fahrt bemerkte Tom sehr bald, daß Gerd vom Kabarett begeistert[6]
war. Zum Beispiel sang er im Auto das Kom(m)ödchen–Lied: 10

> Das was dem Kom(m)ödchen wichtig schien
> Zwischen Honolulu und Berlin
> Wird es ohne Hemmung
> Innere Beklemmung
> Durch den Wochenschau–Kakao 15
> Stets ziehn.[7]

Gerd erzählte auch manches über die Geschichte des Kabaretts. So erfuhr[8]
Tom, daß *cabaret* früher im Französischen[9] einfach „Wirtshaus"[10] bedeutete.
Später, am Ende des neunzehnten Jahrhunderts, meinte man damit die
literarischen Cafés der Bohemiens in Paris. Das erste dieser Art war „le chat 20
noir", also „Die schwarze Katze".[11]

In Deutschland blühte[12] das literarische und bald auch das politische
Kabarett schon vor dem ersten Weltkrieg. Ein bekannter Kabarettist war der
Dramatiker Frank Wedekind. Sein Ensemble hieß „Die 11 Scharfrichter".[13]
Sie machten sich lustig[14] über die Schwächen[15] der Menschen, und oft schok- 25
kierten sie ihre Zeitgenossen[16] sehr. Wedekind schrieb[17] einmal zum Beispiel
ein Gedicht, das begann: „Ich hab' meine Tante[18] geschlachtet."[19]

---

[1] **die Behauptung, –, –en** assertion, statement
[2] **kannte** knew
  from **kennen** to know
[3] **sprach** spoke
  from **sprechen** to speak
[4] **lud . . . ein** invited
  from **ein-laden** to invite
[5] **das „Kom(m)ödchen"** the spelling is a play
  on words: (1) **das Kommödchen** small
  bureau (2) **das Komödchen** little comedy
[6] **begeistert** enthusiastic
[7] **„Das was . . . ziehn"** theme song of the
  Kom(m)ödchen. A fairly literal prose
  translation reads: "What appears to
  the *Kom(m)ödchen* to be important
  between Honolulu and Berlin, it will,

without inhibition and anguish, make
fun of in its news of the week."
[8] **erfuhr** learned, found out
  from **erfahren** to learn, find out
[9] **im Französischen** in French
[10] **das Wirtshaus, –es, ⸚er** inn
[11] **„Die schwarze Katze"** "The Black Cat"
[12] **blühen** to flourish
[13] **der Scharfrichter, –s, –** executioner
[14] **sich lustig machen über** to make fun of
[15] **die Schwäche, –, –n** weakness
[16] **der Zeitgenosse, –n, –n** contemporary
[17] **schrieb** wrote
  from **schreiben** to write
[18] **die Tante, –, –n** aunt
[19] **schlachten** to slaughter

»Die Stachelschweine«

BERLINER LITERARISCHES KABARETT

LEITUNG ROLF ULRICH

German Information Center

Unter den Kabarettisten der Zeit zwischen den beiden Weltkriegen machte sich vor allem Werner Finck einen Namen. Die Nazis fürchteten[20] ihn wegen seiner scharfen[21] Satiren und seiner Respektlosigkeit[22] vor dem Regime. 30 Mehr als einmal kam er ins Gefängnis.[23] Respektlos, aggressiv, kritisch und geistreich[24] sind auch die neuen Kabaretts. Schon ihre Namen zeigen das: „Die Stachelschweine",[25] „Die Wühlmäuse",[26] „Das faule[27] Ei",[28] und — „Das Kom(m)ödchen".

[20] **fürchten** to fear
[21] **scharf** sharp, biting
[22] **die Respektlosigkeit, –, –en** irreverence
[23] **das Gefängnis, –ses, –se** jail
[24] **geistreich** bright, witty

[25] **das Stachelschwein, –s, –e** porcupine
[26] **die Wühlmaus, –, ⁻e** vole, field mouse
[27] **faul** rotten
[28] **das Ei, –s, –er** egg

Fragen und Antworten

1. Was taten Tom und Gerd in Düsseldorf?
   Sie gingen ins Kabarett.
2. Worüber unterhielten sie sich auf dem Heimweg?
   Sie sprachen über die Vorstellung.
3. Was gefiel Tom am besten?
   Ihm gefiel der Sketch über die Amerikanisierung der Sprache.

4. Was fand Gerd großartig?
   Er fand den literarischen Teil (*part*) des Programms großartig.
5. Verstand Tom alles?
   Nein, manchmal fiel es ihm schwer, mitzukommen.
6. Verstehen die Deutschen alles im Kabarett?
   Selbst ihnen fällt das oft schwer.
7. Wem gelang es, die Kabaretts zu schließen?
   Den Nazis gelang es, sie zu schließen.
8. Wer bemerkte, daß Gerd die Parodie gut nachahmen konnte?
   Tom bemerkte es, und auch Gerd selbst.
9. Wozu lud Gerd seinen Freund ein?
   Er lud ihn ein, mit ihm ins Kabarett zu gehen.
10. Von wem erfuhr Tom manches über die Geschichte des Kabaretts?
    Als sie nach Düsseldorf fuhren, erzählte Gerd ihm manches darüber.

Structure and Practice

Explanation of Forms

I. SIMPLE PAST TENSE (II)

The uses of the simple past tense discussed in the last lesson, in connection with weak verbs, apply to strong verbs as well. However, the forms of the strong verbs differ from those of weak verbs.

A. Strong Verbs

In the past tense, strong verbs always have a stem change (which must be memorized) and a characteristic set of endings, as shown in the following examples:

gehen (*to go*)	**sitzen** (*to sit*)
ich **ging**	ich **saß**
du **ging***st*	du **saß***est*
er, sie, es **ging**	er, sie, es **saß**
wir **ging***en*	wir **saß***en*
ihr **ging***t*	ihr **saß***t*
sie **ging***en*	sie **saß***en*
Sie **ging***en*	Sie **saß***en*

Note: Verbs whose past-tense stem ends in an s-sound add an extra **-e-** before the ending in the second person singular: **sitzen, du saßest.**

B. *Werden* and *Sein*

Although **werden** and **sein** are irregular in their present tense, they follow the pattern of strong verbs in the simple past. The past-tense stem of **werden** is **wurde** (because the stem ends in -**e**, the first and third person plural add -**n** instead of -**en**); the past tense stem of **sein** is **war.**

werden (*to become*)	sein (*to be*)
ich **wurde**	ich **war**
du **wurdest**	du **warst**
er, sie, es **wurde**	er, sie, es **war**
wir **wurden**	wir **waren**
ihr **wurdet**	ihr **wart**
sie **wurden**	sie **waren**
Sie **wurden**	Sie **waren**

II. PRINCIPAL PARTS OF VERBS

Like English, German lists three principal parts for most verbs: infinitive, past tense, past participle (English: [*to*] *go, went, gone*). In addition, German lists a fourth principal part, the present tense, for verbs that have a vowel change. Traditionally the third-person singular forms are used for principal parts.

It is important to memorize the principal parts of strong verbs. They supply the information needed to form any tense of the verb. In the following list of strong verbs you have had, most verbs with separable prefixes are omitted, since they have the same stem changes as the basic form of the verb (e.g., **kommen, kam, (ist) gekommen; ankommen, kam . . . an, (ist) angekommen**); the only verbs with separable prefixes that are included are those whose basic form you have not yet had: **anfangen** (*to begin*), **einladen** (*to invite*). Beginning with this lesson, the principal parts of any strong verbs are given in the vocabularies.

INFINITIVE	PAST	PAST PARTICIPLE	PRESENT	ENGLISH
anfangen	fing . . . an	hat angefangen	fängt . . . an	to begin
beginnen	begann	hat begonnen		to begin
bekommen	bekam	hat bekommen		to get, receive
bitten	bat	hat gebeten		to ask, request
bleiben	blieb	*ist* geblieben		to stay, remain
einladen	lud . . . ein	hat eingeladen	lädt . . . ein	to invite
erfahren	erfuhr	hat erfahren	erfährt	to learn, experience

INFINITIVE	PAST	PAST PARTICIPLE	PRESENT	ENGLISH
essen	aß	hat gegessen	ißt	to eat
fahren	fuhr	*ist* (hat) gefahren	fährt	to go, drive
fallen	fiel	*ist* gefallen	fällt	to fall
finden	fand	hat gefunden		to find
fliegen	flog	*ist* (hat) geflogen		to fly
geben	gab	hat gegeben	gibt	to give
gefallen	gefiel	hat gefallen	gefällt	to be pleasing to, to like
gehen	ging	*ist* gegangen		to go
gelingen	gelang	*ist* gelungen		to succeed
halten	hielt	hat gehalten	hält	to hold, stop
heißen	hieß	hat geheißen		to be called, named
helfen	half	hat geholfen	hilft	to help
kommen	kam	*ist* gekommen		to come
laufen	lief	*ist* gelaufen	läuft	to run
lesen	las	hat gelesen	liest	to read
nehmen	nahm	hat genommen	nimmt	to take
schlafen	schlief	hat geschlafen	schläft	to sleep
schließen	schloß	hat geschlossen		to close
schreiben	schrieb	hat geschrieben		to write
schweigen	schwieg	hat geschwiegen		to be silent
sehen	sah	hat gesehen	sieht	to see
sein	war	*ist* gewesen	ist	to be
sitzen	saß	hat gesessen		to sit
sprechen	sprach	hat gesprochen	spricht	to speak
stehen	stand	hat gestanden		to stand
treffen	traf	hat getroffen	trifft	to meet
trinken	trank	hat getrunken		to drink
tun	tat	hat getan		to do
sich unterhalten	unterhielt	hat unterhalten	unterhält	to converse
vergessen	vergaß	hat vergessen	vergißt	to forget
verlieren	verlor	hat verloren		to lose
verschwinden	verschwand	*ist* verschwunden		to disappear
verstehen	verstand	hat verstanden		to understand
werden	wurde	*ist* geworden	wird	to become, get

III. DEPENDENT INFINITIVES WITH *ZU* AND INFINITIVE PHRASES

Most German verbs (except for modals and a few other verbs that will be discussed in a later lesson) require a **zu** with any dependent infinitive used with them.

Modal:

Er **konnte** das nicht **verstehen.**

but:

Das **war** schwer **zu verstehen.**

When the dependent infinitive has a separable prefix, the **zu** is placed between the prefix and the rest of the verb.

Manchmal war es schwer, **mitzukommen.**

Frequently the dependent infinitive is combined with other elements to form an entire infinitive phrase. In such a phrase the infinitive is last, and the whole phrase is set off by a comma.

Er lud ihn ein, **mit ihm ins Kabarett zu gehen.**
He invited him to go to the cabaret with him.
Selbst mir fällt es schwer, **alles zu verstehen.**
Even I find it hard to understand everything.
Wem gelang es, **die Kabaretts zu schließen?**
Who succeeded in closing the cabarets?

IV. IMPERSONAL SUBJECT ES

A number of German verbs and expressions have as their subject the impersonal pronoun **es** which refers to no specific noun. A few of these have equivalent forms in English (**es regnet** — *it's raining;* **es schneit** — *it's snowing*); others function this way in contrast to their English equivalents (**es gelingt mir** — *I succeed*). You have had the following impersonal verbs and expressions:

Es gibt hier keine Geschwindigkeitsbegrenzung.
There is no speed limit here.
Es geht mir genauso.
It's the same with me.
Es fällt mir schwer (leicht), alles zu verstehen.
It's hard (easy) for me to understand everything.
Es gelingt mir nie, ihn zu sehen.
I never succeed in seeing him.

Notice the way these impersonal verbs are used in the following sentences from this lesson:

Mir ging's (ging es) genauso.
I felt the same way.
Gab es das auch während der Nazizeit?
Did that go on during the Nazi period too?

Manchmal **fiel es ihm** schwer, mitzukommen.
Sometimes it was hard for him to follow.

Wem gelang es, die Kabaretts zu schließen?
Who succeeded in closing the cabarets?

Den Nazis gelang es, sie zu schließen.
The Nazis succeeded in closing them.

Word Study and Usage

I. SELBST

A. As Intensifying Pronoun

Selbst is used as an intensifying pronoun, and as such is placed after the noun or pronoun to be stressed. It can be used for all persons and does not change form.

Gerd **selbst** bemerkte, daß er die Parodie sehr gut nachahmen konnte.
*Gerd **himself** noticed that he was able to imitate the parody very well.*

Die Deutschen **selbst** verstehen nicht alles.
*The Germans **themselves** don't understand everything.*

B. Meaning even

When **selbst** precedes a word or phrase, it means *even.*

Selbst mir fällt es oft schwer.
***Even I** often find it hard.*

Selbst während der Nazizeit gab es noch Kabaretts.
***Even during the Nazi period,** there were cabarets.*

II. ALTERNATE POSITION FOR SEPARABLE PREFIX

Although the normal position for separable prefixes in simple tenses is at the end of the clause, they may be placed, for stylistic reasons, before a final prepositional phrase.

Gerd und Tom fahren **zurück** nach Bonn. (*or:* Gerd und Tom fahren nach Bonn **zurück.**)

Class Drills

I. a. Restate the following sentences in the simple past tense:

  1. Ich komme immer zu früh.
     Ich gehe ins Kabarett.
     Ich bin oft bei ihr.
     Ich verliere den Mut.

  2. Du wirst zu streng.
     Du schläfst zu lange.
     Du hilfst mir oft.
     Du kommst um acht Uhr an.

  3. Er fährt nach Bonn zurück.
     Er versteht nicht alles.
     Er tut nichts.
     Er sieht schlecht aus.

  4. Wir laden ihn oft ein.
     Wir finden das Programm großartig.
     Wir halten uns die Ohren zu.
     Wir nehmen an der Tour teil.

  5. Sie unterhalten sich über das Programm.
     Sie schließen nach und nach.
     Sie sprechen über die Vorstellung.
     Sie sitzen im Café.

  6. Du gibst ihm zuviel.
     Er fängt wieder von vorne an.
     Ich esse zuviel.
     Sie schweigen darüber.
     Wir bleiben nicht lange.

b. Restate the sentences in exercise a. in the present perfect tense.

c. Restate the sentences in exercise a. in the past perfect tense.

II. Restate the following sentences, substituting the correct form of the infinitives and infinitive phrases:

  1. Es war schwer, ihn zu verstehen.
        (das glauben)
        (ihm helfen)

(ein Zimmer finden)
(mitkommen)
(wieder anfangen)
(sich das vorstellen)

2. Es gelang ihnen, die Kabaretts zu schließen.
(ihr alles erklären)
(eine Wohnung bekommen)
(die Stadt wieder aufbauen)
(uns nachahmen)

3. Er hat sie gebeten, ins Eßzimmer zu gehen.
(ihn morgen treffen)
(Kaffee und Torte bestellen)
(uns einladen)
(die Bilder abholen)

III. *Restate the following sentences, substituting the correct form of the new object given in English:*

1. Gelang es ihnen, eine Wohnung zu bekommen?
(*he*)
(*you [polite]*)
(*you [sing. fam.]*)
(*she*)
(*the man*)
(*the visiting professor*)
(*the family*)
(*the student [f.]*)
(*the students*)
(*the Americans*)

2. Es fiel mir schwer, alles zu verstehen.
(*he*)
(*they*)
(*we*)
(*she*)
(*I*)
(*the American*)
(*the man*)
(*the student [f.]*)
(*the American [f.]*)
(*the people*)
(*the Americans*)

IV. Restate the following sentences in the present perfect tense:

Es gelingt ihm, das richtige Wort zu finden.
Es fällt mir schwer, alles zu verstehen.
Ich bitte sie, mit mir ins Konzert zu gehen.
Ich lade ihn ein, mit uns in die Mensa zu gehen.
Es ist schwer, immer alles zu verstehen.

Exercises

I. Rewrite the following sentences in the simple past tense:

1. Ich bitte ihn um Auskunft. 2. Wann fängt die Vorstellung an?
3. Er lacht immer über mich. 4. Es geht sehr lustig zu. 5. Sie steht
da und schweigt. 6. Wir amüsieren uns. 7. So heißt es wenigstens
in der Zeitung. 8. Sie ahmt ihn immer nach. 9. Sie helfen ihm und
geben ihm Geld. 10. Ich bemerke es nie. 11. Er hält seine Vorlesung
auf deutsch. 12. Wir trinken Kaffee und essen Torte. 13. Warum
setzt er sich nicht? 14. Ich laufe nach Hause. 15. Er schreibt, wie er
spricht. 16. Holen sie die Bilder ab? 17. Er versteht nichts, und
ihm gelingt nie etwas. 18. Wir kommen um acht Uhr an. 19. Sie
warten auf mich. 20. Er sieht sich alles an, aber nichts gefällt ihm.

II. Rewrite the following sentences, replacing <u>können</u> by <u>gelingen</u>:

EXAMPLE: *Ich konnte die Tür nicht schließen.*
　　　　　Es gelang mir nicht, die Tür zu schließen.

1. Die Stewardeß konnte endlich die Zeitschrift finden. 2. Ich kann
nie das Richtige sagen. 3. Wir können nie gute Aufnahmen machen.
4. Der Student kann manchmal einen guten Platz bekommen. 5. Sie
konnten manches darüber erfahren. 6. Die Leute konnten endlich
Karten dafür bekommen.

III. Translate into English. In sentences 1–5, reproduce the German sentences from your English translations:

1. Mir gefällt es nicht, daß er Sie immer nachahmt. 2. Mancher
Darsteller verlor während dieser Zeit den Mut. 3. So ein Fest hatte
selbst er noch nie erlebt. 4. Wir fuhren pünktlich ab, kamen aber
nicht fahrplanmäßig an. 5. Sie bat uns um Auskunft über den
spanischen Gastprofessor. 6. Bei den Vorlesungen kommt er nicht
immer mit, aber dafür kann er ja nichts. 7. Zum Glück gab es dort

eine Geschwindigkeitsbegrenzung. 8. Haben Sie ihr gar nichts über diese Vorstellung geschrieben? 9. Wir luden ihn ein, an einem Spaziergang durch das historische Viertel der Stadt teilzunehmen. 10. Es ist ihnen nicht gelungen, Auskunft darüber zu bekommen.

IV. *Translate, using the simple past tense:*

1. Even he wrote me a postcard. 2. It was very difficult for her to read it. 3. We ourselves saw it. It was really exceptional. 4. In the beginning I had a good time. 5. They lost everything. 6. Then they had to close their shop. 7. Did he invite you to go to the concert with him? 8. He was a good performer, but his political jokes were very daring. 9. She laughed until she cried. 10. Gradually the censorship became very strict.

V. *Composition. Write ten sentences in the form of a composition on this topic —* „Ein Abend im Kabarett." *For each sentence, use the words given below:*

1. Gerd und Tom Düsseldorf
2. Kabarett Tränen
3. Darsteller politische Witze
4. gefallen Sketch Sprache
5. Gerd Parodie gefallen
6. nachahmen
7. nach der Vorstellung sich unterhalten
8. Tom erfahren Kabarett-Tradition
9. Nazizeit
10. nach 1945 Kabarett werden beliebt

Active Vocabulary

die Amerikanisie-rung, –	Americanization	der Dichter, –s, –	poet, fiction writer
sich (*acc.*) amü-sieren	to enjoy oneself, have a good time	einmalig	unique, exceptional
		erfahren, er-fuhr, hat erfahren, erfährt	to learn, find out
anfangs	in the beginning		
bemerken	to notice		
am besten	best (of all)	fallen, fiel, ist gefallen, fällt	to fall
blasiert	blasé		
das Cocktailge-spräch, –s, –e	conversation at a cocktail party	es fällt mir schwer	I find it hard, it is difficult for me
der Darsteller, –s, –	performer	es geht mir ge-nauso	it's the same with me

gelingen, ge-lang, ist gelungen	to succeed	schwer	difficult; heavy
		selbst	–self; even
		der Sketch, –es, –e	sketch, skit
das Gespräch, –s, –e	conversation	die Sprache, –, –n	language
		streng	severe, strict
gewagt	daring	der Teil, –(e)s, –e	part
großartig	splendid, great	der Ton, –(e)s, ⸚e	tone
das Kabarett, –s, –s *or* –e	cabaret	die Tradition, –, –en	tradition
der Kabarettist, –en, –en	cabaret performer	die Träne, –, –n	tear
		sich (*acc.*) unter-halten (über + *acc.*), unterhielt, hat unter-halten, un-terhält	to converse, talk (about)
die Kabarett-Tra-dition, –	cabaret tradition		
die Kabarettvor-stellung, –, –en	cabaret performance		
das Lachen, –s	laughter	verlieren, ver-lor, hat verloren	to lose
vor Lachen	from laughing		
literarisch	literary	verständlich	understandable
meist-	most	die Vorstellung, –, –en	performance
mit-kommen, kam . . . mit, ist mitgekom-men	to follow; come along		
		der Witz, –es, –e	joke
der Mut, –(e)s	courage	die Zensur, –	censorship
nach und nach	gradually, by and by	zurück-fahren, fuhr . . . zurück, ist zurück-gefahren, fährt . . . zurück	to drive back
nach-ahmen	to imitate		
die Parodie, –, –n	parody		
politisch	political		
schließen, schloß, hat geschlossen	to close		

Sechzehnte Lektion

Review

Reading Practice

Tom schreibt an Fred Johnson.

Lieber Fred,

Dein Brief kam am Montag. Heute abend habe ich etwas Zeit, und so sollst Du gleich von mir hören.

Dein Bericht (*report*) vom Münchner Fasching war besonders interessant. Also geht es in diesen Tagen auch bei Euch sehr lustig zu. Als Du auf der Faschingsfeier warst, habe ich mir den Rosenmontagszug in Köln angesehen. Das ist wirklich ein tolles Fest, und ich wollte natürlich alles mitmachen. Bei dem Umzug mußte ich an unsere „Rosebowl" Parade denken, aber hier war es doch viel wilder und lauter. In Pasadena zum Beispiel tanzt keiner auf der Straße oder brüllt: „Hurrah for Pasadena!" Man hat mir gesagt, daß viele Leute in den zwei oder drei Nächten vor Aschermittwoch gar nicht ins Bett gehen. Ich hatte schon nach einem Tag zuviel. Wir kommen eben aus Wisconsin und sind keine echten Rheinländer.

Warst Du schon einmal in einem Kabarett? Da mußt Du unbedingt hin. Gerd Thiele und ich sind nach Düsseldorf gefahren, und dort haben wir eine Vorstellung des berühmten „Kom(m)ödchens" besucht. Bei manchen der Sketche kamen uns die Tränen vor Lachen. Manchmal habe ich nicht alles verstanden, denn man muß sehr gut über Politik, Literatur, usw. Bescheid wissen. Auch arbeiten die Kabarettisten gerne mit Wortspielen, und das zu verstehen, fällt einem Nichtdeutschen natürlich besonders schwer.

Am Ende der Weihnachtsferien (*Christmas vacation*) habe ich noch schnell einen Ausflug nach Frankfurt am Main gemacht. Es ist vor allem eine Industriestadt mit sehr modernen Geschäftsvierteln, aber es gibt dort auch viel Sehenswertes, zum Beispiel das Goethehaus. Ich mußte wieder an unseren alten Lehrer denken. Er hat ja so oft von seinem Studium in Frankfurt gesprochen. Wenn er vom Goethehaus erzählte, wurde er doch immer melancholisch, weil der Krieg das Viertel um das Rathaus verwüstet (*devastated*) hatte. Wenn ich nach Hause zurückkomme, kann ich ihm erzählen, daß man alles wieder aufgebaut hat. Ich lege eine Aufnahme bei (**beilegen**

225

— *to enclose*). Du siehst, ich sitze am Schreibtisch des Geheimrats (*privy councilor*) Goethe.

Es ist spät geworden, und heute morgen war ich früh auf.

Laß von Dir hören. Bis zum nächsten Brief.

Dein
Tom

Drills

I. PRESENT PERFECT TENSE: WEAK AND STRONG VERBS

Substitute the new subject or verb:

Ich habe doch in Hamburg gearbeitet. (**bleiben**)
Ich bin doch in Hamburg geblieben. (**er**)
Er ist doch in Hamburg geblieben. (**studieren**)
Er hat doch in Hamburg studiert. (**wir**)
Wir haben doch in Hamburg studiert. (**ankommen**)
Wir sind doch in Hamburg angekommen. (**sie** — *they*)
Sie sind doch in Hamburg angekommen. (**wohnen**)
Sie haben doch in Hamburg gewohnt. (**du**)
Du hast doch in Hamburg gewohnt. (**abfahren**)
Du bist doch in Hamburg abgefahren. (**ich**)
Ich bin doch in Hamburg abgefahren. (**warten**)
Ich habe doch in Hamburg gewartet. (**sie** — *she*)
Sie hat doch in Hamburg gewartet. (**landen**)
Sie ist doch in Hamburg gelandet. (**ihr**)
Ihr seid doch in Hamburg gelandet. (**sich amüsieren**)
Ihr habt euch doch in Hamburg amüsiert. (**er**)
Er hat sich doch in Hamburg amüsiert.

II. PAST PERFECT TENSE: WEAK AND STRONG VERBS

Substitute the new subject or verb:

A. Ich hatte es schon gemacht. (**er**)
   Er hatte es schon gemacht. (**finden**)
   Er hatte es schon gefunden. (**wir**)
   Wir hatten es schon gefunden. (**erwähnen**)
   Wir hatten es schon erwähnt. (**du**)
   Du hattest es schon erwähnt. (**anfangen**)
   Du hattest es schon angefangen. (**sie** — *they*)

Sie hatten es schon angefangen. (**fotografieren**)
Sie hatten es schon fotografiert. (**ihr**)
Ihr hattet es schon fotografiert. (**beginnen**)
Ihr hattet es schon begonnen. (**ich**)
Ich hatte es schon begonnen. (**sich ansehen**)
Ich hatte es mir schon angesehen. (**er**)
Er hatte es sich schon angesehen. (**erfahren**)
Er hatte es schon erfahren. (**wir**)
Wir hatten es schon erfahren. (**haben**)
Wir hatten es schon gehabt.

B. Ich war in Berlin gelandet. (**er**)
Er war in Berlin gelandet. (**ankommen**)
Er war in Berlin angekommen. (**wir**)
Wir waren in Berlin angekommen. (**bleiben**)
Wir waren in Berlin geblieben. (**sie** — *she*)
Sie war in Berlin geblieben. (**verschwinden**)
Sie war in Berlin verschwunden. (**sie** — *they*)
Sie waren in Berlin verschwunden. (**sein**)
Sie waren in Berlin gewesen. (**du**)
Du warst in Berlin gewesen.

III. PAST TENSE: WEAK AND STRONG VERBS

Substitute the new subject or verb:

Er saß bei ihnen. (**wir**)
Wir saßen bei ihnen. (**bleiben**)
Wir blieben bei ihnen. (**sie** — *she*)
Sie blieb bei ihnen. (**wohnen**)
Sie wohnte bei ihnen. (**ich**)
Ich wohnte bei ihnen. (**essen**)
Ich aß bei ihnen. (**er**)
Er aß bei ihnen. (**sein**)
Er war bei ihnen. (**wir**)
Wir waren bei ihnen. (**warten**)
Wir warteten bei ihnen. (**sie** — *they*)
Sie warteten bei ihnen. (**anfangen**)
Sie fingen bei ihnen an. (**ich**)
Ich fing bei ihnen an. (**sich entschuldigen**)
Ich entschuldigte mich bei ihnen. (**sie** — *she*)
Sie entschuldigte sich bei ihnen. (**arbeiten**)
Sie arbeitete bei ihnen.

Exercises

I. REFLEXIVE VERBS

In each of the following sentences, substitute the reflexive verb in parentheses for the italicized elements. Use the same tense as in the original sentence.

1. Ich *habe* den Umzug *gesehen*. (**sich ansehen**)
2. Ich *habe* nach ihr *gefragt*. (**sich erkundigen**)
3. Ich *habe* viel Spaß *gehabt*. (**sich amüsieren**)
4. Ich *war nicht sehr froh* darüber. (**sich ärgern**)
5. Ich *habe* mit ihm darüber *gesprochen*. (**sich unterhalten**)
6. Ich kann diese Sache nicht *glauben*. (**sich vorstellen**)

II. SEPARABLE PREFIXES

Rewrite the following sentences, replacing the italicized elements with the substitutes in parentheses. Use the same tense as in the original sentence:

1. Er *hat* die Zeitung *geholt*. (**abholen**)
2. *Sind* Sie *bei* der Feier *gewesen*? (**teilnehmen an** + *dative*)
3. Ich kam gerade, als das Geschäft *schloß*. (**zumachen**)
4. Er *war* krank. (**aussehen**)
5. Wann *beginnt* die Vorlesung? (**anfangen**)
6. Sie *tut* das *auch*. (**mitmachen**)
7. Er *ist* um neun Uhr *nach Hause gefahren*. (**abfahren**)
8. Wann *kommt* er? (**ankommen**)
9. Ich kann nicht immer *folgen*. (**mitkommen**)

III. PAST TENSES: STRONG AND WEAK VERBS, MODALS

Rewrite the following sentences (a) *in the simple past,* (b) *in the present perfect:*

1. Ich gehe oft ins Theater. 2. Wie lange bleibt er dort? 3. Sie bittet ihn darum. 4. Sie fährt nach Bonn, weil sie dort studiert. 5. Er bleibt länger, weil es ihm hier gefällt. 6. Sie laufen nach Hause. 7. Sie erzählt ihm alles. 8. Er versteht sie nicht. 9. Ich besuche ihn nicht, da ich am Montag zurückfahre. 10. Hoffentlich wird alles besser.

IV. *IMPERSONAL* **ES;** **ZU** + *INFINITIVE PHRASES*

Combine the clauses in the following sentences according to the example:

EXAMPLE: **Es gelingt mir nicht oft; ich bekomme einen guten Platz.**
Es gelingt mir nicht oft, einen guten Platz zu bekommen.

1. Es ist schwer; man glaubt diese Geschichte.
2. Es gelingt ihnen nicht; sie ahmen ihn richtig nach.
3. Es fällt mir schwer; ich lerne diese Fachausdrücke.
4. Es gibt nur einen Weg; man erfährt das.

Now rewrite your new sentences in the present perfect tense.

V. *TRANSLATION*

Translate the following sentences into German:

1. He had been right. 2. Are you going by car? 3. She did not like antique furniture (*mögen* [*simple past*]) 4. Why wasn't he able to do that? 5. In the afternoon we do not like to work. 6. Was there something worth seeing? 7. Even I can understand that. 8. You did read it, didn't you? 9. He left at twenty past seven. 10. He told us nothing new. 11. She sat down next to me. 12. Was it difficult for him to do that?

In den Bayerischen Alpen

München

[*Nach dem Besuch im „Haus der Kunst" wandern Tom und Gerd ins Künstlerviertel Schwabing. Gerds Vetter Karl, ein Bildhauer, hat sie eingeladen.*]

TOM — Schwabing, der deutsche Montmartre!

GERD — Besser, der *bayrische* Montmartre. Die Bayern sind nämlich die größten Lokalpatrioten Deutschlands.

TOM — Die Künstlertypen hier sehen genauso aus wie ihre amerikanischen Kollegen.

GERD — Ja, die Kunst wird immer internationaler, und die Künstler werden zahlreicher. Der Betrieb hier ist viel größer als vor einigen Jahren.

TOM — Es ist nun mal Mode, Maler, Dichter oder Schauspieler zu sein. Jeder glaubt an sein schöpferisches Talent.

GERD — Und die Pseudokünstler sind am liebsten dort, wo Kunst zur Tradition gehört. Deswegen ist München der beliebteste Treffpunkt der Boheme.

TOM — Aber ein Stadtteil wie Schwabing hat doch seinen eigenen Reiz: die Ateliers, die Galerien, die engen Gassen. Schade, daß wir nicht länger hier bleiben.

GERD — [*bleibt stehen*] Tom, ich glaube, wir haben uns verlaufen. Am besten rufe ich Karl an. Oder sollen wir lieber mit dem Taxi hinfahren?

TOM — Das wäre wohl am einfachsten.

Munich

[*After their visit to the* Haus der Kunst,[1] *Tom and Gerd stroll to Schwabing, the artists' quarter. Gerd's cousin Karl, a sculptor, has invited them over.*]

TOM — Schwabing, the German Montmartre!

GERD — Better yet, the *Bavarian* Montmartre. You know the Bavarians are the biggest "boosters" of their region in Germany.

TOM — The artist-types here look exactly like their American counterparts.

GERD — Yes, art is getting more and more international, and artists are getting more numerous. There's much more going on here than there was a few years ago.

TOM — Now it's the fashion to be an artist, a poet, or an actor. Everyone believes in his creative talent.

GERD — And pseudoartists like most to be where art is part of the tradition. That's why Munich is the most popular meeting place for the Bohemian world.

TOM — But a section like Schwabing does have its own charm: the studios, the galleries, the narrow streets. Too bad we're not staying here longer.

GERD — [*stops*] Tom, I think we're lost. The best thing to do is call Karl. Or do you think we'd better go there by taxi?

TOM — That would probably be the simplest thing.

[1] **Haus der Kunst:** One of the most important museums in Munich.

Lesestück XVII

„Ich will aus München eine so schöne Stadt machen, daß man Deutschland nicht kennt, wenn man nicht auch München gesehen hat." Das sagte König Ludwig I. (1825–1848) seinen Bayern, und heute stimmt das. München ist mit seinen breiten[1] Straßen, den vielen Theatern, den berühmten Museen[2] und Kunstgalerien die beliebteste Stadt Deutschlands. Mehr 5 Deutsche möchten dort wohnen als irgendwo anders.[3] Es ist also kein Wunder, daß die bayrische Metropole schneller wächst als jede andere Großstadt Deutschlands. Weniger[4] als die Hälfte[5] aller Einwohner[6] sind einheimische[7] Münchner. Ob einheimisch oder nicht, alle Münchner lieben[8] ihre Stadt, sind stolz auf sie und halten[9] sie für[9] die beste aller Städte. Sie sind wirklich 10 die größten Lokalpatrioten nicht nur Deutschlands. Ein Schauspieler sagte einmal: „In München möchte ich immer leben. Wenn nicht in München, dann im Himmel." Der amerikanische Schriftsteller Thomas Wolfe nannte[10] München „eine der wunderbarsten[11] Städte der Welt".

Schauspieler, Schriftsteller, Studenten und Künstler sind besonders gern in 15 dieser „Weltstadt mit Herz", und das war auch schon früher so. In der Münchner Geschichte gibt es viele Dichter– und Künstlergruppen. Vielleicht die berühmteste[12] Malergruppe war der „Blaue Reiter".[13] Im Jahre 1911 gründeten die Maler Franz Marc und Wassily Kandinsky eine Zeitschrift unter diesem Namen. Andere Künstler wie Paul Klee und August Macke 20 kamen dazu. Heute nennen wir sie die ersten Expressionisten. Die Expressionisten stehen in Opposition zu den älteren Schulen, z.B. dem Impressionismus. „Der Impressionist ist das Grammophon der äußeren[14] Welt", sagen sie. Franz Marc schreibt, er will nicht „nach[15] den Gesetzen[16] der Optik mit freundlicher Hilfe der Kamera" malen. Für ihn ist die Kunst „die kühnste[17] 25 Entfernung[18] von der Natur". Am bekanntesten[19] von allen Bildern Franz Marcs sind „Die drei roten[20] Pferde"[21] (1911) und „Turm der blauen

---

[1] **breit** wide, broad
[2] **das Museum, –s, Museen** museum
[3] **irgendwo anders** anywhere else
[4] **weniger** less
  from **wenig** little
[5] **die Hälfte, –, –n** half
[6] **der Einwohner, –s, –** inhabitant
[7] **einheimisch** native
[8] **lieben** to love
[9] **halten für** to consider
[10] **nannte** called
  from **nennen** to call
[11] **wunderbarst–** most wonderful
  from **wunderbar** wonderful

[12] **berühmtest–** most famous
  from **berühmt** famous
[13] **der „Blaue Reiter"** the *Blue Rider*
[14] **äußer–** outer, exterior
[15] **nach** according to
[16] **das Gesetz, –es, –e** law
[17] **kühnst–** boldest
  from **kühn** bold
[18] **die Entfernung, –, –n** departure, distance
[19] **am bekanntesten** best known
[20] **rot** red
[21] **das Pferd, –(e)s, –e** horse

Pferde" (1913). Über diese radikale Art, die Welt zu sehen und zu zeigen, schreibt er: „Wir malen nicht den Wald oder das Pferd, wie sie uns gefallen oder scheinen,[22] sondern wie sie wirklich sind, — ihr absolutes Wesen."[23]   3

Der Expressionismus war der Beginn der modernen Kunst. Von dort führt ein direkter Weg zur abstrakten Malerei[24] unserer Zeit.

---

[22] **scheinen** to appear, seem
[23] **das Wesen, –s, –** being, essence

[24] **die Malerei, –, –en** (art of) painting

German Information Center

George Grosz: Schwere Zeiten

*Franz Marc: **Der Turm der blauen Pferde***

Fragen und Antworten

1. Warum ist der Betrieb in Schwabing größer geworden?
   Es gibt mehr Künstler als vor einigen Jahren.
2. Warum kommen die Pseudokünstler gern nach München?
   Sie gehen am liebsten dorthin, wo die Kunst zur Tradition gehört.
3. Was ist ein beliebter Treffpunkt der Boheme?
   Schwabing, der deutsche Montmartre.
4. Warum heißt Schwabing der deutsche Montmartre?
   Dort gibt es fast so viele Künstler wie in Paris.
5. Warum nennt Gerd es den bayrischen Montmartre?
   Die Bayern sind größere Lokalpatrioten als die anderen Deutschen.
6. Warum gibt es immer mehr „Künstler"?
   Weil jeder glaubt, schöpferisches Talent zu haben.
7. Bleiben Gerd und Tom längere Zeit in München?
   Nein, sie können nicht lange dort bleiben.
8. Warum will Tom mit dem Taxi fahren?
   Das ist einfacher, denn sie haben sich verlaufen.
9. Sind die meisten Einwohner Münchens einheimische Münchner?
   Nein, weniger als die Hälfte sind einheimische Münchner.
10. Wie nannte ein amerikanischer Schriftsteller München?
    Er nannte München „eine der wunderbarsten Städte der Welt".

Structure and Practice

Explanation of Forms

COMPARISON OF ADJECTIVES AND ADVERBS

A. Forms

1. REGULAR FORMATION OF COMPARATIVE AND SUPERLATIVE: German adjectives and adverbs, except for a few irregular ones, form their comparative by adding **-er** and their superlative by adding **-(e)st** to the positive form. The extra **(e)** indicated for the superlative is used

for adjectives and adverbs whose stem ends in **-t, -d,** or an s-sound, in order to facilitate pronunciation.

> schön, schön**er**, schönst-
> interessant, interessant**er**, interessant**est**-
> süß, süß**er**, süß**est**-

Note: The dashes used after the superlatives indicate that the superlative form is never used in German without a declensional ending. This will be explained in the following section under "B. Use."

German has no equivalent to *more* and *most* that English uses to form some comparatives and superlatives. All adjectives and adverbs, even the irregular ones, form their comparative and superlative with the endings given above.

A number of monosyllabic adjectives and adverbs umlaut the stem vowel of both the comparative and superlative. Of these you have met the following:

> alt, **älter, ältest**-
> jung, **jünger, jüngst**-
> kalt, **kälter, kältest**-
> krank, **kränker, kränkst**-
> kurz, **kürzer, kürzest**-
> lang, **länger, längst**-
> oft, **öfter, öftest**-
> warm, **wärmer, wärmst**-

2. IRREGULAR COMPARISON OF ADJECTIVES AND ADVERBS: The following adjectives and adverbs you have had are irregular in the formation of their comparative and superlative:

> ***bald, eher, am ehesten**
> ***gern, lieber, am liebsten**
> **groß, größer, größt**-
> **gut, besser, best**-
> **viel, mehr, meist**-

* These function only as adverbs, never as adjectives. The superlative form given for them as adverbs will be explained in the following section.

B. Use

1. THE COMPARATIVE

a. As an Attributive Adjective: A comparative form used as an attributive adjective (in front of a noun) functions the same way as a positive, that is, it adds adjective endings.

> Die Bayern sind größere Lokalpatrioten als die anderen Deutschen.

> Die Expressionisten stehen in Opposition zu den älteren Schulen.

Note: Exceptions are the comparative of **viel (mehr)** and **wenig (weniger)**, which never add any adjective endings:

> Es gibt **mehr** Künstler als vor einigen Jahren.

  b. As a Predicate Adjective or Adverb: A comparative used as a predicate adjective or adverb functions the same way as a positive, that is, it adds no declensional endings.

> Der Betrieb ist **größer** als vor einigen Jahren.
> Schade, daß wir nicht **länger** bleiben.

2. THE SUPERLATIVE

  a. As an Attributive Adjective: The superlative is used with the definite article and an adjective ending when a noun follows or is definitely understood after it.

> Die Bayern sind **die größten Lokalpatrioten** Deutschlands.
> *The Bavarians are the biggest "boosters" of their region in Germany.*

> München ist **der beliebteste Treffpunkt** der Boheme.
> *Munich is the most popular meeting place for the Bohemian world.*

> Gibt es viele Künstler hier? — Nein, **die meisten** gehen nach München.
> *Are there many artists here? — No, most of them go to Munich.*

  b. As an Adverb: The superlative used as an adverb has a special form, **am ... (e) sten.**

> Sie gehen **am liebsten** dorthin.
> *They like best to go there.*

> **Am besten** rufe ich Karl an.
> *The best thing to do is call Karl.*

c. As a Predicate Adjective: The superlative as a predicate adjective can be used either with the definite article or the **am ... (e)sten** form.

> Von allen Dirigenten ist er **der beste.**
>
> *or:* Von allen Dirigenten ist er **am besten.**
> *Of all the conductors he is the best (one).*
>
> Das wäre wohl **das einfachste.**
>
> *or:* Das wäre wohl **am einfachsten.**
> *That would probably be the simplest thing.*

C. Special Constructions and Uses

1. **so . . . wie** AND **als:** When making comparisons with the positive form of an adjective or adverb, **so . . . wie** is used.

> Dort gibt es fast **so** viele Künstler **wie** in Paris.
> *There are almost **as** many artists there **as** in Paris.*
>
> Die Künstlertypen hier sehen genau**so** aus **wie** ihre amerikanischen Kollegen.
> *The artist-types here look exactly **like** their American counterparts.*

When making comparisons using the comparative form of an adjective or abverb, **als** is used.

> Der Betrieb hier ist größer **als** vor einigen Jahren.
> *There is more going on here **than** there was a few years ago.*
>
> Die Bayern sind größere Lokalpatrioten **als** die anderen Deutschen.
> *The Bavarians are bigger "boosters" of their region **than** the other Germans.*

2. DOUBLE COMPARATIVE: **Immer** before a comparative forms a double comparative.

> Die Kunst wird **immer internationaler.**
> *Art is getting **more and more international.***
>
> Die Stadt wird **immer größer.**
> *The city is getting **bigger and bigger.***

3. COMPARATIVE IN A POSITIVE MEANING: Like English, German can use a comparative in a positive meaning:

> Er war **ein älterer Herr.**
> *He was **an older (elderly) gentleman.***

This form is sometimes rendered in English by using *rather* or *somewhat:*

Gerd und Tom bleiben **längere Zeit** in München.
*Gerd and Tom are staying in Munich **for a rather long (somewhat longer) time.***

Word Study and Usage

I. SPECIAL USE OF PREPOSITION *VOR*

The preposition **vor** used in an expression of time means *ago;* **vor** then governs the dative case.

Ich habe ihn **vor einem Jahr** gesehen.
*I saw him **a year ago.***
Der Betrieb hier ist größer als **vor einigen Jahren.**
*There is more going on here than there was **a few years ago.***

II. *DORT* AND *DORTHIN*

As with **wo** and **wohin,** the difference between **dort** and **dorthin** is a matter of stationary position and change of location.

Die Künstler **sind** am liebsten **dort,** wo die Kunst zur Tradition gehört.
Artists like best to be where art is part of the tradition.

Die Künstler **gehen** am liebsten **dorthin,** wo die Kunst zur Tradition gehört.
Artists like best to go where art is part of the tradition.

Class Drills

I. *Restate each of the following sentences, substituting the comparative form of the given adjectives or adverbs:*

1. Das wäre einfacher.
   (schön)
   (interessant)
   (schwer)
   (verständlich)

        (warm)
        (kurz)
        (gut)
        (groß)

2. Er fährt schneller.
        (schlecht)
        (weit)
        (lange)
        (gut)
        (gern)

3. Das ist der schönere Teil der Stadt.
        (interessant)
        (neu)
        (elegant)
        (modern)
        (schlecht)
        (alt)
        (gut)

II. Restate each of the following sentences, substituting the superlative form of the given adjectives or adverbs:

1. Das ist das modernste Gebäude der Stadt.
        (neu)
        (schön)
        (interessant)
        (bekannt)
        (groß)
        (alt)

2. Die bekanntesten Künstler sind hier.
        (interessant)
        (berühmt)
        (begabt)
        (jung)
        (alt)
        (viel)
        (groß)

3. Das wäre am einfachsten.
        (schnell)
        (schön)
        (interessant)
        (leicht)
        (gut)

4. Er fährt am schnellsten.
(schlecht)
(weit)
(lang)
(gut)
(gern)

III. Answer the following questions with a positive comparison:

EXAMPLE: **Ist er *größer als* sie?**
Nein, er ist *so groß wie* sie.

Ist er intelligenter als sie?
Ist er begabter als sie?
Ist er bekannter als sie?
Ist er älter als sie?
Ist er größer als sie?

IV. Answer the following questions with a comparative:

EXAMPLE: **Ist er *so groß wie* sie?**
Nein, er ist *größer als* sie.

Ist er so intelligent wie sie?
Ist er so bekannt wie sie?
Ist er so begabt wie sie?
Ist er so alt wie sie?
Ist er so groß wie sie?

V. Restate the following sentences, using the double comparative form in place of the original adjective or adverb:

EXAMPLE: **Das Wetter wird *schlecht*.**
Das Wetter wird *immer schlechter*.

Die Kunst wird international.
Die Künstler werden zahlreich.
Diese Gebäude sehen schlecht aus.
Er arbeitet viel.
Viele Künstler kommen nach Schwabing.

Exercises

I. Rewrite the following sentences, changing the adjective to (a) *the comparative and* (b) *the superlative:*

1. Sind die Bayern wirklich große Lokalpatrioten? 2. Er glaubt, daß er großes Talent hat. 3. Er ist ein bekannter Schauspieler. 4. Sie sind durch die kleinen Dörfer gefahren. 5. Wäre das nicht einfach? 6. Viele Musiker gingen nach Wien. 7. Er spielt gut Klavier. 8. Wir blieben lange in Frankfurt. 9. Die Amerikaner kommen gern nach München. 10. Diese Vorstellung hat mir gut gefallen.

II. Rewrite the following sentences, using two forms of the superlative:

EXAMPLE: **Dieses Haus ist *alt*.**
Dieses Haus ist *das älteste*.
Dieses Haus ist *am ältesten*.

1. Dieses Gebäude ist bekannt. 2. Diese Straße ist eng. 3. Dieser Sessel ist schön. 4. Diese Stadt ist berühmt. 5. Dieser Maler ist begabt. 6. Dieses Dorf ist klein.

III. Translate into English. In sentences 1–5, reproduce the German sentences from your English translations:

1. Es wäre wohl am einfachsten, mit dem Taxi hinzufahren. 2. Mir hat der Sketch besser gefallen als ihr. 3. Ein kleinerer Wagen ist oft besser als ein größerer. 4. Die meisten amerikanischen Studenten möchten am liebsten in München studieren. 5. Das gefällt mir nicht besonders; haben Sie nichts Moderneres? 6. Er gehörte zu den berühmtesten Musikern seiner Zeit. 7. Selbst bei kältestem Wetter ist er am Rhein entlang spaziert. 8. Es wurde immer dunkler; endlich bemerkte sie, daß sie sich verlaufen hatte. 9. Vor drei Tagen hast du schlechter ausgesehen. 10. Es ist nun mal Mode, amerikanische Ausdrücke zu gebrauchen.

IV. Translate:

1. What do you like most? 2. I prefer to go there by taxi. 3. He speaks exactly like his cousin, only faster. 4. A year ago she bought the most modern house in the artists' quarter. 5. I found this lecture more strenuous than the seminar. 6. His political jokes are getting more and more daring. 7. I invited him to visit me later. 8. Why

didn't you come sooner?   9. Two days ago I went to (*in*) his studio, but he wasn't there.   10. Many artists prefer to go to Paris (rather) than to Munich.

V. Composition. Write ten sentences in the form of a composition on this topic — „In München." For each sentence, use the words given below:

1. Tom und Gerd   sich ansehen   „Haus der Kunst"
2. dann   Künstlerviertel
3. Karl   einladen   ihn   besuchen
4. Künstlerviertel   Schwabing   heißen
5. manche Leute   der deutsche Montmartre
6. Tom und Gerd   sich unterhalten   Künstler
7. Künstlertypen   Tom   erinnern an
8. Kunst   international   denn   viele Leute   schöpferisches Talent
9. deswegen   Betrieb
10. schwer   Weg   finden   deswegen   sich verlaufen

Active Vocabulary

an-rufen, rief . . . an, hat angerufen	to call (on the telephone)	der Kollege, –n, –n	colleague, counterpart
das Atelier, –s, –s	studio	die Kunst, –, ⸚e	art
der Bayer, –n, –n	Bavarian	der Künstler, –s, –	artist
bayrisch	Bavarian	der Künstlertyp, –s, –en	artist-type
der Betrieb, –s	bustle, activity	der Lokalpatriot, –en, –en	"booster" of one's region
der Bildhauer, –s, –	sculptor	der Maler, –s, –	painter
die Boheme, –	the Bohemian world, Bohemia	die Mode, –, –n	fashion
deswegen	for that reason, therefore	nämlich	namely, you know
		nannte	called
eigen	own	*from* nennen	to call
einheimisch	native	der Reiz, –es, –e	charm, attraction
der Einwohner, –s, –	inhabitant	schade!	too bad!
		der Schauspieler, –s, –	actor
eng	narrow	schöpferisch	creative
die Galerie, –, –n	(art) gallery	der Stadtteil, –s, –e	section of a city
die Gasse, –, –n	street, alley	stehen-bleiben, blieb . . . stehen, ist stehengeblieben	to stop
die Hälfte, –, –n	half		
hin-fahren, fuhr . . . hin, ist hingefahren, fährt . . . hin	to go there, drive there	das Talent, –s, –e	talent
		das Taxi, –s, –s	taxi

der Treffpunkt, –s, –e	meeting place	**der Vetter, –s, –n**	cousin (*m.*)
		wandern	to walk, stroll
sich (*acc.***) verlaufen, verlief, hat verlaufen, verläuft**	to lose one's way	**wäre**	would be
		from **sein**	to be
		wohl	probably
		wunderbar	wonderful
		zahlreich	numerous

Achtzehnte Lektion

Nach Wien

[*Gerd und Tom kommen außer Atem auf dem Münchner Hauptbahnhof an.*]

GERD — Warum sind wir nur so gerannt? Wir haben ja noch zehn Minuten. Siehst du irgendwo unseren Fahrkartenschalter?

TOM — Dort steht „Balkan Expreß", das wird wohl unser Zug sein.

GERD — Ja, das ist er. Da müssen wir auch noch Schlange stehen!

TOM — Es wird nicht lange dauern. [*Sie stellen sich an.*] Balkan Expreß, das klingt wie der Titel eines Kriminalromans.

GERD — Liest du gern Krimis?

TOM — Wenn sie psychologisch gut motiviert sind.

GERD — Ich wußte gar nicht, daß du dich für Psychologie interessierst.

TOM — Eigentlich nur bei Krimis. Hast du welche zu Hause?

GERD — Ein paar. In Wien wirst du ja Onkel Max kennenlernen. Er hat eine richtige Leihbücherei. [*Greift in die Tasche.*] Sag mal, hast *du* den Stadtplan von Wien mitgebracht?

TOM — Ja, er ist im Koffer bei den Büchern.

GERD — Gut, daß du daran gedacht hast. Sonst verirren wir uns dort wie in München.

TOM — Siehst du, wir sind schon an der Reihe. Den Zug verpassen wir bestimmt nicht.

On the Way to Vienna

[*Gerd and Tom arrive out of breath at the main railroad station in Munich.*]

GERD — Why did we run like that? We still have ten minutes. Do you see our ticket window anywhere?

TOM — Over there it says "Balkan Express." That's probably our train.

GERD — Yes, that's it. And we have to wait in line there!

TOM — It won't take long. [*They get in line.*] Balkan Express — that sounds like the title of a mystery novel.

GERD — Do you like whodunits?

TOM — Yes, when they're psychologically well motivated.

GERD — I didn't know that you're interested in psychology.

TOM — Only in mysteries, really. Do you have any at home?

GERD — A few. In Vienna you'll meet Uncle Max. He has a regular lending library. [*Reaches into his pocket.*] Say, did *you* bring the map of Vienna along?

TOM — Yes, it's in the suitcase with the books.

GERD — It's a good thing you thought of it. Otherwise we'd get lost there the way we did in Munich.

TOM — You see — we're next in line. We definitely won't miss the train.

Lesestück XVIII

Auf der Reise nach Wien unterhielten sich die Freunde über dieses und jenes. Es war ganz natürlich, daß sie auch auf Sigmund Freud zu sprechen kamen, denn Freud verbrachte den größten Teil seines Lebens in Wien. Tom fragte sich, was er von den Werken des großen Wissenschaftlers[1] gelesen hatte. Psychologie war nicht sein Hauptfach, aber er kannte zwei der bekann- 5 teren Werke: „Das Unbehagen in der Kultur"[2] und „Totem und Tabu". Er wandte[3] sich an Gerd, und dieser nannte noch andere Titel, besonders die fundamentale „Traumdeutung".[4] Dann sprachen sie über den enormen Ein- fluß Freuds auf das moderne Denken und die moderne Literatur. Wörter wie „Sublimierung", „Frustration", „Fehlleistung",[5] „Libido", „Ich, Es, 10 Über-Ich"[6] sind allen gebildeten[7] Menschen heute bekannt. Nach Freuds Theorie verdrängt[8] der Mensch Erlebnisse,[9] besonders Kindheitserlebnisse, ins Unterbewußtsein.[10] Sie bilden dort Komplexe mit eigener Dynamik und Symbolik. Sie kommen zum Ausdruck in Bildern,[11] vor allem in Traum- bildern. Natürlich ist die Forschung[12] seit Freuds Zeit nicht stehengeblieben, 15 und keiner weiß, was die Zukunft[13] auf diesem Gebiet noch bringen wird. Diese Wissenschaft[14] steht erst am Anfang, und das unbekannte Terrain ist viel größer als das bekannte. Freud aber hat durch seine Theorien über die Bedeutung[15] des Traums, des Sexuellen und des Unterbewußtseins Pionier- arbeit geleistet.[16] 20

Tom freut sich auf[17] die nächsten Tage. Wieviel Neues und Interessantes werden sie bringen? Wird er etwas von dem Glanz[18] der alten Kaiserstadt spüren?[19] Er muß an einen Bekannten denken, dem Wien nicht gefiel, weil die Stadt seiner Meinung nach[20] nur noch von ihrer Vergangenheit[21] lebte. Die nächsten Tage brachten die Antwort. Die Freunde besuchten die vielen 25 Sehenswürdigkeiten,[22] den Stephansdom,[23] den Prater,[24] die Kaffeehäuser, und besonders gern waren sie an den historischen Stätten, die an einige der größten Musiker erinnern: Gluck, Haydn, Mozart, Beethoven, Schubert und,

---

[1] **der Wissenschaftler, –s, –** scholar, learned man, scientist
[2] **„Das Unbehagen in der Kultur"** *Civilization and Its Discontents*
[3] **sich wenden an, wandte, hat gewandt** to turn to
[4] **„Traumdeutung"** *The Interpretation of Dreams*
[5] **die Fehlleistung, –, –en** (Freudian) slip
[6] **Ich, Es, Über-Ich** Ego, Id, Superego
[7] **gebildet** educated
[8] **verdrängen** to suppress
[9] **das Erlebnis, –ses, –se** experience
[10] **das Unterbewußtsein, –s** subconscious
[11] **das Bild, –(e)s, –er** *here* image

[12] **die Forschung, –** research
[13] **die Zukunft, –** future
[14] **die Wissenschaft, –, –en** science
[15] **die Bedeutung, –, –en** meaning, significance
[16] **leisten** to accomplish, render
[17] **sich freuen auf** to look forward to
[18] **der Glanz, –es** splendor
[19] **spüren** to feel, sense
[20] **seiner Meinung nach** according to his opin- ion
[21] **die Vergangenheit, –** past
[22] **die Sehenswürdigkeit, –, –en** sight, place of interest
[23] **der Stephansdom, –s** St. Stephen's Cathedral
[24] **der Prater, –s** famous park in Vienna

Der Walzerkönig Johann Strauß

nicht zu vergessen, der „Walzerkönig"[25] Johann Strauß waren in Wien zu Hause oder hatten hier eine zweite Heimat gefunden. Tom Evans hatte 30 dasselbe Erlebnis wie viele andere Besucher Wiens vor ihm: er verliebte sich in[26] die Stadt, und es fiel ihm schwer, Wien so bald wieder zu verlassen.

[25] **der „Walzerkönig", –s** "King of the Waltz"   [26] **sich verlieben in** to fall in love with

Fragen und Antworten

1. Warum rannten Gerd und Tom so?
   Sie werden wohl nicht gewußt haben, wieviel Uhr es war.
2. Werden die beiden den Zug verpassen?
   Nein, sie haben genug (*enough*) Zeit.
3. Wen kannte Tom noch nicht?
   Den Wiener Onkel kannte er noch nicht.
4. Wofür interessiert sich Tom?
   Er interessiert sich für einen guten Krimi.
5. Wie hat Gerd die Bibliothek (*library*) seines Onkels genannt?
   Er nannte sie eine Leihbücherei.
6. Wer hatte nicht an den Stadtplan gedacht?
   Gerd hatte nicht daran gedacht.
7. Wer dachte an den Stadtplan und brachte ihn mit?
   Tom dachte daran und brachte ihn mit.
8. Wo stellten Tom und Gerd sich an?
   Sie stellten sich am Fahrkartenschalter an.
9. Wer lebte lange in Wien?
   Freud verbrachte dort den größten Teil seines Lebens.
10. Worauf freut sich Tom?
    Er freut sich auf die Kaiserstadt Wien.

Structure and Practice

Explanation of Forms

I. IRREGULAR WEAK VERBS

There is a small group of German verbs that have a stem change in the past tense and past participle but otherwise follow the pattern of weak verbs in the formation of all the tenses. They are called irregular weak verbs. Following is the basic list of these verbs with their principal parts.

INFINITIVE	PAST	PAST PARTICIPLE	ENGLISH
bringen	brachte	hat gebracht	to bring
denken	dachte	hat gedacht	to think
brennen	brannte	hat gebrannt	to burn
kennen	kannte	hat gekannt	to know
nennen	nannte	hat genannt	to name, mention
rennen	rannte	*ist* gerannt	to run
senden	sandte	hat gesandt	to send
wenden	wandte	hat gewandt	to turn
*wissen	wußte	hat gewußt	to know

* In this group only **wissen** has an irregular present tense (see Lesson 3).

In addition to the basic forms listed above, most of these verbs can have various separable and inseparable prefixes on them, which give them different meanings:

mit-bringen	brachte ... mit	hat mitgebracht	to bring along
verbringen	verbrachte	hat verbracht	to spend (time)

II. FUTURE TENSE

A. Formation

Both English and German form the future tense by the use of an auxiliary. English uses *will* or *shall* as the auxiliary (*I shall go, he will go,* etc.); German uses the present tense of **werden** with the dependent infinitive. The infinitive is placed at the end of an independent clause; in dependent clauses the auxiliary is last and the infinitive just before it.

Ich **werde** ihn in Wien **kennenlernen.** *I shall get to know him in Vienna.*

Du **wirst** ihn in Wien **kennenlernen.** *You will get to know him in Vienna.*

Er, sie, es **wird** ihn in Wien **kennenlernen.** *He . . .* etc.
Wir **werden** ihn in Wien **kennenlernen.**
Ihr **werdet** ihn in Wien **kennenlernen.**
Sie **werden** ihn in Wien **kennenlernen.**
Sie (*you*) **werden** ihn in Wien **kennenlernen.**

Since **werden** is also used as an independent verb (meaning *to become*), it is important to note whether it is used by itself or as an auxiliary before determining its meaning.

B. *Use*

In German the future tense is used much less frequently than in English. German tends to use the present tense instead whenever the future time is otherwise clear from the context, and especially if there is an adverbial element indicating future time in the sentence.

> Nach der Vorlesung kaufe ich mir Aspirin.
> *I'll buy some aspirin after class.*
>
> Dann gehen wir zusammen hin.
> *Then we'll go over there together.*

The future tense with **wohl** or **schon** is occasionally used to indicate probability in present time.

> Das **wird wohl** unser Zug **sein.**
> *That is probably our train.*

III. *FUTURE PERFECT TENSE*

A. *Formation*

Future: Ich **werde** ihn **sehen.**
I shall see him.

Future Perfect: Ich **werde** ihn **gesehen haben.**
I shall have seen him.

Like the future tense, the future perfect uses the present tense of **werden** as the auxiliary. The difference between the formation of the future and the future perfect in both English and German is that the future tense uses the present infinitive of the dependent verb (**sehen** — *to see* in the example above), whereas the future perfect uses the perfect infinitive, that is, the past participle and the infinitive of the perfect tense auxiliary (**gesehen haben** — *have seen* in the example above).

> Ich **werde** ihn **gesehen haben.** *I shall have seen him.*
> Du **wirst** ihn **gesehen haben.** *You will have seen him.*
> Er, sie, es **wird** ihn **gesehen haben.** *He . . .* etc.
> Wir **werden** ihn **gesehen haben.**
> Ihr **werdet** ihn **gesehen haben.**
> Sie **werden** ihn **gesehen haben.**
> Sie (*you*) **werden** ihn **gesehen haben.**

> Ich **werde** dann **gegangen sein.** *I shall have gone then.*
> Du **wirst** dann **gegangen sein.** *You will have gone then.*
> Er, sie, es **wird** dann **gegangen sein.** *He . . .* etc.

Wir **werden** dann **gegangen sein.**
Ihr **werdet** dann **gegangen sein.**
Sie **werden** dann **gegangen sein.**
Sie (*you*) **werden** dann **gegangen sein.**

B. Use

The future perfect tense is rarely used to express future time. Its main use is to express probability in past time. **Wohl** or **schon** is then part of the construction.

Sie **werden wohl** nicht **gewußt haben,** wieviel Uhr es war.
*They **probably didn't know** what time it was.*

Word Study and Usage

I. IRGEND-

Irgend- (*some . . . or other*) can be used as a prefix to form a number of combinations. The most common of these are:

irgendwo (somewhere or other)
irgendwie (somehow or other)
irgendwann (sometime or other)

II. PAST PARTICIPLE AS ADJECTIVE

Past participles can be used as adjectives. Like other adjectives, they are uninflected when used as predicate adjectives, but get adjective endings when used attributively.

Ich lese gern Krimis, wenn sie gut **motiviert** sind. (**motivieren —** *to motivate*)
I like to read detective stories if they are well motivated.
Ich bin vollkommen **erschöpft.** (**erschöpfen —** *to exhaust*)
I am completely exhausted.
Er war ein ganz **vergessener** Dichter. (**vergessen —** *to forget*)
He was a completely forgotten poet.

Class Drills

I. a. Restate the following sentences in the simple past tense:

1. Ich kenne ihn nicht.
   Ich nenne das eine Leihbücherei.

Ich denke nicht daran.
Ich bringe den Stadtplan mit.
Ich weiß das nicht.

2. Er rennt immer.
Er kennt den Wiener Onkel nicht.
Er nennt ihn einen Lokalpatrioten.
Er denkt an den Stadtplan.
Er bringt uns etwas mit.
Er weiß das nicht.

3. Wir kennen den Professor nicht.
Wir nennen ihn Tom.
Wir denken oft an ihn.
Wir bringen unseren Onkel mit.
Wir wissen das nicht.

4. Sie rennen immer so.
Sie nennen das eine Skandalgeschichte.
Sie kennen uns nicht.
Sie denken nicht daran.
Sie bringen das Kind mit.
Sie wissen das nicht.

b. Restate the sentences in exercise a. in the present perfect tense.

II. Restate the following sentences in the future tense:

1. Ich verpasse den Zug nicht.
Ich besuche ihn oft.
Ich komme in Wien an.
Ich fahre in München ab.

2. Er kauft sich Aspirin.
Er bekommt Kopfschmerzen.
Er macht alles mit.
Er fährt mit dem Taxi hin.

3. Wir werden alle alt.
Wir rufen Karl an.
Wir machen das Geschäft zu.
Wir kommen ein Stück mit.

4. Sie gehen zum Zahnarzt.
Sie trinken Kaffee.
Sie besuchen das Goethehaus.
Sie holen die Bilder ab.

III. Restate the following sentences, beginning each with <u>Ich weiß,</u> <u>daß</u> . . . :

EXAMPLE: **Er *wird* Kopfschmerzen *bekommen.***
Ich weiß, *daß* er Kopfschmerzen *bekommen wird.*

Er wird sich Aspirin kaufen.
Er wird in Wien ankommen.
Wir werden in München abfahren.
Wir werden den Zug verpassen.
Sie werden das Goethehaus besuchen.
Sie werden ihn oft sehen.
Ich werde Kopfschmerzen bekommen.
Ich werde den Zug verpassen.

IV. Restate the following sentences as past probability, using the future perfect tense:

Er wird es wohl wissen.
Sie werden es wohl mitbringen.
Er wird wohl daran denken.
Er wird ihn wohl kennen.
Sie werden wohl zu Hause sein.
Sie werden wohl dort bleiben.

V. Restate each of the following sentences, substituting the past participle of the new verbs:

1. Alles war schon geschrieben.
          (verlieren)
          (schließen)
          (kochen)
          (bestellen)
          (wiederaufbauen)
          (ausverkaufen)

2. Er war ein verlorener Mann.
          (vergessen)
          (erfahren)

3. Das war eine gut erzählte Geschichte.
          (motivieren)
          (schreiben)

Exercises

I. Rewrite the following sentences in the (a) *simple past and* (b) *present perfect tense:*

1. Woran denken Sie? 2. Er verbringt drei Tage in München. 3. Kennen Sie diesen Studenten? 4. Man nennt ihn einen Pseudokünstler. 5. Er bringt ihr immer etwas Schönes mit. 6. Sie rennen auf den Bahnhof. 7. Das ganze Gebäude brennt. 8. Man sendet den besten Journalisten nach Bonn. 9. Ich weiß das wirklich nicht. 10. Sie wissen nichts davon.

II. Rewrite the following sentences in the future tense:

1. In dieser Stadt verläuft er sich sicher. 2. Er bringt seinen spanischen Freund mit. 3. Sie wartet bis acht Uhr auf dem Flugplatz. 4. Ich frage ihn, ob er die Bilder abholt. 5. Er tut es, weil er viel Geld hat.

III. Rewrite the following sentences in the present tense:

1. Er verlor alles. 2. Sie verstand ihn nicht. 3. Sie haben ihr immer geholfen. 4. Ich fing wieder von vorne an. 5. Wir unterhielten uns darüber. 6. Sie sind nicht lange dort geblieben. 7. Er fuhr bald zurück. 8. Ich habe an der Tour teilgenommen. 9. Sie hat nie etwas getan. 10. Wir sind ins Konzert gegangen. 11. Ich habe gut geschlafen. 12. So hieß es in der Zeitung. 13. Er traf sie vor der Mensa. 14. Sie hat den ganzen Tag gelesen. 15. Wir haben gern im Café gesessen.

IV. Translate into English. In sentences 1–5, reproduce the German sentences from your English translations:

1. Es wird ihm schwer fallen, in allen Vorlesungen mitzukommen. 2. Hoffentlich wird sie sich in München nicht verirren. 3. Am besten rufen Sie mich um acht Uhr zu Hause an. 4. Nach einigen Jahren wird er der beliebteste Dirigent sein. 5. Er wird ihr irgendwie helfen. 6. Ich weiß nicht, an welchem Schalter ich mich anstellen soll. 7. Warum stehen die Leute hier Schlange? Dort steht doch: „Alle Plätze ausverkauft." 8. Ich habe euch nicht verstanden; wie habt ihr das genannt? 9. Warten wir, bis es kühler geworden ist, dann gehen wir zusammen hin. 10. Den größten Teil des Tages wird er wohl in der Bibliothek verbracht haben.

V. Translate:

1. We waited in line. (*simple past*)   2. I won't have time because I want to read a mystery.   3. He had the book in his pocket.   4. I didn't know who she was.   5. We are looking forward to your visit. 6. It will get better soon.   7. I didn't bring the book along because I didn't think of it.   8. He brought his German friend along. (*simple past*)   9. Who's next?   10. They had read it somewhere or other.

VI. Composition. Write ten sentences in the form of a composition on this topic — „Auf dem Münchner Bahnhof." For each sentence, use the words given below:

1. Tom und Gerd   rennen   Bahnhof   aber   genug Zeit
2. sich anstellen   Fahrkartenschalter
3. wollen   verbringen   Tage   Wien
4. Tom   sich freuen auf
5. Tom   gefallen   Name   Zug
6. Balkan Expreß   erinnern an
7. Tom   gern   Krimi
8. Gerds Onkel   auch   sich interessieren   Kriminalroman
9. Wien   Tom   werden   tagsüber   Besichtigungstour   abends   Krimi
10. Tom und Gerd   Wien   nicht verirren   weil   Stadtplan

Active Vocabulary

sich an-stellen	to get in line	**sich freuen auf**	to look forward to
der Atem, –s	breath	(+ *acc.*)	
außer Atem	out of breath	**genug**	enough
der Bahnhof,	railroad station	**greifen, griff,**	to reach
–s, ∸e		**hat ge-**	
die Bibliothek, –,	library	**griffen**	
–en		**der Hauptbahn-**	main railroad station
brennen,	to burn	**hof, –s, ∸e**	
brannte,		**sich interessieren**	to be interested in
hat ge-		**für**	
brannt		**irgendwann**	sometime or other
das Buch, –(e)s,	book	**irgendwie**	somehow or other
∸er		**irgendwo**	anywhere
die Fahrkarte, –,	ticket (railroad, bus,	**kennen-lernen**	to get to know
–n	etc.)	**klingen, klang,**	to sound
der Fahrkarten-	ticket window	**hat ge-**	
schalter, –s, –		**klungen**	
sich freuen	to be happy	**der Koffer, –s, –**	suitcase
		der Krimi, –s, –s	mystery story, crime

= der Kriminal-roman, –s, –e	novel, detective story
die Leihbücherei, –, –en	lending library
mit-bringen, brachte . . . mit, hat mitgebracht	to bring along
motivieren	to motivate
der Onkel, –s, –	uncle
ein paar	a few
die Psychologie, –	psychology
psychologisch	psychological
die Reihe, –, –n	series, number, line
an der Reihe sein	to be next
rennen, rannte, ist gerannt	to run
der Roman, –s, –e	novel
der Schalter, –s, –	counter
Schlange stehen	to stand in line
senden, sandte, hat gesandt	to send
der Stadtplan, –s, ⸚e	city map
stehen, stand, hat ge-standen	to say (in print)
die Tasche, –, –n	pocket
der Titel, –s, –	title
verbringen, verbrachte, hat ver-bracht	to spend (time)
sich verirren	to lose one's way
verpassen	to miss
welche	some, any
wenden, wandte, hat gewandt	to turn

Neunzehnte Lektion

„Der Hauptmann von Köpenick"

[*Tom und Gerd waren stundenlang durch Berlin spaziert und sind dann ins Kino gegangen, um sich auszuruhen. Sie haben den „Hauptmann von Köpenick" gesehen.*]

TOM — Das war ein Film nach meinem Geschmack! Der hat mir gefallen! Wer war der Schauspieler, der die Hauptrolle gespielt hat?

GERD — Heinz Rühmann. Ein ausgezeichneter Komiker. Ich sehe ihn gern spielen. Das war aber auch eine Rolle, in der er sich selbst übertroffen hat. In diesem Film war ich nun schon dreimal, und er ist immer noch amüsant.

TOM — Ich bin froh, daß wir uns haben ausruhen müssen; da habe ich endlich mal einen guten deutschen Nachkriegsfilm sehen können.

GERD — Leider zeigt man zu viele sentimentale Heimatfilme und Wildwestreißer.

TOM — Es gibt ja erstaunlich viele ausländische Filme hier. Und alle synchronisiert. Ich muß immer lachen, wenn ein amerikanischer Star deutsch spricht, Liz Taylor zum Beispiel.

GERD — Das kann ich mir denken. Mir würde der „Hauptmann von Köpenick" auf englisch auch komisch vorkommen. — Sollen wir noch schnell ein Glas Bier trinken?

TOM — Gute Idee, ich habe furchtbaren Durst.

The Captain of Köpenick

[*Gerd and Tom had been walking around through Berlin for hours and then went to the movies to rest. They saw* The Captain of Köpenick.]

TOM — That was my kind of movie. I enjoyed that. Who was the actor that played the leading role?

GERD — Heinz Rühmann. An excellent comedian. I like to see him perform. But in that role he really outdid himself. I've been to this movie three times, and it's still funny.

TOM — I'm glad we had to take a rest. That way I finally got to see a good postwar German movie.

GERD — Unfortunately, they show too many sentimental *Heimat*[1]-movies and Grade B Westerns.

TOM — There certainly are an awful lot of foreign films here. And all of them are dubbed. I always have to laugh when an American movie star speaks German — Liz Taylor, for example.

GERD — I can imagine. *Der Hauptmann von Köpenick* in English would seem funny to me, too. How about a quick glass of beer?

TOM — Good idea. I'm terribly thirsty.

---

[1] **Heimatfilme** — *regional movies.* These are movies that have a particular regional country setting and trivial themes.

Berlin

Lesestück XIX

Leider hat Gerd recht mit seiner Kritik am deutschen Film nach 1945. Es gibt zwar einige gute Filme, aber meistens können die Filmfreunde in Deutschland nur Durchschnittsware[1] sehen, was besonders schmerzt,[2] da die ältere Generation auf eine große Zeit auf diesem Gebiet zurückblicken kann. „Der blaue Engel",[3] „Das Cabinett des Dr. Caligari", „M", aus den zwanziger 5 Jahren, sind Filme, die man heute noch zeigt.

„Der Hauptmann von Köpenick", den Tom sich hat ansehen können, und der ihm so gut gefallen hat, war zuerst ein Drama, in dem der Autor, Carl Zuckmayer, einige Schwächen des Wilhelminischen Deutschlands angreift:[4] die Autoritätsgläubigkeit[5] des Bürgers und den komischen Respekt vor der 10 Militäruniform. Zuckmayer verdankt die Handlung[6] einer wahren Episode. Damals, im Jahre 1906, hatte die ganze Welt über den Schuster[7] Wilhelm Voigt lachen können, der sich über den Uniformenkult des Kaiserdeutschlands lustig machte.

Voigt ist ein armer Mensch, der ein Opfer[8] der Bürokratie geworden ist. 15 Als junger Mann schon landete er im Gefängnis. Nun, nach 20 Jahren, ist er endlich wieder ein freier[9] Mann, aber der Staat[10] will ihn nicht haben und gibt ihm keine Arbeitserlaubnis.[11] Und das ist etwas, was jeder braucht: wer keine „Arbeitserlaubnis" hat, bekommt keine „Aufenthaltsgenehmigung",[12] und wer keine „Aufenthaltsgenehmigung" hat, bekommt keine „Arbeitser- 20 laubnis". Man gibt ihm nicht einmal[13] einen Paß,[14] mit dem er dieses büro-kratische Land verlassen könnte. Nun denkt er sich jenen Streich[15] aus,[16] der ihn so berühmt gemacht hat. Er will sich selbst einen Paß besorgen.[17] Also kauft er sich eine alte Offiziersuniform, hält[18] als falscher Hauptmann eine Gruppe Soldaten auf der Straße an[18] und befiehlt[19] ihnen, in Köpenick, 25 einem Vorort[20] von Berlin, das Rathaus zu besetzen.[21] Alle gehorchen[22] ihm, die Soldaten, der Bürgermeister,[23] die Polizisten.[24] Und warum? Wegen der

---

[1] **die Durchschnittsware, –, –n** mediocre product
[2] **schmerzen** to hurt
[3] **„Der blaue Engel"** *The Blue Angel*
[4] **an-greifen, griff . . . an, hat angegriffen** to attack
[5] **die Autoritätsgläubigkeit, –** (blind) faith in the authorities
[6] **die Handlung, –, –en** plot, action
[7] **der Schuster, –s, –** shoemaker
[8] **das Opfer, –s, –** victim
[9] **frei** free
[10] **der Staat, –(e)s, –en** state
[11] **die Arbeitserlaubnis, –** working permit
[12] **die Aufenthaltsgenehmigung, –, –en** permit of residence

[13] **nicht einmal** not even
[14] **der Paß, Passes, Pässe** passport
[15] **der Streich, –(e)s, –e** prank
[16] **sich** (*dat.*) **aus-denken, dachte . . . aus, hat ausgedacht** to think up, contrive, invent
[17] **sich** (*dat.*) **besorgen** to provide oneself with
[18] **an-halten, hielt . . . an, hat angehalten, hält . . . an** to stop
[19] **befehlen, befahl, hat befohlen, befiehlt** to order
[20] **der Vorort, –s, –e** suburb
[21] **besetzen** to occupy
[22] **gehorchen** (*dat.*) to obey
[23] **der Bürgermeister, –s, –** mayor
[24] **der Polizist, –en, –en** policeman

Hauptmannsuniform. Keiner fragt ihn nach einer Legitimation. Alle respektieren die Uniform. Leider hat unser Schuster kein Glück. Das Rathaus von Köpenick hat gar kein Paßamt,[25] und so bekommt er seinen Paß nicht. 30

Zuckmayer gibt seiner Zeitsatire ein mildes Ende. Voigt geht selbst zum Polizeipräsidenten von Berlin und erzählt ihm die ganze Geschichte. Dieser und sein Stab[26] amüsieren sich sehr darüber, ohne zu merken,[27] daß sie über sich selbst lachen. Sie bewirten[28] ihn mit Rotwein und einem Wurstbrot[29] und geben ihm endlich sogar einen Paß. 35

[25] **das Paßamt, –s, ⁓er** passport office
[26] **der Stab, –(e)s, ⁓e** staff
[27] **merken** to realize, notice

[28] **bewirten** to treat
[29] **das Wurstbrot, –s, –e** cold-cut sandwich

Fragen und Antworten

1. Warum waren Tom und Gerd ins Kino gegangen?
   Sie hatten sich ausruhen müssen.
2. Hat Tom der „Hauptmann von Köpenick" gefallen?
   Ja, das war ein Film, der ihm gefallen hat.
3. Wer hat die Hauptrolle gespielt?
   Heinz Rühmann, den Gerd großartig findet.
4. Wer ist Heinz Rühmann?
   Ein Komiker, dessen Namen jeder Deutsche kennt.
5. Hat Gerd diesen Schauspieler schon oft spielen sehen?
   Ja, den hat er schon oft gesehen.
6. Warum hat Tom in einem synchronisierten Film lachen müssen?
   Er hat Liz Taylor deutsch sprechen hören.
7. Warum hat Tom auch ein Glas Bier gewollt?
   Er hat etwas trinken wollen, weil er Durst hatte.
8. Was für Filme gibt es in Deutschland?
   Es gibt viele ausländische Filme, was Tom erstaunlich findet.
9. Warum hat man Voigt nicht arbeiten lassen?
   Weil er keine Arbeitserlaubnis hatte.
10. Warum wollte Voigt das Rathaus besetzen?
    Um sich einen Paß zu besorgen.

Structure and Practice

Explanation of Forms

I. RELATIVE PRONOUNS

A relative pronoun generally refers back to a noun or pronoun (its antecedent) in a preceding clause. (English: *the man **who** . . . ; the film **that** . . . ; he is the one **whose** name . . . etc.*)

A. Forms

The forms of the relative pronoun for both persons and things are identical with the definite article, except in the genitive case and the dative plural. The following paradigm shows these exceptions in boldface. Notice that the boldface forms, although they are not identical with the definite articles, resemble them closely.

	MASCULINE	FEMININE	NEUTER	PLURAL
Nom.:	der	die	das	die
Acc.:	den	die	das	die
Dat.:	dem	der	dem	**denen**
Gen.:	**dessen**	**deren**	**dessen**	**deren**

Note: German has an alternate relative pronoun, **welcher,** which has the same declension as the **der**-word **welcher.** This alternate is occasionally used in written German instead of the above forms for stylistic reasons, that is, if there are too many definite articles in the sentence. The relative pronoun **welcher,** however, cannot be used in the genitive case.

B. Use

Whereas English may occasionally omit the relative pronoun (*The man* [*whom*] *you see there* . . .), German must always express it.

A relative pronoun agrees in gender and number (*sing.* or *pl.*) with its antecedent; its case is determined by its function (subject, verb object, prepositional object, etc.) in the relative clause.

> Wer war **der Schauspieler, der** die Hauptrolle gespielt hat?
> *Who was the actor that played the leading role?*
>
> **Heinz Rühmann, den** Gerd großartig findet, hat die Hauptrolle gespielt.
> *Heinz Rühmann, who Gerd thinks is marvelous, played the leading role.*
>
> Er ist **ein Komiker, dessen** Namen jeder Deutsche kennt.
> *He's a comedian whose name every German knows.*
>
> Das war **eine Rolle, in der** er sich selbst übertroffen hat.
> *That was a role in which he really outdid himself.*

C. Word Order

Relative clauses are dependent clauses and as such are set off by commas and have the inflected verb last.

Das war ein Film, **der ihm gefallen** *hat.*

Heinz Rühmann, **den Gerd großartig** *findet,* hat die Hauptrolle gespielt.

D. *Indefinite Relative Pronoun* <u>was</u>

In addition to the relative pronoun forms described above, German has a so-called indefinite relative pronoun **was,** which *must* be used *only* when the antecedent is one of the following:

(1) An entire clause:

Es gibt viele ausländische Filme, was Tom erstaunlich findet.

There are many foreign movies, which amazes Tom.

(2) An indefinite neuter pronoun such as **etwas, nichts, alles, viel(es), wenig:**

Das ist **etwas, was** jeder braucht.

That's something that everyone needs.

(3) a superlative adjective used as an abstract noun:

Das ist **das Schönste, was** ich mir vorstellen kann.

That is the most beautiful thing that I can imagine.

II. *THE DEMONSTRATIVE PRONOUN DER*

In German the demonstrative pronoun der (**die, das;** *pl.* **die**), which has exactly the same declension as the relative pronoun shown above, is used in place of the personal pronoun er, sie (*she*), es, sie (*they*) for emphasis. Like the relative pronoun, it agrees in number and gender with its antecedent, and its case is determined by its function in its own clause. (In highly colloquial German, the demonstrative is used with less discrimination and frequently carries no particular emphasis.)

In the following groups of sentences, you see the noun in the first sentence replaced, first by a personal pronoun, and then by the demonstrative:

Die Sinfonie hat mir gefallen.	*I liked the symphony.*
Sie hat mir gefallen.	*I liked it.*
Die hat mir gefallen.	*I liked that* (*one*).

Den Schauspieler hat er oft gesehen.	*He has seen the actor often.*
Ihn hat er oft gesehen.	*He has seen him often.*
Den hat er oft gesehen.	*He has seen* <u>him</u> *often.*

Der used as a demonstrative can be distinguished from the relative pronoun by the word order: whereas relative pronouns cause dependent word order (verb last in the clause), demonstratives do not.

Relative Pronoun:

Es war Heinz Rühmann, **den** Gerd großartig **findet.**
It was Heinz Rühmann, who Gerd thinks is marvelous.

Demonstrative Pronoun:

Es war Heinz Rühmann, **den findet** Gerd großartig.
It was Heinz Rühmann. Gerd thinks <u>he</u>'s marvelous.

III. THE DOUBLE INFINITIVE CONSTRUCTION

A. Modal Auxiliaries in the Perfect Tenses

Modal auxiliaries have two past participles; one uses a **ge-** prefix and a **-t** suffix on the same stem used for the simple past tense; the other has the same form as the infinitive.

INFINITIVE	PAST PARTICIPLES	
	I	II
dürfen	**gedurft**	**dürfen**
können	**gekonnt**	**können**
mögen	**gemocht**	**mögen**
müssen	**gemußt**	**müssen**
sollen	**gesollt**	**sollen**
wollen	**gewollt**	**wollen**

You will recall that modals are usually used with a dependent infinitive; sometimes, however, no dependent infinitive is expressed.

Er **will** ein Glas Bier.   Er **will** ein Glas Bier **trinken.**

In the perfect tenses, past participle I is used when there is no dependent infinitive; past participle II is used when there is a dependent infinitive.

Er **hat** ein Glas Bier **gewollt.**   Er **hat** ein Glas Bier **trinken wollen.**

Er **hatte** ein Glas Bier **gewollt.**   Er **hatte** ein Glas Bier **trinken wollen.**

When past participle II is used, the construction is called a double infinitive, although the modal is not a real infinitive but only looks like one.

B. Double Infinitive with Other Verbs

A few verbs besides the modals function the same way, that is, they can be used independently or with a dependent infinitive without **zu**. The most frequent of these are: **sehen, helfen, hören** and **lassen**.

> Ich **sehe** ihn oft.   Ich **sehe** ihn oft **spielen.**
> *I often see him.*   *I often see him perform.*
> Ich **hörte** sie.   Ich **hörte** sie **sprechen.**
> *I heard her.*   *I heard her speak.*

These verbs, like the modals, have two past participles, one of which resembles the infinitive; this is the one used when a dependent infinitive is present.

> Ich **habe** ihn oft **gesehen.**   Ich **habe** ihn oft **spielen sehen.**
> Ich **hatte** sie **gehört.**   Ich **hatte** sie **sprechen hören.**

C. Word Order in Double Infinitive Constructions

As you can see from the examples above, the auxiliary in independent clauses is in normal second position, and the two infinitives are placed at the end of the clause, the one which is actually a past participle, being last.

In dependent clauses, however, the auxiliary is placed before the two infinitives, not at the very end of the clause, where it would ordinarily be.

> Ich bin froh, daß wir uns **haben** ausruhen müssen.

Note: The same word order rules apply in the future tense when the modals and the verbs listed under B are used with a dependent infinitive.

> Er **wird** es **tun müssen.**
> *He will have to do it.*
> Er weiß, daß er es **wird tun müssen.**
> *He knows that he will have to do it.*

Word Study and Usage

I. ADVERBS AND ADJECTIVES

In English the suffix *-ly* is usually added to adjectives to form adverbs; therefore, the two parts of speech are easily distinguished from each other, even out of context: *beautiful, beautifully; real, really.* In German many adjectives function also as adverbs with no change to distinguish one from the other.

> Sie ist schön.   *She is beautiful.*
> Sie singt schön.   *She sings beautifully.*

Adverbs, however, do not have inflectional endings, and they can thus be distinguished from adjectives in attributive position (i.e., before the noun). Notice the contrast in the following pair of sentences:

> Das ist ein **gut** synchronisierter Film.
> *That is a **well**-synchronized movie.*
> Das ist ein **guter** synchronisierter Film.
> *That is a **good** synchronized movie.*

II. THE SUFFIX -LANG

The suffix **-lang** added to the plural of a noun denoting time means *for.* The new form then functions as an adverb and is, therefore, not capitalized.

> **stundenlang** (for [several] hours)
> **tagelang** (for [several] days)
> **nächtelang** (for [several] nights)
> **minutenlang** (for [several] minutes)

III. UM . . . ZU PLUS AN INFINITIVE

Um used with **zu** and an infinitive forms an infinitive phrase meaning *in order to . . .*

> Sie sind ins Kino gegangen, **um** sich auszuruhen.
> *They went to the movies (in order) to rest.*
> Voigt wollte das Rathaus besetzen, **um** sich einen Paß **zu** besorgen.
> *Voigt wanted to occupy the city hall (in order) to get himself a passport.*

Class Drills

I. Restate the following sentences, substituting the new antecedents:

1. Das war der Film, der uns gefallen hat.
   Ausflug
   Krimi
   Roman

2. Das war die Vorstellung, die uns gefallen hat.
> Feier
> Geschichte
> Vorlesung

3. Das war das Fest, das uns gefallen hat.
> Konzert
> Programm
> Buch

(*Watch the gender of the nouns in the following group and make the appropriate changes in the relative pronouns.*)

4. Das war der Roman, der mir gefallen hat.
> Geschichte
> Programm
> Konzert
> Vorstellung
> Film

5. Das ist ein Film, den er großartig findet.
> Maler
> Dichter
> Schauspieler

6. Das ist eine Schauspielerin, die er großartig findet.
> Geschichte
> Idee
> Parodie

7. Das ist ein Bild, das er großartig findet.
> Fest
> Kabarett
> Buch

(*Watch the gender of the nouns in the following group and make the appropriate changes in the relative pronouns.*)

8. Das ist ein Maler, den er großartig findet.
> Idee
> Parodie
> Fest
> Schauspieler
> Dichter

9. Kennen Sie den Zahnarzt, von dem er spricht?
> Star
> Roman
> Künstler

10. Kennen Sie das Geschäft, von dem er spricht?
    Lied
    Lokal
    Kabarett

11. Kennen Sie die Firma, von der er spricht?
    Galerie
    Straße
    Schauspielerin

(*Watch the gender of the nouns in the following group and make the appropriate changes in the relative pronouns.*)

12. Kennen Sie den Schauspieler, von dem er spricht?
    Lokal
    Firma
    Galerie
    Roman
    Lied

13. Das sind die Romane, die uns gefallen.
    Bilder
    Geschichten
    Bücher

14. Das sind die Dichter, die jeder Deutsche kennt.
    Filme
    Komiker
    Schauspieler

15. Das sind die Lieder, von denen er sprach.
    Künstler
    Konzerte
    Rollen

II. Restate the following pairs of sentences, connecting each pair with the appropriate relative pronoun:

EXAMPLE: **Ich weiß etwas. Er weiß es nicht.**
            Ich weiß etwas, *was* er nicht weiß.

1. Ich weiß etwas. Es wird ihn interessieren.
Ich weiß etwas. Es wird ihm nicht gefallen.
Ich weiß etwas. Es wird ihm komisch vorkommen.
Ich weiß etwas. Er wird es nicht glauben.

2. Sie ist froh darüber. Das finde ich erstaunlich.
Er hat gut gespielt. Es ist kein Wunder.

Die Filme sind synchronisiert. Das gefällt mir nicht.
Man zeigt viele Wildwestfilme. Ich finde es erstaunlich.

III. *Restate the following sentences, replacing the relative pronoun with a demonstrative:*

Das war ein guter Film, der uns gefallen hat.
Er ist ein guter Schauspieler, den ich gern sehe.
Dort ist die Weinstube, von der er immer spricht.
Das sind seine Freunde, denen er es erzählt hat.
Das ist eine Skandalgeschichte, von der er immer spricht.

IV. *Restate the following sentences in the present perfect tense:*

Ich wollte diesen Film sehen.
Er mußte durch Berlin fahren.
Wir durften nichts sagen.
Sie sollten sich den Film ansehen.
Sie konnte sich endlich ausruhen.
Man ließ ihn nicht arbeiten.
Ich sah ihn gern spielen.
Wir hörten ihn oft sprechen.

V. *Restate the following sentences, changing the adverb in each to an adjective:*

EXAMPLE: **Das ist ein *gut* synchronisierter Film.**
Das ist ein *guter* synchronisierter Film.

1. Das ist ein erstaunlich amüsanter Roman.
2. Das steht in dieser furchtbar sentimentalen Geschichte.
3. Er wohnt in einem historisch interessanten Stadtteil.
4. Sie haben ein ungewöhnlich modernes Haus.
5. Er ist ein schöpferisch begabter Mensch.

VI. *Restate the following sentences, forming phrases with* <u>um</u> . . . <u>zu</u> + inf. *from the expressions in parentheses:*

EXAMPLE: **Sie wollen nach München, (die historischen Gebäude sehen)**
Sie wollen nach München, *um die historischen Gebäude zu sehen.*

Sie wollen nach München, (die Galerien besuchen)
(das berühmte Orchester hören)

(an der bekannten Universität studieren)
(sich das Künstlerviertel ansehen)
(das Oktoberfest mitmachen)

Exercises

I. Connect the two sentences by making the second one a relative clause:

1. Ich war in einem alten Film. Er hat mir gefallen. 2. Er ist ein ausgezeichneter Komiker. Ich sehe ihn gern. 3. Das war eine gute Rolle. Darin hat er sich selbst übertroffen. 4. Gehört er zu diesen Leuten? Ihnen hat es nicht gefallen. 5. Kennen Sie das Dorf? Es ist nicht weit von Bonn. 6. Ist das Ihr Fernglas? Sie haben es verloren. 7. Waren Sie in dem Café? Ich habe Ihnen davon erzählt. 8. Das ist die Universität. Er hat sie besucht. 9. Das ist der Professor. Ihm verdanken wir viel. 10. Es gibt viele Studenten hier. Sie wissen nichts darüber. 11. Kennen Sie die Darsteller? Wir haben sie gestern gesehen. 12. Das ist der Roman. Seinen Titel habe ich vergessen. 13. Es gibt hier viele alte Filme. Das finde ich erstaunlich. 14. Ihm gefallen Heimatfilme. Es ist unglaublich. 15. Das ist die Austauschstudentin. Ihr Deutsch ist fehlerlos. 16. Ich habe viele Städte besucht. Ihre Straßen waren nicht sehr gut.

II. Rewrite the following sentences in the simple past tense:

1. Endlich habe ich mich ausruhen müssen. 2. Er hat in ein Jazzkonzert gehen wollen. 3. Sie sind in die Mensa gegangen, weil sie ihn dort haben treffen sollen. 4. Sie haben uns nicht ins Gebäude kommen lassen. 5. Ich bin pünktlich gekommen, da ich ihn etwas habe fragen wollen. 6. Ich habe sie ins Zimmer kommen hören. 7. Wo haben Sie ihn spielen sehen? 8. Sie hat nicht gewußt, daß sie das nicht hat sagen dürfen. 9. Ich habe mich gefreut, daß er sie hat besuchen können. 10. Er ist ins Kino gegangen, weil er sich einen alten Film hat ansehen wollen.

III. Translate into English. In sentences 1–5, reproduce the German sentences from your English translations:

1. Er gehört zu den Dichtern, von denen man heute in allen Zeitungen liest. 2. Die Seminare machen ihm Schwierigkeiten, was ich mir gut vorstellen kann. 3. Endlich habe ich den Schauspieler gesehen,

den Gerd so gut nachahmen kann. 4. Warum hast du nicht an den Stadtplan gedacht? Den brauchen wir bestimmt. 5. Er hat sich die Mauer ansehen wollen, als er in Berlin war. 6. Wir haben stundenlang Schlange stehen müssen, um Karten zu bekommen. 7. So sind eben die Bayern. Die sind die größten Lokalpatrioten. 8. Ich wollte mir den Rosenmontagszug ansehen, was ich aber leider nicht konnte. 9. Ich war auf der Sylvesterparty, an der Tom auch teilgenommen hat. 10. Ich mag psychologische Romane nicht besonders, aber dieser psychologisch sehr gut motivierte Roman hat mir gefallen.

IV. Translate:

1. Finally I was able to get tickets. (*pres. perf.*) 2. That seems funny to me. 3. This (*das*) is a movie that I've seen twice. 4. He is a great comedian! I like him! 5. She didn't go to Bonn because she couldn't. (*pres. perf.*) 6. They didn't let him work since he had no permit. 7. I can imagine that it is giving him trouble. 8. He has never gone to the movies, which I find amazing. 9. These (*das*) are the teachers to whom our university owes a lot. 10. I went to (*in*) the *Mensa* (in order) to wait for him.

V. a. Composition. Write ten sentences in the form of a composition on this topic — „Tom in Berlin." For each sentence, use the words given below:

1. Tom   zuerst   Stadt   ansehen
2. weil   stundenlang   müde
3. Kino   weil   sich ausruhen
4. „Hauptmann von Köpenick"   Nachkriegsfilm   amüsant
5. Heinz Rühmann   Schauspieler   Hauptrolle
6. Gerd   dieser Film   dreimal
7. nach   Kino   sich unterhalten   Film
8. Tom   erstaunlich   ausländisch   synchronisiert
9. Tom   lachen   müssen
10. Durst   Bier

b. Free Composition: Tom writes a letter to a friend about movies in Germany.

Active Vocabulary

amüsant	amusing, funny	**besetzen**	to occupy
die Arbeitserlaub-	working permit	**sich** (*dat.*) **besorgen**	to provide oneself
nis, –			with, get
ausländisch	foreign	**sich** (*dat.*) **denken,**	to imagine
sich (*acc.*) **aus-**	to rest	**dachte, hat**	
ruhen		**gedacht**	

der Durst, –es	thirst
erstaunlich	amazing
froh	happy, glad
furchtbar	terrible
der Geschmack, –s	taste
der Hauptmann, –s, Hauptleute	captain
die Hauptrolle, –, –n	leading role
der Heimatfilm, –s, –e	regional movie
die Idee, –, –n	idea
das Kino, –s, –s	movie theater
der Komiker, –s, –	comedian
komisch	comical, funny
lachen	to laugh
lassen, ließ, hat gelassen, läßt	to let, allow

der Nachkriegsfilm, –s, –e	postwar movie
der Paß, Passes, Pässe	passport
die Rolle, –, –n	role, part
der Star, –s, –s	(movie) star
stundenlang	for hours
synchronisieren	to dub (movie)
übertreffen, übertraf, hat übertroffen, übertrifft	to outdo, excel
vor-kommen (*dat.*), kam . . . vor, ist vorgekommen	to seem
der Wildwestreißer, –s, –	grade B Western movie

Zwanzigste Lektion

Am Checkpoint Charlie

[*Gerd und Tom sitzen im Auto und warten auf die Paßabfertigung.*]

GERD — Es sieht so aus, als ob wir noch lange warten müßten.

TOM — Wir sind anscheinend in die Stoßzeit geraten.

GERD — Es hat keinen Zweck, ungeduldig zu werden.

TOM — Sind die Vopos immer so streng?

GERD — Es kommt darauf an. Vielleicht haben sie heute einen Schmuggler gefaßt.

TOM — [*lächelnd*] Oder gar einen Spion!

GERD — Wer weiß! — Wenn es nur nicht so langsam ginge!

TOM — Zum Essen in Ost-Berlin wird's wohl nicht mehr reichen. Sollen wir ein Picknick im Auto abhalten?

GERD — Warum nicht. Würdest du mal bitte die Brote vom Rücksitz holen? — Danke.

TOM — Die „Dreigroschenoper" wäre kein Vergnügen, wenn ich mittendrin Hunger bekäme. Mir knurrt dann immer der Magen.

GERD — Mir auch.

TOM — Ich bin neugierig auf das Berliner Ensemble. Brecht hat es doch selbst gegründet, nicht wahr?

GERD — Ja. Das ist eine ganz hervorragende Schauspielertruppe. Wenn ich könnte, würde ich öfter hinfahren.

TOM — Ich glaube, da vorne setzt sich die Kolonne in Bewegung.

GERD — Endlich!

At Checkpoint Charlie

[*Gerd and Tom are sitting in the car, waiting for the passport inspection.*]

GERD — It looks as though we might have to wait a long time.

TOM — Evidently we've gotten into the rush hour.

GERD — There's no point in getting impatient.

TOM — Are the *Vopos*[1] always so strict?

GERD — It depends. Maybe today the've caught a smuggler.

TOM — [*smiling*] Or even a spy.

GERD — Who knows? — I wish it wouldn't take so long.

TOM — We probably won't have time to eat in East Berlin. Should we have a picnic in the car?

GERD — Why not? Would you please get the sandwiches from the back seat? — Thank you.

TOM — I wouldn't enjoy the *Threepenny Opera* if I got hungry right in the middle of it. My stomach always growls then.

GERD — Mine too.

TOM — I'm anxious to see the Berlin Ensemble. Brecht started it himself, didn't he?

GERD — Yes. It's really an outstanding acting company. If I could, I would go more often.

TOM — I think the line is starting to move up ahead.

GERD — It's about time.

---

[1] **Vopo:** Abbreviated form of **Volkspolizei** — *people's police*, the name of the East German police.

Seit einigen Tagen sind Gerd und Tom nun schon in Berlin, dieser merkwürdigen[1] und faszinierenden Stadt. Auch ihre Geschichte ist ungewöhnlich. Einmal galt sie als[2] meistgehaßte[3] Stadt der Welt, dann wieder als Zitadelle der Demokratie. Heute ist sie ein politisches Monstrum, weil sie zweigeteilt[4] ist. Von der Mauer, die als scharf bewachte[5] Grenze[6] durch die Stadt geht, hat Präsident Kennedy gesagt: „Es gibt immer noch Dinge auf dieser Welt, die man gesehen haben muß, ehe man sie glauben kann."

Die Entwicklung[7] Berlins war hektischer als die Entwicklung anderer europäischer Hauptstädte. Im 19. Jahrhundert, zum Beispiel, verdreifachte[8] sich die Einwohnerzahl[9] in 50 Jahren. Es war, als ob die Stadt wie ein Magnet die Massen anzöge.[10] Heute wohnen 2,2 Millionen Menschen in West–Berlin, 1,1 Million in Ost–Berlin.

Besonders in den Jahren vor und nach dem ersten Weltkrieg war Berlin eine wirkliche Metropole, ein Zentrum für Politik, Wirtschaft,[11] Presse, Verkehr,[12] Kunst und Wissenschaft. Die „goldenen zwanziger Jahre" sind schon fast legendär geworden. Kein Wunder, daß auch der junge Dramatiker und Theatermann Bert Brecht dort leben wollte. Seine Erlebnisse in einem Kriegslazarett[13] hatten ihn zum Pazifisten gemacht. Nun greift er die Mächte[14] an, die er für den Krieg verantwortlich[15] macht: den Staat, die Parteien, die Kirche, das Militär, die Großindustrie. Brecht will die Gesellschaft reformieren. Wenn er nicht fest[16] glaubte, daß man sie verändern[17] und verbessern[18] könnte, würde er verzweifeln.[19] Auch sein berühmtestes Werk, die „Dreigroschenoper" (1928) soll der verrotteten[20] Gesellschaft einen Spiegel vorhalten. Die ganze Welt sang damals Macky Messers Song:

> Und der Haifisch, der hat Zähne, 25
> Und die trägt er im Gesicht.
> Und Macheath, der hat ein Messer,
> Doch das Messer sieht man nicht.[21]

Brecht glaubt, daß der Marxismus das beste Instrument für eine Gesellschaftsreform ist. Als Marxist kommt er natürlich sofort auf die schwarze 30

---

[1] **merkwürdig** unusual
[2] **gelten als** to be considered
[3] **meistgehaßt** most hated
[4] **zweigeteilt** divided in two
[5] **bewachen** to guard, watch
[6] **die Grenze, –, –n** border
[7] **die Entwicklung, –, –en** development
[8] **verdreifachen** to triple
[9] **die Einwohnerzahl, –, –en** population
[10] **als ob die Stadt . . . anzöge** as if the city attracted
[11] **die Wirtschaft, –** economy
[12] **der Verkehr, –s** traffic

[13] **das Kriegslazarett, –s, –e** military hospital
[14] **die Macht, –, –** power
[15] **verantwortlich** responsible
[16] **fest** firmly
[17] **verändern** to change
[18] **verbessern** to improve, correct, reform
[19] **verzweifeln** to despair
[20] **verrottet** rotten
[21] **„Und der . . . nicht."** a fairly literal prose translation reads: And the shark he has teeth,/And he has them in his face./But Macheath he has a knife,/But one does not see the knife."

Lotte Lenya (rechts) und Ida Krottendorf (links) in Brechts „Mutter Courage"

Liste, als Hitler Kanzler wird. Wie so viele hat er gar keine Wahl: bliebe er[22] in Deutschland, so müßte er mit sofortiger Verhaftung[23] rechnen.[24] Er geht in die Emigration. Über Dänemark, Finnland und Rußland[25] kommt er nach Amerika. In Hollywood erlebt er das Ende des zweiten Weltkrieges. Aber Hollywood, die Traumfabrik,[26] und der Moralist und Reformer Brecht ver- 35 stehen einander nicht, und so kehrt er 1948 nach Europa zurück.

In den Emigrationsjahren schrieb Brecht die Stücke, die zu den besten Dramen der modernen Literatur gehören: „Mutter Courage und ihre Kinder", „Der gute Mensch von Sezuan",[27] „Galileo Galilei", „Der kaukasische Kreidekreis".[28] Seine letzten Jahre verbrachte Brecht in Ost-Berlin, und dort 40 baute er die Theatergruppe auf, die damals eine der besten der Welt war: das Berliner Ensemble.

[22] **bliebe er** if he remained
[23] **die Verhaftung, –, –en** arrest
[24] **rechnen mit** to count on, expect
[25] **Rußland** Russia
[26] **die Traumfabrik, –, –en** dream factory

[27] **„Der gute Mensch von Sezuan"** *The Good Woman of Setzuan*
[28] **„Der kaukasische Kreidekreis"** *The Caucasian Chalk Circle*

Fragen und Antworten

1. Wohin muß man fahren, um das Berliner Ensemble zu sehen?
   Wenn man diese Theatergruppe sehen will, muß man nach Ost-Berlin fahren.
2. Warum wird Gerd ungeduldig?
   Weil die Paßabfertigung heute sehr langsam geht.
3. Geht es am Checkpoint Charlie immer so langsam?
   Nein, es kommt auf die Tageszeit an.
4. Sind die Vopos immer so streng?
   Nein, nur wenn sie Schmuggler oder Spione fassen.
5. Ist Tom neugierig auf das Berliner Ensemble?
   Ja, er ist sehr neugierig darauf.
6. Was könnten die beiden tun, wenn es schneller ginge?
   Kämen sie früh genug nach Ost-Berlin, so würden sie dort essen.
7. Warum muß Tom etwas essen?
   Wenn er im Theater Hunger bekäme, so würde ihm der Magen knurren.
8. Warum kann Gerd nicht oft nach Ost-Berlin?
   Er wohnt in Bonn. Wenn er in West-Berlin wohnte, könnte er öfter hin.
9. Ist Berlin eine politisch interessante Stadt?
   Ja, Berlin spielt eine ungewöhnlich interessante Rolle in der Politik.
10. Was ist die Mauer?
    Das ist die scharf bewachte Grenze zwischen Ost- und West-Berlin.

Structure and Practice

Explanation of Forms

GENERAL SUBJUNCTIVE (I)

The verb tenses you have learned previously were all used to make a statement or ask a question dealing with actual facts. Such tenses are referred to as indicative.

> Haben Sie noch eine deutsche Zeitung?
> *Do you have another German newspaper?*
>
> Alles tanzte auf der Straße.
> *Everyone was dancing in the street.*
>
> Es wird nicht lange dauern.
> *It won't take long.*

In contrast to these indicative tenses, there are subjunctive tenses which, to use general terms, are reserved for conditions that are uncertain, improbable, or unreal. The specific constructions for which the subjunctive is used will be treated in this lesson and Lessons 21 and 23.

English uses the subjunctive for some of the functions that German does, but most English subjunctive forms are not recognizable out of context, since they are identical with indicative forms. Most speakers of English, for example, will classify the words *he lived* as simple past tense. Yet, notice the use of this phrase in the following sentences:

> When *he lived* here, he liked it. (past tense)
> If *he lived* here now, he would like it. (subjunctive)

Obviously the second sentence is not past tense. It is an unreal condition for which English, like German, uses the subjunctive; the *lived* in that sentence refers to present time.

Other subjunctive forms in English are more easily recognizable: *I were* could not possibly be an indicative form; it would only be found where English uses the subjunctive:

> If *I were* you, I would do just that.

German has two different types of subjunctive, each having special uses. In this lesson and the next, the more commonly used forms and constructions, those of the general subjunctive, will be treated.

A. Forms of the General Subjunctive: Present and Future Time

For uncertain, unreal, or improbable conditions in present or future time, German has two tenses: present subjunctive and future subjunctive.

1. PRESENT SUBJUNCTIVE: As in English, German present subjunctive forms are based on the simple past of the indicative (see the English examples above).

   a. Weak Verbs: The present subjunctive of weak verbs looks exactly like the past indicative.

fragen	**arbeiten**
ich **fragte**	ich **arbeitete**
du **fragtest**	du **arbeitetest**
er, sie, es **fragte**	er, sie, es **arbeitete**
wir **fragten**	wir **arbeiteten**
ihr **fragtet**	ihr **arbeitetet**
sie **fragten**	sie **arbeiteten**
Sie **fragten**	Sie **arbeiteten**

   b. Strong Verbs: The present subjunctive of strong verbs is formed by adding the personal endings (italicized below) to the past indicative stem; an umlaut is added to the stem vowel whenever possible.

gehen	**kommen**	**sein**
ich **ging***e*	ich **käm***e*	ich **wär***e*
du **ging***est*	du **käm***est*	du **wär***est*
er, sie, es **ging***e*	er, sie, es **käm***e*	er, sie, es **wär***e*
wir **ging***en*	wir **käm***en*	wir **wär***en*
ihr **ging***et*	ihr **käm***et*	ihr **wär***et*
sie **ging***en*	sie **käm***en*	sie **wär***en*
Sie **ging***en*	Sie **käm***en*	Sie **wär***en*

   c. Modals: The present subjunctive of modals looks like the past indicative, except that those modals which have an umlaut in the infinitive also have one in the subjunctive. (You will recall that modals in the past indicative have no umlauts.) Only the third-person singular (**er**) is given below.

dürfen: er **dürfte**	**müssen:** er **müßte**
können: er **könnte**	**sollen:** er **sollte**
mögen: er **möchte**	**wollen:** er **wollte**

   d. **haben** and **werden**: The irregular verbs **haben** and **werden** in the present subjunctive look just like the past indicative, except for the addition of an umlaut on the stem vowel.

haben: er **hätte**   **werden:** er **würde**

e. Irregular Weak Verbs: The present subjunctive of **bringen** (**er brächte**), **denken** (**er dächte**) and **wissen** (**er wüßte**) looks like the past indicative with the addition of an umlaut on the stem vowel. The other irregular weak verbs (**brennen, nennen,** etc.) are generally avoided in the subjunctive by the use of synonyms or by using the verbs in the future subjunctive (described below).

2. FUTURE SUBJUNCTIVE: The future subjunctive of all verbs is formed by using the present subjunctive of **werden** (**er würde**) as the auxiliary with a dependent infinitive placed at the end of the clause.

Ich **würde** öfter **hinfahren.**   *I would go more often.*
Du **würdest** öfter **hinfahren.**   *You would go more often.*
Er, sie, es **würde** öfter **hinfahren.**   *He . . .* etc.
Wir **würden** öfter **hinfahren.**
Ihr **würdet** öfter **hinfahren.**
Sie **würden** öfter **hinfahren.**
Sie (*you*) **würden** öfter **hinfahren.**

B. Use of the General Subjunctive: Present and Future Time

1. CONTRARY-TO-FACT CONDITIONS: In both English and German, contrary-to-fact statements are expressed by an *if*-clause (condition-clause) and a conclusion-clause. However, not every statement constructed in this way is contrary to fact.

Wenn ich **kann, fahre** ich **hin.**
If I can, I'll drive there.
or: *Whenever I can, I drive there.*
Wenn ich **könnte, würde** ich **hinfahren.**
If I could, I would drive there.

In the first example above, we have a statement that is not contrary to fact; the implication is that there is a possibility the condition may be fulfilled. In the second example, we have a contrary-to-fact statement; the implication is that it is improbable the condition will be fulfilled. The first statement is in the indicative; the second is in the subjunctive.

In the subjunctive statement above, the speaker is referring to present (or future) time. For such present-time constructions, German uses present subjunctive in the condition-clause, and present subjunctive or future subjunctive in the conclusion-clause. (Both are equally correct, but the future is more prevalent in spoken German.)

> Wenn er Hunger **bekäme, knurrte** ihm der Magen.
> *or:* **würde** ihm der Magen **knurren.**
> *If he got hungry, his stomach would growl.*

2. VARIATIONS OF THE CONDITION CONTRARY-TO-FACT CONSTRUCTION, PRESENT TIME: There are circumstances under which we use what might be considered only one or the other of the two clauses of a condition contrary-to-fact statement.

    a. The Condition-Clause Construction: Both German and English can express a contrary-to-fact wish by using a condition-clause in combination with **nur** (*only*); the conclusion is left to the imagination. The present subjunctive is used.

> Wenn es nur nicht so langsam ginge!
> *If only* (or: *I wish*) *it wouldn't take so long.*

(**Nur** is always placed after the subject and after any pronoun objects.)

    b. The Conclusion-Clause Construction: In both German and English, the condition-clause can be left unexpressed in some instances. Either present or future subjunctive may be used in the conclusion-clause.

> Das wäre wohl am einfachsten.
> *or:* Das würde wohl am einfachsten sein.
> *That would probably be the simplest thing.*

Sometimes the conclusion-clause construction is used to make requests more polite.

> **Würdest du** mal bitte die Brote vom Rücksitz holen?
> *Would you please get the sandwiches from the back seat?*
> **Könnten Sie** mir bitte eine deutsche Zeitung geben?
> *Could you please give me a German newspaper?*

3. WORD ORDER VARIATIONS IN CONDITION CONTRARY-TO-FACT STATEMENTS: The **wenn**-clause in a condition contrary-to-fact statement can come first or second; it is a dependent clause, and its inflected verb is always last; the main (conclusion) clause has inverted word order if it comes after the **wenn**-clause.

Wenn ich könnte, **würde ich** öfter hinfahren.
Ich würde öfter hinfahren, wenn ich könnte.

English can on occasion omit the *if;* it is not commonly done and often sounds stiff. If it is omitted, the verb is placed first.

Had he done his work, he would not have this difficulty.

German can omit the **wenn** in any sentence (even in the indicative ones). It is commonly done and does not sound stiff. As in English, the inflected verb is placed first when the **wenn** is omitted.

Wenn er Hunger **bekäme,** (so) würde ihm der Magen knurren.
Bekäme er Hunger, so würde ihm der Magen knurren.

So (or **dann**) is optional before the conclusion clause, but it is usually used in sentences where the **wenn** is omitted. The **so** (or **dann**) does not affect the word order.

Word Study and Usage

I. DEFINITE ARTICLE AS SUBSTITUTE FOR THE POSSESSIVE ADJECTIVE

In German the definite article is used instead of the possessive adjective in referring to parts of the body or articles of clothing when it is clearly understood, from the context, who the "possessor" is.

Er greift in **die Tasche.**
He reaches into his pocket.
Er hat das Fernglas in **der Hand.**
He has the binoculars in his hand.

Often, however, a dative pronoun is used in the sentence to indicate the "possessor."

Mir knurrt dann immer **der Magen.**
My stomach always growls then.
Bekäme er im Theater Hunger, so würde **ihm der Magen** knurren.
If he got hungry in the theater, his stomach would growl.

II. PRESENT PARTICIPLES (ENGLISH -ing FORM OF THE VERB)

The present participle in German is formed by adding **-d** to the infinitive: **lächelnd** (infinitive: **lächeln** — *to smile*), **hervorragend** (infinitive:

hervorragen — *to stand out, project*). These participles are never used in German as verb forms, but only as adjectives or adverbs.

> Das ist eine ganz **hervorragende** Schauspielertruppe.
> *That's a very **outstanding** acting company.*
> Gerd sagt **lächelnd** . . .
> *Gerd says, **smiling** . . .*

Class Drills

I. Restate the following sentences, changing the subject in both clauses, in turn, to <u>er</u>, <u>wir</u>, <u>sie</u> *(they):*

Wenn ich hier bliebe, würde ich ihn besuchen.
Wenn ich Zeit hätte, ginge ich mit.
Wenn ich Karten bekäme, wäre ich froh.
Wenn ich in Berlin wohnte, könnte ich öfter hin.

II. a. Restate the following sentences as contrary-to-fact conditions, using present subjunctive in both clauses:

> EXAMPLE: **Wenn ich Zeit *habe*, *gehe* ich öfter hin.**
> **Wenn ich Zeit *hätte*, *ginge* ich öfter hin.**

Wenn ich Zeit habe, bleibe ich in Berlin.
> ist das sehr einfach
> unterhalte ich mich gern mit ihm
> komme ich auch mit
> sehe ich mir das Ensemble an
> kann ich es tun
> muß ich ihn besuchen

b. Restate the sentences in exercise a. as contrary-to-fact conditions, using future subjunctive in the conclusion-clause:

> EXAMPLE: **Wenn ich Zeit habe, *gehe* ich öfter *hin*.**
> **Wenn ich Zeit hätte, *würde* ich öfter *hingehen*.**

III. Restate the following sentences as contrary-to-fact wishes, adding <u>nur</u>:

> EXAMPLE: **Er kommt bald.**
> **Wenn er nur bald käme!**

Es geht schneller.
Es ist wahr.

Ich habe Mut.
Ich bekomme eine Karte.
Sie fassen den Spion.
Sie besucht uns manchmal.
Wir können ihn verstehen.
Ich darf es tun.
Sie weiß es.

IV. a. Restate the following sentences, omitting the <u>wenn</u> in each:

Wenn ich hier bliebe, so würde ich ihn besuchen.
Wenn sie sich verirrten, so könnten sie mich anrufen.
Wenn wir Zeit hätten, so könnten wir in Ost-Berlin essen.
Wenn ich in Berlin wohnte, so wäre das möglich.
Wenn ich Hunger bekäme, so würde mir der Magen knurren.

b. Restate the original sentences in exercise a., reversing the order of the clauses.

V. Restate the following sentences, using the present participle given as an attributive adjective in front of the noun:

EXAMPLE: **Das war ein Tag! (anstrengend)**
Das war ein *anstrengender* Tag!

Das ist eine Schauspielertruppe. (**hervorragend**)
Lesen Sie bitte die Geschichte! (**folgend**)
Er stand an dem Wasser. (**rauschend**)
Sie setzte sich neben den Mann. (**schweigend**)
Er sah nur noch den Zug. (**abfahrend**)

Exercises

I. Rewrite the following sentences as condition contrary-to-fact statements. Use future subjunctive in the conclusion-clauses.

1. Wenn ich kann, fahre ich öfter hin. 2. Wenn wir warten müssen, essen wir im Auto. 3. Wenn er pünktlich kommt, gehen wir ins Kino. 4. Wenn er hier bleibt, hilft er uns sicher. 5. Wenn das wahr ist, gehe ich auch hin. 6. Wenn er den Zug verpaßt, fährt er mit dem Taxi. 7. Wenn er sich verirrt, ruft er seinen Freund an. 8. Wenn er zu diesen Leuten gehört, glaubt er das auch. 9. Wenn er es weiß, sagt er es mir. 10. Wenn wir Zeit haben, besuchen wir ihn.

II. Rewrite the following requests and suggestions, using the present subjunctive to make them more polite:

1. Können Sie mir dabei helfen?   2. Ist das nicht einfacher?   3. Wissen Sie vielleicht seinen Namen?   4. Werden Sie das für mich tun?
5. Gehen Sie lieber ins Kino?   6. Ist es nicht besser, nichts zu sagen?
7. Haben Sie Zeit dazu?   8. Dürfen wir Sie um Auskunft bitten?
9. Kommen Sie nicht lieber mit uns?   10. Darf ich Sie dazu einladen?

III. Translate into English. In sentences 1–5, reproduce the German sentences from your English translations:

1. Könnten wir nur früher abfahren!   2. Heute hatte er einen ungewöhnlich anstrengenden Tag.   3. Wer weiß, vielleicht ist er froh, daß er nicht mitgefahren ist.   4. Anscheinend hat er so etwas noch nie erlebt.   5. Wenn er kein so guter Schauspieler wäre, könnte er diese Rolle nicht spielen.   6. Wenn es bei der Paßabfertigung etwas schneller ginge, würde es noch zum Essen reichen.   7. Den Schmuggler, nach dem sich die Polizei erkundigte, hat man heute fassen können.
8. Wenn sich die Kolonne da vorne nur endlich in Bewegung setzte!
9. Alles, was die anderen taten, hat er auch mitmachen wollen.   10. Sie hat sich im Kabarett gar nicht amüsiert, was wir uns nicht vorstellen können.

IV. Translate:

1. It depends on the weather.   2. Could you tell me who played the leading part?   3. If he were here, he would help me.   4. Would you have time to go to the concert?   5. If you want to see the Berlin Ensemble, you have to go to East Berlin.   6. That is an unusually good movie.   7. Evidently we have gotten into difficulties.   8. There was no point in waiting for hours.   9. It would seem funny to me if he arrived on time (*pünktlich*).   10. Would you like to read a mystery?

V. a. Composition. Write ten sentences in the form of a composition on this topic — „Nach Ost-Berlin." For each sentence use the words suggested below:

1. Gerd und Tom   wollen   „Dreigroschenoper"
2. hervorragend   Brecht   gründen
3. wenn   Berliner Ensemble   Ost-Berlin
4. zuerst   durch   Paßabfertigung
5. heute   langsam   weil   Stoßzeit
6. Tom   glauben   Vopos   streng   weil   Schmuggler

7. keine Zeit   Essen   Ost-Berlin
8. Brote   Picknick   Auto
9. Tom   müssen   essen   sonst   Magen   knurren
10. endlich   in Bewegung setzen

b. Free Composition: Tom tells a friend about their experience at Checkpoint Charlie.

Active Vocabulary

ab-halten, hielt . . . ab, hat abgehalten, hält . . . ab	to hold, have
als ob	as though
an-kommen auf (+ acc.), kam . . . an, ist . . . angekommen	to depend on
anscheinend	evidently, apparently
bewachen	to guard, watch
sich (*acc.*) **in Bewegung setzen**	to get moving
das Brot, –(e)s, –e	bread, sandwich
„Die Dreigroschenoper"	*The Threepenny Opera*
das Ensemble, –s, –s	ensemble
fassen	to catch
gar	even
geraten in (+ acc.), geriet, ist geraten, gerät	to get into
die Grenze, –, –n	border
gründen	to found, start
hervorragend	outstanding
holen	to get, fetch
knurren	to growl
die Kolonne, –, –n	line, column
lächeln	to smile
langsam	slow
mittendrin	in the middle of it
neugierig sein auf (+ acc.)	to be anxious to (*see, read*, etc.)
die Paßabfertigung, –, –en	passport inspection
das Picknick, –s, –s	picnic
reichen zu	to be sufficient for
der Rücksitz, –es, –e	back seat
scharf	sharp
das Schauspiel, –s, –e	play, drama
die Schauspielertruppe, –, –n	acting company
der Schmuggler, –s, –	smuggler
der Spion, –s, –e	spy
die Stoßzeit, –, –en	rush hour
die Tageszeit, –, –en	time of day
die Theatergruppe, –, –n	acting company
ungeduldig	impatient
das Vergnügen, –s, –	fun, joy
der Vopo, –s, –s = Volkspolizist	"people's police" (East German police)
der Zweck, –(e)s, –e	purpose

German Information Center

Bertolt Brecht

Das Goethe-Schiller-Denkmal

Einundzwanzigste Lektion

Weimar

[*Norbert, Gerds Vetter, hat Tom mit seinem Wagen nach Weimar gebracht, wo sie bei Verwandten wohnen. Tom freut sich auf die Sehenswürdigkeiten, und die beiden wollen gleich eine Besichtigungstour machen.*]

NORBERT — Wenn wir vorgestern angekommen wären, hätten wir meinen Freund Peter noch angetroffen. Der hätte uns sicher herumgeführt. Er hat mal eine Zeitlang hier gewohnt.

TOM — Keine Angst, wir finden uns schon zurecht. Ich habe ja Erfahrung mit fremden Städten.

NORBERT — Jetzt kommen wir bald zum Goethe-Schiller-Denkmal.

TOM — Es kommt mir vor, als ob ich irgendwo ein Bild davon gesehen hätte. Die beiden Klassiker Deutschlands wohnten im gleichen Ort und wurden Freunde — das hat mich schon immer interessiert.

[*Sie biegen um die Ecke.*]

NORBERT — Sehen Sie, da ist das Denkmal.

TOM — Jetzt erinnere ich mich! Es war in einem Schulbuch.

NORBERT — Der Gegensatz zwischen den Persönlichkeiten ist gut dargestellt, nicht wahr? Schiller, der junge, idealistische Freiheitskämpfer; Goethe, der reifere, weltmännische Hofmann. So sah sie das neunzehnte Jahrhundert.

TOM — Hätte ich nur meinen Fotoapparat mitgebracht!

NORBERT — Meine Tante hat sicher einige gute Bilder. Fotografieren ist nämlich ihr Hobby. Sie gibt Ihnen bestimmt eins als Souvenir.

Weimar

[Norbert, Gerd's cousin, has driven Tom to Weimar where they are staying with relatives. Tom is looking forward to the sights, and the two of them are about to go sightseeing.]

NORBERT — If we'd arrived the day before yesterday, my friend Peter would still have been here. I'm sure he would have shown us around. He once lived here for a while.

TOM — Don't worry. We'll find our way around. After all, I have experience with strange cities.

NORBERT — We'll be getting to the Goethe-Schiller monument soon now.

TOM — It seems to me that I've seen a picture of it somewhere. The two classical writers of Germany lived in the same place and were friends. I've always found that interesting.

[They turn the corner.]

NORBERT — Look, there's the monument.

TOM — Now I remember — it was in a textbook.

NORBERT — The contrast between the two personalities is portrayed well, isn't it? Schiller, the young, idealistic fighter for liberty; Goethe, the more mature and sophisticated courtier. That's the way the nineteenth century saw them.

TOM — I wish I had brought my camera along.

NORBERT — My aunt must have a few good pictures. You see, photography is her hobby. I'm sure she'll give you one as a souvenir.

Lesestück XXI

Viele Amerikaner, die den Namen „Weimar" hören, denken dabei an die sogenannte „Weimarer Republik". Man meint damit jenen Staat, der nur vierzehn Jahre existierte (1919–1933) und mit Hitlers „Drittem Reich" zu Ende ging.

Warum „Weimarer" Republik? Die Erklärung ist einfach. Nachdem[1] Deutschland 1918 den Krieg verloren hatte, war der letzte Kaiser geflohen,[2] und man wollte eine neue Verfassung.[3] Natürlich dachte man zuerst daran, sich in Berlin zu versammeln[4] und an einer solchen Verfassung zu arbeiten. Aber für diese Arbeit brauchte man Ruhe[5] und Konzentration, und das hatte man damals in Berlin nicht, sondern es gab Straßenkämpfe[6] und Rebellionen. So wählte die Nationalversammlung das stille Weimar. Dabei[7] spielte ein anderer Grund mit:[8] man hoffte, daß der neue Staat mit dem Geiste[9] Goethes und Schillers identifiziert werden würde, der beiden großen Dichter der deutschen Klassik, die lange Zeit in Weimar gelebt hatten. Man kann also sagen: wenn es damals in Berlin stiller gewesen wäre, so hätte man sich gewiß dort versammelt. Dann sprächen die Historiker heute von der „Berliner Republik".

Am Anfang des 19. Jahrhunderts war Weimar dadurch, daß Goethe und Schiller dort lebten, die geistige[10] Hauptstadt Europas geworden. Studenten und junge Dichter machten richtige Pilgerfahrten dorthin. Johann Wolfgang Goethe und Friedrich Schiller hatten sich 1794 bei einer Vorlesung kennengelernt, und damit begann die Freundschaft,[11] die in der deutschen Literatur berühmt geworden ist. Sie dauerte nur zehn Jahre, denn Schiller starb[12] schon 1805, im Alter[13] von 46 Jahren. Aber sie war für beide Dichter von größter Bedeutung. Aus fast täglicher Zusammenarbeit entstanden[14] Teile von Goethes „Faust", seines Romans „Wilhelm Meisters Lehrjahre",[15] und Balladen und Gedichte. Schillers große klassische Dramen, u.a.[16] „Wallenstein", „Maria Stuart", „Wilhelm Tell", stammen aus[17] dieser Zeit. Man kann also sagen: hätte der Zufall[18] damals die beiden Dichter nicht zusammengeführt, so hätte die deutsche Klassik anders ausgesehen. Diese Freundschaft war eigent-

---

[1] **nachdem** after
[2] **fliehen, floh, ist geflohen** to flee, run away
[3] **die Verfassung, –, –en** constitution
[4] **sich** (*acc.*) **versammeln** to assemble
[5] **die Ruhe, –** quiet, peace
[6] **der Straßenkampf, –s, ⁻e** street fighting
[7] **dabei** at the same time, and yet
[8] **mit–spielen** to play a part
[9] **der Geist, –es** spirit
[10] **geistig** spiritual, intellectual

[11] **die Freundschaft, –, –en** friendship
[12] **sterben, starb, ist gestorben, stirbt** to die
[13] **das Alter, –s** age
[14] **entstehen, entstand, ist entstanden** to come into being, be written
[15] **die Lehrjahre** (*pl.*) apprenticeship
[16] **u.a. = unter anderen** among others
[17] **stammen aus** to originate
[18] **der Zufall, –s, ⁻e** chance, coincidence

lich gar nicht so selbstverständlich, denn die beiden Dichter waren sich sehr unähnlich.[19] Goethe war zehn Jahre älter und kam aus Frankfurt, aus einem wohlhabenden[20] Hause; Schiller stammte aus Süddeutschland,[21] aus einer kleinbürgerlichen[22] Familie; Goethes Hauptinteressen neben der Dichtung waren Naturwissenschaften[23] und Staatskunde,[24] Schillers die Geschichte und die Philosophie; und als Lyriker[25] ist Goethe der Erlebnisdichter,[26] während Schillers Interesse der Gedankenlyrik[27] gilt.[28]

Im 19. Jahrhundert stritt[29] man sich in Deutschland darüber, wer größer sei, Goethe oder Schiller. Goethe selbst hatte schon die vernünftigste[30] Antwort darauf gegeben. Er sagte, die Deutschen „sollten sich freuen, daß überhaupt[31] ein paar Kerle[32] da sind, über die sie streiten können".

---

[19] **unähnlich** dissimilar
[20] **wohlhabend** prosperous
[21] **Süddeutschland** South Germany
[22] **kleinbürgerlich** lower middle class
[23] **die Naturwissenschaft, –, –en** science
[24] **die Staatskunde, –** political science
[25] **der Lyriker, –s, –** lyric poet
[26] **der Erlebnisdichter, –s, –** poet of (inner) experiences

[27] **die Gedankenlyrik, –** contemplative poetry
[28] **gelten** to be directed to
[29] **sich streiten, stritt, hat gestritten** to argue, quarrel
[30] **vernünftig** reasonable, sensible
[31] **überhaupt** at all, in general
[32] **der Kerl, –(e)s, –e** fellow, guy, character

Fragen und Antworten

1. Worauf freut sich Tom?
   Er freut sich darauf, die Stadt Weimar zu besichtigen (*to go sightseeing*).
2. Wer hätte sie herumgeführt, wenn sie früher angekommen wären?
   Peter hätte ihnen sicher die Stadt gezeigt.
3. Wann hätten sie Peter angetroffen?
   Wenn sie vorgestern angekommen wären.
4. Kennt Tom das Denkmal schon?
   Nein, es kommt ihm nur vor, als würde er es kennen.
5. Hat er das Denkmal schon gesehen?
   Nein, aber es kommt ihm vor, als hätte er ein Bild davon gesehen.
6. Was hat man bestimmt gesehen, wenn man in Weimar gewesen ist?
   Wenn man in Weimar war, hat man sicher das Denkmal gesehen.
7. Wo hätte Gerd gewohnt, wenn er auch nach Weimar gekommen wäre?
   Wenn er nach Weimar gekommen wäre, hätte er bei seinen Verwandten gewohnt.
8. Warum tut es Tom leid (*is . . . sorry*), daß er seinen Fotoapparat nicht mitgebracht hat?
   Wenn er ihn mitgebracht hätte, könnte er Aufnahmen machen.

9. Woran erinnert sich Tom, wenn er das Denkmal sieht?
   Er erinnert sich daran, daß er es in einem Schulbuch gesehen hat.
10. In welchem Jahrhundert war das kleine Weimar sehr bekannt?
    Es kommt darauf an, ob man über Politik oder Literatur spricht.

Structure and Practice

Explanation of Forms

I. GENERAL SUBJUNCTIVE (II)

A. Forms of the General Subjunctive: Past Time

For uncertain, unreal, or improbable conditions in past time, German has two tenses: past subjunctive and future perfect subjunctive.

1. PAST SUBJUNCTIVE: The past subjunctive is a compound tense. The present subjunctive of **haben** or **sein** (**er hätte** or **er wäre**) is used as the auxiliary (verbs take the same auxiliary in the subjunctive as they do in the indicative) with the past participle of the main verb.

sehen	**gehen**
ich **hätte gesehen**	ich **wäre gegangen**
du **hättest gesehen**	du **wärest gegangen**
er, sie, es **hätte gesehen**	er, sie, es **wäre gegangen**
wir **hätten gesehen**	wir **wären gegangen**
ihr **hättet gesehen**	ihr **wäret gegangen**
sie **hätten gesehen**	sie **wären gegangen**
Sie **hätten gesehen**	Sie **wären gegangen**

2. FUTURE PERFECT SUBJUNCTIVE: The future perfect subjunctive is similar in form to the future perfect indicative, except that the auxiliary is the present subjunctive of **werden**.

sehen	**gehen**
ich **würde gesehen haben**	ich **würde gegangen sein**
du **würdest gesehen haben**	du **würdest gegangen sein**
er, sie, es **würde gesehen haben**	er, sie, es **würde gegangen sein**
wir **würden gesehen haben**	wir **würden gegangen sein**
ihr **würdet gesehen haben**	ihr **würdet gegangen sein**
sie **würden gesehen haben**	sie **würden gegangen sein**
Sie **würden gesehen haben**	Sie **würden gegangen sein**

B. Use of the General Subjunctive: Past Time

In stating a past-time condition contrary to fact, German uses the past subjunctive in both the **wenn**-clause and the conclusion-clause. The future-perfect subjunctive is an alternate in the conclusion-clause, but it is rarely used because of its awkwardness. The alternate form is given in the example below, since it is sometimes used in written German for stylistic reasons.

> Wenn wir vorgestern **angekommen wären, hätten** wir meinen Freund Peter **angetroffen.**
> *or:* . . . **würden** wir meinen Freund Peter **angetroffen haben.**
> *If we **had arrived** the day before yesterday, my friend Peter **would** still **have been** here.*

If only one of the two clauses (**wenn**-clause or conclusion-clause) is used in referring to past time, the same tense is used.

> Wenn ich nur meinen Fotoapparat **mitgebracht hätte!**
> *I wish I **had brought** my camera along.*
> Peter **hätte** ihnen sicher die Stadt **gezeigt.**
> *Peter certainly **would have shown** them the city.*

The **wenn** may be omitted in past-time conditions and the inflected verb is placed in first position.

> **Wären** wir gestern angekommen, so hätten wir meinen Freund Peter angetroffen.
> **Hätte** ich nur meinen Fotoapparat mitgebracht!

C. Additional Use of the General Subjunctive: <u>als ob</u>, <u>als wenn</u>

Als ob and **als wenn** (alternate forms of the English *as if, as though*) introduce conjectures; these, too, are in the subjunctive.

1. PRESENT TIME: If the **als ob**- (**als wenn**) clause refers to the same time as the verb in the main clause, the present subjunctive is used in the conjecture.

> Es sieht so aus, als ob wir noch lange warten **müßten.**
> *It looks as though we might have to wait a long time.*
> Er sah aus, als ob er krank **wäre.**
> *He looked as though he were sick.*

2. PAST TIME: If the conjecture-clause refers to an earlier time than the verb in the main clause, the past subjunctive is used.

Es kommt mir vor, als ob ich irgendwo ein Bild davon **gesehen hätte.**
It seems to me that (as if) I've seen a picture of it somewhere.

Als ob-clauses are dependent clauses and therefore have the inflected verb last. The **ob,** however, may be omitted; in such cases the inflected verb follows the **als.**

Es sieht so aus, **als müßten** wir noch lange warten.
Er sah aus, **als wäre** er krank.
Es kommt mir vor, **als hätte** ich irgendwo ein Bild davon gesehen.

II. *DA- FOR ANTICIPATION*

A preposition always has an object. This object may be a noun or noun phrase:

Ich denke oft an **die alten Zeiten.** *I often think of the old days.*

Or the object may be a pronoun:

Ich denke oft an **ihn.** *I often think of him.*

The pronoun may refer to an inanimate object (or an event or situation), in which case the pronoun substitute **da(r)-** is attached to the preposition:

Ich denke oft **dar**an. *I often think of it.*

The object of a preposition may also be an entire infinitive phrase or a clause; in such a case a **da(r)-** must be attached to the preposition to anticipate the phrase or clause that follows.

Natürlich dachte man zuerst **daran,** sich in Berlin zu versammeln.
Naturally at first they thought of meeting in Berlin.

Er freut sich **darauf,** die Stadt Weimar zu besichtigen.
He is looking forward to going sightseeing in Weimar.

Er erinnert sich **daran,** daß er es in einem Schulbuch gesehen hat.
He remembers (the fact) that he has seen it in a textbook.

Das kommt **darauf** an, ob man über Politik oder Literatur spricht.
That depends on whether you are talking about politics or literature.

Word Study and Usage

I. *FOREIGN WORDS IN GERMAN*

Like most languages, German occasionally borrows a word from another language, either because it has no exact linguistic equivalent of its own, or simply because foreign influences cause the non-German word to find greater favor than the native word. In the case of borrowed nouns, the gender may or may not be the same as it is in the original language.

The following is a sample list of foreign words you have met, along with their German equivalents (when they exist):

das Auto	der Wagen
das Café	das Kaffeehaus
die Party	die Gesellschaft
der Sketch	(in theater language: no equivalent)
das Theater	das Schauspielhaus
die Tour	der Rundgang, die Rundfahrt
das Hobby	die Liebhaberei, das Steckenpferd
das Picknick	die Landpartie [*archaic*]
das Souvenir	das Reiseandenken

II. ADJECTIVAL NOUNS (II)

German has some nouns which have been derived directly from adjectives. Of these you have had: **der Deutsche, der Bekannte,** and **der Verwandte.** The declension of these nouns follows the adjective-ending pattern, that is, the ending on the noun will depend on whether there is a preceding **der-** or **ein-** word, and on the case in which it is used. A masculine form refers to a man; a feminine form refers to a woman; plural forms refer to people (with no distinction as to male or female).

The nominative forms of these nouns will follow the pattern below:

der Deutsche (the German man)   **die Deutsche** (the German woman)
ein Deutscher (a German man)   **eine Deutsche** (a German woman)

die Deutschen (the German people)
keine Deutschen (no German people)

These nouns can be used in any case and with other **der-** or **ein-**words.

Er ist ein Komiker, dessen Namen **jeder Deutsche** kennt.
He is a comedian whose name every German knows.

Er hat **bei seinen Verwandten** gewohnt.
He lived with his relatives.

They can also be used with no **der-** or **ein-**word preceding; they then take the ending of unpreceded adjectives.

Sie wohnen **bei Verwandten.**
They are living with relatives.

When adjectival nouns are used as neuters, they refer to abstractions.

das Deutsche (that which is German)

In addition to the standard adjectival nouns mentioned above, others can be formed.

EXAMPLES: **der Alte** (the old man), **die Alte** (the old woman), **die Alten** (the old people)

das Interessante (the interesting thing, that which is interesting)

das Natürlichste (the most natural thing, that which is most natural)

Class Drills

I. a. Restate the following condition contrary-to-fact sentences in past time, changing the jetzt *to* gestern:

EXAMPLE: **Wenn er** *jetzt ankäme, wäre* **es besser.**
Wenn er *gestern angekommen wäre, wäre* **es besser** *gewesen.*

Wenn er jetzt anriefe, wäre es besser.
Wenn er es uns jetzt gäbe, wäre es besser.
Wenn er es jetzt hätte, *etc.*
Wenn er jetzt käme,
Wenn er jetzt ginge,
Wenn er jetzt hier wäre,
Wenn er es jetzt bestellte,
Wenn er sich jetzt erinnerte,
Wenn er es jetzt könnte,
Wenn er es jetzt dürfte,
Wenn er es jetzt wüßte,

b. Restate the sentences in exercise a. as past condition contrary-to-fact, using sie *(they) as the subject in place of* er.

II. Restate the second clauses in the following group as the conclusions of past condition contrary-to-fact sentences:

EXAMPLE: **Wenn wir gestern angekommen wären, (es hat keinen Zweck gehabt)**
Wenn wir gestern angekommen wären, *hätte es keinen Zweck gehabt.*

Wenn wir gestern angekommen wären, (er hat uns herumgeführt)
(er hat auf uns gewartet)
(er hat uns die Stadt gezeigt)
(wir haben ihn angetroffen)
(wir haben es gesehen)
(wir haben es gekonnt)
(wir haben es gedurft)
(wir haben Karten bekommen)
(er ist da gewesen)
(es ist uns gelungen)
(wir sind mitgefahren)

III. Restate the following wishes in past time:

EXAMPLE: **Wenn er nur länger *wartete!***
Wenn er nur länger *gewartet hätte!*

Wenn er uns nur besuchte!
Wenn ich mich nur erinnerte!
Wenn ich nur Erfahrung damit hätte!
Wenn es nur schneller ginge!
Wenn er nur mitkäme!
Wenn sie nur nicht so ungeduldig wäre!
Wenn ich es nur könnte!
Wenn ich es nur wüßte!

IV. a. Restate the following sentences, omitting <u>wenn</u>:

Wenn wir gestern angekommen wären, so hätten wir ihn angetroffen.
Wenn ich Erfahrung gehabt hätte, so hätte ich mich zurechtgefunden.
Wenn er mitgekommen wäre, so hätte er das Denkmal gesehen.
Wenn es schneller gegangen wäre, so hätten wir dort gegessen.
Wenn ich gekonnt hätte, so wäre ich öfter hingefahren.

b. Restate the original sentences in exercise a., reversing the order of the clauses.

V. a. Restate each of the following sentences as a conjecture, first in present time, then in past time. Begin each with: <u>Es kommt mir vor, als ob</u> . . . :

EXAMPLE: **Sie hat recht.**
Es kommt mir vor, *als ob sie recht hätte.*
Es kommt mir vor, *als ob sie recht gehabt hätte.*

Sie wohnen hier.
Es interessiert ihn.
Es gefällt ihnen nicht.
Es hat keinen Zweck,
Es ist nicht wahr.
Er kommt nicht.
Es geht nicht.
Sie wird ungeduldig.
Sie können es nicht.
Er weiß es.

b. *Restate the sentences in exercise* a. *as conjectures again, this time omitting the* ob.

VI. a. *Restate the following phrases as infinitive phrase objects according to the example:*

EXAMPLE: **nach Berlin fahren**
Er freut sich darauf, nach Berlin zu fahren.

das Denkmal fotografieren
die Stadt sehen
an der Tour teilnehmen
das Berliner Ensemble besuchen

b. *Restate the following clauses according to the example:*

EXAMPLE: **das Wetter ist gut**
Es kommt darauf an, ob das Wetter gut ist.

er hat recht
er kennt es gut
er hat Erfahrung
sie hat den Fotoapparat mitgebracht

c. *Restate the following clauses according to the example:*

EXAMPLE: **sie kommt zu spät**
Sie kann nichts dafür, daß sie zu spät kommt.

sie macht Fehler
sie kann nicht kochen
sie findet es komisch
sie verpaßt immer den Zug

VII. Restate the following sentences, substituting adjectival nouns formed from the given adjectives:

1. Der Deutsche hat das gesagt.
   (unbekannt)
   (alt)
   (krank)

2. Ein Deutscher hat das gesagt.
   (unbekannt)
   (alt)
   (krank)

3. Die Deutsche hat das gesagt.
   (unbekannt)
   (alt)
   (krank)

4. Die Deutschen haben das gesagt.
   (unbekannt)
   (alt)
   (krank)

5. Das war das Erstaunliche.
   (richtig)
   (großartig)
   (sehenswert)
   (hervorragend)
   (einfachst-)

Exercises

I. Rewrite the following sentences as condition contrary-to-fact statements. Treat the sentences that are in the present tense as present contrary-to-fact conditions, and those in a past tense as past contrary-to-fact conditions:

1. Wenn er nach Bonn kommt, ruft er mich an. 2. Wenn er noch dort wohnt, kann er uns herumführen. 3. Hat er Weimar besucht, so hat er sicher Aufnahmen gemacht. 4. Kommt er pünktlich an, so kann er uns helfen. 5. Ist sie in Köln gewesen, so hat sie den Dom gesehen. 6. Wenn er Durst hat, geht er in ein Lokal. 7. Ist ihm das gelungen, so hat er Glück gehabt. 8. Wenn er den Zug verpaßte, fuhr er mit dem Auto. 9. Wenn die Vorlesung um acht anfing, kam er zu spät. 10. Wenn sie zu lange tanzte, wurde sie müde.

II. Connect the phrases in parentheses with the introductory clause, using <u>als ob</u>. *Watch the tenses in the* <u>als ob</u>-*clauses:*

EXAMPLE: **Er sieht aus, (er war in Florida)**
Er sieht aus, *als ob er in Florida gewesen wäre.*

1. Sie sieht aus, (sie war krank)
    (sie hat Kopfschmerzen)
    (sie hat Angst)

2. Es kommt mir vor, (wir müssen lange warten)
    (er ist kein guter Schauspieler)
    (er hat es gesagt)

3. Sie sprechen so gut deutsch, (sie sind Deutsche)
    (sie waren lange in Deutschland)

4. Er kennt Bonn, (er kommt aus Bonn)
    (er wohnte lange dort)

5. Ich erinnere mich so gut daran, (ich habe es gestern gesehen)
    (ich nahm daran teil)
    (ich sehe es vor mir)

III. Translate into English. In sentences 1–5, reproduce the German sentences from your English translations:

1. Ich freue mich schon darauf, Ihnen die Stadt zu zeigen. 2. Wenn er den Wagen mitgebracht hat, kann er uns vielleicht mitnehmen. 3. Wenn ich wüßte, wie sie heißt, würde ich sie anrufen. 4. Wenn sie den Schmuggler doch nur gefaßt hätten! 5. Wenn es nicht so langsam gegangen wäre, hätten wir den Zug nicht verpaßt. 6. Kommt es Ihnen nicht auch vor, als hätte er das schon früher erwähnt? 7. Hätte ich mich nur daran erinnert, daß er nicht mehr hier wohnt! 8. Hättest du den Stadtplan nicht vergessen, so könnten wir uns leichter zurechtfinden. 9. Warum hat er Sie nicht herumführen wollen? 10. Es sah aus, als wäre es ihr gelungen.

IV. Translate:

1. If you had brought your car along, we would have gone to Weimar. 2. If I had only seen this monument! 3. They looked as if they were exhausted. 4. He is looking forward to seeing you. 5. It depends on where they arrive. 6. It seemed to him that (*als ob*) he had heard something. 7. I know that she did not like it. 8. If he only knew that! 9. He is thinking of calling her. 10. I can't remember it.

11. Do you have relatives in Munich?   12. That was the most natural thing.

V. a. Composition. Write ten sentences in the form of a composition on this topic — „Tom in Weimar." For each sentence use the words suggested below:

1. Tom und Norbert   wohnen
2. die beiden   sich freuen auf   Besichtigungstour machen
3. leider   Peter   antreffen
4. Peter   Freund   Weimar   wohnen
5. wenn   früher   Peter   herumführen   aber Tom   Erfahrung
6. vor allem   Goethe-Schiller-Denkmal
7. Tom   kennen   denn   Bild   Schulbuch
8. schade   Tom   Fotoapparat   sonst   Aufnahmen machen
9. er   werden bekommen   Bild   Tante
10. sie   viele Bilder   weil   Hobby

b. Free Composition. Write a short dialogue — Tom and Norbert's aunt have a conversation in which they discuss Tom's impressions of Germany.

Active Vocabulary

die Angst, –, ⸚e	fear	**fremd**	strange, alien
an-treffen,	to meet	**der Gegensatz,**	contrast
traf . . . an,		**–es, ⸚e**	
hat ange-		**gleich**	the same
troffen,		**herum-führen**	to show around
trifft . . . an		**das Hobby, –s, –s**	hobby
besichtigen	to go sightseeing, visit	**der Hofmann, –s,**	courtier
biegen, bog, ist	to turn, bend	**Hofleute**	
(hat)		**idealistisch**	idealistic
gebogen		**der Klassiker, –s, –**	classical author, classic
dar-stellen	to present, depict, portray	**leid tun**	to be sorry
das Denkmal, –s,	monument	**es tut ihm**	he is sorry
⸚er		**leid**	
die Ecke, –, –n	corner	**der Ort, –(e)s, –e**	place
die Erfahrung, –,	experience	**die Persönlichkeit,**	personality, character
–en		**–, –en**	
sich (*acc.*) **erinnern**	to remember (someone *or* something)	**reif**	mature
(an + acc.)		**das Schulbuch,**	textbook
der Fotoapparat,	camera	**–s, ⸚er**	
–s, –e		**die Sehenswürdig-**	sight, place of interest
der Freiheitskämp-	fighter for liberty	**keit, –, –en**	
fer, –s, –			

das Souvenir, –s, –s   souvenir

die Tante, –, –n   aunt

der Verwandte, –n, –n   relative

vorgestern   the day before yesterday

weltmännisch   sophisticated, gentlemanly

eine Zeitlang   for a while

sich (*acc.*) zurechtfinden, fand ... zurecht, hat zurechtgefunden   to find one's way

Zweiundzwanzigste Lektion

Review

Reading Practice

Tom schreibt an seinen deutschen Freund in den USA.

Lieber Peter,

wenn Du Dir die Briefmarke (*stamp*) auf diesem Brief genau angesehen hättest, wüßtest Du, wo ich bin. „Deutsche Demokratische Republik" steht darauf. Ich bin also im „anderen Deutschland", nämlich in Weimar. Wir sind gerade von einer langen Besichtigungstour durch die Stadt zurückgekommen. Jetzt bin ich müde und muß mich ausruhen. Also der richtige Augenblick zum Briefeschreiben.

In den letzten Wochen habe ich viel erlebt. Ich mache nämlich jetzt am Ende meines Deutschlandjahres eine Rundfahrt durch Mitteleuropa. Ich war in der „heimlichen" Hauptstadt Westdeutschlands, in München, dann in der österreichischen Hauptstadt, Wien, von dort nach der früheren Hauptstadt Deutschlands, nach Berlin, und jetzt bin ich in der quasi-Hauptstadt des europäischen Geistes (*intellect, spirit*) während der Goethezeit. Es sieht so aus, als ob mich nur Hauptstädte interessierten, nicht wahr? Aber das stimmt natürlich nicht ganz. Am Freitag z. B. fahre ich weiter nach Göttingen, das ja sehr idyllisch sein soll, aber kaum hauptstädtisch ist. Von dort geht es nach Bremen oder Hamburg weiter; es kommt darauf an, mit welchem Schiff ich nach Hause zurückfahre. Am liebsten wäre ich noch ein zweites Jahr geblieben, aber leider kann ich das nicht.

Wenn Du mich fragen würdest, welcher Teil Deutschlands mir am besten gefallen hat, so müßte ich wie ein Diplomat antworten: jeder Teil des Landes hat seinen eigenen Reiz. Ich bin neugierig auf den Norden. Den kenne ich ja noch gar nicht, und wie man mir gesagt hat, ist der Gegensatz zwischen Norddeutschland und Süddeutschland erstaunlich.

Alles in allem darf ich sagen, daß mein Jahr hier alle meine Erwartungen (*expectations*) übertroffen hat. In diesen elf Monaten habe ich unglaublich viel gesehen und gelernt. Du siehst also, ich habe mich ein wenig in dieses Land verliebt (*fallen in love*), und ich denke jetzt schon daran, eines Tages zurückzukommen. Selbstverständlich freue ich mich jetzt auf die Heimat, aber der Abschied (*departure*) wird mir doch schwer fallen.

Wir werden uns wohl noch sehen, wenn ich nach Hause zurückkomme, nicht wahr?

Bis dann
Dein
Tom

Drills

I. COMPARATIVE OF ADJECTIVES

Substitute the correct form of the element indicated:

A. Das ist ein schönerer Film. (**gut**)
   Das ist ein besserer Film. (**der**)
   Das ist der bessere Film. (**Rolle**)
   Das ist die bessere Rolle. (**ein**)
   Das ist eine bessere Rolle. (**Kabarett**)
   Das ist ein besseres Kabarett. (**alt**)
   Das ist ein älteres Kabarett. (**der**)
   Das ist das ältere Kabarett.

B. Ich möchte das bessere Zimmer haben. (**ein**)
   Ich möchte ein besseres Zimmer haben. (**modern**)
   Ich möchte ein moderneres Zimmer haben. (**die Wohnung**)
   Ich möchte die modernere Wohnung haben. (**ein**)
   Ich möchte eine modernere Wohnung haben. (**dieser**)
   Ich möchte diese modernere Wohnung haben. (**groß**)
   Ich möchte diese größere Wohnung haben. (**Koffer**)
   Ich möchte diesen größeren Koffer haben. (**Ihr**)
   Ich möchte Ihren größeren Koffer haben.

II. SUPERLATIVE OF ADJECTIVES

Substitute the correct form of the element indicated:

A. Das ist die berühmteste Kirche. (**unser**)
   Das ist unsere berühmteste Kirche. (**Professor**)
   Das ist unser berühmtester Professor. (**alt**)
   Das ist unser ältester Professor. (**das Kind**)
   Das ist das älteste Kind. (**jung**)
   Das ist das jüngste Kind. (**ihr**)

Das ist ihr jüngstes Kind. (**Vetter**)
Das ist ihr jüngster Vetter. (**die Studenten**)
Das sind die jüngsten Studenten. (**gut**)
Das sind die besten Studenten.

B. Sie hat das modernste Haus gekauft. (**klein**)
Sie hat das kleinste Haus gekauft. (**Wagen**)
Sie hat den kleinsten Wagen gekauft. (**schön**)
Sie hat den schönsten Wagen gekauft. (**gut**)
Sie hat den besten Wagen gekauft. (**die Möbel**)
Sie hat die besten Möbel gekauft. (**die Uhr**)
Sie hat die beste Uhr gekauft.

III. RELATIVE PRONOUNS

Substitute the new relative pronoun antecedent:

A. Das war der Film, der uns gefallen hat. (**Vorlesung**)
Das war die Vorlesung, die uns gefallen hat. (**Roman**)
Das war der Roman, der uns gefallen hat. (**Konzert**)
Das war das Konzert, das uns gefallen hat. (**Legende**)
Das war die Legende, die uns gefallen hat.

B. Das ist ein Film, den ich sehen möchte. (**Lokal**)
Das ist ein Lokal, das ich sehen möchte. (**Vorstellung**)
Das ist eine Vorstellung, die ich sehen möchte. (**Stadtteil**)
Das ist ein Stadtteil, den ich sehen möchte. (**Café**)
Das ist ein Café, das ich sehen möchte.

C. Kennen Sie den Professor, von dem er spricht? (**Geschichte**)
Kennen Sie die Geschichte, von der er spricht? (**Romane**)
Kennen Sie die Romane, von denen er spricht? (**Lied**)
Kennen Sie das Lied, von dem er spricht? (**Galerie**)
Kennen Sie die Galerie, von der er spricht? (**Komiker**)
Kennen Sie den Komiker, von dem er spricht?

IV. DOUBLE INFINITIVE

Substitute the new subject or verb:

Ich habe das nicht spielen wollen. (**er**)
Er hat das nicht spielen wollen. (**dürfen**)
Er hat das nicht spielen dürfen. (**wir**)
Wir haben das nicht spielen dürfen. (**können**)
Wir haben das nicht spielen können. (**sie:** *they*)

Sie haben das nicht spielen können. (**mögen**)
Sie haben das nicht spielen mögen. (**ich**)
Ich habe das nicht spielen mögen.

V. GENERAL SUBJUNCTIVE: PRESENT TIME AND PAST TIME

Substitute the new subject or verb:

A. Wenn ich das nur wüßte! (**er**)
   Wenn er das nur wüßte! (**können**)
   Wenn er das nur könnte! (**sie:** *they*)
   Wenn sie das nur könnten! (**bemerken**)
   Wenn sie das nur bemerkten! (**sie:** *she*)
   Wenn sie das nur bemerkte! (**haben**)
   Wenn sie das nur hätte! (**ich**)
   Wenn ich das nur hätte! (**bekommen**)
   Wenn ich das nur bekäme! (**wir**)
   Wenn wir das nur bekämen!

B. Hätte er nur gewartet! (**sie:** *they*)
   Hätten sie nur gewartet! (**mitgehen**)
   Wären sie nur mitgegangen! (**wir**)
   Wären wir nur mitgegangen! (**bleiben**)
   Wären wir nur geblieben! (**ich**)
   Wäre ich nur geblieben! (**fragen**)
   Hätte ich nur gefragt! (**du**)
   Hättest du nur gefragt!

Exercises

I. FUTURE, FUTURE PERFECT, AND WEAK IRREGULAR VERBS

Rewrite the following sentences as (a) present probability (future + <u>wohl</u>), (b) simple past, (c) past probability (future perf. + <u>wohl</u>):

EXAMPLE: **Er nennt keinen Namen.**
Er wird wohl keinen Namen nennen.
Er nannte keinen Namen.
Er wird wohl keinen Namen genannt haben.

1. Sie weiß nichts davon.
2. Sie bringen den Stadtplan mit.
3. Er kennt den Amerikaner nicht.

4. Sie denkt gern daran.
5. Sie rennen auf den Bahnhof.

II. RELATIVE PRONOUNS, PERSONAL PRONOUNS, AND DA- PRONOUN SUBSTITUTES

Rewrite the following sentences, changing them into two sentences:

EXAMPLE: **Hol mal bitte die Brote, die auf dem Rücksitz liegen.**
Hol mal bitte die Brote. Sie liegen auf dem Rücksitz.

1. Das ist der Spion, den sie heute gefaßt haben.   2. Diese Leute, bei denen Tom wohnt, sind Norberts Verwandte.   3. Die beiden wollten auch daran teilnehmen, was aber leider unmöglich war.   4. Ich habe einen Freund in Bonn, bei dem Sie sicher wohnen können.   5. Das ist der Fotoapparat, mit dem ich die Aufnahmen gemacht habe.   6. Ich kenne einen Geschäftsmann dort, der Ihnen bestimmt helfen wird.   7. Der Schauspieler, dessen Namen ich leider vergessen habe, hat großartig gespielt.   8. Hast du das Denkmal gesehen, von dem ich dir erzählt habe?

III. COMPARISON OF ADJECTIVES

Rewrite the following sentences, changing the comparative forms to the positive:

1. Haben Sie keinen besseren Kriminalroman?   2. Er ist ein jüngerer Dichter.   3. Können Sie nicht lauter sprechen?   4. Gehen Sie lieber ins Konzert?   5. Das ist ein einfacheres Gedicht.   6. Er ist ein älterer Herr.   7. Wir haben jetzt kälteres Wetter.   8. Hier gibt es jetzt mehr Künstler.

IV. GENERAL SUBJUNCTIVE

Rewrite the following as conditional sentences that are not contrary to fact. (For past time, use present perfect tense.):

1. Wenn ich Zeit hätte, ginge ich ins Kino.   2. Wenn er es gewußt hätte, so wäre er sicher hingefahren.   3. Wenn wir noch Karten bekämen, könnten wir ins Konzert gehen.   4. Wenn ich länger hier bliebe, würde ich mir den Dom ansehen.   5. Wenn er es tun wollte, könnte er es bestimmt.

V. DOUBLE INFINITIVE

Add the modal indicated and write the sentences in the present perfect tense:

1. Er holt die Bilder ab. (**wollen**)   2. Sie bleibt drei Tage in München. (**müssen**)   3. Wir finden uns nicht zurecht. (**können**)   4. Ich rufe sie nicht an. (**dürfen**)   5. Er fängt früher an. (**sollen**)

VI. TRANSLATION

Translate the following sentences:

1. He is an amazingly talented painter.   2. Three days ago he gave an interesting lecture.   3. I found it somewhere or other.   4. If only it were not so strenuous.   5. It looks as if he has missed the train.   6. I am looking forward to visiting my relatives.   7. We need that in order to work.   8. It is getting darker and darker.   9. They worked for hours. 10. She doesn't drive as fast as he.   11. He has enough money (*das Geld*) in his pocket.   12. Isn't that the easiest thing?

Im Harz

Dreiundzwanzigste Lektion

„Harzreise"

[*Tom und Norbert in einer kleinen Pension in Göttingen. Vor dem Schlafen-gehen.*]

TOM — Was hat Heine über Göttingen gesagt?

NORBERT — Es sei grau und langweilig, sei immer so gewesen und werde auch so bleiben. Viele behaupten, er hätte recht gehabt.

TOM — Typisch Heine. Mir gefällt's hier, und das Harzgebirge soll ja auch sehr idyllisch sein.

NORBERT — Das ist es auch. Es ist noch keine Touristenattraktion, also sozusagen noch unberührt von der Zivilisation.

TOM — Ich freue mich sehr auf unsere „Harzreise" morgen. Schade, daß wir nicht auf den Brocken können.

NORBERT — Es heißt immer, das wäre d e r deutsche Berg. Aber zu sehen gibt's da nicht viel. Haben Sie auch solide Sportschuhe bei sich?

TOM — Ja, mit Frau Thieles Hilfe habe ich für alle Fälle vorgesorgt. Sie meinte, es würde nichts schaden, ein drittes Paar Schuhe einzupacken.

NORBERT — [*gähnt*] Schon zehn. Und morgen wollen wir früh aus dem Bett.

TOM — Gute Nacht, Norbert, angenehme Ruhe.

NORBERT — Danke, gleichfalls.

Harzreise[1]

[*Tom and Norbert in a small* Pension[2] *in Göttingen. Before going to bed.*]

TOM — What did Heine say about Göttingen?

NORBERT — That it was gray and dull, that it had always been that way, and would always stay that way. Many people say he was right.

TOM — Typical for Heine. I like it here; and the Harz mountains are supposed to be very idyllic, too.

NORBERT — And they are. They haven't become a tourist attraction yet, and so they're still, you might say, untouched by civilization.

TOM — I'm looking forward to our *Harzreise* tomorrow. Too bad we can't go up to the *Brocken*.[3]

NORBERT — They always say that it's *the* German mountain. But there's not much to see there. Do you have sturdy walking shoes with you?

TOM — Yes. With Mrs. Thiele's help, I'm prepared for any eventuality. She thought it wouldn't hurt to pack a third pair of shoes.

NORBERT — [*yawns*] Ten o'clock already. And tomorrow we want to get up early.

TOM — Good-night, Norbert. Sleep well.

NORBERT — Thank you; the same to you.

---

[1] *Harzreise:* Name of a famous prose work by Heine. See the reading text of this lesson. [2] **die Pension:** A small, usually family-run establishment that rents rooms to tourists or more permanent guests. [3] **der Brocken:** Famous mountain in the *Harz* range. Legend connects it with witch gatherings. It is located in East Germany.

Lesestück XXIII

Norberts Heine–Zitat,[1] wonach Göttingen grau und langweillig sei, ist noch sehr milde, wenn man es mit anderen Bemerkungen[2] Heines vergleicht.[3] Er war in dieser Stadt nicht glücklich gewesen, weil sie ihm zu provinziell war. Auch hatte ihn das Jurastudium enttäuscht. Kein Wunder, daß er, einer der schärfsten Satiriker unter den deutschen Dichtern, sich über 5 Göttingen und die Göttinger lustig machte. Das geschieht[4] am Anfang des Buches „Die Harzreise".

Heine behauptet, die Stadt sei durch ihre Würste[5] und Universität berühmt (in dieser Reihenfolge[6]). Sie habe 999 Feuerstellen,[7] diverse Kirchen, eine Entbindungsanstalt,[8] einen Karzer,[9] eine Bibliothek und einen Ratskeller,[10] 10 wo das Bier sehr gut sei. (Die Satire liegt natürlich darin, daß er Dinge zusammenstellt, die nicht zusammengehören.) Er gibt den schönen Göttinger Kirchen das plätteste[11] aller Adjektive, „divers", und das einzige,[12] was er wirklich lobt,[13] ist das Bier. Die Stadt sei schön und gefalle einem am besten, wenn man sie mit dem Rücken[14] ansehe. In Göttingen gebe es Studenten, 15 Professoren, Philister und Vieh.[15] Davon sei das Vieh der prominenteste Stand.[16]

Das ist der scharfe, ironische Heine, aber die „Harzreise" ist mehr als nur Gesellschaftssatire. Daneben finden wir auch lyrische Beschreibungen,[17] Traumvisionen, Gedichte von hoher Qualität. Heine selbst sagt, es sei „eine 20 Mischung[18] von Naturschilderung,[19] Witz, Poesie und Washington Irvingscher Beobachtung". Es war eine ganz neue Art[20] von Prosa und damals, 1826, eine Sensation auf dem deutschen Büchermarkt. Viele Leser applaudierten, andere fühlten sich angegriffen, als Heine zum Beispiel über seine Landsleute schrieb, das wäre das Schöne bei den Deutschen: keiner sei so verrückt,[21] daß er 25 nicht noch einen Verrückteren fände, der ihn verstehe.

Wir betrachten Heine heute in seiner Mischung von Ironie, Skepsis, Poesie, Witz und Weltschmerz[22] als einen der ersten modernen Prosaschriftsteller. Auch unter den deutschen Lyrikern gehört er zu den besten. Große Komponisten wie Schubert, Schumann, Brahms und Wolf haben seine Gedichte in 30

---

[1] **das Zitat, –s, –e** quotation
[2] **die Bemerkung, –, –en** remark
[3] **vergleichen, verglich, hat verglichen** to compare
[4] **geschehen, geschah, ist geschehen, geschieht** to happen
[5] **die Wurst, –, ⁻e** sausage
[6] **die Reihenfolge, –** order, sequence
[7] **die Feuerstelle, –, –en** fireplace
[8] **die Entbindungsanstalt, –, –en** maternity ward
[9] **der Karzer, –s, –** student jail
[10] **der Ratskeller, –s, –** cellar restaurant of the city hall

[11] **platt** flat
[12] **einzig** only, single
[13] **loben** to praise
[14] **der Rücken, –s, –** back
[15] **das Vieh, –(e)s** cattle
[16] **der Stand, –(e)s, ⁻e** class, rank
[17] **die Beschreibung, –, –en** description
[18] **die Mischung, –, –en** mixture
[19] **die Naturschilderung, –, –en** description of scenery
[20] **die Art, –, –en** kind, sort, type
[21] **verrückt** crazy, mad
[22] **der Weltschmerz, –es** world–weariness, melancholy

Hunderten von Liedern vertont.[23] E i n Gedicht, das man nicht vertont hat, das aber den Heineschen Witz hervorragend wiedergibt,[24] soll dieses Lesestück beschließen.[25]

> Das Fräulein[26] stand am Meere[27]
> Und seufzte[28] lang und bang,[29]
> Es rührte sie so sehre
> Der Sonnenuntergang.[30]
>
> „Mein Fräulein! sein Sie munter,
> Das ist ein altes Stück;
> Hier vorne geht sie unter
> Und kehrt von hinten zurück.“

[23] **vertonen** to set to music
[24] **wieder-geben, gab . . . wieder, hat wiedergegeben, gibt . . . wieder** to reflect, render
[25] **beschließen, beschloß, hat beschlossen** to conclude
[26] **das Fräulein, –s, –** young lady, Miss
[27] **das Meer, –(e)s,–e** sea, ocean
[28] **seufzen** to sigh
[29] **bang(e)** worried, upset
[30] **„Es . . . Sonnenuntergang“** prose translation: "The sunset moved her so very much."

Fragen und Antworten

1. Was hat Tom Norbert gefragt?
   Er hat ihn gefragt, was Heine über Göttingen gesagt habe.
2. Was hat Heine über Göttingen gesagt?
   Es wäre grau und langweilig, wäre immer so gewesen und würde auch so bleiben.
3. Hat Heine recht gehabt?
   Viele sagen, er habe recht gehabt.
4. Was sagte Tom über die geplante (*planned*) Harzreise?
   Er sagte, er freue sich sehr darauf.
5. Hat Tom solide Sportschuhe bei sich?
   Ja. Er sagt, er habe für alle Fälle vorgesorgt; Frau Thiele habe ihm geholfen.
6. Was sagte Frau Thiele zu Tom?
   Sie sagte, er solle ein drittes Paar Schuhe mitnehmen.
7. Findet Tom Göttingen langweilig?
   Nein, er behauptet, daß es ihm dort gefalle.
8. Ist der Brocken wirklich so interessant?
   Norbert meint, daß es da nicht viel zu sehen gäbe.

9. Was behauptet Heine in der „Harzreise"?

Er schreibt in der „Harzreise": „Göttingen ist durch seine Würste und die Universität bekannt."

Er schreibt in der „Harzreise", daß Göttingen durch seine Würste und die Universität berühmt wäre.

Structure and Practice

Explanation of Forms

SPECIAL SUBJUNCTIVE

In addition to the general subjunctive, explained in two previous lessons, German has another type of subjunctive, referred to as special subjunctive, which is restricted mainly to indirect discourse.

A. Forms of the Special Subjunctive

Like the general subjunctive, the special subjunctive has four tenses: present, past, future, and future perfect. The future perfect special subjunctive is so rare, however, that it will be omitted from our treatment here.

1. PRESENT TENSE: For all verbs except **sein,** the present special subjunctive is formed by adding the basic subjunctive personal endings to the infinitive stem. No verbs have stem changes in this tense.

haben	fahren	sprechen
ich habe	ich fahre	ich spreche
du habest	du fahrest	du sprechest
er, sie, es habe	er, sie, es fahre	er, sie, es spreche
wir haben	wir fahren	wir sprechen
ihr habet	ihr fahret	ihr sprechet
sie haben	sie fahren	sie sprechen
Sie haben	Sie fahren	Sie sprechen

but:

sein

ich sei	wir seien
du sei(e)st	ihr seiet
er, sie, es sei	sie seien
	Sie seien

2. PAST TENSE: The past tense of the special subjunctive is a compound tense. The present special subjunctive of **haben** or **sein** is used as the auxiliary with the past participle of the main verb.

sehen	gehen
ich **habe gesehen**	ich **sei gegangen**
du **habest gesehen**	du **sei(e)st gegangen**
er, sie, es **habe gesehen**	er, sie, es **sei gegangen**
wir **haben gesehen**	wir **seien gegangen**
ihr **habet gesehen**	ihr **seiet gegangen**
sie **haben gesehen**	sie **seien gegangen**
Sie **haben gesehen**	Sie **seien gegangen**

3. FUTURE TENSE: The future tense uses the present special subjunctive of **werden** as the auxiliary with the dependent infinitive.

sehen	gehen
ich **werde sehen**	ich **werde gehen**
du **werdest sehen**	du **werdest gehen**
er, sie, es **werde sehen**	er, sie, es **werde gehen**
wir **werden sehen**	wir **werden gehen**
ihr **werdet sehen**	ihr **werdet gehen**
sie **werden sehen**	sie **werden gehen**
Sie **werden sehen**	Sie **werden gehen**

B. Indirect Discourse

1. IN STATEMENTS: In the following synopsis you will see the changes that take place in English when a quotation is given indirectly.

DIRECT QUOTATION	INDIRECT QUOTATION
He said, "I *am reading* that."	He said that he *was reading* that.
He said, "I *read* that."	
He said, "I *have read* that."	He said that he *had read* that.
He said, "I *had read* that."	
He said, "I *will read* that."	He said that he *would read* that.

This system is, of course, not always adhered to in colloquial English. One is likely to hear, "He said that he's reading that," in place of the first indirect quotation shown above. In other words, there is a tendency in English to use the same verb form in the direct and indirect quotation.

German follows a similar pattern of changing the verb form when restating a quotation indirectly. In the indirect quotation, either the general subjunctive or the special subjunctive (if the form does not look like an indicative) may be used; the subjunctive tense in the indirect quotation is the same as the indicative tense in the direct quotation. Remember, however, that the general subjunctive as well as the special subjunctive have only one past tense. German, like English, does not distinguish among the various past tenses in an indirect quotation. (See English synopsis above.)

In the synopsis below, each indirect quotation is given first in the special subjunctive, then in the general subjunctive.

DIRECT QUOTATION	INDIRECT QUOTATION
Sie sagte: „Er **hat** recht."	Sie sagte, daß er recht **habe.**
	or: daß er recht **hätte.**
Sie sagte: „Er **hatte** recht."	
Sie sagte: „Er **hat** recht **gehabt.**"	Sie sagte, daß er recht **gehabt habe.**
Sie sagte: „Er **hatte** recht **gehabt.**"	*or:* daß er recht **gehabt hätte.**
Sie sagte: „Er **wird** recht **haben.**"	Sie sagte, daß er recht **haben werde.**
	or: daß er recht **haben würde.**

In any of the above examples, the **daß** may be omitted; the verb is then in normal second position.

> Sie sagte, daß er recht gehabt **habe.**
> Sie sagte, er **habe** recht gehabt.

2. IN QUESTIONS: Questions quoted indirectly follow the same pattern as statements as far as tenses are concerned.

> Er fragte: „Was **hat** Heine über Göttingen **gesagt?**"
> Er fragte, was Heine über Göttingen **gesagt habe** (*or **hätte***).

3. IN COMMANDS: In indirectly quoting a command, English uses *should;* German uses the present subjunctive (either general or special) of **sollen.**

> Sie sagte, er **solle** (**sollte**) ein drittes Paar Schuhe einpacken.
> *She said he **should** pack a third pair of shoes.*

4. VARIATIONS IN SPOKEN AND WRITTEN GERMAN: In spoken German the general subjunctive is preferred over the special subjunctive for indirect discourse. In highly colloquial German there is a growing tendency to use the indicative rather than the subjunctive.

In written German, the special subjunctive is preferred, unless the forms are identical with the indicative; both types of subjunctive may be mixed, even within the same quotation.

The advantage of the subjunctive for indirect quotations in writing, and even occasionally in speaking, is that there is then no necessity for the constant reminders that English has to use to indicate that the indirect quotation is continuing: *And then he added . . . ; he said further . . . ;* etc. As long as the German verbs continue to be in the subjunctive, it is clear that the writer or speaker is still quoting indirectly. In the reading text of this lesson, for example, Heine is indirectly quoted concerning the city of Göttingen. At one point the quotation continues for several sentences with no reminders except for the subjunctive verb forms:

> **Die Stadt *sei* schön und *gefalle* einem am besten, wenn man sie mit dem Rücken *ansehe*. Die Göttinger *teile* man in Studenten, Professoren, Philister und Vieh ein. Davon *sei* das Vieh der bedeutendste Stand.**

And even in the dialogue of this lesson, Tom asks: **Was hat Heine über Göttingen gesagt?** Norbert answers in the subjunctive with no introductory verb: **Es *sei* grau und langweilig, *sei* immer so gewesen und *werde* auch so bleiben.** The English equivalent would have to be aided to some extent: [*He said*] *that it was gray and dull, that it had always been that way and would always stay that way."*

Word Study and Usage

I. SPACING OF LETTERS FOR EMPHASIS

In printed German the letters of a word are often double-spaced, instead of italicized, for emphasis.

> Es heißt immer, das wäre d e r deutsche Berg.
> *They always say that it's the German mountain.*

When the word **ein** (in any declensional form) is double-spaced, it means *one* rather than *a* or *an*. In the reading text of this lesson, you will find the following example:

> E i n Gedicht, das man nicht vertont hat . . .
> *One poem which has not been set to music . . .*

II. SPECIAL MEANINGS OF *HEIßEN*

The expression **es heißt** is an impersonal construction that may be used in place of **man sagt** to mean *people say, they say,* or *it is said.*

> Es heißt immer, das wäre d e r deutsche Berg.
> *They always say that it's the German mountain.*

In this impersonal use it may also have the meaning *it says.*

> So heißt es wenigstens in einer Legende.
> *At least that's what it says in a legend.*
> So heißt es in der Zeitung.
> *So it says in the newspaper.*

Class Drills

I. a. Restate the following quotations indirectly, using the special subjunctive, and beginning each indirect quotation with daß:

EXAMPLE: **Sie sagte: „Ich bleibe dort."**
Sie sagte, daß sie dort bleibe.

1. Sie sagte: „Ich freue mich darauf."
   Sie sagte: „Ich erinnere mich daran."
   Sie sagte: „Ich glaube das nicht."
   Sie sagte: „Ich gehe in die Stadt."
   Sie sagte: „Ich nehme daran teil."
   Sie sagte: „Ich bekomme Angst."
   Sie sagte: „Es ist nicht wahr."
   Sie sagte: „Ich habe recht."
   Sie sagte: „Ich kann es tun."
   Sie sagte: „Ich weiß es."

2. Sie sagte: „Ich habe vorgesorgt."
   Sie sagte: „Ich hatte Kopfschmerzen."
   Sie sagte: „Ich freute mich darauf."
   Sie sagte: „Ich wußte es nicht."
   Sie sagte: „Ich hatte ihn angerufen."
   Sie sagte: „Ich bin zu früh gekommen."
   Sie sagte: „Ich war krank."
   Sie sagte: „Ich spazierte am Rhein entlang."
   Sie sagte: „Ich blieb dort."
   Sie sagte: „Ich wurde müde."

3. Sie sagte: „Ich werde ihn sehen."

Sie sagte: „Ich werde daran teilnehmen."
Sie sagte: „Ich werde eine Harzreise machen."
Sie sagte: „Ich werde dort bleiben."

b. Restate indirectly the quotations in exercise a., using the general subjunctive, and omitting the <u>daß</u> *in the indirect quotation.*

II. Restate the following direct questions indirectly, using the general subjunctive:

EXAMPLE: **Er fragte mich: „Haben Sie Zeit?"**
Er fragte mich, ob ich Zeit hätte.

1. Er fragte mich: „Haben Sie schon Bekannte?"
                   „Kommen Sie mit?"
                   „Sind Sie krank?"
                   „Gehen Sie oft ins Kino?"
                   „Wohnen Sie in Bonn?"
                   „Glauben Sie das nicht?"
                   „Wissen Sie das nicht?"
                   „Können Sie das?"

2. Er fragte mich: „Haben Sie das behauptet?"
                   „Haben Sie Schuhe eingepackt?"
                   „Haben Sie gut geschlafen?"
                   „Hatten Sie Zeit dazu?"
                   „Waren Sie gestern dort?"
                   „Sind Sie zu spät gekommen?"

III. a. Restate the following commands indirectly, using the special subjunctive and beginning each with: <u>Er sagte ihm</u> *. . . :*

EXAMPLE: **Besuchen Sie ihn bald!**
Er sagte ihm, er solle ihn bald besuchen.

Bringen Sie den Stadtplan mit!
Rufen Sie ihn an!
Bleiben Sie nicht zu lange!
Sehen Sie sich den Film an!
Packen Sie die Schuhe ein!
Vergessen Sie den Fotoapparat nicht!
Denken Sie daran!
Kommen Sie nicht zu spät!
Ruhen Sie sich aus!

b. Restate indirectly the commands in exercise a., using the general subjunctive and beginning each with: <u>Er sagte ihnen</u> . . . :

EXAMPLE: **Besuchen Sie ihn bald!**
Er sagte ihnen, sie sollten ihn bald besuchen.

Exercises

I. a. Rewrite the following sentences, using the special subjunctive for the indirect quotations:

1. Er sagte, er hätte recht gehabt. 2. Ich fragte ihn, wann er angekommen wäre. 3. Er behauptete, er wäre in der Vorlesung gewesen. 4. Ich sagte ihr, sie sollte mir ein Buch mitbringen. 5. Sie fragten, ob du einen Ausflug gemacht hättest. 6. Er fragte mich, wann sie käme. 7. Er schrieb uns, er könnte nicht vor Semesterbeginn kommen. 8. In der Zeitung heißt es, er wäre ein bekannter Dirigent. 9. Sie sagte, sie wollte es morgen tun. 10. Er schrieb, er würde nach Berlin fahren.

b. Rewrite the sentences in exercise a., using direct quotations.

II. Rewrite the following sentences as indirect discourse, using the general subjunctive. Start each sentence with: <u>Er sagte,</u> . . . :

1. Ich bin froh, daß sie auch nach Bonn kommt.
2. Diese idyllische Stadt wird ihnen sicher gefallen.
3. Den Dom muß ich unbedingt sehen.
4. Mein Freund war letzten Sonntag dort.
5. Er hatte Ost-Berlin besucht.
6. Auf dem Heimweg fuhren sie nach Weimar.
7. Sie sah sich diese historische Stadt an.
8. Bringen Sie bitte die Stadtkarte mit.
9. Schreib mir, wann du ankommst.
10. Gerd wird Tom am Flugplatz abholen.

III. Translate into English. In sentences 1–5, reproduce the German sentences from your English translations:

1. Es hat immer geheißen, es gäbe da nichts zu sehen. 2. Hätte ich das gewußt, so hätte ich vorgesorgt. 3. Er behauptet, er wäre nicht in Ost-Berlin gewesen. 4. Wären wir nur nach Weimar gefahren!

5. Wenn ich nur solide Schuhe bei mir hätte!   6. Sie wird wohl so etwas noch nie gesehen haben.   7. Warum hat man Sie nicht auf den Brocken gehen lassen?   8. Das Dorf, in dem er wohnt, soll sehr idyllisch sein. 9. Sie haben eine Harzreise gemacht, was wir bald auch tun werden. 10. Vor dem Schlafengehen erkundigte er sich nach dem Brocken, von dessen Geschichte er nicht viel wußte.

IV. Translate:

1. He said he liked the town.   2. We told them that they should go by car.   3. It won't hurt to do that.   4. They always say that he is a famous poet.   5. She asked him whether he had lived in a dormitory. 6. I think he is looking forward to it.   7. If you had helped me, I would have done it.   8. Doesn't he look as if he had been ill?   9. If I only had money (*das Geld*) with me.   10. Did she really say that I was right?

V. a. Composition. Write ten sentences in the form of a composition on this topic: — „In Göttingen." For each sentence use the words suggested below:

1. Schlafengehen   Pension   sich unterhalten   Göttingen   Heine
2. Heine   Student   Göttingen
3. Stadt   gefallen   nicht besonders
4. „Harzreise"   viel   ironisch   schreiben   über
5. z. B.
6. Tom   behaupten   Stadt   gefallen
7. Tom   sagen   schade   Brocken
8. Norbert   antworten   nicht interessant
9. weil   morgen   früh   müssen   zu Bett
10. denn   Fußtour   anstrengend

b. Free Composition: While resting on their hike, Tom tells Norbert about his home town. (Use your own home town as a model.)

Active Vocabulary

angenehm	. pleasant	**für alle Fälle**	for any eventuality
behaupten	to maintain, say	**gähnen**	to yawn
das Bett, –(e)s, –n	bed	**das Gebirge, –s, –**	mountains, mountain range
ein-packen	to pack		
der Fall, –(e)s, ∺e	case	**das Geld, –(e)s, –er**	money

gleichfalls!	the same to you, likewise	**der Schuh, –(e)s, –e**	shoe
grau	gray	**solide**	sturdy, strong
es heißt	they (people) say	**sozusagen**	as it were, so to speak
die Hilfe, –, –n	help	**der Sport, –(e)s**	sport
langweilig	boring, dull	**der Sportschuh, –s, –e**	walking shoe
mitnehmen, nahm . . . mit, hat mitgenommen, nimmt . . . mit	to take along	**der Tourist, –en, –en**	tourist
morgen	tomorrow	**die Touristenattraktion, –, –en**	tourist attraction
das Paar, –(e)s, –e	pair	**typisch**	typical
die Pension, –, –en	boarding house	**unberührt**	untouched
planen	to plan	**vor-sorgen**	to prepare, take precautions
die Reise, –, –n	trip	**die Wurst, –, ⸚e**	sausage
die Ruhe, –	rest	**die Zivilisation, –, –en**	civilization
schaden (*dat.*)	to do harm, hurt		

Mainzelmännchen vom ZDF*

* This is one of the favorite cartoon characters that appear briefly between commercials on *Zweites Deutsches Fehrnsehen*.

Vierundzwanzigste Lektion

Fernsehen

[*Tom und Ernst Schmidt, ein ehemaliger Schulkamerad von Gerd, jetzt Reporter beim Deutschen Fernsehen. Sie unterhalten sich über das Fernsehen.*]

ERNST — Sie loben das deutsche System, weil Sie wahrscheinlich nur die guten Programme gesehen haben. Aber neben den Vorteilen hat es auch Nachteile.

TOM — Zugegeben, unser Fernsehen besteht schon länger, und man kann hervorragende Sendungen sehen. Aber eins läßt sich nicht leugnen: unser Reklamesystem läßt viel zu wünschen übrig und ist nicht mit dem deutschen zu vergleichen.

ERNST — Wird wirklich etwa alle zehn Minuten das Programm unterbrochen? Macht man das auch bei Schauspielen?

TOM — Fast ausnahmslos. Und das an der spannendsten Stelle!

ERNST — Läßt sich das denn nicht ändern?

TOM — Es ist schon oft dagegen protestiert worden. Aber so ist es nun mal.

ERNST — Na, und wir beschweren uns über die Fernsehgebühren! Das ist ja das kleinere Übel.

TOM — Zweifellos. Ein Programm ohne Unterbrechung ist wirklich ein Genuß.

ERNST — Vielleicht findet sich in Amerika bald eine Lösung dafür.

TOM — Das wäre sehr zu wünschen.

Television

[*Tom and Ernst Schmidt, a former schoolmate of Gerd's, now a reporter in German television. They are talking about television.*]

ERNST — You praise the German system because you've probably only seen the good programs. But it has its disadvantages as well as its advantages.

TOM — Granted, our television has been in existence longer, and you can see excellent programs. But one thing can't be denied: our system of advertising leaves much to be desired and can't be compared with the German.

ERNST — Are the programs really interrupted about every ten minutes? Do they do that with plays, too?

TOM — Almost always. And at the most exciting part, too.

ERNST — Can't that be changed?

TOM — There have often been protests about it. But that's the way it is.

ERNST — Hm! And we complain about television taxes. That's certainly the lesser evil.

TOM — Without a doubt. An uninterrupted program is really a joy.

ERNST — Maybe they'll find a solution in America soon.

TOM — I wish they would.

Lesestück XXIV

Nicht nur auf dem Gebiet der Reklame ist das deutsche Fernsehen anders als das amerikanische. Auch in den Programmen, den Sendezeiten[1] usw. lassen sie sich kaum miteinander vergleichen. Zum Beispiel kann jeder Amerikaner von 7 Uhr morgens bis 1 Uhr nachts und noch später sein Fernsehgerät[2] anschalten.[3] Irgend etwas wird immer gegeben. Die Deutschen jedoch 5 können an Wochentagen meistens nur von 16 Uhr bis etwa um Mitternacht fernsehen. Eine „Late Late Show" also gibt es nicht und wird es wohl nie geben, obgleich[4] die Sendezeit am Wochenende länger ist.

Im deutschen Fernsehen gibt es fast keine Reklame. Man hat zwar das Werbefernsehen,[5] aber dafür ist eine halbe Stunde am Abend reserviert. In 10 dieser Zeit sieht man nur Werbesendungen, die von vielen Leuten, besonders von Kindern, geschätzt[6] werden, denn sie sind zum Teil ganz lustig und unterhaltend.[7] Die Programme werden nicht wie in Amerika von Auto– und Tabakfirmen, Bierbrauereien[8] und Hundefutterfabrikanten[9] finanziert, sondern vom Publikum. Jeder Besitzer eines Fernsehapparates zahlt[10] 8,50 DM Fernsehge- 15 bühren im Monat, und das Geld wird vom Briefträger[11] eingesammelt.[12] Wer sein Gerät nicht registrieren läßt, wer also „schwarz"[13] sieht und dabei gefaßt wird, wird bestraft.[14] Das kann sehr teuer[15] werden. Im Werbefernsehen sieht man manchmal den Vers:

Schwarzhören und -sehen 20
Kommt teuer zu stehen.[16]

Im Gegensatz zu Amerika, wo die Fernsehgesellschaften[17] Privateigentum[18] sind, oder zu Frankreich,[19] wo sie vom Staat kontrolliert werden, ist das deutsche Fernsehen eine sogenannte „Anstalt des öffentlichen Rechts".[20] Das heißt, weder[21] der Staat, noch[21] Interessengruppen, noch Privatpersonen 25 haben das Recht sich einzumischen.[22] Wie die englische BBC werden die beiden deutschen Fernsehanstalten, das „erste" und das „zweite" Programm,

---

[1] **die Sendezeit, –, –en** time of telecast
[2] **das Fernsehgerät, –s, –e** television set
[3] **an-schalten** to turn on
[4] **obgleich** although
[5] **das Werbefernsehen, –s** telecasting of commercials
[6] **schätzen** to appreciate
[7] **unterhaltend** entertaining
[8] **die Bierbrauerei, –, –en** brewery
[9] **der Hundefutterfabrikant, –en, –en** dog food manufacturer
[10] **zahlen** to pay
[11] **der Briefträger, –s, –** mailman
[12] **ein-sammeln** to collect
[13] **„schwarz"** *here* illegal

[14] **bestrafen** to punish
[15] **teuer** expensive
[16] **„Schwarzhören . . . stehen."** the meaning of this jingle is: "To listen to the radio and to watch television illegally will become expensive."
[17] **die Fernsehgesellschaft, –, –en** television network
[18] **das Privateigentum, –s** private property
[19] **Frankreich** France
[20] **„Anstalt des öffentlichen Rechts"** statutory institution
[21] **weder . . . noch** neither . . . nor
[22] **sich** (*acc.*) **ein-mischen** to interfere, meddle

DIESE WOCHE IM FERNSEHEN

Montag, 25. 10.

20.15 Uhr. ARD. Report (Farbe)

Leitung: Dieter Göbel. „Wer wählt 1973 die FDP?" Eine für die Sendung beim Institut für angewandte Sozialwissenschaft bestellte Analyse soll darüber Auskunft geben. „Report" berichtet außerdem über den Stand des Ermittlungsverfahrens, das wegen der Veröffentlichung geheimer Botschaftspapiere gegen einige Journalisten eingeleitet worden ist. ARD-Korrespondent Edmund Gruber will anläßlich der 2500-Jahr-Feier in Persepolis untersuchen, wie es um die Reformen des Schahs steht.

20.15 Uhr. ZDF. Gesundheitsmagazin „Praxis" (Farbe)

Moderator: Hans Mohl. Die Magazinsendung bringt Beispiele aus der Arbeit von Verhaltenstherapeuten und stellt den in Stockholm entwickelten neuen „Baby-Test im Mutterleib" vor, durch den sich das Geschlecht des Embryos im dritten Monat bestimmen läßt. Außerdem wird über das erste deutsche „Zentrum für die Diagnostik und Therapie chronischer Schmerzzustände" berichtet, das in der Mainzer Universitätsklinik eingerichtet worden ist.

21.00 Uhr. ARD. Dein Staat, das bekannte Unwesen (Farbe)

Mit „Angriffslust statt Poeterei" und „Satire statt Witzeln" will der Hannoveraner Kabarettist Dietrich Kittner in seiner 45-Minuten-Show unter anderem „Lebenshilfe für wohlmeinende Sozialdemokraten" geben.

21.00 Uhr. ZDF. Bestie Mensch

„Wir wünschen Monsieur Renoir, daß er möglichst bald aus dem Sumpfloch des Klassen-Kinos herausfindet", erklärten Pariser Kritiker 1938 nach der

Uraufführung dieses 22. Films von Jean Renoir. Das naturalistische Werk mit Jean Gabin und Simone Simon basiert auf Emile Zolas Roman „La bête humaine" und wird vom ZDF in neuer Synchronisation gezeigt.

21.45 Uhr. ARD. Den Zug verpaßt? (Farbe)

Das Ansehen der deutschen Forschung ist in den letzten Jahren erheblich gesunken. Die Fernseh-Autoren Frederic Vester und Gerhard Henschel suchen die Ursachen dafür in der Bonner Wissenschafts-Politik.

22.50 Uhr. ZDF. Fußnoten

Weil „wir mit einer rein phänomenologischen Betrachtung einer so wichtigen

Frage wie dem Rollenverhalten von Mann und Frau heute nicht mehr weiterkommen", hat der Münchner Filmemacher Edgar Reitz seinen 1967 mehrfach prämiierten Erstlingsfilm „Mahlzeiten" (Photo) umgearbeitet. Die Neufassung, die nun im „Filmforum" vorgestellt wird, soll „das Problem stärker konturieren" und „in einen gesellschaftlichen Zusammenhang stellen".

Dienstag, 26. 10.

11.00 Uhr, ZDF, und 21.00 Uhr, ARD. Staatsbesuch aus den Niederlanden (Farbe)

Königin Juliana und Prinz Bernhard in Bonn.

20.15 Uhr. ZDF. Versuchskaninchen? (Farbe)

1,5 Millionen Engländer sind seit Kriegsende in die „Neuen Städte" umgesiedelt worden, jene perfekt konzipierten Industrie- und Wohnzentren, die von der britischen Regierung in wirtschaftlich unerschlossenen Gebieten

angelegt wurden. Mit den meist aus City-Slums stammenden Bewohnern dieser neuen Siedlungen hat sich ZDF-Mitarbeiter Hans-Dieter Grabe unterhalten.

20.15 Uhr. NDR, RB, SFB (III). Hamburg 6, Karolinenviertel

Das Hamburger Autorenteam Christian Geissler, Hajo Dudda und Lothar Janssen, bekannt durch seine kritischen Features über den Strafvollzug („Ein Jahr Knast", „Sie nennen sich Schießer"), porträtieren diesmal Jugendliche aus dem Karolinenviertel beim Hamburger Schlachthof, einem jener städtischen Bezirke, die wegen der hohen Jugendkriminalität als „Knast-Vorfeld" gelten.

21.15 Uhr. ARD. Sand (Farbe)

In seinem ersten Fernseh-Film arrangiert der Brecht-Schüler Peter Palitzsch nach einem Drehbuch von Tankred Dorst Schlüssel-Szenen aus der Biographie des Schwärmers, Gottsuchers und Mystagogen Carl Ludwig Sand, der zum politischen Mörder wurde: Im März 1819 erstach der Theologiestudent den angeblichen Vaterlandsverräter August von Kotzebue und wurde ein Jahr nach dem Attentat öffentlich in Mannheim enthauptet. „Nur die Spitze einer Sache", so Dorst, wird in den jeweils kühl stilisierten Episoden der Mordvorbereitung fixiert — etwa ein Sand-Besuch in der Anatomie, eine Probe-Predigt, ein Blindekuh-Spiel mit Burschenschaftern oder ein Besuch auf dem Schlachtfeld von Jena, wo Einheimische die Patrioten für Leichenfledderer halten. Das Ergebnis ist ein zum Lehrstück stilisierter Dokumentar-Report von solcher Schönheit und Unverbindlichkeit, daß Palitzschs Absicht, „Aspekte für die heutige Wahrheit" zu bieten und „Menschen auch politisch weiterzubringen", am allzu schillernd aufgetragenen Zeitkolorit scheitert.

Ein deutsches Fernsehprogramm

von einem Verwaltungsrat[23] kontrolliert. Darin sitzen Vertreter[24] der Parteien, der Kirchen, der Gewerkschaften,[25] der Industrie usw.

Bei den Programmen mischt[26] man schwere und leichte Kost.[27] Man sieht öfter als in Amerika ganze Theater– und Opernaufführungen,[28] Gespräche am runden Tisch, Dokumentar– und Nachrichtensendungen wie die abendliche „Tagesschau". Für die Kinder gibt es eine Sendung, die „Das Sandmännchen kommt" heißt. Unterhaltungssendungen sind Quizschaus, Krimis, das heißt, Fernsehspiele mit Detektiven und Verbrechern,[29] und Sportübertragungen.[30] Bei Ereignissen[31] von internationalem Interesse verbinden sich[32] viele europäische Fernsehanstalten in der „Eurovision", zum Beispiel bei den Olympischen Spielen. Im deutschen Fernsehen sind sogar alte Bekannte von CBS, NBC und ABC zu finden, so zum Beispiel „Hawaii Fünf-Null" oder „Bonanza". Selbstverständlich wird dann auf der Pazifik-Insel[33] und auf der Ponderosa deutsch gesprochen.

[23] **der Verwaltungsrat, –s, ⸚e** board of directors
[24] **der Vertreter, –s, –** representative
[25] **die Gewerkschaft, –, –en** labor union
[26] **mischen** to mix
[27] **die Kost, –** diet
[28] **die Aufführung, –, –en** performance

[29] **der Verbrecher, –s, –** criminal
[30] **die Sportübertragung, –, –en** sports telecast
[31] **das Ereignis, –ses, –se** event
[32] **sich verbinden, verband, hat verbunden** to join
[33] **die Insel, –, –n** island

Fragen und Antworten

1. Kann man das amerikanische Reklamesystem mit dem deutschen vergleichen?
   Nein, die beiden lassen sich nicht vergleichen.
2. Was läßt sich nicht leugnen?
   Es ist nicht zu leugnen, daß man die beiden Systeme nicht miteinander vergleichen kann.
3. Wie oft wird das Programm unterbrochen?
   Etwa alle zehn Minuten wird es durch eine Reklamesendung unterbrochen.
4. An welcher Stelle wird die amerikanische Sendung unterbrochen?
   Meistens an der spannendsten Stelle.
5. Ist das nicht zu ändern?
   Vielleicht, aber so ist es nun mal.
6. Was hofft Ernst?
   Er hofft, daß man in Amerika bald eine bessere Lösung finden kann.
   daß in Amerika bald eine bessere Lösung gefunden werden kann.
   daß sich bald eine bessere Lösung finden läßt.
7. Wer finanziert die Programme in Amerika und Deutschland?
   In Amerika werden sie von Firmen finanziert, in Deutschland vom Publikum.

8. Warum wird die Werbesendung von Kindern geschätzt?
   Weil sie zum Teil ganz lustig und unterhaltend ist.
9. Wogegen wird in Deutschland protestiert?
   In Deutschland wird gegen die Fernsehgebühren protestiert.

Structure and Practice

Explanation of Forms

I. PASSIVE VOICE

In the active voice the subject performs the action; in the passive voice the subject receives the action. The difference is illustrated in the following English examples:

Active: This company *finances* the program.

Passive: The program *is* (*being*) *financed* by this company.

A. Formation

To form the passive voice, English uses the appropriate tense of the verb *to be* as an auxiliary with the past participle of the main verb; German uses the verb **werden** as the auxiliary with the past participle of the main verb.

You will recall that the verb **werden** is also used as an independent verb meaning *to become, to get*. In the following synopsis, **werden** is used first independently and then as the passive auxiliary so that you may compare the tense formation. The future perfect is omitted because it is rarely used.

	AS INDEPENDENT VERB	AS PASSIVE VOICE AUXILIARY (with past participle)
Present:	Es **wird** spät. *It is getting late.*	Es **wird** von dieser Firma **finanziert.** *It is* (*being*) *financed by this firm.*
Simple Past:	Es **wurde** spät. *It was getting late.*	Es **wurde** von dieser Firma **finanziert.** *It was* (*being*) *financed by this firm.*
Present Perfect:	Es **ist** spät **geworden.** *It has gotten late.*	Es **ist** von dieser Firma **finanziert worden.** *It has been financed by this firm.*

Past Perfect:	Es **war** spät **geworden.**	Es **war** von dieser Firma **finanziert worden.**
	It had gotten late.	*It had been financed by this firm.*
Future:	Es **wird** spät **werden.**	Es **wird** von dieser Firma **finanziert werden.**
	It will get late.	*It will be financed by this firm.*

As you can see from the synopsis above, the passive voice can occur in any tense, determined by the tense of the auxiliary **werden;** the past participle of the main verb remains constant. The only difference in the forms of **werden** when used independently, and when used as an auxiliary, is that the past participle (**geworden**) is shortened to **worden** in the passive voice.

You will also recall that **werden** has a third use in addition to the two shown above, that is, as the auxiliary for the future tense. In that case it is always in the present tense and has a dependent infinitive.

> Er **wird** uns **besuchen.**   *He will visit us.*

B. Use

1. WITH AGENT OR INSTRUMENT: The performer of the action in the passive voice is the agent. This agent is in the dative case, introduced by the preposition **von.**

   > Das Programm wird **von dieser Firma** finanziert.
   > *The program is financed by this company.*

   The action may be the result of an instrument rather than an agent. This instrument is in the accusative case, introduced by the preposition **durch.**

   > Das Programm wird **durch eine Reklamesendung** unterbrochen.
   > *The program is interrupted by a commercial.*

2. WITHOUT AN AGENT OR INSTRUMENT: The passive voice frequently occurs with no agent or instrument expressed.

   > Das Programm wird alle zehn Minuten unterbrochen.
   > *The program is interrupted every ten minutes.*

3. IMPERSONAL PASSIVE: Some passive sentences have no real subject. For such constructions, English uses an introductory *There is (are)* . . .; German uses a false subject, **es.**

   > **Es** wird dagegen oft protestiert.
   > *There are often protests about it.*

If the impersonal passive sentence begins with some other element, or if it is a question, the false subject **es** is omitted, and no subject at all is expressed.

> In Deutschland wird gegen die Fernsehgebühren protestiert.
> Wird in Deutschland dagegen protestiert?

4. MODALS WITH A PASSIVE INFINITIVE: Modals, normally used with dependent infinitives, can also be used with passive infinitives; the passive infinitive consists of a past participle and the infinitive of **werden.**

> **Kann** in Amerika eine bessere Lösung **gefunden werden?**
> *Can a better solution **be found** in America?*

II. SUBSTITUTES FOR PASSIVE VOICE

In spoken German the passive voice is not used frequently. When a sentence in the passive voice has an agent expressed, there is no difference in meaning between it and its active equivalent, and the active is usually preferred.

> Passive: Warum wird die Werbesendung von Kindern geschätzt?
> *Why is the advertising program liked by children?*

> Active: Warum schätzen Kinder die Werbesendung?
> *Why do children like the advertising program?*

As you can see in the examples above, the passive agent (**von Kindern**) becomes the active subject (**Kinder**); the passive subject (**die Werbesendung**) becomes the active object (**die Werbesendung**).

In addition, there are a few special active constructions that can be used in place of the passive voice.

A. The Impersonal Pronoun <u>man</u>

The impersonal pronoun **man** has been treated earlier (see Lesson 5, "Word Study and Usage"). It can be used in place of any passive construction that has no agent.

Passive:	Alle zehn Minuten **wird das Programm unterbrochen.**	*The program is interrupted every ten minutes.*
Substitute **man:**	**Man unterbricht** alle zehn Minuten **das Programm.**	
Impersonal Passive:	**Es wird** oft dagegen **protestiert.**	*There are often protests about it.*
Substitute **man:**	**Man protestiert** oft dagegen.	

B. *Reflexives*

A reflexive may, at times, be used in place of a passive-voice sentence that has no agent.

Passive: Vielleicht **wird** bald eine Lösung **ge-** } *Perhaps a so-*
     funden. } *lution will be*
Reflexive: Vielleicht **findet sich** bald eine Lösung. } *found soon.*

C. *sich lassen with a Dependent Infinitive*

The verb **sich lassen** used with a dependent infinitive can be substituted for a passive construction that includes **können**.

Passive: Eine bessere Lösung **kann** viel- } *Perhaps a better*
     leicht **gefunden werden.** } *solution can be*
sich lassen: Eine bessere Lösung **läßt sich** } *found.*
     vielleicht **finden.**

Passive: Eins **kann** nicht **geleugnet** } *One thing can't be*
     werden. } *denied.*
sich lassen: Eins **läßt sich** nicht **leugnen.** }

D. *sein + zu + Dependent Infinitive*

The verb **sein** used with **zu** and a dependent infinitive is also a substitute for a passive construction that includes **können** or **müssen**.

Passive: Die beiden **können** nicht **vergli-** } *The two can't be*
     chen werden. } *compared.*
Sein + zu   Die beiden **sind** nicht **zu verglei-** }
 + Inf.:   **chen.**

Word Study and Usage

In the expressions *a friend of mine, a schoolmate of Gerd's*, English uses a possessive after *of;* German uses the preposition **von** followed by a dative noun or pronoun, or just the proper name.

Er ist ein Schulkamerad **von Gerd.**
He is a schoolmate of Gerd's.
Das ist ein Freund **von mir.**
That's a friend of mine.

Class Drills

I. **Restate the following sentences, substituting the past participle of the given verbs:**

1. Das wird oft gespielt.
   (sagen)
   (glauben)
   (brauchen)
   (fotografieren)
   (erwähnen)
   (behaupten)
   (darstellen)
   (nennen)
   (tun)
   (unterbrechen)
   (vergleichen)
   (schreiben)
   (vergessen)
   (lesen)
   (trinken)

2. Es wird hier viel getanzt.
   (lachen)
   (zeigen)
   (feiern)
   (fotografieren)
   (lesen)
   (trinken)
   (singen)

II. a. **Restate the following sentences in the passive voice:**

1. Der Student unterbricht die Vorlesung.
   Der Dichter stellt es dar.
   Der Reporter erwähnt das oft.
   Die Firma finanziert das Programm.
   Das Publikum finanziert das Fernsehen.
   Die Kinder schätzen die Werbesendung.
   Die Leute vergessen das.
   Die Amerikaner loben das deutsche System.

2. Er unterbricht die Vorlesung.
   Er stellt es dar.
   Er erwähnt das oft.

Sie finanziert das Programm.
Sie lobt das System.
Sie vergißt es immer.
Wir schätzen das.
Wir behaupten das immer.
Sie schätzen die Werbesendung.
Sie finanzieren das Fernsehen.

b. *Restate the sentences in exercise a., first in the past passive,
   then in the present perfect passive.*

*III. Form questions from the following impersonal passive state-
ments.*

EXAMPLE: **Es wird darüber geschwiegen.**
          Wird darüber geschwiegen?

Es wird dagegen protestiert.
Es wird hier oft getanzt.
Es wird hier viel fotografiert.
Es wird nie davon gesprochen.
Es wird an diesem Tag nie gearbeitet.

*IV. Restate the following sentences, using an active construction
with* <u>man</u>:

EXAMPLE: **Das wird oft behauptet.**
          Man behauptet das oft.

Das wird nicht geleugnet.
Das wird manchmal erwähnt.
Diese Sendung wird geschätzt.
Eine Lösung wird gefunden.
Der Professor wird oft unterbrochen.
Der Film wird nicht gezeigt.
Es wird dagegen protestiert.
Es wird hier oft getanzt.

*V. a. Restate the following sentences, using an active construction
with* <u>sich lassen</u>:

EXAMPLE: **Das *kann behauptet werden.***
          Das *läßt sich behaupten.*

Das kann getan werden.
Das kann geleugnet werden.

Das kann gesagt werden.
Das kann geändert werden.
Die Lösung kann gefunden werden.
Der Ton kann nachgeahmt werden.
Das System kann geändert werden.
Die beiden können verglichen werden.
Die Schwierigkeiten können nicht geleugnet werden.
Diese Filme können synchronisiert werden.

b. Restate the sentences in exercise a., again using <u>sich lassen</u>, this time in the past tense.

VI. Restate the following sentences, using <u>sein</u> + <u>zu</u> + infinitive in place of the passive construction:

EXAMPLE: **Es *kann* nicht damit *verglichen werden*.**
         Es *ist* nicht damit *zu vergleichen*.

Es kann nicht entschuldigt werden.
Es kann nicht geleugnet werden.
Es kann nicht gefunden werden.
Es kann nicht geändert werden.
Was kann hier getan werden?
Was kann hier gesagt werden?

VII. Restate the following sentence, substituting the correct form of the noun or pronoun given in English:

Er ist ein Freund von mir.
          (*his*)
          (*hers*)
          (*ours*)
          (*theirs*)
          (*my father's*)
          (*my mother's*)
          (*her cousin's*)
          (*their sister's*)
          (*Gerd's*)
          (*Peter's*)

Exercises

I. Rewrite each sentence three times, using (a) <u>man</u>, (b) <u>sich lassen</u>, (c) <u>sein</u> + <u>zu</u> + infinitive, in place of the passive voice:

1. Keine bessere Lösung konnte gefunden werden.   2. Von hier aus kann der Berg nicht gesehen werden.   3. Ist es wahr, daß der Schmuggler nicht gefaßt werden konnte?   4. Ich weiß nicht, ob dieser Film synchronisiert werden kann.   5. Das kann hier nicht erwähnt werden. 6. Dieser Komiker kann nicht nachgeahmt werden.   7. Darüber kann nicht viel gesagt werden.   8. Kann das als richtig betrachtet werden? 9. Das kann nicht entschuldigt werden.   10. Das System konnte nicht geändert werden.

II. Rewrite the following sentences in the active voice, using **man** as the subject:

1. Bis in die Nacht wurde getanzt.   2. Auf der Party ist viel gesungen und getrunken worden.   3. Dagegen ist oft protestiert worden. 4. Darüber war viel gelacht worden.   5. Wir können nicht arbeiten, weil oben gefeiert wird.   6. Wissen Sie, ob dort protestiert wird?   7. Hier darf nicht fotografiert werden.   8. Davon wird hier nicht gesprochen. 9. Daran wurde nicht gedacht.   10. Es ist leider darüber geschrieben worden.

III. Translate into English. In sentences 1–5, reproduce the German sentences from your English translations:

1. Wer weiß, warum das Kabarett geschlossen wurde.   2. Darüber war viel geschrieben worden.   3. Durch diese Sendung ist er endlich bekannt geworden.   4. Die Tür ließ sich nicht schließen.   5. Ich weiß nicht, wie lange oben getanzt wurde.   6. Es wäre besser gewesen, wenn das nicht erwähnt worden wäre.   7. Könnten Sie mir sagen, für welches Instrument das geschrieben wurde?   8. Dieses Programm, das von der Firma finanziert wird, wird von vielen geschätzt.   9. Wenn alle das verstehen sollen, muß es lauter gesagt werden.   10. Er behauptete, das wäre nicht oft genug gespielt worden.

IV. Translate:

1. I believe that a solution can be found. (*four ways*)   2. I like to talk (*sich unterhalten*) about it.   3. There was a lot of laughing. 4. This has been written by a reporter.   5. That's the way it has been. 6. He is complaining about the performance.   7. How long has this newspaper been in existence?   8. It would be nice if a solution could be found.   9. He was a friend of hers.   10. He became famous and was praised by all people.

V. a. Composition. Write ten sentences in the form of a composition on this topic: — „Tom und Ernst unterhalten sich über das Fernsehen." ***For each sentence use the words suggested below:***

1. Tom   Schulkamerad   kennengelernt
2. heißen   Ernst Schmidt   arbeiten   Reporter
3. Tom   sich unterhalten   mit Ernst   Fernsehen
4. Tom   sich beschweren   Reklamesystem
5. er   behaupten   nicht vergleichen
6. alle zehn Minuten   unterbrechen   Programm
7. viele Leute   protestieren   aber   nicht ändern
8. Ernst   erzählen   Deutschland   es gibt   Fernsehgebühren
9. die Deutschen   dagegen   protestieren   aber   das kleinere Übel
10. die beiden   hoffen   Lösung   finden

b. Free Composition: Tom writes a letter to a German friend about his discussion with Ernst Schmidt.

Active Vocabulary

ändern	to change	**das Publikum, –s**	public, audience
ausnahmslos	without exception	**die Reklame, –,**	advertisement
sich (*acc.*) **be-**	to complain	**–en**	
schweren		**das Reklamesy-**	system of advertising
bestehen, be-	to exist	**stem, –s, –e**	
stand, hat		**der Reporter, –s, –**	reporter
bestanden		**schätzen**	to appreciate
ehemalig	former	**das Schauspiel, –s,**	play, drama
etwa	about, let us say	**–e**	
das Fernsehen, –s	television	**die Schule, –, –n**	school
die Fernsehge-	television tax, fee	**der Schulkamerad,**	schoolmate
bühr, –,		**–en, –en**	
–en		**die Sendung, –,**	telecast, broadcast,
finanzieren	to finance	**–en**	program
die Gebühr, –, –en	fee	**spannend**	exciting, suspenseful
der Genuß, –sses,	joy, pleasure	**die Stelle, –, –n**	place, spot, part
–sse		**das System, –s, –e**	system
der Kamerad, –en,	friend, comrade	**zum Teil**	in part, partly
–en		**das Übel, –s, –**	evil
leugnen	to deny	**unterbrechen,**	to interrupt
loben	to praise	**unterbrach,**	
die Lösung, –, –en	solution	**hat unter-**	
der Nachteil, –s,	disadvantage	**brochen,**	
–e		**unterbricht**	
protestieren	to protest		

die Unterbre- chung, –, –en	interruption	wünschen zu wünschen übrig lassen	to wish, desire to leave to be desired
unterhaltend	entertaining	zu-geben,	to admit, grant
vergleichen, verglich, hat ver- glichen	to compare	gab . . . zu, hat zu-ge- geben, gibt . . . zu	
der Vorteil, –s, –e	advantage	zugegeben!	granted!
wahrscheinlich	probable, likely	zweifellos	doubtless, undoubt- edly
die Werbesen- dung, –, –en	television commercial		

Fünfundzwanzigste Lektion

Hamburg

[*Tom wartet in einem in der Nähe des Hafens gelegenen kleinen Restaurant auf die Thieles. Sie wollen sich von ihm verabschieden, ehe er mit dem Schiff nach England weiterfährt. Sabine kommt als erste an.*]

SABINE — Guten Tag, Tom, du siehst ja glänzend aus, braun gebrannt!

TOM — Guten Tag, Sabine, du hast dich auch gut erholt.

SABINE — Entschuldige bitte die Verspätung. Wir hatten eine kleine Panne vor Hamburg.

TOM — Es ist doch nichts passiert?

SABINE — Nein, nein, nur ein Reifenschaden. Meine Eltern und Gerd lassen sich entschuldigen. Sie wollen dir noch ein Abschiedsgeschenk in Hamburg kaufen. Ich habe dir auch eine Kleinigkeit mitgebracht.

[*Gibt ihm ein Bündel Zeitungen, Zeitschriften und Illustrierte.*]

TOM — Vielen Dank, Sabine. „Der Spiegel", „Der Stern", „Die Welt", „Die Zeit", „Frankfurter Allgemeine" . . . Du hast ja den ganzen Zeitungsstand aufgekauft!

SABINE — Damit du auf der Überfahrt dein Deutsch nicht verlernst.

TOM — Es tut mir leid, daß mein allzu kurzer Aufenthalt hier schon zu Ende ist. So ein Jahr vergeht ja wie im Fluge.

SABINE — Vielen Dank für deine Karten aus Weimar und Göttingen. Wurde an der Grenze streng kontrolliert?

TOM — Nein, es ging alles glatt.

SABINE — Komm, Tom, Gerd hat uns ein besonders elegantes Restaurant ausgesucht.

Hamburg

[*Tom is waiting for the Thieles in a small restaurant located near the harbor. They want to say good-by to him before he leaves by ship for England. Sabine arrives first.*]

SABINE — Hello, Tom. You look great, all tanned.

TOM — Hello, Sabine. You look well, too.

SABINE — Please excuse us for being late. We had a little car trouble before we got to Hamburg.

TOM — Nothing happened, did it?

SABINE — No, no, just a flat tire. My parents and Gerd send their apologies. They want to buy you a farewell gift in Hamburg. I've brought you a little something, too.

[*She gives him a bundle of newspapers and magazines.*[1]]

TOM — Thank you very much, Sabine. *Der Spiegel, Der Stern, Die Welt, Die Zeit,* the *Frankfurter Allgemeine* . . . you bought out the whole newspaper stand.

SABINE — So that you don't forget your German on your trip back.

TOM — I'm sorry that my stay here is over. It was much too short. A year like this really flies by.

SABINE — Thank you for your cards from Weimar and Göttingen. Was there strict inspection at the border?

TOM — No, everything went smoothly.

SABINE — Let's go, Tom. Gerd has picked out an especially elegant restaurant for us.

---

[1] **Illustrierte:** Picture magazines, very popular in Germany.

346

Die Hamburger nennen ihre Stadt stolz „Freie und Hansestadt Hamburg", „frei", weil sie seit fast 1000 Jahren eine Stadtrepublik ist, und „Hansestadt" nach dem im 13. Jahrhundert gegründeten Städtebund.[1] Wir finden dieses Wort noch heute in der Lufthansa erhalten. Nur noch Hamburg und Bremen sind wirkliche Hansestädte, Stadtstaaten, die von einem von der Bürger- 5 schaft[2] gewählten Bürgermeister regiert[3] werden. Die dem Bürgermeister zur Seite stehende Stadtregierung nennt sich „Senat". Der demokratische Geist findet im Hamburger Rathaus seinen Ausdruck darin, daß der Sitzungssaal[4] des Senats kein Stockwerk[5] über sich hat. „Nur Gott steht über dem Senat." Als der letzte deutsche Kaiser, der eitle[6] und ehrgeizige[7] Wilhelm II. 10 (Regierungszeit 1888–1918), einmal Hamburg besuchte, redete der Bürger- meister ihn mit „lieber Bundesgenosse"[8] an.[9] Darüber freuten sich die Ham- burger sehr, „Willy–Kaiser" aber gar nicht. Die alten Hamburger Patri- zierfamilien nahmen auch keine Adelstitel[10] vom Kaiser an. Stolz sagten sie, ein Hamburger könne nicht erhoben[11] werden. 15

Eine andere von Hamburgern gern gehörte Bezeichnung[12] ist „Hamburg, das Tor[13] zur Welt". Mit dieser etwas poetischen Umschreibung[14] meinen sie ihren Hafen. Hamburg steht nach New York, London und Rotterdam an vierter Stelle unter den großen Seehäfen[15] der Welt. Seit Jahrhunderten ist Hamburg eine Handelsstadt. Ihre reichen Kaufleute[16] fühlen sich als 20 Aristokraten und nennen sich manchmal „königliche Kaufleute". Sie geben[17] auch heute noch den Ton[17] in der Gesellschaft an.[17] Angeblich[18] typische Adjektive für das Benehmen[19] der Gäste auf einer Hamburger Party sind „reserviert", „kühl"[20] und „steif".[21] In der Hamburger Aussprache[22] sagt man „s–teif". Von den Hamburgerinnen heißt es, man sähe sie immer nur mit 25 Hut[23] und Handschuhen und fast immer im Kostüm.[24]

In der Nachkriegszeit ist Hamburg eine Art Pressestadt geworden. Von den fünf Zeitungen und Zeitschriften, die Sabine gekauft hat, erscheinen[25] vier in Hamburg. Dabei sind die Unterschiede in Qualität und Niveau enorm,

---

[1] **der Städtebund, –s, ⸚e** league of cities
[2] **die Bürgerschaft, –** citizens
[3] **regieren** to govern
[4] **der Sitzungssaal, –s, –säle** council cham- ber
[5] **das Stockwerk, –s, –e** floor, story
[6] **eitel** vain
[7] **ehrgeizig** ambitious
[8] **der Bundesgenosse, –n, –n** confederate, fel- low member of the confederation
[9] **an-reden** to address
[10] **der Adelstitel, –s, –** title of nobility
[11] **erheben, erhob, hat erhoben** to elevate, exalt
[12] **die Bezeichnung, –, –en** expression, designa- tion

[13] **das Tor, –(e)s, –e** gate
[14] **die Umschreibung, –, –en** paraphrase
[15] **der Seehafen, –s, ⸚** seaport
[16] **der Kaufmann, –s, Kaufleute** merchant
[17] **den Ton an-geben, gab . . . an, hat an- gegeben, gibt . . . an** to set the tone
[18] **angeblich** supposedly, allegedly
[19] **das Benehmen, –s** conduct, manners
[20] **kühl** stand–offish
[21] **steif** stiff
[22] **die Aussprache, –, –n** pronunciation
[23] **der Hut, –(e)s, ⸚e** hat
[24] **das Kostüm, –s, –e** (woman's) suit
[25] **erscheinen, erschien, ist erschienen** to ap- pear, be published

Hamburg

von der intellektuellen „Die Zeit" bis zum Sensationsblatt[26] „Bild Zeitung". 30
Von der letzteren sagt man im Scherz,[27] wenn man sie schräg[28] halte, so laufe
das Blut[29] heraus.

Mit den Hamburger und anderen Zeitungen unter dem Arm steht Tom
Evans an der Reling des Schiffes, das ihn nach England und dann nach
Amerika bringen wird. Als die Türme der Hansestadt kleiner werden und 35
endlich verschwinden, setzt er sich und beginnt zu lesen. Aus dem von
Sabine mitgebrachten Bündel nimmt er eine Zeitschrift und setzt das fort,[30]
womit er in Aufgabe 1 angefangen hat: die Lektüre des „Spiegels".

[26] **das Sensationsblatt, –s, ⸚er** yellow press,
  sensational newspaper
[27] **der Scherz –es, –e** joke, jest
[28] **schräg** slanted
[29] **das Blut, –(e)s** blood
[30] **fort-setzen** to continue

Fragen und Antworten

1. Wer wartet in Hamburg auf die Thieles?
   Der glänzend aussehende, braun gebrannte Tom.
2. Wo wartet Tom?
   Er wartet in einem kleinen Restaurant, das in der Nähe des Hafens liegt.

348

3. Was tut Tom leid?
   Daß sein Aufenthalt, der allzu kurz war, schon zu Ende ist.
4. Was möchte Sabine wissen?
   Sie möchte wissen, ob an der Grenze streng kontrolliert worden ist.
5. Wurde streng kontrolliert?
   Nein, es wurde nicht streng kontrolliert.
6. Hatte Tom an der Grenze Schwierigkeiten?
   Nein, alles ging glatt.
7. War die Panne schlimm?
   Nein, es war nur ein Reifenschaden; nichts ist passiert.
8. Warum kommen die Thieles nach Hamburg?
   Sie wollen Tom nicht wegfahren lassen, ohne ihm auf Wiedersehen zu sagen.
9. Wer regiert die Hansestädte?
   Ein Bürgermeister, der von der Bürgerschaft gewählt wird.

Structure and Practice

Explanation of Forms

I. THE EXTENDED ADJECTIVE

English can place a limited number of modifiers in front of a noun. The modifier can be a simple adjective:

> a young poet

or several adjectives:

> an unknown, young poet

or it can sometimes be extended to include an adverb:

> a fairly unknown, young poet

but this is about as far as English can go; more elaborate modifiers in English have to be placed after the noun.

> a young poet, fairly unknown in this city

In written German there is almost no limit to the number of modifying elements that can precede the noun. All the modifiers in the last English example given above can, in German, precede the noun.

ein in dieser Stadt ziemlich unbekannter junger Dichter

Thus, in the introduction to the dialogue of this lesson, you find the sentence:

Tom wartet in einem in der Nähe des Hafens gelegenen kleinen Restaurant.

Tom is waiting in a small restaurant (which is) located near the harbor.

A native German reading this sentence does not stop to rearrange it in his mind. He accepts the extended adjective construction as a unit and, after more contact with it, you will also be able to do this. Extensive practice reading such sentences aloud with proper intonation and sentence rhythm will help you to develop a feeling for the construction. Until then, a few clues as to how to handle these constructions will help.

Step 1. Read along until you come to a point in the sentence where you would ordinarily expect a noun, that is, after a simple modifier such as an article, **der**-word, **ein**-word, or simple adjective. In reading the last German example given above, you reach a point at which you expect a noun, and instead find a prepositional phrase:

Tom wartet in einem . . .

Step 2. Locate the noun which you would expect to find there. This noun may be preceded by a simple adjective, as in the same example:

Tom wartet in einem . . . kleinen Restaurant.

Step 3. Rearrange the intervening elements into a relative clause.

Tom wartet in einem kleinen Restaurant, das in der Nähe des Hafens liegt.

Tom is waiting in a small restaurant (which is) located near the harbor.

This relative-clause construction is a frequent substitute for the extended adjective, especially in spoken German.

Elaborate extended adjective constructions are restricted mainly to expository prose where compressed style is sought. With a few exceptions, most writers of fiction avoid them.

In spoken German, elaborate extended adjective constructions are rare, but even there, they go beyond the limits which English allows. The following sentence from the dialogue of this lesson is a case in point:

Es tut mir leid, daß mein allzu kurzer Aufenthalt hier schon zu Ende ist.

The literal translation is awkward in English: "I am sorry that my much too short stay here is over." Even a relative clause would sound too stiff for spoken English: "I am sorry that my stay here, which was much too short, is over." This German sentence is best rendered in English by two short sentences: "I am sorry that my stay here is over. It was much too short."

II. GRAMMATICAL *ES*

The pronoun **es** can sometimes be used as a false subject, when the real subject is not placed first for stylistic reasons. This **es** has no meaning. The real subject, in such a case, is placed after the verb.

> **Es** ist **nichts** passiert.   *Nothing happened.*
> **Es** ging **alles** glatt.   *Everything went smoothly.*

If the real subject (or any other element) is placed first, the **es** is omitted.

> **Nichts** ist passiert.
> **Alles** ging glatt.

Word Study and Usage

I. OHNE . . . ZU + INFINITIVE

Ohne used with **zu** and an infinitive has the meaning *without . . . ing.*

> Sie wollen Tom nicht wegfahren lassen, **ohne** ihm auf Wiedersehen **zu sagen.**
> *They don't want to let Tom leave **without saying** good-by to him.*

II. PROPER NAMES WITH THE DEFINITE ARTICLE

Proper names must be used with a definite article when they are modified.

> **Der** glänzend aussehende, braun gebrannte **Tom** wartet auf die Thieles.
> *Tom, who is tanned and looks great, is waiting for the Thieles.*

Class Drills

I. Restate the following sentences, adding progressively before the noun each of the modifiers given:

EXAMPLE: **Er sitzt in einer Weinstube. (alt)**
Er sitzt in einer *alten* Weinstube. (bekannt)
Er sitzt in einer *bekannten alten* Weinstube. (in dieser Stadt)
Er sitzt in einer *in dieser Stadt bekannten alten* Weinstube.

1. Er ist ein Dirigent. (berühmt)
   (sehr)
   (in Deutschland)

2. Das ist der Skandal. (alt)
   (erwähnt)
   (von ihm)
   (gestern)

3. Die Vopos fassen ihn sicher. (kontrollierend)
   (am Checkpoint Charlie)
   (heute)

II. *Restate the following sentences, omitting the false subject* <u>es</u>:

Es ist nichts passiert.
Es ist alles besser geworden.
Es ging alles glatt.
Es war etwas nicht ganz richtig.
Es waren viele Studenten dort.
Es stand eine interessante Geschichte in der Zeitung.

III. *Complete the following sentence by forming infinitive phrases after* <u>ohne</u>, *using the expressions in parentheses:*

EXAMPLE: **Er ging weg, ohne (sich danach erkundigen)**
Er ging weg, *ohne sich danach zu erkundigen.*

Er ging weg, ohne (sich verabschieden)
   (ein Wort sagen)
   (sie begrüßen)
   (auf Wiedersehen sagen)
   (sie fragen)
   (dagegen protestieren)
   (sie ansehen)
   (den Koffer mitnehmen)

Exercises

I. Rewrite the following sentences in the present perfect tense:

1. Von manchen Leuten wird das behauptet.   2. Es wird kalt.
3. Hier wird oft gesungen.   4. Das läßt sich ändern.   5. Wie ist das
zu machen?   6. Er wird immer bekannter.   7. Was wird dort gespielt?
8. Dafür läßt sich keine Lösung finden.   9. Ich weiß, daß das oft
vergessen wird.   10. Sie wird oft angerufen.   11. Es wird sehr streng
kontrolliert.   12. Da ist nichts zu sehen.   13. Wird oft dagegen protestiert?   14. Die Stadt wird sehr berühmt.   15. Das wird oft erwähnt.

*II. Rewrite the following sentences, using a relative clause accord-
ing to the example:*

EXAMPLE: **Mein leider allzu kurzer Aufenthalt ist zu Ende.**
**Mein Aufenthalt, der leider allzu kurz war, ist zu
Ende.**

1. Er ist ein glänzend aussehender junger Mann.   2. Neben mir saß
ein sehr erschöpft aussehendes junges Mädchen.   3. Mein allzu langes
Semester ist jetzt zu Ende.   4. Er wartet in einem in der Nähe der
Universität gelegenen Lokal.   5. Der in München wohnende berühmte
Maler ist ein Vetter von ihm.

III. Translate:

1. Der in Amerika sehr bekannte Dirigent kommt morgen nach Bonn.
2. Ist bei der Paßabfertigung alles glatt gegangen?   3. Sie sagte, es sei
nur ein Reifenschaden und gar nichts sei passiert.   4. Suchen wir ein
besonders elegantes Restaurant aus!   5. Wenn mein Aufenthalt nur
nicht schon zu Ende wäre!   6. Wissen Sie, warum heute nicht kontrolliert worden ist?   7. Der leider schlecht synchronisierte Film hat ihm
nicht gefallen.   8. Das von Brecht selbst gegründete Theater ist in Ost-
Berlin.   9. Er bat den am Eingang zum Hörsaal stehenden Studenten
um Auskunft.   10. Das ist der nach dem Krieg wieder aufgebaute
Stadtteil Frankfurts.

IV. Translate:

1. Are you sorry that your stay is over?   2. My parents send their
apologies.   3. The restaurant that you picked out is very elegant.
4. Was there inspection yesterday?   5. I am glad that everything is going smoothly.   6. May I say good-by?   7. The semester seems to fly by.

8. He wanted to buy you a gift.   9. Visit us before you leave for America.   10. I hope that nothing will happen.

V. Composition. In the form of a letter from Tom to a friend in Munich describe some of Tom's experiences on his trip from Berlin to Hamburg via Weimar and Göttingen.

Active Vocabulary

der Abschied, –s	farewell, departure	kontrollieren	to check, inspect
das Abschiedsge-schenk, –s, –e	farewell gift	liegen, lag, hat gelegen	to lie, be situated
allzu	much too	die Panne, –, –n	car trouble, break-down
der Aufenthalt, –s, –e	stay, sojourn	passieren, ist passiert	to happen
auf-kaufen	to buy out	regieren	to govern
aus-suchen	to pick out, select	der Reifen, –s, –	tire
braun ge-brannt	sun tanned	der Reifenscha-den, –s, ˵	flat tire
das Bündel, –s, –	bundle	das Restaurant, –s, –s	restaurant
der Bürgermeister, –s, –	mayor	der Schaden, –s, ˵	damage
die Bürgerschaft, –	citizens	der Stand, –(e)s, ˵e	stand, booth
damit (*subord. conj.*)	so that	die Überfahrt, –, –en	crossing, passage, trip
die Eltern (*pl.*)	parents	sich (*acc.*) verab-schieden (von)	to say good-by (to)
sich (*acc.*) entschul-digen lassen	to send one's apolo-gies		
sich (*acc.*) erholen	to rest, recuperate	vergehen, ver-ging, ist vergangen	to pass by (time), go by
der Flug, –(e)s, ˵e	flight		
das Geschenk, –s, –e	gift	verlernen	to forget, unlearn
glänzend	splendid	die Verspätung, –, –en	lateness
glatt	smooth	wählen	to elect
der Hafen, –s, ˵	port, harbor	der Zeitungsstand, –s, ˵e	newspaper stand
die Illustrierte, –n, –n	picture magazine		
die Kleinigkeit, –, –en	small thing, trifle		

Appendix

Pronunciation

The following is a summary of the German sound system with examples of each sound. Wherever there is some similarity to an English sound, this is indicated, but keep in mind that in most cases these similarities are only approximations, not exact equivalents. German has a number of sounds that have no close parallels in English. Whenever possible, the formation of these sounds is described. The only way to learn to pronounce German correctly, however, is by imitation of your instructor or the voices on the tapes.

I. *VOWELS*

A. *Simple Vowels*

In German, simple vowels are always "pure," clear vowels (e.g., *i* in *in* or *e* in *he*), never diphthongs or "gliding" vowels (e.g., *i* in *glide* or *o* in *so*).

German vowels can be long or short. As a rule, they are short in unaccented syllables, or when followed by two or more consonants; they are long when they are doubled, followed by an **h** (which is not pronounced), or when followed by a single consonant. There are, of course, exceptions to this general rule.

1. LONG **a:**
   (similar to the *a* in *calm*)

   kam (*came*)
   Saal (*hall*)
   nahm (*took*)

   SHORT **a:**
   (similar to the *u* in *cut*)

   hat (*has*)
   dann (*then*)
   kann (*is able to*)

2. LONG **e:**
   (no English equivalent)

   gegen (*against*)
   Tee (*tea*)
   nehmen (*to take*)

   SHORT **e:**
   (similar to *e* in *get*)

   kennen (*to know*)
   Ende (*end*)
   Bett (*bed*)

unstressed **e**: similar to *e* in *the;* only used in unstressed syllables:

> **kennen**
> **End**e
> **dunkel**

3. LONG **i**:
(often spelled **ie**; similar to *i* in *machine*)

> **ihm** (*to him*)
> **Maschine** (*machine*)
> **nie** (*never*)

SHORT **i**:
(similar to *i* in *hit*)

> **bitte** (*please*)
> **blind** (*blind*)
> **bis** (*until*)

4. LONG **o**:
(no English equivalent)

> **Boot** (*boat*)
> **ohne** (*without*)
> **Ton** (*sound*)

SHORT **o**:
(no English equivalent)

> **Gott** (*God*)
> **oft** (*often*)
> **Bonn**

5. LONG **u**:
(similar to *oo* in *loot*)

> **gut** (*good*)
> **tun** (*to do*)
> **Mut** (*courage*)

SHORT **u**:
(similar to *u* in *put*)

> **und** (*and*)
> **muß** (*has to*)
> **unten** (*downstairs*)

B. *Umlauted Vowels*

The so-called umlauted vowels are modifications of the vowels **a**, **o**, and **u**. Umlauted vowels can also be short or long.

1. LONG **ä**:
(similar to *a* in *fare*)

> **käme** (*would come*)
> **nähme** (*would take*)
> **Nähe** (*vicinity*)

SHORT **ä**:
(identical in pronunciation with the German short **e**)

> **Gäste** (*guests*)
> **hätte** (*would have*)
> **Kämme** (*combs*)

2. LONG **ö**:
(no English equivalent; pronounce German long **e** as in **Tee** but with lips rounded and protruded)

SHORT **ö**:
(no English equivalent; pronounce German short **e** as in **Bett** but with lips rounded and protruded)

mögen (*to like*)   **können** (*to be able to*)
schön (*nice*)   **öffnen** (*to open*)
Möbel (*furniture*)   **Köln** (*Cologne*)

3. LONG **ü**:   SHORT **ü**:
(no English equivalent; pro-   (no English equivalent; pronounce German long **i** as in **ihm**   nounce German short **i** as
but with lips rounded and pro-   in **bis** but with lips rounded
truded)   and protruded)

kühl (*cool*)   **müssen** (*to have to*)
üben (*to practice*)   **Bündel** (*bundle*)
müde (*tired*)   **Bütte** (*tub*)

Note: **y** is a vowel sound in German; it is pronounced like **ü**:

typisch

C. *Diphthongs*

1. **au**:
(similar to *ou* in *house*)

Haus (*house*)
aus (*out*)
auf (*on*)

2. **ei, (ai, ay, ey**:   rare):
(similar to *i* in *like*)

ein (*a*)   **Mai** (*May*)
mein (*my*)   **Bayern** (*Bavaria*)
nein (*no*)   **Mayer** (*proper name*)

3. **eu, äu**:
(similar to *oi* in *coin*)

heute (*today*)   **läuft** (*runs*)
deutsch (*German*)   **Häute** (*skins*)
Leute (*people*)

II *CONSONANTS*

A. *Simple Consonants*

1. **f, h, k, m, n, p, t,** AND x: pronounced as in English

2. **b, d, g:**   same as English, except in final position where they are close to **p, t,** and **k** respectively. The German **g** is always a hard *g*.

ob (*whether*)   **General** (*general*)
und (*and*)   **Genitiv** (*genitive*)
Tag (*day*)

-ig in final position has the same sound as **ch** in **ich** (see **B.1.** below)

3. **j:**   always pronounced like *y* in *yes:*

ja (*yes*)
Juni (*June*)
Juli (*July*)

4. **l:**   always pronounced with tip of the tongue behind upper front teeth; similar to the initial *l* as in *land:*

Land (*country*)
alle (*all*)
leben (*live*)
hell (*light*)

5. **r:**   "uvular" **r**; no equivalent in English; keep tip of your tongue behind lower front teeth and produce a gargling sound:

Raum (*space*)
lehren (*to teach*)
lernen (*learn*)

In final position, the **r** is "slurred," as in British pronunciation of *father:*

mir (*to me*)
hier (*here*)
Kinder (*children*)

6. **s:**   before vowels, similar to *z* (voiced *s*) in *zoo;* otherwise like *s* (voiceless *s*) in *see:*

sagen (*to say*)   **ist** (*is*)
so (*so*)   **bis** (*until*)
lesen (*to read*)   **Haus** (*house*)

ss is always voiceless:

> **müssen** (*to have to*)
> **lassen** (*to let*)
> **essen** (*to eat*)

ß = **ss** and is used after long vowels, diphthongs, and in final position in the syllable.

7. **v:** pronounced like *f:*

> **Vater** (*father*)
> **vor** (*before*)
> **viel** (*much*)

in some words of foreign origin, **v** is pronounced like *v* in English:

> **November**
> **Universität** (*university*)

8. **w:** similar to English *v:*

> **Wasser** (*water*)
> **bewundern** (*to admire*)

9. **z:** pronounced like *ts* in *nuts:*

> **Zahl** (*number*)
> **zehn** (*ten*)
> **zu** (*to*)

B. *Consonant Combinations*

1. **ch:** no English equivalent

   a) after front vowels (**e, i, eu, äu, ä, ü, ö**): with mouth open, press tip of tongue behind lower front teeth and try to pronounce *sh* without moving lips; or: pronounce the initial *h* in *Hughes:*

   > **ich** (*I*)
   > **Küche** (*kitchen*)
   > **Köchin** (*cook*)
   > **Nächte** (*nights*)

b) after back vowels (**a, o, u, au**): this **ch** sound is made in back of the mouth; keep tip of tongue behind lower front teeth and produce a very gentle gargling sound:

Nacht (*night*)
acht (*eight*)
lachen (*to laugh*)
Kuchen (*cake*)

Note: final **–ig** is pronounced like the **ch** in **ich**:

König (*king*)
wenig (*little*)

ch in initial position before **a, o,** or a consonant is pronounced *k:*

Chor (*choir*)
Chrom (*chrome*)
Charakter (*character*)

chs is pronounced *ks:*

nächst (*next*)
wächst (*grows*)

2. **ck:**   pronounced like *k:*

Ecke (*corner*)

3. **dt:**   pronounced like *t:*

sandte (*sent*)
wandte (*turned*)

4. **gn:**   both **g** and **n** are pronounced:

Gnade (*mercy*)

5. **kn:**   both **k** and **n** are pronounced:

Knie (*knee*)
Knoten (*knot*)
Knall (*bang*)

6. **pf:**   both **p** and **f** are pronounced:

Pfeffer (*pepper*)
Pfanne (*pan*)

7. **ps:** both **p** and **s** are pronounced:

> **Psalm** (*psalm*)
> **Psychologie** (*psychology*)

8. **ph:** pronounced like *f:*

> **Philosophie**

9. **qu:** pronounced *kv:*

> **Qual** (*torture*)
> **bequem** (*comfortable*)

10. **sch:** pronounced like *sh* in *she:*

> **schön** (*nice*)
> **Schule** (*school*)

11. **sp:** in initial position in the syllable, pronounced *shp:*

> **Spion** (*spy*)
> **spielen** (*to play*)
> **Spaß** (*joke*)

in medial or final position, pronounced *sp:*

> **Wespe** (*wasp*)

12. **st:** in initial position in the syllable, pronounced *sht:*

> **Stadt** (*city*)
> **Stein** (*stone*)
> **Student** (*student*)

in medial or final position, pronounced *st:*

> **Gast** (*guest*)
> **Reste** (*remains*)

13. **th:** pronounced *t:* **Theater** (**th** is rare in German; it is found in words of foreign origin and proper names)

14. **tz:** pronounced like *ts:*

> **sitzen** (*to sit*)
> **Platz** (*place*)
> **jetzt** (*now*)

Note: the **t** in **–tion** is also pronounced *ts:*

Nation
Konversation

III. *ACCENT*

Most German words have the accent on the stem: **kommen** (*to come*), **Lufthansa.** Most foreign words or words of foreign origin carry the stress on the syllable that is accented in the foreign language: **Amérika, Student, studiéren.** Because there are many additional factors that influence accentuation, for example, accented or unaccented prefixes, it is important that you imitate your instructor or the voices on the tapes.

Note that in German each word in a sentence is pronounced separately, that is, the words do not run together. Compare:

Guten/Tag   Good day   **Wie/oft . . .**   How often . . .

Stress, rhythm, and intonation in the sentence are best learned by listening to the spoken language.

Noun Declension

CLASS I

No ending in plural; some add umlaut

Consists of:

1. masculine and neuter nouns ending in **-el, -er, -en (der Vater, die Väter)**
2. neuter nouns with diminutive suffixes **-chen** and **-lein (das Mädchen, die Mädchen)**
3. neuter nouns with **Ge-** prefix and **-e** suffix **(das Gebäude, die Gebäude)**
4. only two feminine nouns **(die Mutter, die Mütter; die Tochter, die Töchter)**

Sample declension:

	SINGULAR	PLURAL
NOM.	**der Vater**	**die Väter**
ACC.	**den Vater**	**die Väter**
DAT.	**dem Vater**	**den Vätern**
GEN.	**des Vaters**	**der Väter**

CLASS II

Plural adds **-e;** some add umlaut

Consists of:

1. most monosyllabic masculine nouns **(der Gast, die Gäste)**
2. some monosyllabic feminine nouns **(die Stadt, die Städte)**
3. a few monosyllabic neuter nouns **(das Jahr, die Jahre)**
4. some polysyllabic masculine and neuter nouns **(das Konzert, die Konzerte; der Ausdruck, die Ausdrücke)**

Sample declension:

	SINGULAR	PLURAL
NOM.	der Krieg	die Kriege
ACC.	den Krieg	die Kriege
DAT.	dem Krieg	den Kriegen
GEN.	des Krieges	der Kriege

CLASS III

Plural adds **-er;** add umlaut whenever possible

Consists of:

1. most monosyllabic neuter nouns **(das Haus, die Häuser)**

2. some monosyllabic masculine nouns **(der Mann, die Männer)**

Sample declension:

	SINGULAR	PLURAL
NOM.	das Haus	die Häuser
ACC.	das Haus	die Häuser
DAT.	dem Haus	den Häusern
GEN.	des Hauses	der Häuser

CLASS IV

Plural adds **-n** or **-en;** no umlaut

Consists of:

1. most feminine nouns **(die Schwester, die Schwestern; die Tür, die Türen)**

2. masculine nouns ending in **-or (der Professor, die Professoren)**

3. weak masculine nouns **(der Student, die Studenten)**

Sample declensions:

	SINGULAR	PLURAL	*(weak noun)* SINGULAR	PLURAL
NOM.	die Tür	die Türen	der Student	die Studenten
ACC.	die Tür	die Türen	den Studenten	die Studenten
DAT.	der Tür	den Türen	dem Studenten	den Studenten
GEN.	der Tür	der Türen	des Studenten	der Studenten

CLASS V

Plural adds **-s;** no umlaut

Consists of:

1. many foreign nouns **(das Auto, die Autos; das Kino, die Kinos)**

2. family names **(die Schmidts)**

Sample declension:

	SINGULAR	PLURAL
NOM.	**das Auto**	**die Autos**
ACC.	**das Auto**	**die Autos**
DAT.	**dem Auto**	**den Autos**
GEN.	**des Autos**	**der Autos**

MIXED NOUNS

Some masculine and neuter nouns have a strong declension in the singular (genitive adds **-(e)s**) and a weak declension in the plural (plural adds **-(e)n**). These nouns add no umlaut in the plural.

Sample declension:

	SINGULAR	PLURAL
NOM.	**der Staat**	**die Staaten**
ACC.	**den Staat**	**die Staaten**
DAT.	**dem Staat**	**den Staaten**
GEN.	**des Staates**	**der Staaten**

IRREGULAR NOUNS

There are a few irregular nouns that are actually nouns of Class I, but they have dropped the final **-n** in the nominative singular. They take no umlaut.

Sample declension:

	SINGULAR	PLURAL
NOM.	**der Name**	**die Namen**
ACC.	**den Namen**	**die Namen**
DAT.	**dem Namen**	**den Namen**
GEN.	**des Namens**	**der Namen**

Verbs

I. AUXILIARY VERBS

	INFINITIVE	
haben (*to have*)	sein (*to be*)	werden (*to become*)
	PRESENT PARTICIPLE	
habend	seiend	werdend
	PAST PARTICIPLE	
gehabt	gewesen	geworden
	PRESENT INDICATIVE	
ich habe	ich bin	ich werde
du hast	du bist	du wirst
er hat	er ist	er wird
wir haben	wir sind	wir werden
ihr habt	ihr seid	ihr werdet
sie haben	sie sind	sie werden
Sie haben	Sie sind	Sie werden
	PAST INDICATIVE	
ich hatte	ich war	ich wurde
du hattest	du warst	du wurdest
er hatte	er war	er wurde

wir hatten
ihr hattet
sie hatten
Sie hatten

wir waren
ihr wart
sie waren
Sie waren

wir wurden
ihr wurdet
sie wurden
Sie wurden

PRESENT PERFECT INDICATIVE

ich habe gehabt
du hast gehabt
er hat gehabt
wir haben gehabt
ihr habt gehabt
sie haben gehabt
Sie haben gehabt

ich bin gewesen
du bist gewesen
er ist gewesen
wir sind gewesen
ihr seid gewesen
sie sind gewesen
Sie sind gewesen

ich bin geworden
du bist geworden
er ist geworden
wir sind geworden
ihr seid geworden
sie sind geworden
Sie sind geworden

PAST PERFECT INDICATIVE

ich hatte gehabt
du hattest gehabt
er hatte gehabt
wir hatten gehabt
ihr hattet gehabt
sie hatten gehabt
Sie hatten gehabt

ich war gewesen
du warst gewesen
er war gewesen
wir waren gewesen
ihr wart gewesen
sie waren gewesen
Sie waren gewesen

ich war geworden
du warst geworden
er war geworden
wir waren geworden
ihr wart geworden
sie waren geworden
Sie waren geworden

FUTURE INDICATIVE

ich werde haben
du wirst haben
er wird haben
wir werden haben
ihr werdet haben

ich werde sein
du wirst sein
er wird sein
wir werden sein
ihr werdet sein

ich werde werden
du wirst werden
er wird werden
wir werden werden
ihr werdet werden

sie werden werden	sie werden sein	sie werden haben
Sie werden werden	Sie werden sein	Sie werden haben

FUTURE PERFECT INDICATIVE

ich werde geworden sein	ich werde gewesen sein	ich werde gehabt haben
du wirst geworden sein	du wirst gewesen sein	du wirst gehabt haben
er wird geworden sein	er wird gewesen sein	er wird gehabt haben
wir werden geworden sein	wir werden gewesen sein	wir werden gehabt haben
ihr werdet geworden sein	ihr werdet gewesen sein	ihr werdet gehabt haben
sie werden geworden sein	sie werden gewesen sein	sie werden gehabt haben
Sie werden geworden sein	Sie werden gewesen sein	Sie werden gehabt haben

PRESENT SPECIAL SUBJUNCTIVE

ich werde	ich sei	ich habe
du werdest	du seiest	du habest
er werde	er sei	er habe
wir werden	wir seien	wir haben
ihr werdet	ihr seiet	ihr habet
sie werden	sie seien	sie haben
Sie werden	Sie seien	Sie haben

PRESENT GENERAL SUBJUNCTIVE

ich würde	ich wäre	ich hätte
du würdest	du wärest	du hättest
er würde	er wäre	er hätte
wir würden	wir wären	wir hätten
ihr würdet	ihr wäret	ihr hättet
sie würden	sie wären	sie hätten
Sie würden	Sie wären	Sie hätten

PAST SPECIAL SUBJUNCTIVE

ich habe gehabt	ich sei gewesen	ich sei geworden
du habest gehabt	du seiest gewesen	du seiest geworden
er habe gehabt	er sei gewesen	er sei geworden
wir haben gehabt	wir seien gewesen	wir seien geworden
ihr habet gehabt	ihr seiet gewesen	ihr seiet geworden
sie haben gehabt	sie seien gewesen	sie seien geworden
Sie haben gehabt	Sie seien gewesen	Sie seien geworden

PAST GENERAL SUBJUNCTIVE

ich hätte gehabt	ich wäre gewesen	ich wäre geworden
du hättest gehabt	du wärest gewesen	du wärest geworden
er hätte gehabt	er wäre gewesen	er wäre geworden
wir hätten gehabt	wir wären gewesen	wir wären geworden
ihr hättet gehabt	ihr wäret gewesen	ihr wäret geworden
sie hätten gehabt	sie wären gewesen	sie wären geworden
Sie hätten gehabt	Sie wären gewesen	Sie wären geworden

FUTURE SPECIAL SUBJUNCTIVE

ich werde haben	ich werde sein	ich werde werden
du werdest haben	du werdest sein	du werdest werden
er werde haben	er werde sein	er werde werden
wir werden haben	wir werden sein	wir werden werden
ihr werdet haben	ihr werdet sein	ihr werdet werden
sie werden haben	sie werden sein	sie werden werden
Sie werden haben	Sie werden sein	Sie werden werden

FUTURE GENERAL SUBJUNCTIVE

ich würde werden
du würdest werden
er würde werden
wir würden werden
ihr würdet werden
sie würden werden
Sie würden werden

ich würde sein
du würdest sein
er würde sein
wir würden sein
ihr würdet sein
sie würden sein
Sie würden sein

ich würde haben
du würdest haben
er würde haben
wir würden haben
ihr würdet haben
sie würden haben
Sie würden haben

FUTURE PERFECT SPECIAL SUBJUNCTIVE

ich werde geworden sein
du werdest geworden sein
er werde geworden sein
wir werden geworden sein
ihr werdet geworden sein
sie werden geworden sein
Sie werden geworden sein

ich werde gewesen sein
du werdest gewesen sein
er werde gewesen sein
wir werden gewesen sein
ihr werdet gewesen sein
sie werden gewesen sein
Sie werden gewesen sein

ich werde gehabt haben
du werdest gehabt haben
er werde gehabt haben
wir werden gehabt haben
ihr werdet gehabt haben
sie werden gehabt haben
Sie werden gehabt haben

FUTURE PERFECT GENERAL SUBJUNCTIVE

ich würde geworden sein
du würdest geworden sein
er würde geworden sein
wir würden geworden sein
ihr würdet geworden sein
sie würden geworden sein
Sie würden geworden sein

ich würde gewesen sein
du würdest gewesen sein
er würde gewesen sein
wir würden gewesen sein
ihr würdet gewesen sein
sie würden gewesen sein
Sie würden gewesen sein

ich würde gehabt haben
du würdest gehabt haben
er würde gehabt haben
wir würden gehabt haben
ihr würdet gehabt haben
sie würden gehabt haben
Sie würden gehabt haben

IMPERATIVE

habe!	sei!	werde!
habt!	seid!	werdet!
haben Sie!	seien Sie!	werden Sie!

II. MODAL AUXILIARIES AND WISSEN

PRESENT INDICATIVE

	dürfen	können	mögen	müssen	sollen	wollen	wissen
ich	darf	kann	mag	muß	soll	will	weiß
du	darfst	kannst	magst	mußt	sollst	willst	weißt
er	darf	kann	mag	muß	soll	will	weiß
wir	dürfen	können	mögen	müssen	sollen	wollen	wissen
ihr	dürft	könnt	mögt	müßt	sollt	wollt	wißt
sie	dürfen	können	mögen	müssen	sollen	wollen	wissen
Sie	dürfen	können	mögen	müssen	sollen	wollen	wissen

PAST INDICATIVE

	dürfen	können	mögen	müssen	sollen	wollen	wissen
ich	durfte	konnte	mochte	mußte	sollte	wollte	wußte
du	durftest	konntest	mochtest	mußtest	solltest	wolltest	wußtest
er	durfte	konnte	mochte	mußte	sollte	wollte	wußte
wir	durften	konnten	mochten	mußten	sollten	wollten	wußten
ihr	durftet	konntet	mochtet	mußtet	solltet	wolltet	wußtet
sie	durften	konnten	mochten	mußten	sollten	wollten	wußten
Sie	durften	konnten	mochten	mußten	sollten	wollten	wußten

PRESENT PERFECT INDICATIVE

ich habe gedurft (gekonnt, gemocht, gemußt, gesollt, gewollt, gewußt)
du hast gedurft (gekonnt, gemocht, gemußt, gesollt, gewollt, gewußt)
etc.

PAST PERFECT INDICATIVE

ich hatte gedurft (gekonnt, gemocht, gemußt, gesollt, gewollt, gewußt)
du hattest gedurft (gekonnt, gemocht, gemußt, gesollt, gewollt, gewußt)
etc.

FUTURE INDICATIVE

ich werde dürfen (können, mögen, müssen, sollen, wollen, wissen)
du wirst dürfen (können, mögen, müssen, sollen, wollen, wissen)
etc.

FUTURE PERFECT INDICATIVE

ich werde gedurft (gekonnt, gemocht, gemußt, gesollt, gewollt, gewußt) haben
du wirst gedurft (gekonnt, gemocht, gemußt, gesollt, gewollt, gewußt) haben
etc.

PRESENT SPECAL SUBJUNCTIVE

ich dürfe	ich könne	ich möge	ich müsse	ich solle	ich wolle	ich wisse
du dürfest	du könnest	du mögest	du müssest	du sollest	du wollest	du wissest
etc.						

PRESENT GENERAL SUBJUNCTIVE

ich dürfte	ich könnte	ich möchte	ich müßte	ich sollte	ich wollte	ich wüßte
du dürftest	du könntest	du möchtest	du müßtest	du solltest	du wolltest	du wüßtest
etc.						

PAST SPECIAL SUBJUNCTIVE

ich habe gedurft (gekonnt, gemocht, gemußt, gesollt, gewollt, gewußt)
du habest gedurft (gekonnt, gemocht, gemußt, gesollt, gewollt, gewußt)
etc.

PAST GENERAL SUBJUNCTIVE

ich hätte gedurft (gekonnt, gemocht, gemußt, gesollt, gewollt, gewußt)
du hättest gedurft (gekonnt, gemocht, gemußt, gesollt, gewollt, gewußt)
etc.

FUTURE SPECIAL SUBJUNCTIVE

ich werde dürfen (können, mögen, müssen, sollen, wollen, wissen)
du werdest dürfen (können, mögen, müssen, sollen, wollen, wissen)
etc.

FUTURE GENERAL SUBJUNCTIVE

ich würde dürfen (können, mögen, müssen, sollen, wollen, wissen)
du würdest dürfen (können, mögen, müssen, sollen, wollen, wissen)
etc.

FUTURE PERFECT SPECIAL SUBJUNCTIVE

ich werde gedurft (gekonnt, gemocht, gemußt, gesollt, gewollt, gewußt) haben
du werdest gedurft (gekonnt, gemocht, gemußt, gesollt, gewollt, gewußt) haben
etc.

FUTURE PERFECT GENERAL SUBJUNCTIVE

ich würde gedurft (gekonnt, gemocht, gemußt, gesollt, gewollt, gewußt) haben
du würdest gedurft (gekonnt, gemocht, gemußt, gesollt, gewollt, gewußt) haben
etc.

III. *SUMMARY OF WEAK AND STRONG VERBS*

A. Active

		INFINITIVE	
fragen	**arbeiten**	**sehen**	**gehen**
		PRESENT PARTICIPLE	
fragend	**arbeitend**	**sehend**	**gehend**
		PAST PARTICIPLE	
gefragt	**gearbeitet**	**gesehen**	**gegangen**
		PRESENT INDICATIVE	
ich frage	**ich arbeite**	**ich sehe**	**ich gehe**
du fragst	**du arbeitest**	**du siehst**	**du gehst**
er fragt	**er arbeitet**	**er sieht**	**er geht**

wir fragen	wir arbeiten	wir sehen	wir gehen
ihr fragt	ihr arbeitet	ihr seht	ihr geht
sie fragen	sie arbeiten	sie sehen	sie gehen
Sie fragen	Sie arbeiten	Sie sehen	Sie gehen

PAST INDICATIVE

ich fragte	ich arbeitete	ich sah	ich ging
du fragtest	du arbeitetest	du sahst	du gingst
er fragte	er arbeitete	er sah	er ging
wir fragten	wir arbeiteten	wir sahen	wir gingen
ihr fragtet	ihr arbeitetet	ihr saht	ihr gingt
sie fragten	sie arbeiteten	sie sahen	sie gingen
Sie fragten	Sie arbeiteten	Sie sahen	Sie gingen

PRESENT PERFECT INDICATIVE

ich habe gefragt	ich habe gearbeitet	ich habe gesehen	ich bin gegangen
du hast gefragt	du hast gearbeitet	du hast gesehen	du bist gegangen
er hat gefragt	er hat gearbeitet	er hat gesehen	er ist gegangen
wir haben gefragt	wir haben gearbeitet	wir haben gesehen	wir sind gegangen
ihr habt gefragt	ihr habt gearbeitet	ihr habt gesehen	ihr seid gegangen
sie haben gefragt	sie haben gearbeitet	sie haben gesehen	sie sind gegangen
Sie haben gefragt	Sie haben gearbeitet	Sie haben gesehen	Sie sind gegangen

PAST PERFECT INDICATIVE

ich hatte gefragt	ich hatte gearbeitet	ich hatte gesehen	ich war gegangen
du hattest gefragt	du hattest gearbeitet	du hattest gesehen	du warst gegangen
er hatte gefragt	er hatte gearbeitet	er hatte gesehen	er war gegangen

wir hatten gefragt wir hatten gearbeitet wir hatten gesehen wir waren gegangen
ihr hattet gefragt ihr hattet gearbeitet ihr hattet gesehen ihr wart gegangen
sie hatten gefragt sie hatten gearbeitet sie hatten gesehen sie waren gegangen
Sie hatten gefragt Sie hatten gearbeitet Sie hatten gesehen Sie waren gegangen

FUTURE INDICATIVE

ich werde fragen ich werde arbeiten ich werde sehen ich werde gehen
du wirst fragen du wirst arbeiten du wirst sehen du wirst gehen
er wird fragen er wird arbeiten er wird sehen er wird gehen
wir werden fragen wir werden arbeiten wir werden sehen wir werden gehen
ihr werdet fragen ihr werdet arbeiten ihr werdet sehen ihr werdet gehen
sie werden fragen sie werden arbeiten sie werden sehen sie werden gehen
Sie werden fragen Sie werden arbeiten Sie werden sehen Sie werden gehen

FUTURE PERFECT INDICATIVE

ich werde gefragt haben ich werde gearbeitet haben ich werde gesehen haben ich werde gegangen sein
du wirst gefragt haben du wirst gearbeitet haben du wirst gesehen haben du wirst gegangen sein
er wird gefragt haben er wird gearbeitet haben er wird gesehen haben er wird gegangen sein
wir werden gefragt haben wir werden gearbeitet haben wir werden gesehen haben wir werden gegangen sein
ihr werdet gefragt haben ihr werdet gearbeitet haben ihr werdet gesehen haben ihr werdet gegangen sein
sie werden gefragt haben sie werden gearbeitet haben sie werden gesehen haben sie werden gegangen sein
Sie werden gefragt haben Sie werden gearbeitet haben Sie werden gesehen haben Sie werden gegangen sein

IMPERATIVE

frage! arbeite! sieh! gehe!
fragt! arbeitet! seht! geht!
fragen Sie! arbeiten Sie! sehen Sie! gehen Sie!

PRESENT SPECIAL SUBJUNCTIVE	PRESENT GENERAL SUBJUNCTIVE	PAST SPECIAL SUBJUNCTIVE
ich gehe	ich ginge	ich sei gegangen
du gehest	du gingest	du seiest gegangen
er gehe	er ginge	er sei gegangen
wir gehen	wir gingen	wir seien gegangen
ihr gehet	ihr ginget	ihr seiet gegangen
sie gehen	sie gingen	sie seien gegangen
Sie gehen	Sie gingen	Sie seien gegangen

PRESENT SPECIAL SUBJUNCTIVE	PRESENT GENERAL SUBJUNCTIVE	PAST SPECIAL SUBJUNCTIVE
ich sehe	ich sähe	ich habe gesehen
du sehest	du sähest	du habest gesehen
er sehe	er sähe	er habe gesehen
wir sehen	wir sähen	wir haben gesehen
ihr sehet	ihr sähet	ihr habet gesehen
sie sehen	sie sähen	sie haben gesehen
Sie sehen	Sie sähen	Sie haben gesehen

PRESENT SPECIAL SUBJUNCTIVE	PRESENT GENERAL SUBJUNCTIVE	PAST SPECIAL SUBJUNCTIVE
ich arbeite	ich arbeitete	ich habe gearbeitet
du arbeitest	du arbeitetest	du habest gearbeitet
er arbeite	er arbeitete	er habe gearbeitet
wir arbeiten	wir arbeiteten	wir haben gearbeitet
ihr arbeitet	ihr arbeitetet	ihr habet gearbeitet
sie arbeiten	sie arbeiteten	sie haben gearbeitet
Sie arbeiten	Sie arbeiteten	Sie haben gearbeitet

PRESENT SPECIAL SUBJUNCTIVE	PRESENT GENERAL SUBJUNCTIVE	PAST SPECIAL SUBJUNCTIVE
ich frage	ich fragte	ich habe gefragt
du fragest	du fragtest	du habest gefragt
er frage	er fragte	er habe gefragt
wir fragen	wir fragten	wir haben gefragt
ihr fraget	ihr fragtet	ihr habet gefragt
sie fragen	sie fragten	sie haben gefragt
Sie fragen	Sie fragten	Sie haben gefragt

PAST GENERAL SUBJUNCTIVE

ich hätte gefragt	ich hätte gearbeitet	ich hätte gesehen	ich wäre gegangen
du hättest gefragt	du hättest gearbeitet	du hättest gesehen	du wärest gegangen
er hätte gefragt	er hätte gearbeitet	er hätte gesehen	er wäre gegangen
wir hätten gefragt	wir hätten gearbeitet	wir hätten gesehen	wir wären gegangen
ihr hättet gefragt	ihr hättet gearbeitet	ihr hättet gesehen	ihr wäret gegangen
sie hätten gefragt	sie hätten gearbeitet	sie hätten gesehen	sie wären gegangen
Sie hätten gefragt	Sie hätten gearbeitet	Sie hätten gesehen	Sie wären gegangen

FUTURE SPECIAL SUBJUNCTIVE

ich werde fragen	ich werde arbeiten	ich werde sehen	ich werde gehen
du werdest fragen	du werdest arbeiten	du werdest sehen	du werdest gehen
er werde fragen	er werde arbeiten	er werde sehen	er werde gehen
wir werden fragen	wir werden arbeiten	wir werden sehen	wir werden gehen
ihr werdet fragen	ihr werdet arbeiten	ihr werdet sehen	ihr werdet gehen
sie werden fragen	sie werden arbeiten	sie werden sehen	sie werden gehen
Sie werden fragen	Sie werden arbeiten	Sie werden sehen	Sie werden gehen

FUTURE GENERAL SUBJUNCTIVE

ich würde fragen	ich würde arbeiten	ich würde sehen	ich würde gehen
du würdest fragen	du würdest arbeiten	du würdest sehen	du würdest gehen
er würde fragen	er würde arbeiten	er würde sehen	er würde gehen
wir würden fragen	wir würden arbeiten	wir würden sehen	wir würden gehen
ihr würdet fragen	ihr würdet arbeiten	ihr würdet sehen	ihr würdet gehen
sie würden fragen	sie würden arbeiten	sie würden sehen	sie würden gehen
Sie würden fragen	Sie würden arbeiten	Sie würden sehen	Sie würden gehen

FUTURE PERFECT SPECIAL SUBJUNCTIVE

ich werde gefragt haben	ich werde gearbeitet haben	ich werde gesehen haben	ich werde gegangen sein
du werdest gefragt haben	du werdest gearbeitet haben	du werdest gesehen haben	du werdest gegangen sein
er werde gefragt haben	er werde gearbeitet haben	er werde gesehen haben	er werde gegangen sein
wir werden gefragt haben	wir werden gearbeitet haben	wir werden gesehen haben	wir werden gegangen sein
ihr werdet gefragt haben	ihr werdet gearbeitet haben	ihr werdet gesehen haben	ihr werdet gegangen sein
sie werden gefragt haben	sie werden gearbeitet haben	sie werden gesehen haben	sie werden gegangen sein
Sie werden gefragt haben	Sie werden gearbeitet haben	Sie werden gesehen haben	Sie werden gegangen sein

FUTURE PERFECT GENERAL SUBJUNCTIVE

ich würde gefragt haben	ich würde gearbeitet haben	ich würde gesehen haben	ich würde gegangen sein
du würdest gefragt haben	du würdest gearbeitet haben	du würdest gesehen haben	du würdest gegangen sein
er würde gefragt haben	er würde gearbeitet haben	er würde gesehen haben	er würde gegangen sein
wir würden gefragt haben	wir würden gearbeitet haben	wir würden gesehen haben	wir würden gegangen sein
ihr würdet gefragt haben	ihr würdet gearbeitet haben	ihr würdet gesehen haben	ihr würdet gegangen sein
sie würden gefragt haben	sie würden gearbeitet haben	sie würden gesehen haben	sie würden gegangen sein
Sie würden gefragt haben	Sie würden gearbeitet haben	Sie würden gesehen haben	Sie würden gegangen sein

B. *Passive*

PRESENT INDICATIVE

ich werde gefragt	ich werde gesehen
du wirst gefragt	du wirst gesehen
er wird gefragt	er wird gesehen
wir werden gefragt	wir werden gesehen
ihr werdet gefragt	ihr werdet gesehen
sie werden gefragt	sie werden gesehen
Sie werden gefragt	Sie werden gesehen

PAST INDICATIVE

ich wurde gefragt	ich wurde gesehen
du wurdest gefragt	du wurdest gesehen
er wurde gefragt	er wurde gesehen
wir wurden gefragt	wir wurden gesehen
ihr wurdet gefragt	ihr wurdet gesehen
sie wurden gefragt	sie wurden gesehen
Sie wurden gefragt	Sie wurden gesehen

PRESENT PERFECT INDICATIVE

ich bin gefragt worden	ich bin gesehen worden
du bist gefragt worden	du bist gesehen worden
er ist gefragt worden	er ist gesehen worden
wir sind gefragt worden	wir sind gesehen worden
ihr seid gefragt worden	ihr seid gesehen worden
sie sind gefragt worden	sie sind gesehen worden
Sie sind gefragt worden	Sie sind gesehen worden

PAST PERFECT INDICATIVE

ich war gefragt worden	ich war gesehen worden
du warst gefragt worden	du warst gesehen worden
er war gefragt worden	er war gesehen worden
wir waren gefragt worden	wir waren gesehen worden
ihr wart gefragt worden	ihr wart gesehen worden
sie waren gefragt worden	sie waren gesehen worden
Sie waren gefragt worden	Sie waren gesehen worden

FUTURE INDICATIVE

ich werde gefragt werden
du wirst gefragt werden
er wird gefragt werden
wir werden gefragt werden
ihr werdet gefragt werden
sie werden gefragt werden
Sie werden gefragt werden

ich werde gesehen werden
du wirst gesehen werden
er wird gesehen werden
wir werden gesehen werden
ihr werdet gesehen werden
sie werden gesehen werden
Sie werden gesehen werden

FUTURE PERFECT INDICATIVE

ich werde gefragt worden sein
du wirst gefragt worden sein
er wird gefragt worden sein
wir werden gefragt worden sein
ihr werdet gefragt worden sein
sie werden gefragt worden sein
Sie werden gefragt worden sein

ich werde gesehen worden sein
du wirst gesehen worden sein
er wird gesehen worden sein
wir werden gesehen worden sein
ihr werdet gesehen worden sein
sie werden gesehen worden sein
Sie werden gesehen worden sein

PRESENT SPECIAL SUBJUNCTIVE

ich werde gefragt
du werdest gefragt
etc.

ich werde gesehen
du werdest gesehen
etc.

PRESENT GENERAL SUBJUNCTIVE

ich würde gefragt
du würdest gefragt
etc.

ich würde gesehen
du würdest gesehen
etc.

PAST SPECIAL SUBJUNCTIVE

ich sei gesehen worden
du seiest gesehen worden
etc.

ich sei gefragt worden
du seiest gefragt worden
etc.

PAST GENERAL SUBJUNCTIVE

ich wäre gesehen worden
du wärest gesehen worden
etc.

ich wäre gefragt worden
du wärest gefragt worden
etc.

FUTURE SPECIAL SUBJUNCTIVE

ich werde gesehen werden
du werdest gesehen werden
etc.

ich werde gefragt werden
du werdest gefragt werden
etc.

FUTURE GENERAL SUBJUNCTIVE

ich würde gesehen werden
du würdest gesehen werden
etc.

ich würde gefragt werden
du würdest gefragt werden
etc.

FUTURE PERFECT SPECIAL SUBJUNCTIVE

ich werde gesehen worden sein
du werdest gesehen worden sein
etc.

ich werde gefragt worden sein
du werdest gefragt worden sein
etc.

FUTURE PERFECT GENERAL SUBJUNCTIVE

ich würde gefragt worden sein du würdest gefragt worden sein etc.	ich würde gesehen worden sein du würdest gesehen worden sein etc.

IV. *REFLEXIVE VERBS*

PRESENT TENSE

sich amüsieren (*to enjoy oneself*)	**sich helfen** (*to help oneself*)
ich amüsiere mich	ich helfe mir
du amüsierst dich	du hilfst dir
er amüsiert sich	er hilft sich
wir amüsieren uns	wir helfen uns
ihr amüsiert euch	ihr helft euch
sie amüsieren sich	sie helfen sich
Sie amüsieren sich	Sie helfen sich

SELECTIVE LIST OF REFLEXIVE VERBS

sich (ACC.) **amüsieren** (*to enjoy oneself*)
sich (DAT.) **ansehen** (*to [have a] look at*)
sich (ACC.) **ärgern** (*to be annoyed*)
sich (ACC.) **ausruhen** (*to rest*)
sich (ACC.) **beschweren** (*to complain*)
sich (DAT.) **besorgen** (*to provide oneself with, get*)
sich (DAT.) **denken** (*to imagine*)
sich (ACC.) **entschuldigen** (*to excuse oneself*)
sich (ACC.) **erholen** (*to recuperate, rest*)
sich (ACC.) **erkundigen** (*to inquire*)

sich (ACC.) **erinnern** (*to remember*)
sich (ACC.) **freuen** (*to be happy*)
sich (ACC.) **setzen** (*to sit down*)
sich (ACC.) **unterhalten** (*to converse*)
sich (ACC.) **verabschieden** (*to say good-by, take leave*)
sich (ACC.) **verirren** (*to lose one's way*)
sich (ACC.) **verlaufen** (*to lose one's way*)
sich (DAT.) **vorstellen** (*to imagine*)
sich (ACC.) **zurechtfinden** (*to find one's way*)

V. *VERBS WITH DATIVE OBJECTS (SELECTIVE LIST)*

antworten   (*to answer*)
befehlen   (*to order, command*)
danken   (*to thank*)
folgen   (*to follow*)
gefallen   (*to be pleasing to, like*)
gehorchen   (*to obey*)

gehören   (*to belong to*)
gelingen   (*to succeed*)
glauben   (of persons) (*to believe*)
helfen   (*to help*)
passen   (*to fit, be suitable*)
schaden   (*to do harm, hurt*)

VI. *PRINCIPAL PARTS OF VERBS*

The following is a list of all strong and irregular verbs (including modals and mixed verbs) used actively in this book.

INFINITIVE	PAST	PRESENT	PAST PARTICIPLE	ENGLISH
abfahren	fuhr . . . ab	fährt . . . ab	*ist* abgefahren	*leave, depart*
abhalten	hielt . . . ab	hält . . . ab	hat abgehalten	*hold*
anfangen	fing . . . an	fängt . . . an	hat angefangen	*begin*
ankommen	kam . . . an		*ist* angekommen	*arrive*
anrufen	rief . . . an		hat angerufen	*call (telephone)*
ansehen	sah . . . an	sieht . . . an	hat angesehen	*look at*
antreffen	traf . . an	trifft . . . an	hat angetroffen	*meet*
aufsein	war . . auf	ist . . . auf	*ist* aufgewesen	*be up*
aussehen	sah . . . aus	sieht . . . aus	hat ausgesehen	*look, appear*
beginnen	begann		hat begonnen	*begin*
bekommen	bekam		hat bekommen	*get, receive*
bestehen	bestand		hat bestanden	*exist*
biegen	bog		*ist* (hat) gebogen	*turn, bend*
bitten	bat		hat gebeten	*ask, request*
bleiben	blieb		*ist* geblieben	*stay, remain*
brennen	brannte		hat gebrannt	*burn*
bringen	brachte		hat gebracht	*bring*
denken	dachte		hat gedacht	*think*
dürfen	durfte	darf	hat gedurft	*be allowed to*
einladen	lud . . . ein	lädt . . . ein	hat eingeladen	*invite*
erfahren	erfuhr	erfährt	hat erfahren	*learn, experience*
essen	aß	ißt	hat gegessen	*eat*
fahren	fuhr	fährt	*ist* (hat) gefahren	*go, drive*
fallen	fiel	fällt	*ist* gefallen	*fall*

INFINITIVE	PAST	PAST PARTICIPLE	PRESENT	ENGLISH
finden	fand	hat gefunden		find
fliegen	flog	*ist* (hat) geflogen	fliegt	fly
geben	gab	hat gegeben	gibt	give
gefallen	gefiel	hat gefallen	gefällt	be pleasing to
gehen	ging	*ist* gegangen		go
gelingen	gelang	*ist* gelungen		succeed
geraten	geriet	*ist* geraten	gerät	get (into)
greifen	griff	hat gegriffen		grasp, reach
haben	hatte	hat gehabt	hat	have
halten	hielt	hat gehalten	hält	hold, stop
heimkommen	kam . . . heim	*ist* heimgekommen		come home
heißen	hieß	hat geheißen		be called, named
helfen	half	hat geholfen	hilft	help
hinfahren	fuhr . . . hin	*ist* hingefahren	fährt . . . hin	go, drive there
hingehen	ging . . . hin	*ist* hingegangen		go there
kennen	kannte	hat gekannt		know
klingen	klang	hat geklungen		sound
kommen	kam	*ist* gekommen		come
können	konnte	hat gekonnt	kann	be able to
lassen	ließ	hat gelassen	läßt	let, allow
lesen	las	hat gelesen	liest	read
liegen	lag	hat gelegen		lie, be situated
mitbringen	brachte . . . mit	hat mitgebracht		bring along
mitkommen	kam . . . mit	*ist* mitgekommen		come along
mitnehmen	nahm . . . mit	hat mitgenommen	nimmt . . . mit	take along
mögen	mochte	hat gemocht	mag	like (to)
müssen	mußte	hat gemußt	muß	have to, must

INFINITIVE	PAST	PAST PARTICIPLE	PRESENT	ENGLISH
nachsehen	sah . . . nach	hat nachgesehen	sieht . . . nach	*look up, check*
nehmen	nahm	hat genommen	nimmt	*take*
nennen	nannte	hat genannt		*name, call*
rennen	rannte	*ist* gerannt		*run*
schlafen	schlief	hat geschlafen	schläft	*sleep*
schließen	schloß	hat geschlossen		*close*
schreiben	schrieb	hat geschrieben		*write*
schweigen	schwieg	hat geschwiegen		*be silent*
sehen	sah	hat gesehen	sieht	*see*
sein	war	*ist* gewesen	ist	*be*
senden	sandte	hat gesandt		*send*
sitzen	saß	hat gesessen		*sit*
sollen	sollte	hat gesollt	soll	*be supposed to*
sprechen	sprach	hat gesprochen	spricht	*speak*
stehen	stand	hat gestanden		*stand*
stehenbleiben	blieb . . . stehen	*ist* stehengeblieben		*stop*
teilnehmen	nahm . . . teil	hat teilgenommen	nimmt . . . teil	*take part*
treffen	traf	hat getroffen	trifft	*meet*
trinken	trank	hat getrunken		*drink*
tun	tat	hat getan		*do*
übertreffen	übertraf	hat übertroffen	übertrifft	*outdo, excel*
unterbrechen	unterbrach	hat unterbrochen	unterbricht	*interrupt*
sich unterhalten	unterhielt	hat unterhalten	unterhält	*converse*
verbringen	verbrachte	hat verbracht		*spend (time)*
vergehen	verging	*ist* vergangen		*pass by, go by*
vergessen	vergaß	hat vergessen	vergißt	*forget*
vergleichen	verglich	hat verglichen		*compare*

INFINITIVE	PAST	PAST PARTICIPLE	PRESENT	ENGLISH
sich verlaufen	verlief	hat verlaufen	verläuft	*lose one's way*
verlieren	verlor	hat verloren		*lose*
verschwinden	verschwand	*ist* verschwunden		*disappear*
verstehen	verstand	hat verstanden		*understand*
vorkommen	kam . . . vor	*ist* vorgekommen		*seem*
weiterfahren	fuhr . . . weiter	*ist* weitergefahren	fährt . . . weiter	*drive on, continue*
wenden	wandte	hat gewandt		*turn*
werden	wurde	*ist* geworden	wird	*become*
wissen	wußte	hat gewußt	weiß	*know*
wollen	wollte	hat gewollt	will	*want (to)*
zugeben	gab . . . zu	hat zugegeben	gibt . . . zu	*admit, grant*
zugehen	ging . . . zu	*ist* zugegangen		*go on, happen*
zuhalten	hielt . . . zu	hat zugehalten	hält . . . zu	*hold closed*
sich zurechtfinden	fand . . . zurecht	hat zurechtgefunden		*find one's way*

Declension of Der-Words

	MASC.	FEM.	NEUT.	PL.	MASC.	FEM.	NEUT.	PL.
NOM.	der	die	das	die	dieser	diese	dieses	diese
ACC.	den	die	das	die	diesen	diese	dieses	diese
DAT.	dem	der	dem	den	diesem	dieser	diesem	diesen
GEN.	des	der	des	der	dieses	dieser	dieses	dieser

The **der**-words are:

> **dieser** (*this*)
> **jeder**   (*each, every;* pl. **alle**)
> **jener**   (*that*)
> **mancher** (*many a;* pl. *some*)
> **solcher** (*such a;* pl. *such*)
> **welcher** (*which*)

Declension of Ein-Words

	MASC.	FEM.	NEUT.	PL.	MASC.	FEM.	NEUT.	PL.
NOM.	ein	eine	ein	—	mein	meine	mein	meine
ACC.	einen	eine	ein	—	meinen	meine	mein	meine
DAT.	einem	einer	einem	—	meinem	meiner	meinem	meinen
GEN.	eines	einer	eines	—	meines	meiner	meines	meiner

	MASC.	FEM.	NEUT.	PL.
NOM.	unser	unsere	unser	unsere
ACC.	unseren	unsere	unser	unsere
DAT.	unserem	unserer	unserem	unseren
GEN.	unseres	unserer	unseres	unserer

The **ein**-words are:

> **ein**   (*a, an*)
> **mein** (*my*)
> **dein** (*your* [sing. fam.])
> **sein** (*his, its*)
> **ihr**   (*her, its*)
> **unser** (*our*)
> **euer** (*your* [pl. fam.])
> **ihr**   (*their*)
> **Ihr**   (*your* [polite])
> **kein** (*no, not a, not any*)

Attributive Adjective Declension

After a definite article or any *der-word*

	MASC.	FEM.	NEUT.	PL.
NOM.	der neue Wagen	die alte Firma	das moderne Haus	die modernen Häuser
ACC.	den neuen Wagen	die alte Firma	das moderne Haus	die modernen Häuser
DAT.	dem neuen Wagen	der alten Firma	dem modernen Haus	den modernen Häusern
GEN.	des neuen Wagens	der alten Firma	des modernen Hauses	der modernen Häuser

After an indefinite article or any *ein-word*

	MASC.	FEM.	NEUT.	PL.
NOM.	ein neuer Wagen	eine alte Firma	ein modernes Haus	keine modernen Häuser
ACC.	einen neuen Wagen	eine alte Firma	ein modernes Haus	keine modernen Häuser
DAT.	einem neuen Wagen	einer alten Firma	einem modernen Haus	keinen modernen Häusern
GEN.	eines neuen Wagens	einer alten Firma	eines modernen Hauses	keiner modernen Häuser

Not preceded by a *der-word* or an *ein-word*

	MASC.	FEM.	NEUT.	PL.
NOM.	heißer Tee	eisgekühlte Limonade	kaltes Bier	bekannte Lehrer
ACC.	heißen Tee	eisgekühlte Limonade	kaltes Bier	bekannte Lehrer
DAT.	heißem Tee	eisgekühlter Limonade	kaltem Bier	bekannten Lehrern
GEN.	heißen Tees	eisgekühlter Limonade	kalten Biers	bekannter Lehrer

Comparison of Adjectives and Adverbs

The comparative of adjectives and adverbs is formed by adding **-er** to the stem:

> **Diese Geschichte ist interessant*er* als die andere.**
> **Das ist eine interessant*ere* Geschichte.**

The superlative of attributive adjectives is formed by adding **-(e)st** to the stem:

> **Das ist die interessant*este* Geschichte.**

The superlative of predicate adjectives can be formed two ways:

> **Diese Geschichte ist die interessant*este*.**
> **Diese Geschichte ist *am* interessant*esten*.**

The superlative of adverbs is formed with **am . . . (e)sten:**

> **Er fährt *am* schnell*sten*.**

Adjectives with Umlaut in Comparative and Superlative

> **alt, älter, ältest-**
> **jung, jünger, jüngst-**
> **kalt, kälter, kältest-**
> **krank, kränker, kränkst-**
> **kurz, kürzer, kürzest-**
> **lang, länger, längst-**
> **oft, öfter, öftest-**
> **scharf, schärfer, schärfst-**
> **warm, wärmer, wärmst-**

Irregular Comparatives and Superlatives

> **bald, eher, am ehesten**
> **gern, lieber, am liebsten**
> **groß, größer, größt-**
> **gut, besser, best-**
> **viel, mehr, meist-**

Pronouns

I. PERSONAL PRONOUNS

NOM.	ich	du	er	sie	es	wir	ihr	sie	Sie
ACC.	mich	dich	ihn	sie	es	uns	euch	sie	Sie
DAT.	mir	dir	ihm	ihr	ihm	uns	euch	ihnen	Ihnen
GEN.	(meiner)	(deiner)	(seiner)	(ihrer)	(seiner)	(unser)	(euer)	(ihrer)	(Ihrer)

II. *INTERROGATIVE PRONOUNS* (**wer** and **was**)

NOM.	**wer**	**was**
ACC.	**wen**	**was**
DAT.	**wem**	—
GEN.	**wessen**	—

III. *RELATIVE PRONOUNS* (**der** and **welcher**)

	M.	F.	N.	PL.	M.	F.	N.	PL.
NOM.	**der**	**die**	**das**	**die**	**welcher**	**welche**	**welches**	**welche**
ACC.	**den**	**die**	**das**	**die**	**welchen**	**welche**	**welches**	**welche**
DAT.	**dem**	**der**	**dem**	**denen**	**welchem**	**welcher**	**welchem**	**welchen**
GEN.	**dessen**	**deren**	**dessen**	**deren**	*(dessen)*	*(deren)*	*(dessen)*	*(deren)*

Prepositions

Governing the Accusative (Selective List)

durch	*(through)*
für	*(for)*
gegen	*(against)*
ohne	*(without)*
um	*(around)*

Governing the Dative (Selective List)

aus	*(out of, from)*
bei	*(at, with, near)*
mit	*(with)*
nach	*(after, to)*
seit	*(since, for* [with time]*)*
von	*(from, of)*
zu	*(to)*

Governing the Dative and Accusative

an	*(at, to, on)*
auf	*(on, to, at)*
hinter	*(behind)*
in	*(in, into, to)*
neben	*(next to)*

über	(*over, above, across*)
unter	(*under, among*)
vor	(*in front of*)
zwischen	(*between*)

Governing the Genitive (Selective List)

anstatt	(*instead of*)
trotz	(*in spite of*)
während	(*during*)
wegen	(*because of*)

CONTRACTIONS OF PREPOSITIONS WITH DEFINITE ARTICLES

with *das*: **ans, aufs, durchs, fürs, ins, ums**
  also colloquially: **gegens, hinters, nebens, übers, unters, vors, zwischens**

with *dem*: **am, beim, im, vom, zum**
  also colloquially: **hinterm, überm, unterm, vorm**

with *der*: **zur**

Conjunctions

Coordinating Conjunctions (Selective List)

aber	(*but*)
denn	(*because, for*)
oder	(*or*)
sondern	(*but rather*)
und	(*and*)

Subordinating Conjunctions (Selective List)

als	(*when, as*)
da	(*since*)
daß	(*that*)
ob	(*whether*)
obgleich	(*although*)
obwohl	(*although*)
während	(*while*)

weil	(*because, since*)
wenn	(*when* [*ever*], *if*)
wie	(*as*)

Word Order

POSITION OF VERB

In an independent clause the inflected verb must be the second element.

Er *arbeitet* seit Jahren bei der Firma Opel.
Seit Jahren *arbeitet* er bei der Firma Opel.
Bei der Firma Opel *arbeitet* er seit Jahren.

Infinitives and past participles are placed at the end of the clause.

Er hat bei der Firma Opel *gearbeitet*.
Er will bei der Firma Opel *arbeiten*.

In a dependent clause the inflected verb is in final position.

Ich weiß, daß er bei der Firma Opel *arbeitet*.
Ich weiß, daß er bei der Firma Opel gearbeitet *hat*.
Ich weiß, daß er bei der Firma Opel arbeiten *will*.

In questions the verb precedes the subject.

Arbeitet er bei der Firma Opel?
Wann hat er bei der Firma Opel gearbeitet?

In commands the verb is placed first.

Laufe nicht so schnell!
Lauft nicht so schnell!
Laufen Sie nicht so schnell!

SEPARABLE PREFIXES

A separable prefix is placed at the end of the clause.

Er nimmt an der Tour *teil*.

It is attached to its past participle or infinitive at the end of the clause.

Er hat an der Tour *teilgenommen*.
Er will an der Tour *teilnehmen*.

WORD ORDER OF OBJECTS

The indirect object precedes the direct object unless the direct object is a pronoun.

Er erzählt *seinem Gast eine Legende.*
Er erzählt *ihm eine Legende.*
Er erzählt *sie ihm.*

WORD ORDER OF ADVERBS

The sequence of adverbs in the predicate is TIME, MANNER, PLACE.

T　　　　　　M　　　　　P

Er fährt <u>vor Semesterbeginn</u> <u>mit seinem Gast</u> <u>nach Köln.</u>

German-English Vocabulary

This vocabulary includes all the words in the active and visible vocabularies. Personal pronouns, articles and some obvious cognates are omitted.

Nouns are listed with their genitive and plural endings (in that order): **der Tag, −(e)s, −e.** Strong and irregular verbs are given with their auxiliaries and principal parts. Weak verbs that take **sein** are indicated as: **landen(sein)**; all others take **haben.**

Adjectives and adverbs that take an umlaut in the comparative and superlative are indicated: **alt (ä)**; those with irregular comparatives and superlatives are shown: **gut (besser, best-).**

Separable prefixes are indicated by a hyphen: **mit-machen.**

A number in brackets, after a word from the active vocabularies, indicates the lesson in which the word is used for the first time.

der **Abend, −s, −e** [5] evening
    am Abend in the evening
    eines Abends one evening
das **Abendessen, −s, −** [5] dinner, evening meal
    abendlich (*every*) evening
    abends [14] in the evening(s)
    aber [1] but
    ab-fahren, fuhr . . . ab, ist abgefahren, fährt . . . ab [13] to leave, depart
    abgemacht! [8] agreed! all right! settled!
    ab-halten, hielt . . . ab, hat abgehalten, hält . . . ab [20] to hold, have
    ab-holen [13] to pick up, fetch
der **Abschied, −s, −e** [25] farewell, departure
das **Abschiedsgeschenk, −s, −e** [25] farewell gift
    absolut [10] absolute
    acht [7] eight
    acht- [10] eighth

der **Adelstitel, −s, −** title of nobility
    akademisch academic
der **Akkord, −s, −e** chord
    alle [4] all
    allerdings to be sure; it is true
    allerlei [7] all kinds of (things)
    alles [10] everything; [14] (*coll.*) everyone
    allgemein general
    allmählich [9] gradual
    allzu [25] much too
    als [1] as, as a
    als (*after comparative*) [9] than
    als (*subord. conj.*) [9] when
    als ob (*subord. conj.*) [20] as though
    also [1] so, thus
    alt (ä) [2] old
das **Alter, −s** age
    altmodisch [3] old-fashioned
der **Amerikaner, −s, −** [1] the American
die **Amerikanisierung, −** [15] Americanization
    amüsant [19] amusing, funny
sich (*acc.*) **amüsieren** [15] to enjoy one-

self, have a good time
an (+ *dat./acc.*) [*7*]   at, to, on
ander- [*4*]   other
   die **anderen** [*2*]   the others
ändern [*24*]   to change
anders als   different from
der **Anfang, –s, ⸚e**   beginning
an-fangen, fing . . . an, hat angefangen, fängt . . . an [*14*]   to begin
anfangs [*15*]   in the beginning
angeblich   supposed, alleged
angenehm [*23*]   pleasant
angesehen   respected, esteemed
an-greifen, griff . . . an, hat angegriffen   to attack
die **Angst, –, ⸚e** [*21*]   fear
an-halten, hielt . . . an, hat angehalten, hält . . . an   to stop
an-klagen   to accuse
an-kommen, kam . . . an, ist angekommen [*13*]   to arrive
an-kommen auf (+ *acc.*), **kam . . . an, ist angekommen** [*20*]   to depend on
an-reden   to address
an-rufen, rief . . . an, hat angerufen [*17*]   to call (*on the telephone*)
an-schalten   to turn on
anscheinend [*20*]   evident, apparent
sich (*dat.*) **an-sehen, sah . . . an, hat angesehen, sieht . . . an** [*14*]   to (have a) look at
die **Ansichtskarte, –, –n** [*13*]   picture postcard
„**Anstalt des öffentlichen Rechts**"   statutory institution
anstatt (+ *gen.*) [*9*]   instead of
sich (*acc.*) **an-stellen** [*18*]   to get in line
anstrengend [*10*]   strenuous
antik [*3*]   antique
an-treffen, traf . . . an, hat angetroffen, trifft . . . an [*21*]   to meet
die **Antwort, –, –en**   answer
antworten (*dat.*)   to answer
an-ziehen, zog . . . an, hat angezogen   to attract
applaudieren   to applaud
der **April, –s** [*12*]   April
apropos [*13*]   speaking of
arbeiten [*1*]   to work
der **Arbeiter, –s, –**   worker

die **Arbeitserlaubnis, –** [*19*]   working permit
das **Arbeitszimmer, –s, –** [*3*]   study
die **Architektur, –, –en** [*3*]   architecture
sich (*acc.*) **ärgern** [*14*]   to be annoyed
arm (ä)   poor
der **Arm, –(e)s, –e** [*5*]   arm
der **Armleuchter, –s, –**   candelabrum
die **Art, –, –en**   manner, way(s), type, kind
der **Arzt, –es, ⸚e** [*13*]   physician
der **Aschermittwoch, –s, –e** [*14*]   Ash Wednesday
das **Aspirin, –s** [*14*]   aspirin
das **Atelier, –s, –s** [*17*]   studio
der **Atem, –s** [*18*]   breath
   außer Atem [*18*]   out of breath
auch [*1*]   also, too
das **Audimax = Auditorium Maximum** [*8*]   main lecture hall
auf (+ *dat./acc.*) [*1*]   on, to, at
auf-bauen [*13*]   to build up, construct
der **Aufenthalt, –s, –e** [*25*]   stay, sojourn
die **Aufenthaltsgenehmigung, –, –en**   permit of residence
die **Aufführung, –, –en**   performance
die **Aufgabe, –, –n**   lesson
auf-kaufen [*25*]   to buy out
die **Aufnahme, –, –n** [*13*]   photograph, snapshot
auf-nehmen, nahm . . . auf, hat aufgenommen, nimmt . . . auf   to receive, house
auf-sein, war . . . auf, ist aufgewesen, ist . . . auf [*12*]   to be up, be out of bed
der **Augenblick, –s, –e** [*8*]   moment
der **August, –s** [*12*]   August
aus (+ *dat.*) [*1*]   out of, from
sich (*dat.*) **aus-denken, dachte . . . aus, hat ausgedacht**   to think up, contrive, invent
der **Ausdruck, –s, ⸚e** [*10*]   expression
der **Ausflug, –s, ⸚e** [*4*]   outing, excursion
ausgezeichnet [*7*]   excellent
die **Auskunft, –, ⸚e** [*8*]   information
ausländisch [*19*]   foreign
ausnahmslos [*24*]   without exception
sich (*acc.*) **aus-ruhen** [*19*]   to rest
aus-sehen, sah . . . aus, hat ausgesehen, sieht . . . aus [*14*]   to look, appear

die **Aussicht, –, –en** [*4*] view
die **Aussprache, –, –n** pronunciation
aus-suchen [*25*] to pick out, select
der **Austauschstudent, –en, –en** [*8*] exchange student
aus-verkaufen [*7*] to sell out
das **Auto, –s, –s** [*2*] automobile
die **Autobahn, –, –en** [*2*] super highway
die **Autobiographie, –, –n** autobiography
das **Autofahren, –s** [*4*] driving
der **Autor, –s, –en** author
die **Autorität, –, –en** [*10*] authority
die **Autoritätsgläubigkeit, –** (*blind*) faith in the authorities

das **Bad, –(e)s, ⁔er** [*3*] bathroom, bath
die **Bahn, –, –en** [*2*] lane, track, way
der **Bahnhof, –s, ⁔e** [*18*] railroad station
bald (eher, am ehesten) [*3*] soon
bang(e) worried, upset
die **Bank, –, ⁔e** [*4*] bench
der **Bau, –s** construction
der **Baubeginn, –s** beginning of construction
der **Bayer, –n, –n** [*17*] Bavarian
bayrisch [*17*] Bavarian
bedeuten to mean, signify
die **Bedeutung, –, –en** meaning, significance
beeindruckt impressed
befehlen (*dat.*), **befahl, hat befohlen, befiehlt** to order, command
begabt [*7*] talented
begeistert enthusiastic
der **Beginn, –s** [*5*] beginning
beginnen, begann, hat begonnen [*8*] to begin
die **Begrenzung, –, –en** [*2*] limitation, limit
begrüßen [*2*] to greet, welcome
behaupten [*23*] to maintain, claim, say
die **Behauptung, –, –en** assertion, statement
bei (+ *dat.*) [*1*] at, [*4*] with, near
beide [*2*] both
die beiden [*2*] the two
beinah (e) almost
das **Beispiel, –s, –e** [*9*] example

zum Beispiel [*9*] for example
bekannt [*7*] well-known
der **Bekannte, –n, –n** (*adjectival noun*) [*10*] acquaintance, friend
die **Bekanntschaft, –, –en** acquaintance
bekommen, bekam, hat bekommen [*7*] to get, receive, obtain
belegen [*8*] to sign up for, take, register for (*a course*)
beliebt [*10*] popular
bemerken [*15*] to notice
die **Bemerkung, –, –en** remark
das **Benehmen, –s** conduct, manners
beobachten [*12*] to watch, observe
der **Berg, –(e)s, –e** [*4*] mountain
berühmt [*5*] famous
besetzen [*19*] to occupy
Bescheid wissen (in + *dat.*) [*7*] to be informed (in a *field*)
beschließen, beschloß, hat beschlossen to conclude; decide
die **Beschreibung, –, –en** description
sich (*acc.*) **beschweren (über** + *acc.*) [*24*] to complain (about)
besichtigen [*21*] to go sightseeing, visit
die **Besichtigungstour, –, –en** [*13*] sightseeing tour
der **Besitzer, –s, –** owner
besonders [*5*] especially
sich (*dat.*) **besorgen** [*19*] to provide oneself with, get
bestehen, bestand, hat bestanden [*24*] to exist
bestellen [*5*] to order
bestimmt [*8*] certain, definite
bestrafen to punish
der **Besuch, –s, –e** [*13*] visit
besuchen [*4*] to visit
der **Besucher, –s, –** visitor, tourist
der **Beton, –s** concrete
betrachten als [*9*] to consider
der **Betrieb, –s** [*17*] bustle, activity
das **Bett, –(e)s, –en** [*23*] bed
bevor (*subord. conj.*) before
bewachen [*20*] to guard, watch
sich (*acc.*) **in Bewegung setzen** [*20*] to get moving
bewirten to treat
die **Bezeichnung, –, –en** expression, designation
die **Bibliothek, –, –en** [*18*] library

biegen, bog, ist (hat) gebogen [*21*] to turn, bend

das **Bier, –(e)s, –e** [*10*] beer

die **Bierbrauerei, –, –en** brewery

das **Bild, –(e)s, –er** [*5*] picture; image

der **Bildhauer, –s, –** [*17*] sculptor

die **Biographie, –, –n** biography

bis [*2*] to, until

bis (*subord. conj.*) until

bitte [*13*] you are welcome; [*3*] please

bitten (um), bat, hat gebeten [*8*] to ask (for)

blasiert [*15*] blasé

das **Blei, –s** lead

bleiben, blieb, ist geblieben [*3*] to stay

das **„Bleigießen", –s** pouring of molten lead into water

blühen to flourish

das **Blut, –(e)s** blood

der **Bogen, –s, –** arch

die **Boheme, –** [*17*] the Bohemian world, Bohemia

der **Bohemien, –s, –s** Bohemian

böse bad, wicked

brauchen [*9*] to need

braun gebrannt [*25*] sun-tanned

brechen, brach, hat gebrochen, bricht to break

breit wide, broad

brennen, brannte, hat gebrannt [*18*] to burn

der **Brief, –(e)s, –e** [*13*] letter

der **Briefträger, –s, –** mailman

bringen, brachte, hat gebracht [*12*] to bring

das **Brot, –(e)s, –e** [*20*] bread; sandwich

der **Bruder, –s, ⸚** [*5*] brother

die **Brüderschaft, –** [*5*] brotherhood

brüllen [*14*] to roar, shout

das **Buch, –(e)s, ⸚er** [*18*] book

der **Büchermarkt, –s** book-market

das **Bündel, –s, –** [*25*] bundle

der **Bundesgenosse, –n, –n** confederate, fellow member of the confederation

die **Bundeshauptstadt, –** [*2*] capital of the Federal Republic

die **Bundesrepublik, –** Federal Republic

die **Burg, –, –en** [*4*] castle

der **Bürger, –s, –** citizen; bourgeois

der **Bürgermeister, –s, –** [*25*] mayor

die **Bürgerschaft, –** [*25*] citizens

die **Bürokratie, –, –n** bureaucracy

die **Büttenrede, –, –n** funny speech (*mostly improvised, delivered during carnival. The speaker stands in a "Bütt" i.e., a vat.*)

das **Café, –s, –s** [*13*] café

chinesisch [*10*] Chinese

der **Chor, –(e)s, ⸚e** [*14*] chorus, choir

die **Christenheit, –** Christianity

die **Chronik, –, –en** [*9*] chronicle

das **Cocktailgespräch, –s, –e** [*15*] conversation at a cocktail party

d.h. (das heißt) i.e. (that is)

da [*1*] there

da (*subord. conj.*) [*8*] since

dabei at the same time, and yet

damals [*9*] then; at that time; in those days

damit (*subord. conj.*) [*25*] so that

der **Dampfer, –s, –** [*13*] steamer, ship

Dänemark Denmark

der **Dank, –(e)s** [*1*] thanks

vielen Dank [*1*] thank you very much

danke! [*7*] thank you!

danken (*dat.*) to thank

dann [*3*] then

dar-stellen [*21*] to present, depict, portray

der **Darsteller, –s, –** [*15*] performer

darum [*1*] therefore, for that reason

das [*1*] that

daß (*subord. conj.*) [*8*] that

das **Datum, –s, Daten** date

dauern [*8*] to last

dazu-kommen, kam . . . dazu, ist dazugekommen to join, be added

decken [*12*] to set (*the table*)

dein [*5*] your (*sing. fam.*)

die **Demokratie, –, –n** democracy

denken (an + acc.), dachte, hat gedacht [*7*] to think (of)

sich (*dat.*) **denken, dachte, hat gedacht** [*19*] to imagine

das **Denkmal, –s, ⸚er** [*21*] monument

denn [*5*] because, for

deswegen [*17*] for that reason, therefore

deuten to interpret, read
deutsch [1] German
der **Deutsche, –n, –n** (*adjectival noun*)
[1] German (citizen)
Deutschland [1] Germany
der **Dezember, –s** [12] December
der **Dialekt, –s, –e** dialect
der **Dichter, –s, –** [15] poet, fiction
writer
die **Dichtung, –, –en** poetry
der **Diener, –s, –** servant, footman
dieser [5] this
der **Dienstag, –s, –e** [7] Tuesday
die **Dienstzeit, –, –en** tour of duty
das **Ding, –(e)s, –e** [13] thing
vor allen Dingen [13] above all,
especially
der **Diplomat, –en, –en** diplomat
direkt [1] direct
der **Dirigent, –en, –en** [7] conductor
doch yet, nevertheless, but
das **Dokument, –s, –e** document
der **Dom, –(e)s, –e** [5] cathedral
der **Donnerstag, –s, –e** [7] Thursday
das **Dorf, –(e)s, ⁻er** [2] village
dort [3] there
der **Dozent, –en, –en** university lecturer,
instructor
der **Drache, –n, –n** [4] dragon
der **Drachenfels** [4] *lit.* dragon's cliff
(*name of mountain on the
Rhine*)
das **Drama, –s, Dramen** drama, play
der **Dramatiker, –s, –** dramatist, play-
wright
der **Dreikönigsschrein, –s** shrine of the
Three Wise Men
dreizehn [7] thirteen
dritt- [10] third
drüben [4] over there
dunkel [9] dark
durch (+ *acc.*) [2] through
die **Durchschnittsware, –, –n** mediocre
product
dürfen, durfte, hat gedurft, darf [3]
to be allowed to
der **Durst, –es** [19] thirst
die **Dynamik, –** dynamics

eben [14] just
echt [14] real, genuine
die **Ecke, –, –n** [21] corner
ehe (*subord. conj.*) [13] before

ehemalig [24] former
eher [8] rather
der **Ehrendoktor, –s, –en** honorary doctor
ehrgeizig ambitious
das **Ei, –s, –er** egg
eigen [17] own
eigentlich [4] actual
einander each other
einfach [10] simple
der **Einfluß, Einflusses, Einflüsse** influence
der **Eingang, –s, ⁻e** [8] entrance
einheimisch [17] native
das **Einheitskunstwerk, –s, –e** (*not translatable*) work of art combining
the skills of all the participants
einige [10] some, a few
**ein-laden, lud . . . ein, hat einge-
laden, lädt . . . ein** [7] to
invite
einmal [2] once
einmalig [15] unique, exceptional
sich (*acc.*) **ein-mischen** to interfere,
meddle
ein-packen [23] to pack
ein-sammeln to collect
der **Einwohner, –s, –** [17] inhabitant
die **Einwohnerzahl, –, –en** population
einzig only, single
eisgekühlt [10] cold, iced
eitel vain
elf eleven
die **Eltern** (*pl.*) [25] parents
emigrieren (sein) to emigrate
das **Ende, –s, –n** end
endlich [9] at last, finally
eng [17] narrow
englisch [8] English
auf englisch [8] in English
enorm enormous
das **Ensemble, –s, –s** [20] ensemble
die **Entbindungsanstalt, –, –en** maternity ward
die **Entfernung, –, –en** distance; departure
entlang [12] along
entschuldigen [8] to excuse
sich (*acc.*) **entschuldigen lassen** [25] to
send one's apologies
entstehen, entstand, ist entstanden
to come into being
enttäuschen to disappoint

die **Entwicklung, –, –en** development
das **Ereignis, –ses, –se** event
  erfahren, erfuhr, hat erfahren, erfährt [*15*] to learn, find out, experience
die **Erfahrung, –, –en** [*21*] experience
  erfassen to catch, grasp
  erhalten, erhielt, hat erhalten, erhält to preserve, maintain
  erheben, erhob, hat erhoben to elevate, exalt
sich (*acc.*) **erholen** [*25*] to rest, recuperate
  erinnern (an + acc.) [*7*] to remind (of)
sich (*acc.*) **erinnern (an + acc.)** [*21*] to remember (*someone* or *something*)
  erkennen, erkannte, hat erkannt to recognize, perceive
  erklären to explain, declare
die **Erklärung, –, –en** explanation
sich (*acc.*) **erkundigen** [*14*] to inquire
die **Erlaubnis, –** permission
  erleben [*14*] to experience
das **Erlebnis, –ses, –se** experience
der **Erlebnisdichter, –s, –** poet of (*inner*) experiences
  erscheinen, erschien, ist erschienen to appear, be published
  erschöpft [*14*] exhausted
  erst (*adv.*) [*8*] only, not until
  erst- [*8*] first
    zum erstenmal [*7*] for the first time
  erstaunlich [*19*] amazing.
  erwähnen [*9*] to mention
  erzählen [*3*] to tell, narrate
der (das) **Essay, –s, –s** essay
  essen, aß, hat gegessen, ißt [*13*] to eat
das **Essen, –s, –** [*3*] meal
das **Eßzimmer, –s, –** [*3*] dining room
  etwa [*24*] about, approximately
  etwas [*7*] something; [*10*] somewhat; [*10*] a little
    so etwas [*14*] such a thing
  euer [*5*] your (*pl. fam.*)
  europäisch [*10*] European
der **Expressionismus, –** expressionism
der **Expressionist, –en, –en** expressionist

das **Fach, –(e)s, ⁻er** [*8*] field, specialty

der **Fachausdruck, –s, –e** [*10*] technical term
  fahren, fuhr, ist (hat) gefahren, fährt [*1*] to drive, go
die **Fahrkarte, –, –n** [*18*] ticket (*railroad, bus, etc.*)
der **Fahrkartenschalter, –s, –** [*18*] ticket window
  fahrplanmäßig [*13*] as scheduled, on schedule
die **Fahrt, –, –en** [*13*] trip
die **Fakultät, –, –en** branch of university learning and teaching
der **Fall, –(e)s, ⁻e** [*23*] case
    für alle Fälle [*23*] for any eventuality
  fallen, fiel, ist gefallen, fällt [*15*] to fall
    es fällt mir schwer [*15*] I find it hard, it is difficult for me
  falsch false, wrong
die **Familie, –, –n** [*1*] family
die **Farbe, –, –n** color
der **Fasching, –s** carnival, Schrovetide
  fassen [*20*] to catch
  fast [*4*] almost
der **Fastnachtsonntag, –s, –e** [*14*] Sunday before Lent
  faszinieren to fascinate
  faul rotten
der **Februar, –s** [*12*] February
der **Fehler, –s, –** [*10*] mistake
  fehlerlos [*8*] flawless, perfect
die **Fehlleistung, –, –en** (*Freudian*) slip
die **Feier, –, –n** [*12*] celebration, party
  feiern [*12*] to celebrate
der **Feind, –(e)s, –e** enemy
das **Fenster, –s, –** window
das **Fernglas, –es, ⁻er** [*4*] binoculars
das **Fernsehen, –s** [*24*] television
  fern-sehen, sah . . . fern, hat ferngesehen, sieht . . . fern to watch television
die **Fernsehgebühr, –, –en** [*24*] television tax, fee
das **Fernsehgerät, –s, –e** television set
die **Fernsehgesellschaft, –, –en** television network
  fertig [*1*] finished
  fest firm
das **Fest, –es, –e** [*12*] celebration, festival
die **Festung, –, –en** [*19*] fortress
der **Feudalherr, –n, –en** feudal lord

die **Feuersgefahr, –, –en** fire hazard
die **Feuerstelle, –, –n** fireplace
das **Feuerwerk, –s, –e** fireworks
die **Figur, –, –en** shape
der **Film, –(e)s, –e** [4] film, movie(s)
finanzieren [24] to finance
finden, fand, hat gefunden [4] to
find
die **Firma, –, Firmen** [1] firm, company
das **Fleisch, –es** flesh; meat
fliegen, flog, ist (hat) geflogen [1] to
fly
fliehen, floh, ist geflohen to flee,
run away
der **Flug, –(e)s, ⸚e** [25] flight
der **Fluggast, –(e)s, ⸚e** [1] airline passenger
der **Flugplatz, –es, ⸚e** [1] airport
das **Flugzeug, –s, –e** [1] airplane
flüssig liquid
folgen (sein) (*dat.*) [4] to follow
die **Form, –, –en** form
formell formal
forschen to do research
die **Forschung, –** research, scholarship
der **Fortschritt, –s, –e** progress
fort-setzen to continue
der **Fotoapparat, –s, –e** [21] camera
die **Fotografie, –, –n** [5] photograph
fotografieren, [13] to take a photograph
die **Frage, –, –n** question
fragen [1] to ask
Frankreich France
im Französischen in French
die **Frau, –, –en** [3] woman; Mrs.
das **Fräulein, –s, –** young lady; Miss
frei free
der **Freiheitskämpfer, –s, –** [21] fighter
for liberty
der **Freitag, –s, –e** [7] Friday
fremd [21] strange, alien
der **Fremdenführer, –s, –** guide
sich (*acc.*) **freuen** [18] to be happy
sich (*acc.*) **freuen auf** (+ *acc.*) [18] to
look forward to
sich (*acc.*) **freuen über** (+ *acc.*) to enjoy,
be happy about
der **Freund, –(e)s, –e** [5] friend
freundlich friendly, kind
die **Freundschaft, –, –en** friendship
der **Friede(n), –ns** peace
froh [19] happy, glad

früh [8] early
früher former
wie früher as in the past
die **Frühgotik, –** early Gothic period
(*in art and architecture*)
das **Frühstück, –s, –e** [12] breakfast
der **Frühstückstisch, –es, –e** [12] breakfast table
führen [4] to lead
einen Krieg führen to fight a war
fünf [5] five
für (+ *acc.*) [1] for
furchtbar [19] terrible
fürchten to fear
der **Fuß, –es, ⸚e** [12] foot
zu Fuß [12] on foot
die **Fußtour, –, –en** [4] hike
der **Fußweg, –s, –** [4] footpath

gähnen [23] to yawn
die **Galerie, –, –n** [17] (*art*) gallery
ganz [2] whole, entire
gar [20] even
gar nicht [14] not at all
gar nichts [12] nothing at all
die **Gasse, –, –n** [17] street, alley
der **Gast, –es, ⸚e** [2] guest
der **Gasthörer, –s, –** [8] auditor
der **Gastprofessor, –s, –en** [8] visiting
professor
das **Gebäude, –s, –** [13] building
geben, gab, hat gegeben, gibt [2] to
give
es gibt [2] there is, are
das **Gebiet, –s, –e** [7] field, subject
gebildet educated
das **Gebirge, –s, –** [23] mountains,
mountain range
geboren born
gebrauchen [10] to use
die **Gebühr, –, –en** [24] fee
die **Gedankenlyrik, –** contemplative
poetry
das **Gedicht, –s, –e** [10] poem
gefallen (*dat.*), **gefiel, hat gefallen,
gefällt** [4] to be pleasing to, like
das **Gefängnis, –ses, –se** jail
das **Gefühl, –s, –e** feeling
gegen (+ *acc.*) [2] against
der **Gegensatz, –es, ⸚e** [21] contrast
gehen, ging, ist gegangen [3] to go
es geht mir genau so [15] it's the
same with me

gehorchen (*dat.*)   to obey
gehören (zu) (*dat.*) [9]   to belong to
die **Geige, –, –n** [7]   violin
der **Geist, –es, –er**   spirit; ghost
geistig   spiritual, intellectual
geistreich   bright, witty
das **Geld, –(e)s, –er** [23]   money
gelegentlich [7]   occasional, at the first opportunity
der **Geliebte, –n, –n**   lover, beloved
gelingen (*dat.*), **gelang, ist gelungen** [15]   to succeed
gelten als, galt, hat gegolten, gilt   to be considered
das **Gelübde, –s, –**   vow
gemeinsam [4]   in common
gemütlich [10]   comfortable
genau [2]   exact
genauso [2]   just the same
die **Generation, –, –en**   generation
das **Genie, –s, –s**   genius
genug [18]   enough
der **Genuß, Genusses, Genüsse** [24]   joy, pleasure
gerade [4]   just
das **Gerät, –s, –e**   set, apparatus
geraten in (+ *acc.*), **geriet, ist geraten, gerät** [20]   to get into
gern(e) (lieber, am liebsten) [3]   gladly
gespannt sein auf (+ *acc.*)   to be excited about
das **Geschäft, –s, –e** [2]   business, store
der **Geschäftsmann, –s, Geschäftsleute** [2]   business man
geschehen, geschah, ist geschehen, geschieht   to happen
das **Geschenk, –s, –e** [25]   gift
die **Geschichte, –, –n** [9]   story; [1] history
der **Geschmack, –s** [19]   taste
die **Geschwindigkeit, –, –en** [2]   speed
die **Geschwindigkeitsbegrenzung, –, –en** [2]   speed limit
die **Gesellschaft, –, –en**   society
die **Gesellschaftsreform, –, –en**   social reform
die **Gesellschaftssatire, –, –n**   social satire
das **Gesellschaftsspiel, –s, –e**   party game
das **Gesetz, –es, –e**   law
das **Gespräch, –s, –e** [15]   conversation
die **Gestalt, –, –en**   shape

gestern [14]   yesterday
das **Getränk, –s, –e** [10]   drink, beverage
gewagt [15]   daring
die **Gewerkschaft, –, –en**   labor union
gewiß [9]   certain
gießen, goß, hat gegossen   to pour
der **Glanz, –es**   splendor
glänzend [25]   splendid
das **Glas, –es, ⁻er** [5]   glass
glatt [25]   smooth
glauben (*dat. of persons*) [3]   to believe
gleich [13]   directly, at once; [21] same
gleichfalls! [23]   the same to you! likewise
das **Glück, –(e)s** [9]   luck, fortune
zum Glück [9]   fortunately
glücklich   happy
golden   gold(en)
gotisch   Gothic
der **Gott, –(e)s, ⁻er**   god
das **Grammophon, –s, –e**   phonograph
grau [23]   gray
greifen, griff, hat gegriffen   to span (a chord), [18] grasp
die **Grenze, –, –n** [20]   border
groß (größer, größt-) [8]   big, great
großartig [15]   splendid, great
die **Großindustrie, –**   heavy industry
der **Großvater, –s, ⁻**   grandfather
gründen [20]   to found, start
gründlich   thorough
die **Gründung, –, –en**   founding
die **Gruppe, –, –n**   group, squad
der **Gruß, –es, ⁻e**   greeting, regards
grüßen   to give regards, greet
gut (besser, best-) [1]   good, well

haben, hatte, hat gehabt, hat [1]   to have
der **Hafen, –s, ⁻** [25]   port, harbor
halb [8]   half
halbfertig   half-finished
die **Hälfte, –, –n** [17]   half
die **Halle, –, –n** [7]   hall, auditorium
halten, hielt, hat gehalten, hält [8]   to hold; give (*a lecture*)
halten für   to consider
die **Hand, –, ⁻e** [5]   hand
die **Handels- und Industriestadt, –, ⁻e**   commercial and industrial city

die **Handlung, –, –en** plot, action
hängen [5] to hang, link
harmonisch harmonious
hart (ä) hard
der **Hauptbahnhof, –s, ∸e** [18] main railroad station
das **Hauptfach, –s, ∸er** [1] major subject
das **Hauptinteresse, –s, –n** main interest
der **Hauptmann, –s, Hauptleute** [19] captain
das **Hauptquartier, –s, –e** headquarters
die **Hauptrolle, –, –n** [19] leading role
die **Hauptstadt, –, ∸e** [2] capital
das **Haus, –es, ∸er** [1] house
nach Hause [2] home
zu Hause [1] at home
der **Hausbau, –s** construction of a house
der **Haustyrann, –en, –en** domestic tyrant
die **Hausuniform, –, –en** livery
das **Heer, –(e)s, –e** army
heilig holy
die **Heimat, –** home town, home, homeland
der **Heimatfilm, –s, –e** [19] regional movie
heim-kommen, kam . . . heim, ist heimgekommen [12] to come home
heimlich secret
der **Heimweg, –s, –e** [12] way home
das **Heimweh, –s** homesickness, nostalgia
heiraten to marry
heiß [10] hot
heißen, hieß, hat geheißen [1] to be called, named
es heißt [4] they (people) say
helfen (*dat.*), **half, hat geholfen, hilft** [3] to help
der **Herr, –n, –en** [1] gentleman; Mr.
herum-führen [21] to show around
hervorragend [20] outstanding
das **Herz, –ens, –en** heart
herzlich cordial
heulen to hoot, scream, whistle
heute [7] today
heutig present
hier [2] here
die **Hilfe, –, –n** [23] help
der **Himmel, –s** sky; heaven
hin [5] there
hin-fahren, fuhr . . . hin, ist hinge-

fahren, fährt . . . hin [17] to go there, drive there
hinter (+ *dat./acc.*) [7] behind
der **Historiker, –s, –** historian
historisch [9] historical
das **Hobby, –s, –s** [21] hobby
hoch (höher, höchst-) high
die **Hochschule, –, –n** academy, university
die **Hochzeit, –, –en** wedding
hoffen [13] to hope
hoffentlich [7] I hope, hopefully, it is to be hoped
höflich polite
der **Hofmann, –s, Hofleute** [21] courtier
der **Hoforganist, –en, –en** court organist
die **Höhe, –, –n** [4] peak, top
der **Höhepunkt, –s, –e** high point, climax
holen [20] to get, fetch
das **Holz, –es, ∸er** wood
hören [7] to hear
der **Hörer, –s, –** listener; student
der **Hörsaal, –s, –säle** [8] lecture hall
das **Hotel, –s, –s** [9] hotel
humoristisch humorous
humorlos lacking a sense of humor
der **Hundefutterfabrikant, –en, –en** dog-food manufacturer
der **Hunger, –s** [12] hunger
Hunger haben [12] to be hungry
der **Hut, –(e)s, ∸e** hat

idealistisch [21] idealistic
die **Idee, –, –n** [19] idea
die **Ideologie, –, –n** ideology
idyllisch [9] idyllic
ihr [5] her, its; their
Ihr [3] your (*polite*)
die **Illustrierte, –n, –n** [25] picture magazine
immer [5] always
immer noch still
immer wieder again and again
der **Impressionismus, –** impressionism
in (+ *dat./acc.*) [1] in, into, in
die **Industrie, –, –n** industry
der **Ingenieur, –s, –e** engineer
die **Innendekoration, –, –en** interior decorating
inner- inner, interior
die **Insel, –, –n** island

das **Instrument, –s, –e** [7] instrument
interessant [5] interesting
das **Interesse, –s, –n** interest, concern
die **Interessengruppe, –, –n** special interest group
interessieren [8] to interest
sich (*acc.*) **interessieren für** [18] to be interested in
irgendwann [18] sometime or other
irgendwie [18] somehow or other
irgendwo [18] anywhere, somewhere or other
irgendwo anders anywhere else
die **Ironie, –** irony
ironisch [9] ironic
italienisch Italian

ja [1] yes
das **Jahr, –(e)s, –e** [9] year
das **Jahresende, –s** year's end
das **Jahrhundert, –s, –e** [9] century
der **Januar, –s** [12] January
jawohl [13] yes (*indeed*)
der **Jazz, –es** [7] jazz
die **Jazz-Sinfonie, –, –n** [7] jazz symphony
jeder [2] each, every
jener [5] that
jetzt [3] now
der **Journalist, –en, –en** journalist
die **Jugend, –** youth
der **Juli, –s** [12] July
jung (ü) [1] young
der **Juni, –s** [2] June
das **Jurastudium, –s** study of law
der **Jurist, –en, –en** [8] jurist, student of law

das **Kabarett, –s, –s** *or* **–e** [15] cabaret
der **Kabarettist, –en, –en** [15] cabaret performer
die **Kabarett-Tradition, –** [15] cabaret tradition
die **Kabarettvorstellung, –, –en** [15] cabaret performance
der **Kaffee, –s** [12] coffee
der **Kaiser, –s, –** emperor
kalt (ä) [10] cold
die **Kamera, –, –s** camera
der **Kamerad, –en, –en** [24] friend, comrade
der **Kamin, –s, –e** [10] fireplace
kämpfen to fight

das **Kapitel, –s, –** chapter
der **Karneval, –s, –e** [14] carnival
der **Karnevalsschlager, –s, –** hit tune at carnival time
die **Karte, –, –n** [7] ticket, card
der **Karzer, –s, –** student jail
das **Katerfrühstück, –s, –e** [14] breakfast for hangover victims
das **Katheder, –s, –** lectern
die **Kathedrale, –, –n** cathedral
die **Katze, –, –n** cat
kaufen [7] to buy
der **Kaufmann, –s, Kaufleute** merchant
kaum [8] scarcely, hardly
kein [1] no, not a, not any
kennen, kannte, hat gekannt [1] to know
kennen-lernen [18] to get to know
der **Kerl, –(e)s, –e** fellow, guy, character
die **Kerze, –, –n** candle
der **Kilometer, –s, –** [2] kilometer
das **Kind, –(e)s, –er** [4] child
das **Kindheitserlebnis, –ses, –se** childhood experience
das **Kino, –s, –s** [19] movie theater
die **Kirche, –, –n** [5] church
die **Kirchenglocke, –, –n** churchbell
klar [14] clear, plain
na klar! [14] of course, certainly
klar-machen to make clear
die **Klassik, –** classical age
der **Klassiker, –s, –** [21] classical author, classic
klassisch [7] classical
klatschen to applaud
das **Klavier, –s, –e** [7] piano
das **Kleid, –(e)s, –er** garment, dress; (*pl.*) clothing
klein [2] small
kleinbürgerlich lower middle class
die **Kleinigkeit, –, –en** [25] small thing, trifle
klingen, klang, hat geklungen [18] to sound
klopfen to knock, rap
das **Kloster, –s, ⸚** cloister
die **Klosterglocke, –, –en** cloister bell
der **Klubsessel, –s, –** [10] armchair
knurren [20] to growl
kochen [12] to cook, boil
der **Koffer, –s, –** [18] suitcase
der **Kollege, –n, –n** [17] colleague, counterpart

die **Kolonne, –, –n** [*20*] line, column
der **Komiker, –s, –** [*19*] comedian
komisch [*19*] comical, funny
der **Komplex, –es, –e** complex
kommen, kam, ist gekommen [*1*] to come
kommerziell commercial
der **Kommilitone, –n, –n** [*5*] fellow-student
komponieren to compose
der **König, –s, –e** [*10*] king
königlich royal
können, konnte, hat gekonnt, kann [*3*] can, to be able to
können für etwas [*9*] can help it
ich kann nichts dafür [*9*] I can't help it
das **Konservatorium, –s, Konservatorien** [*7*] conservatory
konstruieren to construct
der **Kontrast, –es, –e** [*3*] contrast
kontrollieren [*25*] to check, inspect
das **Konzert, –s, –e** [*7*] concert
dié **Konzertpause, –, –n** [*7*] concert intermission
die **Kopfschmerzen** (*pl.*) [*14*] headache
die **Kost, –** diet
das **Kostüm, –s, –e** (*woman's*) suit
kräftig [*12*] strong; substantial; nourishing
krank (ä) [*14*] sick
der **Krieg, –(e)s, –e** [*8*] war
das **Kriegslazarett, –s, –e** military hospital
der **Krimi, –s, –s = der Kriminalroman** [*18*]
der **Kriminalroman, –s, –e** [*18*] mystery story, crime novel
die **Kritik, –, –en** criticism
kritisch critical
die **Krönungszeremonie, –, –n** coronation ceremony
die **Küche, –, –n** [*3*] kitchen
kühl [*10*] cool
kühn bold
die **Kultur, –, –en** culture, civilization
kulturell cultural
die **Kunst, –, –e** [*17*] art
der **Künstler, –s, –** [*17*] artist
der **Künstlertyp, –s, –en** [*17*] artist-type
das **Künstlerviertel, –s, –** [*17*] artists' quarter
kurz (ü) [*4*] short

lächeln [*20*] to smile
lachen [*19*] to laugh
das **Lachen, –s** [*15*] laughter
vor Lachen [*15*] from laughing
die **Lage, –, –n** [*8*] situation
die **Lampe, –, –n** lamp
das **Land, –(e)s, ⁓er** [*2*] country
landen (sein) [*1*] to land
der **Landsmann, –s, Landsleute** compatriot
lang(e) (ä) [*2*] long
langsam [*20*] slow
der **Langschläfer, –s, –** [*12*] sleepyhead
langweilig [*23*] boring, dull
der **Lärm, –(e)s** noise
lassen, ließ, hat gelassen, läßt [*19*] to let, allow; cause
das **Latein, –s** Latin
lateinisch Latin
laufen, lief, ist gelaufen, läuft [*2*] to run
laut [*14*] loud
läuten to ring, toll
leben [*4*] to live
das **Leben, –s, –** life
Lebewohl sagen to bid farewell
legendär legendary
die **Legende, –, –n** [*4*] legend
legen to lay, place
den Grundstein legen to lay the corner stone
lehren to teach
der **Lehrer, –s, –** [*10*] teacher
die **Lehrjahre** (*pl.*) apprenticeship
leicht [*1*] easy; light
das **Leid, –(e)s** suffering, sorrow
leid tun [*21*] to be sorry
es tut ihm leid [*21*] he is sorry
leider [*1*] unfortunately
die **Leihbücherei, –, –en** [*18*] lending library
leisten to accomplish, render
die **Lektüre, –, –n** [*1*] reading material
lernen [*12*] to learn
lesen, las, hat gelesen, liest [*7*] to read; [*8*] lecture
der **Leser, –s, –** reader
letzt- [*8*] last
leugnen [*24*] to deny
die **Leute** (*pl.*) [*9*] people
das **Licht, –(e)s, –er** light
lieb dear
lieben to love

sich (*acc.*) **lieben**   to love each other
   lieber [7]   rather
das **Lied, –(e)s, –er** [10]   song
liegen, lag, hat gelegen [25]   to lie,
   be situated
die **Limonade, –, –en** [10]   lemonade,
   soda, soft drink
links   to (on) the left
die **Liste, –, –n**   list
literarisch [15]   literary
die **Literatur, –, –en**   literature
loben [24]   to praise
das **Lokal, –s, –e** [8]   restaurant, inn
der **Lokalpatriot, –en, –en** [17]   "booster"
   of one's region
die **Lösung, –, –en** [24]   solution
die **Lufthansamaschine, –, –n** [1]   airplane of the Lufthansa (*the German airline*)
lustig [12]   merry, gay, funny
sich **lustig machen über** (+ *acc.*)   to
   make fun of
die **Lyrik, –**   lyric poetry
der **Lyriker, –s, –**   lyric poet

machen [3]   to make, do
die **Macht, –, ⁻e**   power
das **Mädchen, –s, –** [4]   girl
der **Magen, –s, – *or* ⁻** [12]   stomach
der **Mai, –s** [12]   May
der **Maler, –s, –** [17]   painter
die **Malerei, –, –en**   (art of) painting
man [2]   one
mancher [5]   many a (*pl.* some)
manchmal [2]   sometimes
der **Mann, –(e)s, ⁻er** [2]   man
der **März, –es** [12]   March
der **Marxismus, –**   Marxism
die **Maschine, –, –n** [1]   machine
das **Maschinenzeitalter, –s**   age of the
   machine, era of technology
der **Maskenball, –s, ⁻e** [14]   fancy-dress
   ball
die **Masse, –, –n**   mass
die **Mauer, –, –n** [4]   wall
der **Mauerrest, –(e)s, –e** [4]   remains of
   a wall
das **Meer, –(e)s, –e**   sea, ocean
mehr [3]   more
mein [1]   my
meinen [7]   to mean, think
die **Meinung, –, –en**   opinion
meistgehaßt   most hated

die **Mensa, –, Mensen** [8]   students' dining hall (university)
der **Mensch, –en, –en** [9]   man, human
   being
merken   to notice, realize
merkwürdig   strange, peculiar, unusual
das **Metall, –s, –e**   metal
das **Metaphysische, –n**   realm of the
   metaphysical
die **Metropole, –, –n**   metropolis
das **Militär, –s**   military, army
die **Militäruniform, –, –en**   military uniform
die **Minute, –, –n** [8]   minute
mischen   to mix
die **Mischung, –, –en**   mixture
mit (+ *dat.*) [4]   with
**mit-bringen, brachte . . . mit, hat
   mitgebracht** [18]   to bring along
mit-führen   to carry along
**mit-kommen, kam . . . mit, ist mit-
   gekommen** [15]   to follow; [13]
   come along
das **Mitleid, –s**   sympathy, pity
mit-machen [14]   to join in
**mit-nehmen, nahm . . . mit, hat mit-
   genommen, nimmt . . . mit** [23]
   to take along
**mit-schreiben, schrieb . . . mit, hat
   mitgeschrieben**   to write down,
   take down
mit-spielen   to play a part
der **Mittag, –s, –e** [8]   noon
mittags [14]   at noon
das **Mittelalter, –s** [4]   Middle Ages
mittendrin [20]   in the middle of it
die **Mitternacht, –**   midnight
der **Mittwoch, –s, –e** [7]   Wednesday
die **Möbel** (*pl.*) [3]   furniture
möbliert   furnished
die **Mode, –, –n** [17]   fashion
modern [3]   modern
modernisieren   to modernize
mögen, mochte, hat gemocht, mag
   [3]   to like (to)
der **Monat, –s, –e** [13]   month
das **Monstrum, –s, Monstren**   monster
der **Montag, –s, –e** [7]   Monday
moralisch   moral
morgen [23]   tomorrow
der **Morgen, –s, –** [12]   morning
morgens [14]   in the morning(s)

motivieren [*18*]   to motivate
müde [*4*]   tired
munter [*12*]   awake; lively
das **Museum, –s, Museen**   museum
die **Musik, –** [*7*]   music
musikalisch [*7*]   musical
der **Musiker, –s, –** [*7*]   musician
müssen, mußte, hat gemußt, muß [*3*]   must, to have to
der **Mut, –(e)s** [*15*]   courage
die **Mutter, –, ≃** [*12*]   mother

na! [*10*]   well! now then!
nach (+ *dat.*) [*1*]   to; [*3*] after; according to
nach und nach [*15*]   gradually, by and by
nach-ahmen [*15*]   to imitate
nachdem (*subord. conj.*)   after
nachher [*2*]   afterward
die **Nachkriegsentwicklung, –**   postwar development
der **Nachkriegsfilm, –s, –e** [*19*]   postwar movie
der **Nachmittag, –s, –e** [*8*]   afternoon
heute nachmittag [*8*]   this afternoon
die **Nachricht, –, –en**   news
nach-sehen, sah . . . nach, hat nachgesehen, sieht . . . nach [*7*]   to look up, check
nächst-   next
die **Nacht, –, ≃e** [*14*]   night
der **Nachteil, –s, –e** [*24*]   disadvantage
die **Nähe, –** [*8*]   vicinity
der **Name, –ns, –n** [*1*]   name
nämlich [*17*]   namely, you know
die **Nationalversammlung, –, –en**   national assembly
natürlich [*13*]   natural
die **Naturschilderung, –, –en**   description of nature
die **Naturwissenschaft, –, –en**   science
der **Nazi, –s, –s**   Nazi
die **Nazizeit, –** [*9*]   Nazi period
neben (+ *dat./acc.*) [*1*]   next to
das **Nebenfach, –s, ≃er** [*1*]   minor subject
nehmen, nahm, hat genommen, nimmt [*1*]   to take
nein [*1*]   no
nennen, nannte, hat genannt [*2*]   to call, name
neu [*2*]   new

neugierig sein auf (+ *acc.*) [*20*]   to be anxious to (*see, read, etc.*)
das **Neujahr, –s** [*12*]   New Year
der **Neujahrsmorgen, –s** [*12*]   New Year's morning
nicht [*1*]   not
nicht einmal   not even
nicht mehr   no longer
nichts [*2*]   nothing
nie [*14*]   never
noch nie [*14*]   never (before)
noch [*1*]   still
noch ein [*1*]   another
noch nicht [*13*]   not yet
der **November, –s** [*12*]   November
die **Nonne, –, –n** [*4*]   nun
nun   now
nur [*3*]   only

ob (*subord. conj.*) [*4*]   whether
und ob! [*4*]   and how!
oben [*3*]   above; upstairs
obgleich (*subord. conj.*)   although
oder [*7*]   or
die **Offiziersuniform, –, –en**   officer's uniform
oft (ö) [*3*]   often
ohne (+ *acc.*) [*2*]   without
ohne . . . zu [*25*]   without . . . .-ing
das **Ohr, –(e)s, –en** [*14*]   ear
der **Oktober, –s** [*12*]   October
der **Onkel, –s, –** [*18*]   uncle
die **Optik, –**   optics
das **Orchester, –s, –** [*7*]   orchestra
die **Orgel, –, –n**   organ
der **Ort, –(e)s, –e** [*21*]   place
das *or* die **Ostern**   Easter

das **Paar, –(e)s, –e** [*23*]   pair
ein paar [*18*]   a few
die **Panne, –, –n** [*25*]   car trouble, breakdown
der **Papst, –es, ≃e**   Pope
parfümiert   perfumed
der **Parlamentarier, –s, –**   parliamentarian
die **Parodie, –, –n** [*15*]   parody
die **Partei, –, –en**   (*political*) party
der **Paß, Passes, Pässe** [*19*]   passport
die **Paßabfertigung, –, –en** [*20*]   passport inspection
das **Paßamt, –s, ≃er**   passport office
passen (*dat.*)   to fit, be suitable

passieren (sein) [25]   to happen
die **Patrizierfamilie, –, –n**   patrician family
die **Pause, –, –n** [7]   pause, intermission
die **Pension, –, –en** [23]   boarding house
der **Pensionär, –s, –e**   retired person
die **Persönlichkeit, –, –en** [21]   personality, character
das **Pferd, –(e)s, –e**   horse
die **Pfirsichbowle, –, –n**   punch made with peaches
die **Phantasie, –, –n**   imagination
der **Philister, –s, –**   Philistine, nonacademic person
die **Philosophie, –, –n**   philosophy
das **Picknick, –s, –s** [20]   picnic
der **Pilger, –s, –**   pilgrim
die **Pilgerfahrt, –, –en**   pilgrimage
die **Pionierarbeit, –, –en**   pioneering work
der **Plan, –(e)s, ⁻e**   plan
planen [23]   to plan
platt   flat
der **Platz, –es, ⁻e** [1]   place, plaza; [8] seat
die **Poesie, –**   poetry
poetisch   poetic
die **Politik, –** [1]   politics
der **Politiker, –s, –** [2]   politician, statesman
politisch [15]   political
der **Polizist, –en, –en**   policeman
prahlen [3]   to boast
praktisch   practical
der **Präsident, –en, –en**   president
der **Prater, –s**   famous park in Vienna
die **Presse, –**   press
die **Pressestadt, –, ⁻e**   city of the press
privat [1]   private
das **Privateigentum, –s**   private property
die **Privatperson, –, –en**   private person
der **Professor, –s, –en** [2]   professor
das **Programm, –s, –e** [7]   program
prophezeien   to prophesy, predict
die **Prosa, –**   prose
Prost! [5]   cheers! your health! (*informal toast*)
protestieren [24]   to protest
provisorisch   temporary
der **Pseudokünstler, –s, –** [17]   pseudoartist
die **Psychologie, –** [18]   psychology
psychologisch [18]   psychological

das **Publikum, –s** [24]   public, audience
der **Punkt, –(e)s, –e** [9]   point, spot
pünktlich [13]   punctual
die **Pünktlichkeit, –** [13]   punctuality

die **Qualität, –, –en**   quality

rasen   to rage, rave
das **Rathaus, –es, ⁻er** [13]   city hall
der **Ratskeller, –s, –**   cellar restaurant of the city hall
die **Ratte, –, –n**   rat
das **Rauschen, –s** [9]   rushing, rustle, murmur
die **Realität, –, –en**   reality
rechnen mit   to count on, expect
recht [1]   right
das **Recht, –(e)s, –e**   law, jurisprudence; right
recht haben [1]   to be right
rechts   to (on) the right
regieren [25]   to govern
die **Regierung, –, –en**   government
an die Regierung kommen   to come into power
das **Reich, –(e)s, –e**   empire
reichen zu [20]   to be sufficient for
reif [21]   mature
der **Reifen, –s, –** [25]   tire
der **Reifenschaden, –s, ⁻** [25]   flat tire
die **Reihe, –, –n** [18]   series, number, line
an der Reihe sein [18]   to be next
die **Reihenfolge, –**   order, sequence
die **Reise, –, –n** [23]   trip, journey
der **Reiz, –es, –e** [17]   charm, attraction
die **Reklame, –, –n** [24]   advertisement
das **Reklamesystem, –s, –e** [24]   system of advertising
die **Reling, –**   railing
die **Reliquie, –, –n**   relic
die **Rennbahn, –, –en** [2]   race track
rennen, rannte, ist gerannt [18]   to run
der **Reporter, –s, –** [24]   reporter
die **Respektlosigkeit, –, –en**   irreverence
das **Restaurant, –s, –s** [25]   restaurant
der **Rheindampfer, –s, –** [13]   Rhine boat
die **Rheinfahrt, –, –en** [13]   Rhine trip
das **Rheinland, –s**   Rhineland
der **Rheinländer, –s, –** [14]   Rhinelander
der **Rheinwein, –s, –e** [4]   Rhine wine
richtig [4]   right, correct

das **Richtige, –n** [4] the right thing
riesig [12] gigantic, immense, enormous
der **Ring, –(e)s, –e** ring
der **Ritter, –s, –** [4] knight
die **Rolle, –, –n** [19] role, part
der **Roman, –s, –e** [18] novel
der **Romantiker, –s, –** Romantic writer
romantisch [4] romantic
die **Rose, –, –n** rose
der **Rosenmontagszug, –s, ⁔e** [14] parade on the Monday before Lent
rot red
der **Rücken, –s, –** back
der **Rücksitz, –es, –e** [20] back seat
die **Ruhe, –** [23] rest, quiet, peace
rühren to move, touch
die **Ruine, –, –n** [4] ruin
der **Rum, –s, –s** [10] rum
rund round
der **Rundgang, –s, ⁔e** [3] tour
Rußland Russia

der **Saal, –(e)s, Säle** [8] room, hall
die **Sache, –, –n** [9] thing, matter, incident
die **Sage, –, –n** [4] legend
sagen [4] to say
die **geschlagene Sahne, –** whipped cream
der **Samstag, –s, –e** [7] Saturday
das **Sandmännchen, –s, –** little sandman
der **Satiriker, –s, –** satirist
schade! [17] too bad!
der **Schaden, –s, ⁔** [25] damage
schaden (*dat.*) [23] to do harm, hurt
der **Schalter, –s, –** [18] counter
scharf (ä) [20] sharp
der **Scharfrichter, –s, –** executioner
scharren to scrape
    mit den Füßen scharren to scrape one's feet
schätzen [24] to appreciate
die **Schau, –, –en** show, spectacle
das **Schauspiel, –s, –e** [24] play, drama
der **Schauspieler, –s, –** [17] actor
die **Schauspielertruppe, –, –n** [20] acting company
scheinen, schien, hat geschienen to appear, seem
der **Scherz, –es, –e** joke, jest
das **Schiff, –(e)s, –e** [12] ship
die **Schiffssirene, –, –n** ship's siren
schlachten to slaughter

schlafen, schlief, hat geschlafen, schläft [12] to sleep
das **Schlafengehen, –s** going to bed
das **Schlafzimmer, –s, –** [3] bedroom
der **Schlager, –s, –** popular song
Schlange stehen [18] to stand in line
schlecht [14] bad
schließen, schloß, hat geschlossen [15] to close
schlimm [9] bad, evil
das **Schloß, Schlosses, Schlösser** [4] castle, palace
die **Schloßruine, –, –n** [4] castle ruin
schmecken [10] to taste
schmerzen to hurt
der **Schmuggler, –s, –** [20] smuggler
schnell [2] fast, quick
schockieren to shock
schon [3] already
schon! [9] that's true!
schön [8] beautiful
schöpferisch [17] creative
schräg slanted
schreiben, schrieb, hat geschrieben [10] to write
der **Schreibtisch, –(e)s, –e** [13] desk
der **Schrein, –(e)s, –e** shrine
der **Schriftsteller, –s, –** writer
der **Schuh, –(e)s, –e** [23] shoe
das **Schulbuch, –s, ⁔er** [21] textbook
die **Schule, –, –n** [24] school
der **Schulkamerad, –en, –en** [24] schoolmate
der **Schuster, –s, –** shoemaker
schwach (ä) weak, feeble
die **Schwäche, –, –n** weakness
schwarz (ä) black
„schwarz" illegal
das **„schwarze Brett"** bulletin board
schweigen, schwieg, hat geschwiegen [9] to be silent
schwer [15] difficult; heavy
schwer-fallen (*dat.*)**, fiel . . . schwer, ist schwergefallen, fällt . . . schwer** [15] to be hard
die **Schwester, –, –n** [3] sister
die **Schwierigkeit, –, –en** [10] difficulty
sechs [7] six
der **Seehafen, –s, ⁔** seaport
sehen, sah, hat gesehen, sieht [2] to see
sehenswert [13] worth seeing, remarkable

die **Sehenswürdigkeit, –, –en** [21] sight, place of interest
sehr [3] very
sein [3] his, its
sein, war, ist gewesen, ist [1] to be
seit (+ *dat.*) [2] since; [4] for
die **Seite, –, –n** [4] side; aspect; page
der **Sekt, –(e)s, –e** champagne
selbst [15] self; even
selbstverständlich [3] of course; certain
das **Semester, –s, –** [5] semester
der **Semesterbeginn, –s** [5] beginning of the semester
das **Seminar, –s, –e** [10] seminar
der **Senat, –s** senate
senden, sandte, hat gesandt [18] to send
die **Sendezeit, –, –en** time of telecast
die **Sendung, –, –en** [24] telecast, broadcast, program
das **Sensationsblatt, –s, ⸚er** yellow press, sensational newspaper
der **September, –s** [12] September
servieren to serve
der **Sessel, –s, –** [10] easy chair
setzen to put, place
sich (*acc.*) **setzen** [14] to sit down
seufzen to sigh
das **Sexuelle, –n** sexual
sicher [3] sure, certain
siebt-, siebent- [10] seventh
siebzig [2] seventy
die **Sinfonie, –, –n** [7] symphony
singen, sang, hat gesungen to sing
die **Sitte, –, –n** custom, habit
sitzen, saß, hat gesessen [3] to sit
der **Sitzungssaal, –s, –säle** council chamber
der **Skandal, –s, –e** [9] scandal
die **Skandalgeschichte, –, –n** [9] scandal
die **Skepsis, –** scepticism
der **Sketch, –(e)s, –e** [15] sketch, skit
so [1] so, such
so ein [4] such a
so ... wie [2] as ... as
sofortig immediate
sogar [13] even
der **Sohn, –(e)s, ⸚e** [7] son
solcher [5] such a
der **Soldat, –en, –en** soldier
solide [23] sturdy, strong
sollen, sollte, hat gesollt, soll [3] shall, to be supposed to

der **Sommer, –s, –** summer
sondern but (*on the contrary*)
der **Sonnabend, –s, –e** [7] Saturday
der **Sonnenaufgang, –s, ⸚e** sunrise
der **Sonnenuntergang, –s, ⸚e** sundown
sonst [5] otherwise
sonst ein [7] some other
der **Sonntag, –s, –e** [7] Sunday
das **Souvenir, –s, –s** [21] souvenir
sozusagen [23] as it were, so-to-speak
Spanien Spain
spanisch [10] Spanish
spannend [24] exciting, suspenseful
der **Spaß, –es, ⸚e** [4] fun
es macht mir Spaß [4] I enjoy it
zum Spaß [5] for fun
spät [4] late
spazieren (sein) [12] to walk (*leisurely*), stroll
der **Spaziergang, –s, ⸚e** [9] stroll, walk
der **Spiegel, –s, –** [1] mirror (*name of a German weekly magazine*)
spielen [7] to play
der **Spion, –s, –e** [20] spy
der **Sport, –(e)s** [23] sport
der **Sportschuh, –s, –e** [23] walking shoe
die **Sportübertragung, –, –en** sports telecast
die **Sprache, –, –n** [15] language
sprechen, sprach, hat gesprochen, spricht [1] to speak
spüren to feel, sense
der **Staat, –(e)s, –en** state
die **Staatskunde, –** political science
der **Stab, –(e)s, ⸚e** staff
das **Stachelschwein, –s, –e** porcupine
die **Stadt, –, ⸚e** [2] city
der **Städtebund, –s, –e** league of cities
der **Stadtplan, –s, ⸚e** [12] city map
die **Stadtplanung, –** city planning
der **Stadtteil, –s, –e** [17] section of a city
der **Stahl, –(e)s** steel
das **Stahlrohr, –s, –e** steel tubing
der **Stand, –(e)s, ⸚e** class, rank; [25] stand, booth
das **Ständchen, –s, –** [12] serenade
der **Star, –s, –s** [19] (movie) star
die **Stätte, –, –n** [9] spot, place
statt-finden, fand ... statt, hat stattgefunden to take place
stehen, stand, hat gestanden [7] to

stand; [*18*] say (in print)

stehen-bleiben, blieb . . . stehen, ist stehengeblieben [*17*]   to stop

steif   stiff

die **Stelle, –, –n** [*24*]   place, spot, part

der **Stephansdom, –s**   St. Stephen's Cathedral

die **Sterbeglocke, –, –n**   funeral bell

sterben, starb, ist gestorben, stirbt   to die

die **Stewardeß, –, Stewardessen** [*1*]   stewardess

der **Stil, –(e)s, –e**   style

still [*9*]   quiet

stimmen [*3*]   to be correct

die **Stimmung, –, –en**   mood

das **Stockwerk, –s, –e**   floor, story

stolz (auf + acc.) [*7*]   proud (of)

die **Stoßzeit, –, –en** [*20*]   rush hour

die **Straße, –, –n** [*2*]   road, street

der **Straßenkampf, –s, ∸e**   street fighting

der **Streich, –(e)s, –e**   prank

der **Streicher, –s, –** [*7*]   player of a stringed instrument

streiten, stritt, hat gestritten   to argue, quarrel

streng [*15*]   severe, strict

das **Stück, –(e)s, –e** [*13*]   piece, part, bit; (*theater*) play

der **Student, –en, –en,** [*1*]   student

das **Studentenheim, –s, –e** [*1*]   dormitory

studieren [*1*]   to study

das **Studium, –s**   study, studying

die **Stunde, –, –n** [*8*]   hour

stundenlang [*19*]   for hours

die **Sublimierung, –, –en**   sublimation

suchen nach   to seek, look for

Süddeutschland   South Germany

süß [*10*]   sweet

der **Sylvester, –s**   New Year's Eve

der **Sylvesterabend, –s, –e** [*12*]   New Year's Eve

die **Sylvesterfeier, –, –n** [*12*]   New Year's Eve celebration

die **Sylvesterparty, –, –s** [*12*]   New Year's Eve party

die **Symbolik, –** symbolism

synchronisieren [*19*]   to dub (*movie*)

das **System, –s, –e** [*24*]   system

der **Tag, –(e)s, –e** [*2*]   day

die **„Tagesschau", –**   daily news telecast

die **Tageszeit, –, –en** [*20*]   time of the day

täglich   daily

tagsüber [*14*]   during the day

das **Talent, –s, –e** [*17*]   talent

der **Tannenbaum, –s, ∸e**   Christmas tree

die **Tante, –, –n** [*21*]   aunt

tanzen [*12*]   to dance

die **Tasche, –, –n** [*18*]   pocket

tatsächlich [*14*]   real, actual

das **Taxi, –s, –s** [*17*]   taxi

der **Tee, –s, –s** [*10*]   tea

der **Teil, –(e)s, –e** [*15*]   part

zum Teil [*24*]   in part, partly

teilnahmsvoll [*14*]   concerned, sympathetic

teil-nehmen (an + dat.), nahm . . . teil, hat teilgenommen, nimmt . . . teil [*13*]   to take part, participate (in)

das **Terrain, –s, –s**   terrain

die **Terrasse, –, –n** [*3*]   terrace

teuer   expensive

die **Textilien** (*pl.*)   textiles

das **Theater, –s, –**   theater

die **Theatergruppe, –, –n** [*20*]   acting company

das **Thema, –s, Themen**   subject, topic

die **Theorie, –, –n**   theory

der **Tisch, –es, –e** [*12*]   table

der **Titel, –s, –** [*18*]   title

die **Tochter, –, ∸** [*4*]   daughter

toll [*14*]   mad, wild

der **Ton, –(e)s, ∸e** [*15*]   tone

den Ton an-geben, gab . . . an, hat angegeben, gibt . . . an   to set the tone

das **Tor, –(e)s, –e**   gate

die **Torte, –, –n** [*13*]   cake, pastry, pie

tot   dead

die **Tour, –, –en** [*4*]   tour

der **Tourist, –en, –en** [*23*]   tourist

die **Touristenattraktion, –, –en** [*23*]   tourist attraction

die **Tradition, –, –en** [*15*]   tradition

traditionell   traditional

tragen, trug, hat getragen, trägt   to bear; to wear

die **Träne, –, –n** [*15*]   tear

transponieren   to transpose, transport

der **Traum, –(e)s, ∸e**   dream

das **Traumbild, –s, –er**   dream, image, vision

die **Traumfabrik, –, –en** dream factory
treffen, traf, hat getroffen, trifft [8] to meet
der **Treffpunkt, –s, –e** [17] meeting place
treu true, faithful
trinken, trank, hat getrunken [5] to drink
trocken dry
trotz (+ *gen.*) [9] in spite of
tun, tat, hat getan [5] to do
die **Tür, –, –en** [3] door
der **Turm, –(e)s, ⁓e** [4] tower
typisch [23] typical

u.a. (unter anderen) among others
das **Übel, –s, –** [24] evil
üben to practice
über (+ *dat./acc.*) [7] over, above; [2] about
die **Überfahrt, –, –en** [25] crossing, passage, trip
der **Übergang, –s, ⁓e** transition
überhaupt at all, in general
überraschen to surprise
der **Übersetzer, –s, –** translator
übertreffen, übertraf, hat übertroffen, übertrifft [19] to outdo, excel
übrigens [2] by the way
die **Uhr, –, –en** [5] clock, watch; o'clock
um (+ *acc.*) [2] at; around
die **Umschreibung, –, –en** paraphrase
umsonst in vain
umständlich [5] formal, fussy
der **Umzug, –s, ⁓e** [14] parade
unähnlich dissimilar
unbedingt [5] absolute, by all means
unbekannt unknown
unberührt [23] untouched
und [2] and
ungeduldig [20] impatient
ungefähr [2] approximate
ungewöhnlich [12] unusual
unglaublich [9] unbelievable
der **Uniformenkult, –s** worship of the uniform
die **Universität, –, –en** [1] university
unmodern out of date
unmöglich impossible
unser [5] our
unten [3] below; downstairs
unter (+ *dat./acc.*) [7] under, among
das **Unterbewußtsein, –s** subconscious

unterbrechen, unterbrach, hat unterbrochen, unterbricht [24] to interrupt
die **Unterbrechung, –, –en** [24] interruption
sich (*acc.*) **unterhalten, unterhielt, hat unterhalten, unterhält** [15] to converse, talk about
unterhaltend [24] entertaining
der **Unterschied, –s, –e** difference

der **Vater, –s, ⁓** [2] father
sich (*acc.*) **verabschieden (von)** [25] to say good-by (to)
verändern to change
verantwortlich responsible
verbessern to improve, correct, reform
sich **verbinden, verband, hat verbunden** to connect, join
die **Verbindung, –, –en** union
der **Verbrecher, –s, –** criminal
verbringen, verbrachte, hat verbracht [18] to spend (*time*)
verdanken [3] to owe
verdrängen to suppress
verdreifachen to triple
die **Verfassung, –, –en** constitution
die **Vergangenheit, –** past
vergehen, verging, ist vergangen [25] to pass by (*time*), go by
vergessen, vergaß, hat vergessen, vergißt [3] to forget
vergleichen, verglich, hat verglichen [24] to compare
das **Vergnügen, –s, –** [20] fun, joy, pleasure
die **Verhaftung, –, –en** arrest
sich (*acc.*) **verirren** [18] to lose one's way
der **Verkehr, –s** traffic
verlassen, verließ, hat verlassen, verläßt to leave
sich (*acc.*) **verlaufen, verlief, hat verlaufen, verläuft** [17] to lose one's way
verlernen [25] to forget, unlearn
sich (*acc.*) **verlieben (in** + *acc.*) to fall in love (with)
verlieren, verlor, hat verloren [15] to lose
vernünftig reasonable
verpassen [18] to miss
verrottet rotten
verrückt crazy, mad

der **Vers, –es, –e** verse
sich (*acc.*) **versammeln** to assemble
verschwinden, verschwand, ist ver-
schwunden [9] to disappear
die **Verspätung, –, –en** [25] lateness
verständlich [15] understandable
verstehen, verstand, hat verstanden
[10] to understand
der **Versuch, –s, –e** attempt
vertonen to set to music
vertreiben, vertrieb, hat vertrieben
to drive out, expel
der **Vertreter, –s, –** representative
der **Verwaltungsrat, –s, ⸚e** board of directors
der **Verwandte, –n, –n** (*adjectival noun*)
[21] relative
verwüsten to devastate, wreck
Verzeihung! [1] pardon me!
verzweifeln (sein) to despair
der **Vetter, –s, –n** [17] cousin (*m.*)
das **Vieh, –s** cattle
viel (mehr, meist-) [1] much
viele (mehr, meist-) [3] many
vieles [14] many things
vielleicht [7] perhaps
das **Viertel, –s, –** [8] quarter, section
die **Viola, –, Violen** viola
die **Visitenkarte, –, –n** calling card
das **Volk, –(e)s, ⸚er** people
das **Volksfest, –es, –e** public festival
voll full (of)
die **Vollendung, –** completion
vollkommen [14] complete
von (+ dat.) [2] of, from
von . . . aus [13] from
der **Vopo, –s, –s = Volkspolizist** [20]
People's Police
vor (+ dat./acc.) [3] in front of;
[17] ago
vor allem [7] especially, above all
voraus [13] beforehand
im voraus [13] in advance
vorbei [8] over, finished
vorgestern [21] the day before yesterday
die **Vorhalle, –, –n** [7] lobby
vor-kommen (*dat.*)**, kam . . . vor,**
ist vorgekommen [19] to seem
die **Vorlesung, –, –en** [8] lecture
das **Vorlesungsverzeichnis, –ses, –se** university catalogue
der **Vormittag, –s, –e** [14] forenoon,
morning
vormittags [14] in the morning(s),
before noon
vorn(e) [14] in front
von vorn(e) [14] over again
der **Vorname, –ns, –n** [5] first name
der **Vorort, –s, –e** suburb
vor-sorgen [23] to prepare, take pre-
cautions
sich (*dat.*) **vor-stellen** [14] to imagine
die **Vorstellung, –, –en** [15] performance
der **Vorteil, –s, –e** [24] advantage
vor-ziehen, zog . . . vor, hat vorgezo-
gen to prefer
wachsen, wuchs, ist gewachsen,
wächst to grow
der **Wagen, –s, –** [1] car, wagon
wählen [25] to choose; elect
wahr [5] true, truly
nicht wahr? [5] isn't it so?
während (+ gen.) [9] during
während (*subord. conj.*) while
wahrscheinlich [24] probable, likely
das **Wahrzeichen, –s, –** [5] landmark
der **Wald, –(e)s, ⸚er** [4] forest
der **„Walzerkönig", –s** "King of the
Waltz"
die **Wand, –, ⸚e** [5] wall
wandern (sein) [17] to walk, stroll
wann [2] when
warm (ä) [10] warm
warnen to warn
warten [1] to wait
warten auf (+ acc.) [7] to wait for
warum [3] why
was [1] what
was für [3] what kind of, what a
das **Wasser, –s, –** [9] water
der **Wasserweg, –s, –e** waterway
wecken [12] to wake
weder . . . noch neither . . . nor
weg away
der **Weg, –(e)s, –e** [1] way
wegen (+ gen.) [9] because of
die **Weihnacht(en), –** [12] Christmas
weil (*subord. conj.*) [8] because,
since
der **Wein, –(e)s, –e** [4] wine
der **Weinberg, –s, –e** [4] vineyard
die **Weinstube, –, –n** [5] *lit.* "wine room"
weit [2] far
weiter-arbeiten to continue to work
weiter-fahren, fuhr . . . weiter, ist

(hat) weitergefahren, fährt . . . weiter [*13*] to drive on, continue

weiter-gehen, ging . . . weiter, ist weitergegangen to continue, go on

welcher [*3*] which

welche [*18*] some, any

die **Welt, –, –en** [*8*] world

weltbekannt [*5*] world-renowned, famous

der **Weltkrieg, –s, –e** [*8*] world war

weltmännisch [*21*] sophisticated, gentlemanly

die **Weltpolitik, –** world politics

der **Weltschmerz, –es** world-weariness, melancholy

wenden, wandte, hat gewandt [*18*] to turn

sich (*acc.*) **wenden an** (+ *acc.*), **wandte, hat gewandt** to turn to

wenig [*7*] little

wenigstens [*4*] at least

wenn (*subord. conj.*) [*8*] if, whenever

wer [*1*] who

das **Werbefernsehen, –s** telecasting of commercials

die **Werbesendung, –, –en** [*24*] television commercial

werden, wurde, ist geworden, wird [*5*] to become

etwas werden [*13*] to turn out (*well*)

das **Werk, –(e)s, –e** work

das **Wesen, –s, –** being, essence

wetten [*13*] to bet

das **Wetter, –s, –** [*10*] weather

wichtig important

wie [*1*] how; like

wie (*subord. conj.*) [*2*] as

wieder again

wieder-geben, gab . . . wieder, hat wiedergegeben, gibt . . . wieder to reflect, render

das **Wiedersehen, –s** [*8*] meeting again

auf Wiedersehen! [*8*] good-by (*for the present*)

wieso [*3*] in what way

wieviel Uhr [*8*] what time

um wieviel Uhr [*8*] at what time

der **Wildwestreißer, –s, –** [*19*] Grade B Western

wirken [*3*] to have an effect

wirklich [*3*] real

die **Wirtschaft, –** economy

wirtschaftlich [*8*] economic

das **Wirtschaftszentrum, –s, –zentren** economic center

das **Wirtshaus, –es, ⁓er** inn

wissen, wußte, hat gewußt, weiß [*3*] to know

die **Wissenschaft, –, –en** science

der **Wissenschaftler, –s, –** scholar, learned man, scientist

der **Witz, –es, –e** [*15*] joke; wit

wo [*1*] where

die **Woche, –, –n** week

das **Wochenende, –s, –n** week-end

der **Wochentag, –s, –e** weekday

woher [*4*] from where

wohin [*2*] where (to)

wohl [*17*] probably

wohlhabend prosperous

wohnen [*1*] to live

die **Wohnung, –, –en** [*3*] apartment; dwelling; house

das **Wohnzimmer, –s, –** [*3*] living room

wollen, wollte, hat gewollt, will [*1*] to want (to)

das **Wort, –(e)s, –e** [*10*] word

das **Wörterbuch, –s, ⁓er** dictionary

die **Wühlmaus, –, ⁓e** vole, field mouse

das **Wunder, –s, –** [*14*] wonder, miracle

wunderbar [*17*] wonderful

das **Wunderkind, –s, –er** child prodigy

sich (*acc.*) **wundern** to be surprised

wünschen [*24*] to wish, desire

zu wünschen übrig lassen [*24*] to leave to be desired

die **Wurst, –, ⁓e** [*23*] sausage

das **Wurstbrot, –s, –e** sandwich

zahlen to pay

zahlreich [*17*] numerous

der **Zahnarzt, –es, ⁓e** [*13*] dentist

zeigen [*5*] to show

die **Zeile, –, –n** line

die **Zeit, –, –en** [*5*] time

zur Zeit at the time

der **Zeitgenosse, –n, –n** contemporary

eine Zeitlang [*21*] for a while

die **Zeitschrift, –, –en** [*1*] magazine

die **Zeitung, –, –en** [*1*] newspaper

der **Zeitungsstand, –s, ⁓e** [*25*] newspaper stand

die **Zensur, –** [*15*] censorship
das **Zentrum, –s, Zentren** center
die **Zeremonie, –, –n** [*5*] ceremony
das **Ziel, –(e)s, –e** destination, goal
　ziemlich [*5*] rather, quite
das **Zimmer, –s, –** [*1*] room
die **Zitadelle, –, –n** citadel
das **Zitat, –s, –e** quotation
die **Zivilisation, –, –en** [*23*] civilization
der **Zoll, –(e)s, ⁻e** [*9*] customs
　zu (+ *dat.*) [*3*] to, at
　zu [*1*] too
das **Zuckerwasser, –s** sugar water
　zueinander [*5*] to each other
　zuerst [*3*] first, at first
der **Zufall, –s, ⁻e** chance, coincidence
der **Zug, –(e)s, ⁻e** [*13*] train
　zu-geben, gab . . . zu, hat zuge-
　　geben, gibt . . . zu [*24*] to ad-
　　mit, grant
　　zugegeben! [*24*] granted
　zu-gehen, ging . . . zu, ist zuge-
　　gangen [*12*] to go on, happen
　　es geht lustig zu [*12*] there is a
　　lot of fun
　zu-halten, hielt . . . zu, hat zuge-

　　halten, hält . . . zu [*14*] to
　　hold closed, keep closed
die **Zukunft, –** future
　zu-machen [*13*] to close
sich (*acc.*) **zurecht-finden, fand . . . zu-**
　　recht, hat zurechtgefunden [*21*]
　　to find one's way
　zurück-fahren, fuhr . . . zurück, ist
　　(hat) zurückgefahren, fährt . . .
　　zurück [*15*] to drive back
　zurück-kehren (sein) to return
　zusammen [*8*] together
die **Zusammenarbeit, –** co-operation,
　　team work
der **Zustand, –, ⁻e** condition, state
　zu-winken (*dat.*) to wave at
der **Zweck, –(e)s, –e** [*20*] purpose
　zwei [*2*] two
　zweifellos [*24*] doubtless, undoubt-
　　edly
　zweigeteilt divided in two
　zweit- second
　　zum zweiten Mal for the second
　　time
　zwischen (+ *dat./acc.*) [*7*] between

English-German Vocabulary

This vocabulary includes the words needed for English-German exercises. Omitted are personal pronouns, articles, possessive adjectives, and prepositions with several German equivalents.

Nouns are listed with their genitive and plural endings (in that order): **der Tag, −(e)s, −e.** Strong and irregular verbs are given with their auxiliaries and principal parts. Weak verbs that take **sein** are indicated; all others take **haben.**

Separable prefixes are indicated by a hyphen: **vor-kommen.**

to be able to können, konnte, hat gekonnt, kann
about über (+ *acc.*)
after nach (+ *dat.*)
afternoon der Nachmittag, −s, −e
  afternoons nachmittags
  this afternoon heute nachmittag
again wieder
against gegen (+ *acc.*)
ago vor (+ *dat.*)
airport der Flugplatz, −es, −e
to be allowed to dürfen, durfte, hat gedurft, darf
along entlang
always immer
amazing erstaunlich
American der Amerikaner, −s, −
American amerikanisch
and und
antique antik
anything etwas
to arrive an-kommen, kam . . . an, ist angekommen
artist der Künstler, −s, −
artists' quarter das Künstlerviertel, −s, −
as . . . as so . . . wie
as if als ob (*subord. conj.*)
to ask fragen

to ask for bitten um (+ *acc.*), bat, hat gebeten
aspirin das Aspirin, −s

bad schlimm
to be sein, war, ist gewesen, ist
beautiful schön
because weil (*subord. conj.*), denn
to become werden, wurde, ist geworden, wird
bedroom das Schlafzimmer, −s, −
before ehe (*subord. conj.*)
to begin beginnen, begann, hat begonnen; an-fangen, fing . . . an, hat angefangen, fängt . . . an
from the beginning (over again) von vorn(e)
in the beginning anfangs
to believe glauben (*dat. of persons*)
big groß
binoculars das Fernglas, −es, −er
book das Buch, −(e)s, −er
to brag prahlen
breakfast table der Frühstückstisch, −es, −e
to bring along mit-bringen, brachte . . . mit, hat mitgebracht
brother der Bruder, −s, −

420

businessman der Geschäftsmann, –s, Geschäftsleute
but aber
to buy kaufen
by von (+ *dat.*); mit (+ *dat.*) (*vehicle*)
by the way übrigens

café das Café, –s, –s
to call nennen, nannte, hat genannt
to call (*on the telephone*) an-rufen, rief
   . . . an, hat angerufen
can können, konnte, hat gekonnt, kann
   can help it können für etwas
capital die Hauptstadt, –, ⸚e
car der Wagen, –s, –; das Auto, –s, –s
castle die Burg, –, –en
cathedral der Dom, –(e)s, –e
to celebrate feiern
censorship die Zensur, –
century das Jahrhundert, –s, –e
certainly selbstverständlich
classical klassisch
to close schließen, schloß, hat geschlossen; zu-machen
to come kommen, kam, ist gekommen
comedian der Komiker, –s, –
to complain sich (*acc.*) beschweren
complete vollkommen
concert das Konzert, –s, –e
conditions die Lage, –
conductor der Dirigent, –en, –en
to consider betrachten als
to be correct stimmen
cousin (*m.*) der Vetter, –s, –n

daring gewagt
dark dunkel
day der Tag, –(e)s, –e
   all day den ganzen Tag
to depend on an-kommen auf (+ *acc.*),
   kam . . . an, ist angekommen
difficult schwer
   it is difficult (for) es fällt (*dat.*)
   schwer
difficulty die Schwierigkeit, –, –en
direct direkt
to do tun, tat, hat getan; machen
dormitory das Studentenheim, –s, –e
downstairs unten, nach unten
to drive fahren, fuhr, ist (hat) gefahren,
   fährt

easy leicht
economic wirtschaftlich
eight acht
elegant elegant
to enjoy: (I enjoy it) es macht mir Spaß
enough genug
ensemble das Ensemble, –s, –s
entrance der Eingang, –s, ⸚e
especially besonders
even selbst; sogar
every jeder
everything alles
evidently anscheinend
exact genau
excellent ausgezeichnet
exceptional einmalig
exchange student der Austauschstudent,
   –en, –en
excuse me! Verzeihung!
exhausted erschöpft
to exist bestehen, bestand, hat bestanden

family die Familie, –, –n
famous berühmt
far weit
fast schnell
finally endlich
to find finden, fand, hat gefunden
first erst-
   for the first time zum erstenmal
first name der Vorname, –ns, –n
to fly fliegen, flog, ist (hat) geflogen
to follow folgen (sein) (*dat.*)
for für (+ *acc.*)
for hours stundenlang
forest der Wald, –(e)s, ⸚er
to forget vergessen, vergaß, hat vergessen, vergißt
four vier
friend der Freund, –(e)s, –e
from von (+ *dat.*); aus (+ *dat.*)
front: in front of vor (+*dat./acc.*)
fun der Spaß, –es, ⸚e
   for fun zum Spaß
funny komisch
furniture die Möbel (*pl.*)

German deutsch
Germany Deutschland
to get (become) werden, wurde, ist geworden, wird
to get (receive) bekommen, bekam, hat
   bekommen

to get into   geraten in (+ *acc.*) geriet, ist geraten, gerät
gift   das Geschenk, –s, –e
to give   geben, gab, hat gegeben, gibt
to give trouble   Schwierigkeiten machen
to give (a lecture)   (eine Vorlesung) halten, hielt, hat gehalten, hält
to be glad   sich (*acc.*) freuen
gladly   gern(e)
to go   gehen, ging, ist gegangen; fahren, fuhr, ist gefahren, fährt; fliegen, flog, ist geflogen
good   gut
good-by   auf Wiedersehen
gradually   nach und nach
great   groß

to happen   passieren (sein)
to have   haben, hatte, hat gehabt, hat
to have to   müssen, mußte, hat gemußt, muß
to have a good time   sich (*acc.*) amüsieren
to hear   hören
to help   helfen (*dat.*), half, hat geholfen, hilft
here   hier
hike   die Fußtour, –, –en
home   nach Hause
to hope   hoffen
   I hope   hoffentlich
house   das Haus, –es, ⸚er
   at my (his, *etc.***) house**   bei mir (ihm, *etc.*)
how   wie
to hurt, harm   schaden (*dat.*)

if   wenn (*subord. conj.*)
ill   krank
to imagine   sich (*dat.*) vor-stellen; sich (*dat.*) denken, dachte, hat gedacht
in order to   um . . . zu
information   die Auskunft, –, ⸚e
to inspect   kontrollieren
interesting   interessant
to invite   ein-laden, lud . . . ein, hat eingeladen, lädt . . . ein
ironic   ironisch

joke   der Witz, –es, –e
June   der Juni, –s

kitchen   die Küche, –, –n

to know   kennen, kannte, hat gekannt; wissen, wußte, hat gewußt, weiß
late   spät
later   später
to laugh   lachen
   I laugh until I cry   mir kommen die Tränen vor Lachen
leading part   die Hauptrolle, –, –n
to leave (for)   ab-fahren (nach), fuhr . . . ab, ist abgefahren, fährt . . . ab
lecture   die Vorlesung, –, –en
lecture hall   der Hörsaal, –s, Hörsäle
legend   die Sage, –, –n; die Legende, –, –n
to let (allow)   lassen, ließ, hat gelassen, läßt
letter   der Brief, –(e)s, –e
like   wie
to like   gefallen (*dat.*), gefiel, hat gefallen, gefällt; mögen, mochte, hat gemocht, mag
   I like to drive   ich fahre gern
to live   wohnen
living room   das Wohnzimmer, –s, –
long   lange
to look (appear)   aus-sehen, sah . . . aus, hat ausgesehen, sieht . . . aus
to look at   sich (*dat.*) an-sehen, sah . . . an, hat angesehen, sieht . . . an
to look forward to   sich (*acc.*) freuen auf (+ *acc.*)
to lose   verlieren, verlor, hat verloren
a lot   viel

to make   machen
many   viele
many a   mancher
may   dürfen, durfte, hat gedurft, darf
to meet   treffen, traf, hat getroffen, trifft
Mensa   die Mensa, –, Mensen
to mention   erwähnen
to miss   verpassen
mistake   der Fehler, –s, –
modern   modern
Monday   der Montag, –s, –e
money   das Geld, –(e)s
monument   das Denkmal, –s, ⸚er
more   mehr
most   meist-, am meisten
   to like most   am besten gefallen (*dat.*)
movie   der Film, –(e)s, –e
movies (movie theater)   das Kino, –s, –s
Mr.   Herr

Mrs. Frau
must müssen, mußte, hat gemußt, muß
  must not nicht dürfen
mystery story der Kriminalroman, –s, –e

name der Name, –ns, –n
  my name is ich heiße
natural natürlich
to need brauchen
never nie
new neu
newspaper die Zeitung, –, –en
next to (+ *dat./acc.*) neben
to be next an der Reihe sein
nice schön
nine neun
no kein
no! nein!
not nicht
nothing nichts
now nun, jetzt

o'clock Uhr
old alt
on auf (+ *dat./acc.*), an (+ *dat./acc.*)
oneself selbst
only nur
or oder
orchestra das Orchester, –s, –
other ander-
outing der Ausflug, –s, ⸚e
to be over zu Ende sein
to owe verdanken

painter der Maler, –s, –
parents die Eltern (*pl.*)
park der Park, –(e)s, –s
people die Leute (*pl.*)
performer der Darsteller, –s, –
performance die Aufführung, –, –en
perhaps vielleicht
permit die Erlaubnis, –
to pick out aus-suchen
to pick-up ab-holen
picture das Bild, –(e)s, –er
plane das Flugzeug, –s, –e
to play spielen
please bitte
pocket die Tasche, –, –n
poet der Dichter, –s, –
to be no point in keinen Zweck haben
political politisch
popular beliebt

postcard die Karte, –, –n
to praise loben
pretty (quite, rather) ziemlich
professor der Professor, –s, –en
program das Programm, –s, –e

quarter das Viertel, –s, –
  a quarter of ein Viertel vor
  a quarter past ein Viertel nach

to read lesen, las, hat gelesen, liest
really wirklich
relative der Verwandte, –n, –n
to **remember** (*someone or something*)
  sich (*acc.*) erinnern (an + *acc.*)
to remind (of) erinnern (an + *acc.*)
reporter der Reporter, –s, –
restaurant das Restaurant, –s, –s
Rhine der Rhein, –(e)s
Rhine trip die Rheinfahrt, –, –en
to ride fahren, fuhr, ist gefahren, fährt
to be right recht haben; stimmen
room das Zimmer, –s, –

to say sagen
to say good-by sich (*acc.*) verabschieden
scandal der Skandal, –s, –e
seat der Platz, –es, ⸚e
second (moment) der Augenblick, –s, –e
second zweit-
to see sehen, sah, hat gesehen, sieht
  see you! auf Wiedersehen!
to seem vor-kommen (*dat.*), kam . . . vor,
  ist vorgekommen
to seem to fly by wie im Fluge vergehen,
  verging, ist vergangen
semester das Semester, –s, –
seminar das Seminar, –s, –e
to send one's apologies sich (*acc.*) entschuldigen lassen, ließ, hat gelassen,
  läßt
to serenade ein Ständchen bringen,
  brachte, hat gebracht
to set (the table) (den Tisch) decken
seven sieben
shall sollen, sollte, hat gesollt, soll
ship das Schiff, –(e)s, –e
to show zeigen
side die Seite, –, –n
since (*prep.*) seit (+ *dat.*)
since (*conj.*) da (*subord. conj.*); weil
  (*subord. conj.*)
to sit sitzen, saß, hat gesessen

to sit down sich (*acc.*) setzen
six sechs
six-thirty halb sieben
to sleep schlafen, schlief, hat geschlafen, schläft
small klein
smooth glatt
so so
solution die Lösung, –, –en
something etwas
somewhere or other irgendwo
soon bald
to be sorry leid tun, tat, hat getan
to speak sprechen, sprach, hat gesprochen, spricht
speed limit die Geschwindigkeitsbegrenzung, –, –en
to stand stehen, stand, hat gestanden
to start an-fangen, fing . . . an, hat angefangen, fängt . . . an
stay der Aufenthalt, –s, –e
to stay bleiben, blieb, ist geblieben
still noch
store das Geschäft, –s, –e
strenuous anstrengend
strict streng
student der Student, –en, –en
studio das Atelier, –s, –s
such so
to be supposed to sollen, sollte, hat gesollt, soll
symphony die Sinfonie, –, –n

to take nehmen, nahm, hat genommen, nimmt
to take a look (look something up) nachsehen, sah . . . nach, hat nachgesehen, sieht . . . nach
to take part (in) teil-nehmen (an + *dat.*), nahm . . . teil, hat teilgenommen, nimmt . . . teil
to take (a trip) (eine Fahrt) machen
talented begabt
to talk, converse sich (*acc.*) unterhalten, unterhielt, hat unterhalten, unterhält
taxi das Taxi, –s, –s
teacher der Lehrer, –s, –
technical term der Fachausdruck, –s, –e
to tell erzählen; sagen
than als
to thank danken (*dat.*)
thank you very much vielen Dank
that das; daß (*subord. conj.*)

that is the way it is so ist es nun mal
then dann
there dort, da
there is es gibt
to think denken, dachte, hat gedacht; glauben
to think of denken an (+ *acc.*) dachte, hat gedacht
third dritt-
this dieser; das
three drei
through durch (+ *acc.*)
through (finished) fertig
ticket die Karte, –, –n
time die Zeit, –, –en
on time pünktlich
tired müde
today heute
too zu
town die Stadt, –, –e
train der Zug, –(e)s, –e
Tuesday der Dienstag, –s, –e
twenty zwanzig
twice zweimal
two zwei

unbelievable unglaublich
to understand verstehen, verstand, hat verstanden
unfortunately leider
university die Universität, –, –en
unusual ungewöhnlich
upstairs oben
to use gebrauchen

very sehr
to visit besuchen
visit der Besuch, –s, –e

to wait (for) warten (auf + *acc.*)
to wait in line Schlange stehen, stand, hat gestanden
to wake (someone) wecken
to walk (stroll) spazieren (sein)
to want wollen, wollte, hat gewollt, will
to watch beobachten
weather das Wetter, –s
Wednesday der Mittwoch, –s, –e
well gut
what was
what kind of was für
what time wieviel Uhr
at what time um wieviel Uhr

when wenn (*subord. conj.*); als (*subord. conj.*)

where wo; wohin

whether ob (*subord. conj.*)

which welcher

who wer

why warum

with mit (+ *dat.*), bei (+ *dat.*)

without ohne (+ *acc.*)

to work arbeiten

worse schlimmer

worth seeing sehenswert

to write schreiben, schrieb, hat geschrieben

would like möchte(n)

year das Jahr, –(e)s, –e

yesterday gestern

Index

427